BRITISH ROYAL YACHTS

A Complete Illustrated History

With a Foreword by H.R.H. The Duke of Edinburgh

Tony Dalton

HALSGROVE

First published in Great Britain in 2002

British Library Cataloguing-in-Publication Data
A CIP record for this title is available from the British Library

ISBN 1 84114 130 5

HALSGROVE
PUBLISHING, MEDIA AND DISTRIBUTION

Halsgrove House
Lower Moor Way
Tiverton, Devon EX16 6SS
Tel: 01884 243242
Fax: 01884 243325
email sales@halsgrove.com
website www.halsgrove.com

Printed in Hong Kong by Regal Printing Limited

FOREWORD

BRITISH ROYAL YACHTS

By H.R.H. The Duke of Edinburgh

For a thousand years Kings and Queens of Britain have used ships for war or pleasure and to visit distant parts of their island kingdoms and lately to their far-flung Empire.

This book traces the long succession of vessels designed or adapted for Royal use. It is a reminder of the lengthy period when the seas around our coasts provided our highways to the world; highways for exploration and trade, for economic and imperial expansion and for emigration. The Royal Yachts symbolised our dependence on the seas and reminded everyone that Britain was a maritime nation.

Kings and Governments recognised these factors and successive Royal Yachts were designed and built to the highest standards and the latest technology as symbols of British maritime achievements.

The decommissioning of HMY *Britannia* in 1997 brought that chapter in British history to a symbolic end. Appropriately, the last occasion of her ceremonial life was the handover of Hong Kong which marked the end of the Empire.

The author has done his homework and the result is a fascinating and detailed account of Royal Yachts of all sizes – some used in war, some for official duties and some for pleasure, which have served British Heads of State over 1000 years.

HMY *Britannia* was the last of a distinguished line and I am pleased that her contribution has been so well-documented.

Philip

For Gheikie, Ziz and Mother, who made it all possible

CONTENTS

PART TWO – THE STEAM YACHTS

ACKNOWLEDGEMENTS

In several years of research so many people have given their unstinting help that I cannot possibly mention them all – if they have gone unrecorded, I am none the less appreciative.

I am especially grateful to the Royal Yacht Britannia Trust for their generous research grant, which enabled me to donate my royalties to naval charities. And to Simon Butler, the Publisher, and his team at Halsgrove, who have not only produced a superb book from my random sheets of paper, but who have also made a donation to the same naval charities.

Many collections, museums and firms kindly gave permission to reproduce material and – exceptionally – waived their normal fees. Without this the book could not have been published, so I am particularly grateful to them: The National Maritime Museum; the Royal Collection Trust; the Royal Archives; the National Museums of Scotland; the British Museum; the Imperial War Museum; Nederlands Scheepvaartmuseum, Amsterdam; the Ministry of Defence/Crown Copyright Agent; Beken Maritime Services; Devonport Management Ltd; The Illustrated London News Picture Library; Topham Picturepoint; the Council of the Society for Nautical Research; Colin M. Baxter, for his superbly detailed paintings; John Munford, Colin Moodie and Arthur Saluz for their designs/drawings of proposed Royal Yachts; and Eric Thorburn, for his excellent interior photographs of *Britannia*.

Where photographs are credited with Crown Copyright/MoD they are reproduced with the permission of the Controller of Her Majesty's Stationery Office.

The charts on pages 125 and 126 are reproduced from charts in the Admiralty Collection by permission of the Controller of Her Majesty's Stationery Office and the UK Hydrographic Office. Further information on the Admiralty Collection can be obtained from the Product Manager, Admiralty Collection, UK Hydrographic Office, Admiralty Way, Taunton, Somerset TA1 2DN.

I am indebted for Chapter 9 to *The Rise and Fall of Parkgate, Passenger Port for Ireland, 1686-1815* by Geoffrey Place, published by The Chetham Society at Manchester University Press in 1994.

Those individuals I would particularly like to thank are as follows, but in no especial order: The family of the late Paymaster Commander Charles Gavin, Royal Navy, for the access to his papers and photographs; Mrs J.S. Dalglish for photographs and permission to quote from *The Life Story of a Fish*; Lawrence Philips, RD, TD, for much research, help and permission to reproduce his photographs from Pembroke Dockyard Archives; the late Captain John Mott, MVO, Royal Navy; A.V. Pelly Esq., LVO, for permission to quote extensively from his father's book and letters, and to reproduce photographs; Geoffrey Jarvis; Lady Dugdale, DCVO, JP, DL; Mrs K.G. Smith and Coaker; Admiral Sir William O'Brien, KCB, DSC; Commodore A.J.C. Morrow, CVO, Royal Navy; John Stockman; Pat Caws; Bill

Hunt; Dr Norman Macdougall, for his help on 'Royal Yachts in Scotland'; David Taylor and Colin Starkey of the National Maritime Museum; Alison Harvey-Wood, formerly at The National Library of Scotland; C. Lloyd Esq, Surveyor of the Queen's Pictures; Bob Downie, Director of The Royal Yacht Britannia; Frank Walton; 'Fiona from The Printshop'; Charles Judge; Captain C.H.H. Owen, Royal Navy; Maldwin Drummond, OBE, JP, DL, Hon DSc, for permission to quote from *Salt Water Palaces*; Lt Cdr A.W.A. Stevens, MBE, Royal Navy, for his reminiscences as a boy seaman in the 'V & A'; The Corporation of the Hull Trinity House; Mrs Carola Zogolovitch for permission to use the sketches by her late father, Sir Hugh Casson; Colin Bowden; Rear Admiral C.H. Layman CB, DSO, LVO, for much encouragement, advice and practical help over the years of research; Clive Watts, for his all-important suggestion of Halsgrove as the publisher; 'Dixie' Deane, mainspring of the Association of Royal Yachtsman; Major Grant Walker, U.S. Naval Academy, Annapolis; Captain Ian Sutherland, Royal Navy; Mrs Joy Donner, for her encyclopaedic fund of naval knowledge; Paul Reynolds; Rebecca, Iona, James and Tomas for endless patience in photocopying and finding reference books; and most importantly of all, my wife Georgina, who has never once said 'Bother the Royal Yachts' although she must often have felt it!

Tony Dalton
Maolachy, November 2001

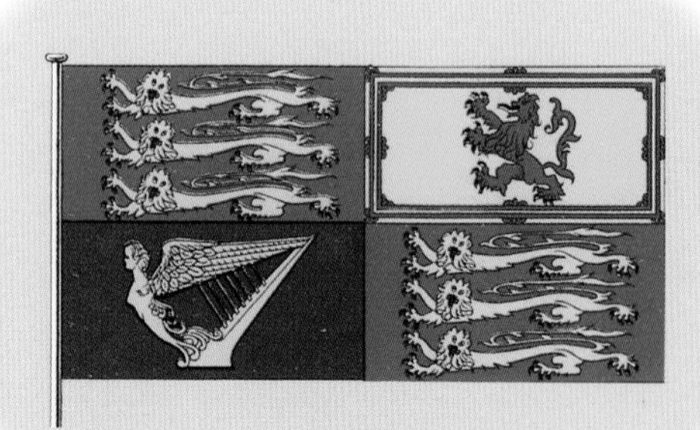

Royal Standard.

PART ONE

THE SAILING YACHTS

THE KING'S SHIPS

ANGLO-SAXONS TO THE EARLY STUARTS

Royal Yacht – more correctly at this period royal warship; a vessel of State, used by the sovereign to impress or subdue, and employed to convey royalty, ambassadors and other great persons, often from one kingdom to another.

It is obviously right and proper that the sovereign of a maritime nation should have at his or her disposal a vessel in every way fitted for the ceremonial and official duties of such an exalted office. Thus, although the term 'yacht' did not come into use until the mid-1600s, there were of course vessels which were used for the personal service of the King long before this.

Although it is tempting to list any vessel associated with royalty, this section is guided by the definition of a Royal Yacht above. Thus the early 'Royal Yachts', more correctly termed vessels of State, served much the same purpose as did their modern counterparts. They would, however, not have been reserved solely for the use of royalty, but also for commerce and war as circumstances dictated; but their accommodation and appearance would often be modified for the carriage of royalty or other great officials.

In Anglo-Saxon times the 'King's Ships' are described as 'long ships', with elevated prows and sterns, usually ornamented with figures of men, birds, lions and other animals, which were often gilded. These vessels were mainly propelled by oars, and they were steered by oars, one on each quarter. Some had a single mast with a large square sail, on royal vessels dyed purple, and in the King's own ship the hull was divided into five compartments. In the foremost the King's standard-bearers were quartered; next came the general storeroom; then the room for sails and tackle; then the arms chest and quarters for the warriors; and astern of all the great cabin for the accommodation of the sovereign.[1]

The captain acted as helmsman, and the crew consisted of 50 to 60 men. Harold, King of Norway, presented one such vessel to King Athelstan (924-939). The head of it was wrought in gold, the sails were of purple canvas, and the deck was elegantly wrought all round with gold.[2] King Edgar (944-975) enjoyed 'sommer progresses and [his] yerely chiefe pastimes were the sailing round about this whole isle of Albion'.[3]

William the Conqueror (1066-1087) led the fleet for the invasion of England in his own vessel, the MORA, given to him by his wife Matilda. The Bayeux Tapestry shows the ship as larger than the others, with ten men embarked, although there were certainly more than that. The prow is ornamented with a lion's head, and at the stern is an effigy of a boy blowing a horn. At the masthead is a cross of gold, below that a banner of white charged with a gold cross within a blue border. There is a single sail, the sheet of which is held by the steersman, and the sail was dyed in vertical stripes of red, brown, red. The captain was one Stephen

William the Conqueror (1066-1087). From The Bayeux Tapestry.

Fitz-Erard, and for his service Fitz-Erard was granted exemption from taxation on his house at Southampton. As for Matilda, she was given the county of Kent by William for providing him with the MORA; not a bad bargain!

William Rufus (1087-1100) crossed the Channel many times in his battle to retain Normandy. He once made his pilots put to sea in rough weather with the exhortation 'whether they had ever heard of a King being drowned'.[4]

In Norman and Plantagenet times there was little difference between the ship-of-war and the merchant ship; indeed when not otherwise required the King was in the habit of hiring out his ships for commerce. Gun armaments were as yet unknown, so the men fought from raised platforms in the bow and stern – the fore castle and the after castle.

The King's Ships were generally the personal property of the King, who usually directed their movements and operations himself, embarking in whichever ship he chose. But there was one ship kept for his own use, or the conveyance of distinguished persons, the Royal Yacht of the time. The Esnecca, or 'Snekkja', was originally a type of long, fast galley; as a class of ship it appears to have lasted into the fifteenth century, but no reliable picture of it has survived. The captain, or nauclerus, of the King's Esnecca was a man of importance, and what was more, both officers and men were liveried – that is, were paid fixed salaries; 12d a day for the captain, and 3d a day for seamen.

King Henry I (1100-1135), who had been residing in Normandy, decided to return to England with all his family, and the King departed first, on 25 November 1120. The seventeen-year-old Prince William, Henry's only legitimate heir, embarked later with his natural brother and sister on LE BLANCHE NEF. With them were some 140 of the flower of the young nobility of England and Normandy; with their servants they totalled nearly 300 in all. The vessel was commanded by Thomas Fitz-Stephen, grandson of the man who steered the Conqueror's ship, but the crew, and probably most of the passengers, were the worse for wine. The ship struck a rock and soon foundered, with the loss of all lives save one – 'Berauld, a butcher of Rouen'. King Henry, we are told, 'was never seen to smile again'.[5]

As the Kings of England ruled over the greater part of France there was a need for a regular despatch service across the Channel between England and Normandy. Usually kept at one of the Cinque Ports, the King's Esnecca was an ideal vessel for this purpose. There are definite records of royal use: in 1166 for the passage of Henry II across the Channel; in 1174, when Henry embarked from Portsmouth for Normandy, taking with him as prisoner William the Lion of Scotland; in 1176, the King's daughter crossed to go to Sicily, and in 1184 the Duke of Saxony and the Queen crossed the Channel.

Richard I (1189-1199) fitted out a fleet of galleys and transports for the Crusades, which he led himself. His own favourite ship was the TRENCH LE MER, or 'Cleave the Sea', and he was present on board her at the naval battle at Acre against the Saracens in 1191. On returning overland to England he was captured, and on his release he embarked in the TRENCH LE MER in March 1194 at Antwerp and sailed for England – and as every Kevin Costner fan knows, the King arrived just in time for the marriage of his cousin, Maid Marian, to Robin Hood.

In the reign of King John (1199-1216) the Archdeacon of Taunton, one William de Wrotham, was appointed Chief Keeper of the King's Ships, responsible for safe custody of the ships and maintenance of the seaports from Romney to Southampton. In 1210 the commander of the Royal Yacht, or as he was then called, Master of the King's Great Galley, was one Richard of London.[6]

The Cinque Ports, however, were starting to silt up, and with the Court often at Winchester it was decided in May 1212 to establish a base for the King's Ships at Portsmouth. Directions were given for the construction of slips for the galleys, the building of storehouses, and a strong wall to enclose them all: 'and this was to be done at once, lest the galleys or their stores should be injured during the ensuing winter'.[7] Even before this official establishment of Portsmouth Dockyard the harbour was no stranger to royalty, for several Kings embarked there for France. Indeed it is said that King Stephen, after a particularly rough passage back, landed on the western shore of the harbour and called it thankfully 'God's Port' – the Gosport of today.

The records of Henry III (1216-1272) often show the King's Great Ship or the King's Galley mentioned by name, thus the QUEEN and the CARDINAL, the latter captured from the Portuguese. The King hired out his Great Ship when not required for his own use, and in 1232 John Blanchboilly had custody of the QUEEN for life. In exchange for an annual rental of fifty marks he could trade wherever he liked, but was responsible for the ship's upkeep, and at his death she was to be restored to the King in as good a state as when Blanchboilly received her. When not in service the King's Ships were placed on slipways in covered buildings, and were based at the Cinque Ports as well as Portsmouth.[8] In 1230 the royal arms are shown embroidered on the sail; the royal banner was red, with three gold lions, a device first adopted by Richard I after the Crusades. The Cross of St George was added by Henry V after the Battle of Agincourt.[9]

In the accounts of 1227 the sum of £11 was paid to the Master of the King's Great Ship and galleys at Portsmouth, at the rate of 6d a day to the master and 3d a day to each sailor. In the following year 4s 6d was paid 'for the making of some sort of chamber in the said ship to put our said effects in'. In 1242 orders were given for 'convenient cabins or chambers, wainscotted' to be built in a ship taking the King and Queen to Poitou and Gascony. Twenty ships were to accompany them, and provisions obtained from the Bishopric of Winchester.[10]

Edward I (1272-1307) negotiated the marriage to his son of The Maid of Norway, heiress of Scotland, and in 1290 the King's butler provisioned the Royal Yacht for the voyage – 'going to Yarmouth to take there a great ship, and to store the same with divers things necessary to send it to Norway to bring to England the lady Margaret'. The provisions included wine, ale, corn, beef, pork, bacon, stock-fish, sturgeon, herrings, lampreys, almonds, rice, beans, peas, onions, leeks, cheese, nuts, salt, vinegar, mustard, pepper, cummin-seed, ginger, cinnamon, figs, raisins, saffron, ginger-bread, wax torches, tallow candles, cressets, lanthorns, napkins, wood, biscuit, a banner of the King's arms and a silken streamer. Although the total charge was only £29 2s 11d, this amounted to six years' wages for a seaman. The crew consisted of a master, 40 sailors and a boy, plus five envoys with their retinue and 18 horses. All these preparations came to nought however, as on the return voyage the ship was wrecked and the Maid of Norway drowned, thus dashing Edward's plans of uniting England and Scotland dynastically.[11]

The reign of Edward II (1307-1327) was one of intimate connection between the English and French Courts, and in November 1307 the Warden of the Cinque Ports was ordered to prepare ships for the King's personal conveyance, together with his retinue, his pavilion and tents. Edward was claiming his bride, Isabel, only daughter of Philip of France, and the marriage was celebrated with great splendour at Boulogne in January 1308.

Edward III (1327-1377) was almost continually at war with France, thus necessitating much voyaging across the Channel. His Great Ships appear to have had their headquarters at Sandwich, and one is named as the GEORGE. He embarked in her at Sandwich in 1342, and as was the custom, handed the great seal to the Chancellor, and made the Duke of Cornwall custodian in his absence. Five years later Calais surrendered, but on his return to Sandwich, Edward's fleet was dispersed by a storm, and many knights drowned. He is said to have exclaimed, 'O blessed Mary, holy Lady, why is it and what does it portend, that in going to France I enjoy a favourable wind, a calm sea and all things prosper with me, but that in returning to England all kinds of misfortunes befal me?' – a question raised in the years since by many cross-Channel passengers.[12]

Piracy was then very common on the high seas, and the interference this caused to peaceful trade between countries was a frequent occasion of war. So in 1350 Edward determined to punish the Spaniards and assembled a fleet off Winchelsea, with himself on board the THOMAS, and the Prince of Wales and his brother the Earl of Richmond, then only ten, in another ship. When the look-out sighted the whole Spanish fleet he exclaimed, 'I see so many, as God may help me I cannot count them.' As befits one of the greatest warrior Kings, Edward clearly enjoyed the battle, for he ordered his helmsman, 'Lay me against that Spaniard who is coming, for I wish to joust with him.' So fierce was the battle the King's ship the THOMAS was sunk under him, and he was forced to transfer to a captured Spanish one, but the outcome was complete victory for the English fleet, and became known as 'Les Espagnols sur Mer'.[13]

The King's own ships the THOMAS and the CHRISTOPHER – the latter the most celebrated ship for her size and beauty – were cogs, the first-class vessel of the fourteenth century. The crew of the cog THOMAS consisted of a master, two constables, two carpenters, 124 sailors, and eight boys. In addition she probably carried 60 or more soldiers and archers, and was thus from 200 to 220 tons burden.[14] Incidentally, the master of the ship was known as the 'cogswain', from which we get the present word coxswain.[15]

There is also mention of a 'fluve' class of ship, for in 1345 King Edward took passage to Flanders in his fluve the SWALLOW. Fluves were large, flat vessels, drawing little water, and thus ideal for embarking and landing troops, horses and stores in Flanders and the Low Countries.

Two other vessels of Edward's reign are worthy of mention. The galley LA PHILIPPA had one mast (cost £10) and yard (cost £3), with a sail dyed red, a bowsprit, one large anchor weighing 1100lbs, five small anchors and 80 oars (this was at a time when a master carpenter earned 6d per day, and a labourer 2½d per day).[16] And in August 1372 the King embarked at Sandwich in the GRACE DE DIEU to cruise along the coast of Normandy and Brittany.

Henry IV's (1399-1413) own cog, the JOHN, was distinguished by having on top of the mast a crown and sceptre, together with his crest, the lion of England crowned; and her capstan was ornamented with three fleur-de-lis. Her sail was embroidered with the King's arms, and from the mast flew, in addition to the royal banner, two streamers and eight guidons. In 1400 one of the King's barges was painted red, adorned with collars and garters of gold, each collar containing a fleur-de-lis, and each garter a leopard. Another barge was painted black and carved with ostrich feathers, the scroll being gilt.[17]

When in late 1402 a ship was sent to Brittany to bring to England Joan of Navarre, the affianced wife of Henry IV, orders were given for the construction of offices or cabins for the buttery, pantry, spicery, ewery, and the chandlery. But Henry neglected to make arrangements for paying the crew, and the lords sent to accompany Joan had to pay the men from their own pockets. Joan embarked at Camaret on 13 January 1403, intending to make for Southampton, but after a rough passage of five days she was only too glad to disembark at Falmouth.[18]

In the summer of 1406 the newly created Admiral in the North, Nicholas Blackburn, conveyed the Princess Philippa across the North Sea for her marriage to King Eric of Denmark. Piracy was then rife, and the Princess's ship carried two guns, 40 pounds of powder, 40 stone shot, 40 wads, 24 bows, 40 sheaves of arrows, 40 pavises (probably pavesses; shields used to line the fore and after castles as protection from small arms fire). They were made of poplar, which did not splinter; later they were highly decorated with armorial designs. Also listed were four touches (perhaps firing-irons) and two fire-pans.[19]

In 1414 Henry V (1413-1422) asserted his claim to France and immediately began preparations for war. By the following August he had assembled a fleet of 1400 vessels at Southampton together with 6000 men-at-arms and 24 000 archers. On Saturday 10 August the King embarked in the TRINITY ROYAL and at once ordered the sail yard to be hoisted to the middle of the mast, indicating he was ready to put to sea.

The fleet in fact sailed on Sunday, and by Wednesday most of the army had landed at Harfleur. After Agincourt was won Henry embarked at Calais on 16 November, reaching Dover late on the same day. The return passage of the victorious army and all their prisoners was exceptionally rough, the fleet was in part dispersed, and two ships sank with all hands. The most distinguished of the captive French noblemen were on the King's ship, and it is said they considered their sufferings on the day of battle to be nothing to the seasickness they endured on passage to England. Henry was unaffected, for he appeared before them as composed as when on land.[20]

Throughout his reign Henry V maintained a fleet of about 35 ships, each being described as 'of the tower', the medieval equivalent of HMS – His Majesty's Ship. The King's own ship, the GRACE A DIEU, had a 'mesan' in addition to her 'great mast', the first appearance of a two-masted ship in English waters.[21] Henry was the last monarch recorded as using purple sails; he sailed from France to England in the KING'S CHAMBER, which carried a sail of purple silk, embroidered in gold with the arms of England and France.[22]

That the ships were the personal property of the King is shown by one of the first orders of the Council for the infant Henry VI (1422-1461), whereby it sold nearly all the King's Ships in order to pay off debts incurred by his late father. A strange decision, as Henry inherited the crowns of both France and England, necessitating much crossing of the Channel. And so decimated was the Royal Navy by the sale of its ships that the total expenditure on the service for the two years ending 31 August 1439, was a mere £8 9s 7d. The policing of the Narrow Seas, such as it was, was carried out by contractors, who paid their masters 6d a day, and the seamen 1s 6d a week, and the same in victuals.[23] Henry failed to hold France, and in the later years of his reign became embroiled in the Wars of the Roses, before finally being murdered in the Tower on the orders of Edward IV. Though Edward IV (1461-1483) was much involved in naval affairs with his campaigns in France, little is recorded of the ships he used personally.

UNDER THE TUDORS

In 1500 the plague was raging in London, so Henry VII (1485-1509) and his family went to Calais, arriving there on 8 May, and returning about the end of June.[24]

After the Wars of the Roses one begins to hear of gilded barges, Royal Yachts in all but name, which took part in pageants on the Thames, and one such greeted the arrival of Catherine of Aragon, betrothed to Arthur, Prince of Wales.

The KATHERINE PLEASAUNCE, of a hundred tons, was laid down at Deptford in 1514, and being the King's special ship was artistically decorated. She probably conveyed, and certainly accompanied, Henry VIII (1509-1547) to Calais in 1520 when he met Francis I King of France, in what afterwards became known as the Field of the Cloth of Gold.[25] Surprisingly, it was to be over three hundred years before the next meeting of an English and French sovereign, in 1843, with the visit of Queen Victoria on board her new steam yacht VICTORIA & ALBERT to King Louis Phillipe at Treport.

The painting below shows the HENRY GRACE A DIEU, (second from right) Royal Standards flying, conveying the King from Dover to Boulogne on 31 May 1520. The decks are crowded with men-at-arms and trumpeters, the sails and pennants are of cloth of gold, and the King, in crimson and gold, is seen standing on the upper deck. From each of the four angles of the forecastle flies the Royal Standard of England, the staff of each standard being surrounded by a fleur-de-lis. The ship's quarters, sides and tops are hung with targets, all charged differently.[26] However it is now known the HENRY GRACE A DIEU was refitting in the Thames at the time, so the picture was painted after the event.

In 1546 the GALIE SUBTILE is shown as being equipped for the special use of royalty but with the dominions on the Continent gone and the sea fraught with dangers, a heavily armed ship was the most suitable vessel for the few occasions on which royalty embarked.

HENRY GRACE A DIEU, 1514

'The departure of Henry VIII from Dover for Boulogne, 1520.' The painting is at Hampton Court, although the artist is unknown.

Gavin wrote[27] that Queen Elizabeth I (1558-1603), last of the Tudors, never left the shores of England save for sheltered expeditions on the Thames. But there is some evidence that she had built the RAT O' WIGHT for her own use at Shamford, on the Isle of Wight.[28] Her father, Henry VIII, had built two forts, then called cows, on either side of the Medina estuary to protect the island; Shamford in due course was renamed Cowes, and the western fort, 'enlarged and softened into domesticity', became the headquarters of the Royal Yacht Squadron in 1858.

There is a Van de Velde drawing of a heavily armed ship inscribed KING ELIZABETH'S SHIP, sometimes erroneously ascribed as a Royal Yacht of Queen Elizabeth. The inscription probably refers to Elizabeth Queen of Bohemia, daughter of James VI & I, who assisted with money and ships the Royalist fleet against the Commonwealth. The word 'King' in the inscription is an ancient joke, for it was customary after the death of Elizabeth I to refer to her as 'King' and James I as 'Queen'.[29] Whether this arose from his abhorrence of violence and preference for diplomacy to war, or his predilection for young men, is not recorded.

KING ELIZABETH'S SHIP

James VI & I (1603-1625) inherited from Elizabeth not only the Crown of England to add to that of Scotland, but also the nucleus of a navy that had destroyed the ambitions of the most powerful monarch on earth. James however preferred diplomacy to war, and made peace with Spain. Thereafter the navy fell into disrepair, whilst its affairs were handled by dishonest and incompetent officials. The seas became so dangerous that the coasts of Devon and Cornwall were regularly raided by 'Turks' from North Africa who carried off young men for the slavery of the galleys. The 'Dunkirkers' even levied a toll on ships using the Thames.

Among the first royal vessels to be built solely for pleasure was the DISDAIN, given in 1604 by James I to his ten-year-old son Henry, Prince of Wales. She was built by Commissioner Phineas Pett, one of a great family of shipwrights, who wrote in his memoirs:

> About January 15th 1604, a letter was sent post-haste to Chatham from my Honourable Lord Admiral Howard, [Lord High Admiral] commanding me with all possible speed to build a little vessel for the young Prince Henry to disport himself in about London Bridge, and acquaint his Grace with shipping and the manner of that element; setting me down the proportions and the manner of garnishings, which

> was to be like the work of the ARK ROYAL, battlementwise. This little ship was in length 25 feet by the keel, and in breadth 12 feet, garnished with painting and carving, both within board and without, very curiously, according to his Lordship's directions.
>
> (ARK ROYAL was Lord Howard of Effingham's flagship which took part in the fight against the Spanish Armada.)

Pett 'wrought night and day by torch and candle' and the little ship was launched on 6 March, 'with a noise of drums, trumpets, and such like ceremonies'. She was sailed round from Chatham and was taken 'right against the Tower before the King's lodgings' where she was visited by Prince Henry and the Lord High Admiral who 'took pleasure in beholding the ship, being furnished at all points with ensigns and pennants'. A day or two later Prince Henry 'with a great bowle of wine, christened the ship and called her by the name of DISDAIN'[30] (see facing page).

In 1608 Prince Henry, then fourteen, visited Woolwich to view the PRINCE ROYAL being built, and the King nominally presented it to his son. In the years since completing the DISDAIN Phineas Pett had been accused of using bad timber in building his ships, and frauds in giving receipts for stores. But Prince Henry stood by him at the trial, Pett was acquitted, and continued to build the King's Ships, including the PRINCE ROYAL, at that time the largest ship ever built.

The day of the launch came, 24 September 1610, a wild, storm-tossed day, and as high water approached it became obvious the launch should be delayed until the wind dropped. The King was absent, suffering from 'a surfeit of grapes', but the Queen, Prince Henry, Princess Elizabeth and Prince Charles were all on the stand, and an attempt was made to launch the ship. The dock gates, however, which were too narrow, 'pent her in so straight that she stuck fast between them', and she settled in the mud until the next high tide floated her off.[31]

The PRINCE ROYAL was one of the few men-of-war built by James I, the finest and most heavily armed ship of the time, with 55 guns. She was highly decorated with carving, painting and gilding; badges and coats of arms adorned her stern, whilst great carved lions' heads surrounded the gunports. Indeed her designer, Phineas Pett, was accused of making a showpiece rather than a man-of-war.

The DISDAIN was so popular with the royal children that the King, in June 1612, ordered Pett to build a new small ship for the Prince, a pinnace which was also to act as tender to the great ship. A pinnace at that date was not a ship's boat, but a sea-going vessel, ship-rigged; her dimensions were to be 72 feet long, 24 feet beam and 11 feet draught.[32]

That winter Frederick V, Elector Palatine of the Rhine, came to London to marry Henry's sister, the Princess Elizabeth. There were feasts and banquets and plays to celebrate the occasion, but young Henry enjoyed none of these, for he lay dying of typhoid fever. As for the pinnace, she never left the stocks. Nothing further is recorded of the DISDAIN, apart from her appearing in the list of the navy in 1618 rated at 30 tons burden.

The PRINCE ROYAL was such a magnificent vessel she was the obvious first choice for use by royalty, and in 1613 the newly-wed Princess Elizabeth and Frederick sailed from Rochester to Flushing in the ship. This was an important voyage dynastically, for from their daughter Sophia and her husband, the Elector of Hanover, descended the future sovereigns of Britain.

Ten years later in 1623 the PRINCE ROYAL, now named the PRINCE, carried home the new Prince of Wales from a visit to Spain. He had been on a romantic but fruitless attempt to claim his bride, and the future Charles I was escorted by a fleet of the largest ships of the period. There is a large oil painting by

PRINCE ROYAL, 1610

Adam Willaerts – 'Embarkation of the Elector Palatine and his bride Princess Elizabeth at Dover.' The small ship on the extreme left is possibly the DISDAIN, *given in 1604 by James I to his ten-year-old son. Willaerts was a Dutch painter who may have come over with the Elector.*

Facing: *SOVEREIGN OF THE SEAS, 1637*

Sir Peter Lely –'The Sovereign of the Seas with Peter Pett.' Peter Pett was barely twenty-seven years old when appointed Master Builder of the SOVEREIGN OF THE SEAS, *the first English three-decker. However, he came from a long line of master shipwrights stretching back to the fifteenth century noted for their knowledge, experience and judgement. Phineas Pett, builder of the* DISDAIN, *had eight sons by his first wife and besides building numerous men-of-war of all classes, the Petts built 14 Royal Yachts for Charles II alone.*

H.C.V. Vroom in Hampton Court Palace which shows the PRINCE, escorted by the 1st rates DEFENCE and ST ANDREW, entering Portsmouth Harbour on 5 October.[33]

Charles I (1625-1649) added the SOVEREIGN OF THE SEAS to the fleet in 1637, again designed by Phineas Pett, this time aided by his son Peter. At 232 feet overall length and armed with 100 guns on her three decks she was a true man-of-war, but her decorations were more in keeping with a Royal Yacht. Van Dyck provided the drawings, and Gerard Christmas, the King's master-carver, ornamented her from bow to stern. The £6691 spent on interior and exterior joinerwork, carving, painting and gilding, would have paid for a 40-gun ship complete. The SOVEREIGN OF THE SEAS fought in many battles during her sixty-year life before being accidentally destroyed by fire at Chatham.

The Ship Money levy which Charles I reintroduced made economic sense, for it enabled a standing navy to be maintained, instead of the ramshackle affair by which the monarch provided ships in times of need. The cost was also to be spread throughout the land, but this much-hated tax was one of the reasons leading to the Civil War. Ironically it was Oliver Cromwell who ultimately made the tax acceptable, reforming the navy, making it more efficient, and clearing home waters of the pirates who infested them. However, much of the Commonwealth's revenue came from the confiscated estates and assets of Royalists; once this windfall had been absorbed in maintaining large numbers in the army and the navy, arrears of pay again became the norm. By 1659 the Navy Board owed £500 000 in wages alone.

ROYAL YACHTS IN SCOTLAND

The use in Scotland of 'Royal Yachts' followed much the same pattern as in England; that is, the sovereign often had one favourite vessel, usually fitted out for his use for a specific occasion. If this use were infrequent – as was often the case – furnishings such as tapestries, linen and plate would be brought from his palaces for the event. There are entries in the accounts of the Lord High Treasurer for Scotland of various sums paid for refitting and furnishing vessels for such use.

In the mid-1100s the Hebrides and west coast of Scotland were effectively a separate kingdom, although nominally owing suzerainty to the King of Scots. Birlinns were oared galleys with a single square-sail hoisted when the wind was right; undoubtedly the one used by the chief would have been finer and more elaborately decorated than the rest.

Somerled, Lord of the Isles (c.1126-1164), gained the bride he wanted by tampering with the royal galley, for he wished to marry the Princess Ragnhildis, daughter of Olaf the Red, King of the Isle of Man, Islay, Mull and the Isles south of Ardnamurchan. The story goes that he arranged with a friend, who just happened to be Olaf's foster-brother, to bore holes in the royal galley, and stop them with buttered thole pins. When in due course the galley began to sink, Somerled was able to rescue Olaf, and claim his daughter in marriage as a pourboire.[1]

After the Scots' defeat at the battle of Halidon Hill on 19 July 1333, the boy King David II (1329-1371), together with his Queen and two sisters, fled to France. I doubt whether there was time to prepare all but the most basic accommodation on whichever ship conveyed them to safety and seven years of exile.

James III (1452-1488), owned among other ships the YELLOW CARVEL of some 300 tons, described in 1475 as 'the King's own carvel'; for a time she was commanded by the famous – or infamous – Sir Andrew Wood of Largo.[2] When war threatened in 1488 James fled north, but returned to face the Border lairds, led by his fifteen-year-old son, at Sauchieburn on 11 June. Defeated, the King escaped from the battlefield, but failed to make it to the YELLOW CARVEL lying waiting in the Forth, for James 'fell into the hands of vile persons and was slain'.[2a] Unable to rescue her royal owner, the YELLOW CARVEL, along with Sir Alexander Wood's FLOWER, picked up other survivors from the battle and conveyed them across the Forth to safety.

History gives much credit to James IV (1488-1513) for building up the Scots Navy, but his aim was equally for diplomatic reasons as for defence of the realm. He constructed the MARGARET and the GREAT MICHAEL as vessels of state as much as for war, and they thus merit inclusion as Royal Yachts, or more accurately royal warships.

James IV owned or hired many ships, and upwards of £10 000 (Scots) a year was spent on his fleet. In 1495 he sailed in the CHRISTOPHER from Dumbarton up the Sound of Mull to Mingary Castle, where four chieftains made submission to him. The royal ship TREASURER was used for conveying the French herald, Mountjoy, to Denmark; and in 1507 the TREASURER was used to convey to France the King's son Alexander Stewart, archbishop of St Andrews. The GABRIEL, manned by Frenchmen but paid for by James, was employed in conveying the French ambassador on his journeys to and from Scotland, for there was much negotiation between James and King Louis XII of France.[3]

Whilst James was restrained on land by the 1497 Anglo-Scottish treaty of 'Perpetual Peace', the terms left him a loophole at sea, and this he exploited by the building of a navy with French money, shipwrights and timber.

Left: *A model of the GREAT MICHAEL, 1511*

Built by James IV as much for diplomacy as for war, the GREAT MICHAEL *was by one account 'the greatest ship that ever sailed in England or France'.*

It was thus slightly ironic that his first great ship, the MARGARET, was named after his wife, Margaret Tudor, and may well have led to the Anglo-Scots 'naval race' and the building in England of the MARY ROSE in 1509. The MARGARET was launched at Leith in 1505, and was at that time the principal ship in James's navy, much used by the King himself; he and the Queen dined on board, with tapestries brought from Falkland Palace for the occasion.

On the eve of St Andrew's Day, 30 November 1512, the French ambassador, Charles de Tocque, Seigneur de la Mothé, arrived during a fierce storm, and was amazed to see a great capital ship lying at Blackness close to the MARGARET. This was the GREAT MICHAEL, 'the greattest scheip that ewer saillit in Ingland or France',[4] launched in October the previous year. Although one doubts the contemporary account that the ship was 12 score feet long and 35 feet broad between her walls, which were each 10 feet thick, the GREAT MICHAEL was about 1000 tons, and carried a crew of 300 men.

The King had sailed in her that June up the Firth to Bo'ness, and on 3 August he and the Queen dined on board, again surrounded by tapestries brought from Falkland Palace for the occasion.[4a] This ship was to be the culmination of James' naval diplomacy, and he duly received the French ambassador on board, where the latter presented his credentials. So impressed was the Seigneur that his report back to France led Louis to request the services of the GREAT MICHAEL and other ships of the Scots Navy in his forthcoming war with England. In that kingdom Henry VIII was also impressed, and it is probable that, not to be outdone by the Scots, he ordered the building of the HENRY GRACE A DIEU in competition to the GREAT MICHAEL.

The GREAT MICHAEL was duly hired to Louis XII, and following Henry VIII's invasion of France in June 1513 the Scots fleet sailed from the Forth on 25 July. They sailed north and west to raid Carrickfergus, stopped over-long at Ayr, and eventually arrived at Brest to join the French fleet about the middle of September.

By then, however, James IV was dead, killed at Flodden on 6 September in a battle he should have won in a war he should not have entered. In Edinburgh, those ruling for the infant James V had no wish to maintain a ruinously expensive navy, and the GREAT MICHAEL was sold to the French for £18 000 (Scots) – about half her cost of building. James IV's great vessel of State had been in Scots service for only two and a half years, yet her effect in pre-war propaganda was considerable. Those ambassadors who had seen her were left in no doubt as to her size and power; those kings who had not were given the impression of something heavily-armed, vast and menacing. She was to be the grandest Scots vessel of state, and the best remembered.

On his death at Flodden, James IV seems to have left but two ships of his own, the JAMES and the MARGARET; James V (1513-1542) as a minor does not appear to have made any personal use of them.

During a raid on the Isle of Man in 1533 MacDonald of Islay and Maclean of Duart took as a prize the English ship MARY WILLOUGHBY (also known as MARY WILLBYE). At something over 300 tons she was not to be compared to the GREAT MICHAEL, but she remained the largest ship in the fleet of James V. He immediately claimed the vessel, and travelled to Inveraray in September to collect her, remaining in the vicinity a month before sailing in her to Dumbarton in October. There James left the MARY WILLOUGHBY, giving orders for a refit that was to cost the substantial sum of £500 – this at a time when his income was about £30 000.

In July 1536 James V decided to pay an unofficial visit to France to view his intended bride, the daughter of the Duke of Vendome – and, incidentally, bring back her much needed dowry of a hundred thousand crowns. He set sail with a small retinue in a single vessel, but encountered such storms that when he was asleep, 'those who accompanied him commanded the pilot to turn the sails for Scotland… so that when the King awoke he found himself near his own harbours upon the Forth'.[5]

The King was furious, but later that year he again set sail, this time with a small fleet of seven ships, including the SALAMANDER, MARY WILLOUGHBY and MORISAT (possibly French). Whether the SALAMANDER at that time belonged to James V is unclear, but she certainly did on the King's return voyage. In October the SALAMANDER sailed to Scotland with Lords Erskine and Rothes, before returning to Dieppe early the following year.

James, however, was so disgusted at the sight of his poor ugly, misshapen fiancée that he refused to marry her. 'Some circumstance not explained in history caused the match to be broken off. Probably (the King) discovered on his arrival that the affections of the princess had been previously engaged by a rival of inferior rank, and had the generosity to resign her reluctant hand. It is at least certain that no quarrel took place, as he gave away the princess in marriage to the Count de Beauvais before he left France…'[6]

Francis I of France shrewdly reoffered his own third daughter Madeline, whom the Scots had previously refused. They were married on New Year's Day 1557, and in addition to the dowry Francis gave James 12 war-horses with full accoutrements, several suits of gilded armour and two ships, the SALAMANDER and the MORSENER.[7]

The SALAMANDER was the personal emblem of the French King, and there is no doubt the SALAMANDER ship was luxuriously fitted out; she is frequently marked in the Treasurer's accounts post-1537 as 'the King's ship'. James and his new Queen sailed home to Scotland in the SALAMANDER, master Thomas Richardson, but within three months the climate had killed the delicate Madeline. James V's notorious parsimony was shown on the return voyage, for John Barton had to tip the seamen of the SALAMANDER 'in the absence of his grace's purse', and it took an age for him to obtain repayment.[8]

Three years later, in 1540, James made a cruise in the SALAMANDER, whose master was John Ker, around Orkney and the Western Isles. Almost all the nobility were ordered to attend upon the King, including the Earls of Argyll, Huntly, Atholl, Arran, Errol, Moray, Cassilis and the Earl Marischal; and Lord Maxwell,

Admiral of Scotland. There were 16 ships in all, including the King's ship 'the SALAMANDRY which the French king gave him,' the MARY WILLOUGHBY, merchant ships for the lords and gentlemen, three ships for victuals, a 'howk' [hulk] for baggage, and a well-trimmed bark to be the 'scurior' before the fleet. There were 3-4000 men embarked, for this was to be a show of strength to the unruly Western Isles, a visit to 'the north and south isles for the ordouring of thame in justice and gude policy'. The record of expenses includes 12s for grey cloth to line a coloured coat for the King 'quhen he zeid [went] to the Ilis'. Someone must have warned him that the wind might be cold when he rounded Cape Wrath.

The fleet sailed in early June, James having delayed for the safe birth of his son James by Mary of Guise on 22 May. This was a royal progress, intended to impress the further reaches of the kingdom, and the King dined on gold plate to the sound of music; for on a progress, whether by sea or land, he expected to be entertained with as much splendour as if in his own palace. The voyage ended in mid-August at Dumbarton, and was adjudged a great success in strengthening the King's hold on his outlying regions.[9]

Mary Queen of Scots (1542-1567) was affianced to the Dauphin of France at the tender age of five, and it was considered safer to send her to France out of Henry VIII's way until she was old enough to marry. In 1548 King Henry of France sent his own royal galley to Leith to embark the Queen, but so strong was the conceived threat from Henry VIII that the galleys were sent north about Scotland to Dumbarton. From there the longer route to France could be run through seas less well policed by the English fleet. Mary embarked on 29 July 1548, but the small fleet waited several days for good weather before sailing; but as Monsieur de Brézé wrote to Mary's mother, Mary of Guise:

> We were almost compelled on two or three occasions to return to port at Dumbarton, and one night about ten leagues from the Cape of Cornwall when the sea was wondrous wild, with the biggest waves I ever saw, to our great consternation the rudder of our galley was broken. Nevertheless our Lord was pleased to intervene, so that we replaced the rudder almost at once in spite of the heavy sea that was running.[10]

The English fleet was successfully avoided and Mary landed at Roscoff on 13 August.

Thirteen years and a day were to pass before she set out to return to Scotland, at eighteen already a widow, her husband the King of France having died eight months previously. On Wednesday 14 August 1681, Mary prepared to sail from Calais in a French galley, Elizabeth I thrice having refused her safe passage through England. Shortly before embarking Mary witnessed a fishing boat founder with all hands, and commented, 'What a sad augury for a journey.'[11] The small fleet sailed, however, and the English Ambassador wrote to Queen Elizabeth on 19 August that his servant at Calais had seen 'the Queen of Scotland haling out of that haven on the 14th inst. about noon, with two galleys and two great ships'.[12] Surprisingly, the English fleet did not intercept Mary, merely saluting her galley and checking the other ships for pirates, and Mary landed at Leith on 19 August after a calm and misty voyage. The Queen's horses fared less well, as the ship carrying them landed at Tynemouth, and the horses were impounded for a month as they had no passports!

James VI (1567-1625) had married by proxy the fourteen-year-old Anne of Denmark in the autumn of 1589. The GIDEON, flagship of the Danish Navy, was prepared for the journey to Scotland, and the largest cabin hung with tapestries, a bed installed for Anne, and a pallet for her personal maid. Escorted by 13 ships-of-war the GIDEON sailed on 1 September, but encountered three tempestuous storms in sequence, and although once in sight of Scotland they were driven back relentlessly. The GIDEON was under-ballasted, her timbers leaked, and huge waves broke over the ship; three cannon broke loose, killing eight men and narrowly missing Anne. With two feet of water in the hold Admiral Munk was finally forced to run for the safety of the Norwegian fjords. Much to her relief, after seven weeks at sea, Anne set foot on dry land and repaired to Oslo, there to wait for spring and the chance of calmer seas.

An increasingly anxious James sent out a small convoy to seek for news, and at last, on 10 October a battered and storm-tossed Danish ship arrived from Norway. James ordered the Earl of Bothwell, Admiral of

Scotland to sail with six ships to rescue Queen Anne, but the Council flatly declined the expense. So James decided to go himself in Chancellor Maitland's small ship 'with such ships as he [Maitland] and some other loyal subjects could furnish...[13]

It was a brave (some would say foolhardy) decision of James to cross the North Sea at that time of year, especially as Maitland's ship was of only 130 tons. She was also crowded with the officers and attendants appointed to serve Queen Anne, as well as 'all the minions of the King's stables and bedchamber'. There was to be no shortage of food, 'for all these ships, specially the Chancellor's, is so furnished and fraught with good and delicate victual as it was thought strange of so many live cattle and pulleyn, so much banqueting stuff, so much wine of all sorts'.[13a]

James sailed about 22 October. Within six days he was in Norway, within a month he had married Anne. In the New Year they were in Denmark, where he found the company so convivial he remained until spring, drinking, hunting and arguing with learned men. James and Anne finally sailed for Scotland on 21 April 1590, again in the GIDEON, and again they experienced storms, although not so ferocious, for they landed at Leith on May Day to a tumultuous reception. But for Anne, much as she loved her mother and brother in Denmark, the memories of her North Sea crossings were such that she never ventured on the sea again.[13b]

James VI of Scotland inherited the English Crown from Elizabeth I in 1603, thus becoming James I of England. He chose to claim his new crown by proceeding overland, and never again left his two kingdoms. James shamefully neglected the navy he inherited, as is detailed above.

CHARLES II (1660-1685)

THE PRINCIPAL YACHTS

Royal Yacht – a ship built at the royal pleasure, marked by specially luxurious fittings, and at the service of the monarch for business of State, for cruising, for pleasure, as an adjunct of the fleet, and even for racing.

As young men avoiding the Roundheads, both Charles II – then the Prince of Wales – and his brother James, Duke of York, enjoyed sailing in open boats around the Scilly and Channel Islands. In the summer of 1646 Charles had a boat built at St Malo, borrowing money from the Governor of Jersey to pay for her. She had twelve pairs of oars, two masts, and was gaily decorated, the first of some two dozen vessels he was to commission during his lifetime. During later exile in Holland the brothers discovered the pleasures of yachting, for the Dutch had developed these small craft to a high standard of comfort and luxury.

All through the early 1600s yachts had accompanied every Dutch fleet that put to sea, serving as advice boats with their speed, manoeuvrability and good sea-keeping qualities. They were used to carry passengers or despatches over short distances, for exploration, or to escort captured ships back to port. The term comes from jaght, a seventeenth-century term formed on jagen, to hunt or chase. A jachtship was a 'ship for chasing', which soon became anglicized to yacht, but the term suggests they were originally privateers, rather than pleasure boats.

In Holland the rivers and canals were the highroads from one province to another, from one town to the next, and so yachts were used by persons of rank as ordinary means of transport as well as for pleasure. The Dutch yachts had been brought to a high degree of comfort, with much decoration, carving, gilding and paintwork, all of which appealed to Charles. He and his brother soon became competent helmsmen.

John Evelyn noted in his diary for 1 October 1661 that 'yachts [were] vessels not known amongst us till the Dutch East India Company presented that curious piece to the King; being excellent sailing vessels'. But as early as 1613 Phineas Pett recorded the term 'yoathe' in his autobiography. And we find in the household accounts for Herstmonceux Castle in Sussex for the year 1643/4 the sum of £6 paid to 'George Richardson for making a dock at Pemsie (Pevensey) for my lord's yought' (Francis Lennard, Lord Dacre).[1]

At his Restoration in 1660 Charles II commenced the first stage of his journey home in a yacht which had formerly belonged to his brother-in-law, the Prince of Orange, who had died in 1650. It was undoubtedly the finest of the 13 large yachts and numerous smaller vessels which accompanied him as he set out on the first stage to England. The interiors of the cabins were decorated and gilded, whilst some of the best artists of the time had been engaged in making beautiful paintings and sculptures with which to embellish them.

The King boarded the yacht at Breda, together with his sister, the widowed Princess of Orange, and her young son (the future William III); in the many other yachts were the Duke of York and the notables who had shared Charles's exile.

The journey by yacht ended at Rotterdam, the King and his party crossing overland to Scheveningen, where the English fleet was anchored off. Charles immediately embarked in the NASEBY, and the Royal Standard, the Lord High Admiral's flag, and the Union flag were broken out – the first recorded time a sovereign had flown these three flags on board a man-of-war. Gavin comments, 'as though the Royal Standard at the main proclaimed, "I am, by the Grace of God, Charles the Second, King of England"; the Union flag at the mizzen, "I am the King of Great Britain"; and the Anchor flag at the fore, "I am Charles, King of England, and Lord High Admiral of the English Fleet".'

'With a fresh gale and most happy weather,' recorded Pepys, 'we set sail for England.' During the passage to Dover the King in the great cabin gave instructions for the names of ships bearing Cromwellian significance to be changed. This renaming of ships also occurred quite often with Royal Yachts, making some of them particularly awkward to trace.

With the Restoration, Charles II took over an impressive fleet of 154 vessels, which he renamed the Royal Navy. He also took over impressive debts, for the seamen alone were owed £400 000, some having not been paid for three years.[2] He appointed the twenty-seven-year-old Samuel Pepys to the Navy Board, and although the old problems – shortage of money, inefficiency and corruption – were constantly to the fore, Pepys slowly began to achieve order and efficiency.

To this fleet were added 26 yachts between 1660 and 1688, but it must not be assumed they were solely for royal use. Charles tended to have one main vessel of the time, the others being laid up, transferred to general service or engaged on special duties, such as the MERLIN and MONMOUTH surveying the coast of Britain. The Lord Lieutenant of Ireland, the Commissioners of the Dockyards and the Governor of the Isle of Wight all had yachts attached to their appointments. When on general service the yachts were in active commission, as shown by the sinking of the HENRIETTA and the capture of the KATHERINE in the Dutch Wars. And being small, the yachts were quick, if not necessarily cheap, to build, and so were used to appraise the evolving science of naval architecture as trial ships for larger men-of-war.

The list of principal Royal Yachts gives some idea where the King's affection lay at the time of their building. MARY for his sister, the Princess Royal; KATHERINE for his future Queen; HENRIETTA after his favourite sister Minette, Duchess of Orleans, whose husband was brother to the King of France; CLEVELAND after his favourite of the moment, Barbara Villiers, Duchess of Cleveland; CHARLOT, for the Countess of Litchfield, his second daughter by the Duchess of Cleveland; MONMOUTH for his son, the Duke of Monmouth, by Lucy Walter; PORTSMOUTH after another favourite, Louise de Kéroualle, newly created Duchess of Portsmouth; and FUBBS from her nickname.

Charles had appeared so pleased with the yacht in which he voyaged from Breda that the Burgomaster of Amsterdam begged for the city to be allowed to present the King with a similar one. On His Majesty graciously accepting, a vessel was purchased from the Admiralty Board of the Netherlands, and suitably prepared for Charles.

She was a typical Dutch State yacht, magnificently painted below, and ornate with gilded carvings, particularly round the stern cabin, with its high coach roof and side windows. She was broad in the beam, of shallow draught, cutter or 'yacht'-rigged, and fitted with lee-boards to enable her to be sailed to windward. Eight small guns could be fired from the circular gunports, with their carved and gilded port wreaths. The Royal Arms of England were on the stern, under three elaborate stern lanterns, and the figurehead was a unicorn.

MARY

Built c.1658 in Holland for the Dutch Admiralty.

Length on gundeck	–	Length by the keel	52 feet
Beam	19 feet	Depth in hold	7 feet 7 inches
Tons burden	100	Crew	20 peace 30 war
Guns	8 three-pounders		

Draught 10 feet with leeboards down; actual draught probably about 3 feet.[3]
Named after the King's sister, the Princess Royal, mother of William III.
1660 presented by the City of Amsterdam to Charles II.
1661 transferred to general service.
1675 4 April, wrecked off Holyhead.

MARY, 1660

The extraordinary detail of this drawing by Willem Van de Velde the Elder displays his artistic skills at their best. The Dutch States provided him with a small vessel in which to follow the fleet and record naval actions. He came to England about 1665, and was appointed marine painter to the King in 1674.

MARY left for England on 12 August 1660 under the command of Captain John De Geus, and on arrival in the Thames was named by Charles MARY, after his sister, the Princess Royal. MARY was the first true Royal Yacht as we understand the term.

Pepys's Diary, 15 August 1660:

> To the office, and after dinner by water to White Hall, where I found the King gone this morning by five of the clock to see a Dutch pleasure-boat [MARY] below bridge, where he dines, and my Lord (Sandwich) with him. The King do tire all his people that are about him with early rising since he come.

8 November 1660:

> On board the yacht, which is indeed the finest thing I saw for neatness and room in so small a vessel. Mr Pett is to make one to outdo this for the honour of the country, which I fear he will scarce better.

Mr (afterwards Sir Anthony) Deane, Master Shipwright of Woolwich Dockyard, and Commissioner of the Navy, told Pepys that, 'in the year '60 the Dutch gave His Majesty a yacht called the MARY whence came the improvements of our present yachts, for until that time we had not heard such a name in England.'[4]

But the MARY remained in the personal service of the King for little more than a year before being handed over to the navy for general service. Her build and sea-worthiness made her ideal for the short seas of the Irish Channel, 'for the sea is so short and broken that Holland built ships are found the fittest for that passage'.[5] So she was employed carrying important passengers of State between Parkgate on the River Dee or Holyhead to Dublin, as well as anti-privateering duties in the Irish Channel.

The MARY was wrecked on the foggy night of 4 April 1675 (25 March, Julian calendar) when, at about 2 am, she struck a rock near the present Skerries lighthouse, seven miles from Holyhead. She carried a crew of 28 and 46 passengers in her small hull, including the Earl of Ardglass, the Earl of Meath, and his son Lord Ardee. As she settled she listed heavily, and her mast touched the rocks of the Skerries, enabling 39 of those on board the overcrowded vessel to scramble ashore. However, 35 were lost, including the Captain, Boatswain and the Earl of Meath; those on the rocks were rescued after two days by a Wicklow vessel.[6]

KATHERINE

Built 1661 at Deptford.		Surveyor Commissioner Pett.	
Length on gundeck	–	Length by the keel	49 feet
Beam	19 feet	Depth in hold	–
Tons burden	94	Crew	30
Guns	8 three-pounders	Estimated cost £1335	

Named after Katherine of Braganza, Infanta of Portugal.
In August 1673 she was captured by the Dutch, but returned in November the following year. Thereafter assigned to the service of the Ordnance.

Within three months of the MARY's arrival Charles ordered a new yacht to be built at Deptford by Commissioner Pett. There was no doubt the arrival of the MARY stimulated English shipwrights, and the new yacht was to be of deeper draught for English waters – which obviated the need for leeboards – and finer underwater lines.

The KATHERINE was named after Katherine of Braganza, Infanta of Portugal, to whom Charles was affianced. She had been escorted from Portugal by the Earl of Sandwich on board the first-rate ROYAL CHARLES, and was married to the King in Portsmouth on 22 May 1661.

Charles took a keen interest in the building of this yacht, as did Pepys, who wrote in his diary for 13 January 1661:

> To the Globe for dinner, and then with Commissioner Pett to his lodgings there, (which he hath for the present, while he is in building the King's yacht, which will be a very pretty thing, and much beyond the Dutchman's).

And on the 15th:

> The King hath been this afternoon at Deptford to see the yacht that Commissioner Pett is building, which will be very pretty, as also that his brother at Woolwich is making. (ANNE.)

KATHERINE was not entirely satisfactory; she had been ballasted with lead shot from the Tower of London, but on 4 June Commissioner Pett requisitioned from Chatham Dockyard 'New sails and four tons of musket-shot required for ballast.'[7] This meant a complete new suit of sails within two months of launching, but as the first yacht to be built she must surely have been regarded somewhat as a trial-horse. KATHERINE was rigged with one mast, a mainsail with a long gaff and no boom, a square topsail, and two headsails – a rig typical of Royal Yachts of that period.

KATHERINE, 1661

This drawing by Willem Van de Velde the Elder shows the 'fine yellow-painted (figure) head supported by sea-nymphs and goddesses, ...for two feet below the rails it is covered with costly sculptures and gold-painted carvings of grotesque figures and plants. (The stern) boasts three round gilded lanterns (and) a maiden in stately dress... finely carved and gilded'.

The KATHERINE continued in service until August 1673, when she was captured by the Dutch at the battle of Texel. Nicholas Witsen, later Burgomaster of Amsterdam, described her most fully at the time of her capture, and his account gives us a detailed record of the yacht.[8] She was restored to England in November the following year, as a present from the Prince of Orange to one Alderman Backwell. By then, however, the King was building a new KATHERINE, and the old yacht was usually assigned to the service of the Ordnance.

In 1677 the KATHERINE was among the fleet of yachts accompanying the honeymoon voyage of William of Orange and Princess Mary, (later King William and Queen Mary) daughter of James, Duke of York.

HENRIETTA

Built 1663 at Woolwich.		Surveyor Christopher Pett.	
Length on gundeck	–	Length by the keel	52 feet
Beam	19 feet 5 inches	Depth in hold	7 feet
Tons burden	104	Crew	30
Guns	8 three-pounders		

Named after the King's mother (1609-1669) or sister Minette, the Duchess of Orleans (1631-1660); probably the latter.[9]
1673 sunk at the Battle of Texel.

The estimated cost of the HENRIETTA was £1335, but this was probably for the hull alone, and her final ready-for-sea cost is more likely to have been £3640 (at £35/ton).[10]

The King personally supervised the design of HENRIETTA, and her fitting out was the result of much careful thought. To reduce cost, the cabins were hung with gilded leather instead of the usual elaborate carved decorations to ceilings and bulkheads. Three copper chimneys were fitted, one for a marble fireplace.

For some reason, possibly because of increased sail area, HENRIETTA required considerable ballast; 16 tons of shot and 13 tons of lead being originally supplied. But a further 16 tons were needed, and to economise the Navy Board suggested stone ballast. Christopher Pett replied indignantly, 'If stones are used it will half fill the cabins and would make her run to leeward.'[11]

On 10 August 1663 Christopher Pett wrote to the Navy Commissioners and begged that the launch might be delayed until the next spring tides, when her rigging and sails might be more forward. And again on 31 August he wrote that he had chosen a mast for the King's new yacht, but wanted the three (poop) lanterns, which His Majesty would expect to see up at the launching, and they were the most difficult to make.

There is a story told of HENRIETTA that when she was afloat, but not actually finished, she was flying all her colours, when a boat passed which refused to strike to the colours. The royal crew, in high dudgeon at this perceived insult to the King, promptly seized the hapless boat. The matter was referred to the King, who ordered the boat to be restored, as he was not on board the HENRIETTA at the time, and so his colours should not have been flying.

Soon the HENRIETTA was put to use, for on 5 September 1662 Pepys wrote:

> With the Duke (of York); where all our discourse of war in the highest measure. Prince Rupert was with us; who is fitting himself to go to sea in the Heneretta.

Edward Byrd, Master Shipwright at Woolwich, when writing to the Navy Board about some repairs for the yacht commented, 'The King has more affection for the HENRIETTA than all the rest.' Indeed in March 1671, at Sheerness, the King personally inspected the fitting of milled-lead sheathing to the yacht as protection against worms. She was one of the first vessels so to be fitted, but it was not a great success, as the iron fastenings caused corrosion to set up. It is possible this may have weakened the fastenings, for the HENRIETTA was sunk in 1673 at the Battle of Texel in the Third Dutch War.

By 1664 it was apparent that the old quarrel between the English and the Dutch was breaking out again, especially after the English occupied New Amsterdam and renamed it New York. As Monck said, 'The trade of the world is too little for us two, therefore one must down.'

By March next year the two countries were at war, and the Royal Yachts played their part as despatch vessels to the fleet. However, by the autumn of 1666 the fleet was leaky, lacking masts and spars, and above all men. The Privy Council recommended the Great Ships be laid up for the winter in the Thames and Medway, for no funds were available, even for the sailors' pay; pay tickets were dishonoured, while the men were angry and in mutinous mood.
Pepys, 31 October 1666:

> The seamen grow very rude... and no one with justice can blame them, we owing them so much money, and their familys must starve if we do not give them money, or they procure upon their tickets from some people that will trust them. ...the business of the navy standing wholly still. No credit, no goods sold us, nobody will trust us.

The winter of 1666 came and went, spring passed, summer was at hand, and still the King's Great Ships were laid up in the Medway, idle and apparently forgotten. Then on 9 June 1667 the Dutch under De Ruyter arrived and sailed up the river, piloted by English deserters furious at those who had withheld their pay:

> '...he himself did hear many Englishmen on board the Dutch ships speaking to one another in English; and that they did cry and say, "We did heretofore fight for tickets; now we fight for dollars!"'[12]

The Dutch captured the ROYAL CHARLES, burnt three great warships and shamed the nation. But Pepys could not help noting in his diary for 21 June 1667 a tit-bit of scandal:

> The night the Dutch burnt our ships the King did sup with my Lady Castlemayne at the Duchess of Monmouth's, and they were all mad in hunting a poor moth.

Peace with the Dutch, for a time at least, was signed later that year, but it was three years before Charles ordered the building of another principal yacht. This one, the CLEVELAND, was the first of several yachts to be named after one of his many mistresses.

Charles II's interest was not confined just to the yachts, but also in the ships of the navy and the dockyards and organisations that supplied them. He encouraged the nobility and gentry to send their sons to sea, thus raising the standard of the officers. He knighted many of the senior captains and those who had distinguished themselves, as well as senior shipbuilders and dockyard officials. In the words of a pamphlet published in 1705:

> (The King) himself frequently went aboard his Men of War and Yachts, and sometimes cruised in the Channel; by that means bringing the whole Court to sea, not only for a passage, but a kind of sejour; so that in his days it was become a mode at Court to discourse of Naval Affairs, the Captains of Men of War meeting there many of their acquaintance, scarce any of the courtiers not having been at sea, either with the King or the Duke of York.[13]

CLEVELAND

Built 1671 at Portsmouth.		Surveyor Sir Anthony Deane.	
Length on gundeck	–	Length by the keel	53 feet 4 inches
Beam	19 feet 4 inches	Depth in hold	7 feet 9 inches
Tons burden	107	Crew	730
Guns	8 three-pounders		

Named after the Duchess of Cleveland.
January 1685 to the service of the Office of Ordnance.
25 January 1715 paid off and sold shortly afterwards.

Barbara Villiers was the wife of Roger Palmer, and about 1690, when aged eighteen, she became the willing mistress of Charles II; Palmer, as recompense, was created Earl of Castlemaine. Hectoring and spendthrift, her amours were notorious, but in August 1670 Charles created her Duchess of Cleveland, Countess of Southampton and Baroness Nonsuch. More of a golden handshake really, as she was soon to be ousted by Louise de Kéroualle.

Pepys was much enamoured of her, 'I went away not weary with looking at her.' And to his 'great solace and content' he once observed Lady Castlemaine's 'smocks and linen petticoats' on the line!

Charles continued the tradition of naming yachts after his favourites by later christening the CHARLOT of 1677 for the Countess of Litchfield, his daughter by the Duchess of Cleveland.

For the first few years of her life the CLEVELAND was the yacht mostly used by King Charles. He made many visits to his fleet and dockyards, for he was most keen to raise the profile of the navy. By showing royal interest he assured his courtiers and the captains and officers of ships of the high regard in which he held the navy, and thus attracted a greater number of suitable men into the service.

The King would embark at Greenwich or some other port on the Thames, and accompanied by the other yachts carrying officials of State, he would proceed to where the fleet was anchored. One well-recorded visit to the fleet was on 6 June 1672, after the Battle of Solebay, and is detailed overleaf.

CLEVELAND, 1671

From the studios of Van de Velde the Younger in 1689 – 'Royal Yachts at sea in a storm.' The painting may well represent an earlier event. The yacht in the foreground may be the CLEVELAND, *her mainsail brailed up in the strong wind. Beyond her is a two-deck ship flying the Royal Standard at the main. In the background are three more yachts and another ship.*

In July 1678 Sir Anthony Deane was sent to France to accompany the two yachts he had built at Portsmouth for Louis XIV. The affair was viewed with suspicion in England, for Pepys and Deane were charged with sending plans and drawings of ships to the French, an indication of how valuable yacht design had become.

In 1685 the CLEVELAND was transferred to service of the Office of Ordnance, paid off 25 January 1715 and sold.

VISIT OF CHARLES II TO THE FLEET, 6 JUNE 1672, AFTER THE BATTLE OF SOLEBAY

Charles II would pay frequent visits to the fleet, partly out of personal interest, and partly to inspire the men; if he was unable to pay them, at least he could encourage them. After the Battle of Solebay against the Dutch, on 29 May 1672 (OS), the English and French fleets retired to the Medway to refit, and on 5 June lay at anchor in the Swin under the command of James, Duke of York; the day was hazy with a 'fresh gale' blowing from the south-west. Royal Yachts were commonly used in times of war, and in this instance the KITCHEN, Captain William Wright, was attached to the fleet. On 3 June she was sent upriver to Gravesend; on the 5th her log[14] reads:

THE FLEET, 1672

Willem Van de Velde the Younger – 'Visit to the Fleet.' In the left foreground is the ANNE *yacht, stern to. Broadside is the* CLEVELAND, *in which Charles II had come down the Thames, and which he has just left; a man is aloft hauling down the standard. The Duke of York is on board the flagship, HMS* PRINCE, *with the King's boat alongside. The* KITCHEN *is astern of the Prince, and on the extreme right is part of a Dutch bezan, possibly the* BEZAN.

> att 7 A Clocke the King Cam downe and went on Boord of the Cleveland yacht so we Cam to sail and att 3 afternoon we Cam to An Anckor. In shore was the fleate not Being Com up.

(The naval day changed at noon, so by the time the King boarded the PRINCE it was 6 June.) Charles was accompanied by the KATHERINE, ANNE, KITCHEN and probably BEZAN, as well as other yachts for the numerous courtiers invariably in attendance. As soon as the CLEVELAND came in sight of the fleet the Duke of York on board the PRINCE caused his standard to be struck. The King went on board the flagship, at which moment the Royal Standard was hoisted at the main, the 'Red Standard with anchor' (Lord High Admiral's Standard) at the fore, and the Union flag at the mizzen.

The King conducted a Council of War on board the PRINCE, and remained with the fleet for several days, as is shown by the KITCHEN'S log of 9 June:

> Att one in the Morning we waied with Littell wind... the Ann and Cleveland in our Company Being Bound up (river) with the King att 9 att night wee Cam to An Anckor... (near Woolwich).

Once Charles had completed his inspection the fleet proceeded to sea in search of the Dutch fleet.

CORONELLI'S YACHT

In 1673 the Italian hydrographer Coronelli published a drawing of an English Royal Yacht. From this contemporary illustration and later Admiralty draughts one can establish the normal layout of Royal Yachts.

In Coronelli's drawing a short ladder leads from the maindeck to a lobby, with the King's cabin to starboard. Right aft is the great cabin or Queen's cabin with a four-poster bed and side windows; there appears to be a bulkhead with an arched doorway leading into a closet. This is strange, for it would have blocked the light from the stern windows. Beneath these two cabins is stowage for ship's gear. The stateroom is amidships, the full width of the vessel, reached from the lobby by a companionway, and lit by a skylight on deck. It is highly decorated, with paintings hung on the ship's sides, and has a table secured to the deck. Forward of this is the lords' room, then the galley, and finally the officers' and men's quarters. One is immediately reminded of the description by Nicholas Witsen, later Burgomaster of Amsterdam, when the Dutch captured the KATHERINE yacht.
4 September 1673:

> One goes down some steps into two rooms aft, the foremost is a brave hall, painted all round with works of art, gilded and decorated with carvings; the after cabin which one enters from the other is up a step or two; here there is a nice bedstead, and it looks out aft with windows being decorated all round with gold leather. Above this room, which is raised some feet above the deck, stands the helmsman, the iron tiller is conveniently bent so that it can be handled by a man standing upright. The after end of the roof over this stern cabin is higher than the fore end for the sake of appearance. Below these two rooms in the bottom of the ship are spaces for stowing rigging gear and tools. In the fore hall is a staircase with a door by which one goes down into a room whose floor is the ship's bottom; through this one enters another, and thus reaches the caboose which is the fore part of the ship; these rooms have beds all round, separated by screens painted with the King's arms and gilded.

Coronelli's drawing is not the KATHERINE, as she was yacht-rigged i.e. one mast. But the first principal yacht to be ketch-rigged, the FUBBS, was not built until 1682, nine years after the publication of Coronelli's drawing, which remains unidentified.

Gavin quotes Keltridge's list of ship's rigging as showing the MERLIN (1666) and KITCHEN (1670) as being galliots i.e. with a lateen-mizzen; so they are both possible contenders for Coronelli's yacht. It is unlikely that the MERLIN, never a principal Royal Yacht, would be so highly equipped as in Coronelli's drawing.

There is also a Van de Velde drawing showing the KITCHEN with but a single mast. She was in any case built as a floating galley for other Royal Yachts, and would not have had the accommodation shown.

KATHERINE II

Built 1674 at Chatham.		Surveyor Phineas Pett.	
Length on gundeck	–	Length by the keel	56 feet
Beam	21 feet 4 inches	Depth in hold	8 feet 6 inches
Tons burden	135	Crew	30
Guns	8 three-pounders		

Named after KATHERINE captured by the Dutch 1673.
Estimated cost £1550.
1720 rebuilt.

The first KATHERINE had been captured by the Dutch in 1673, and although she was returned the following year, Charles had already given orders for a replacement. She was built at Chatham by Phineas Pett, cousin of Commissioner Peter Pett who had built the first KATHERINE in 1661.

Her estimated cost was £1550, but this was probably only the hull and rigging; guns, colours and decoration would have been extra, for as in modern yacht-building, the art is to keep the initial estimate low!

Above: *CORONELLI'S YACHT, 1673*

Left: *KATHERINE II, 1674*

At the National Maritime Museum is a rigged model of a Stuart Royal Yacht c.1674 which probably represents the KATHERINE. *Known as 'Mrs Montagu's model,' from the donor, it represents a design for one of the 14 large yachts built by Charles II. The decorations of the stern are not, however, identical with any of those sketched and named by the Van de Veldes, although the dimensions correspond very closely with those of the* KATHERINE *and the* PORTSMOUTH. *As actually built, nearly all these Stuart Royal Yachts carried a large carving of the royal arms in the stern. The figure of a draped woman and two naked boys, which here take the place of that design, seem to indicate that the present model represents a projected rather than a completed vessel. The carving, which is excellently preserved, is delicate and elaborate, the sleeping boys above the windows of the cabin being particularly charming. The mast, gaff and lower yard are all original, whilst the sails and rigging have been added by the museum. From the quality of carving, and a Van de Velde drawing of the stern of the* KATHERINE *it is probable the model represents the yacht.*[15]

Facing: *PORTSMOUTH, 1674*

Van de Velde the Elder – 'The Portsmouth yacht at anchor.' The PORTSMOUTH *is here shown at anchor, her mainsail half-brailed, and her square topsail aback in the very light air. A common pendant flies from the masthead, and the deck is crowded with people, but the occasion is not known. The painting is dated 1675; the hull almost certainly painted by Van de Velde the Elder, but the mast and sails by the Younger.*

KATHERINE is shown as one of eight Royal Yachts in service when William and Mary assumed the throne from the deposed James II in 1688, and one of seven in service in 1703, shortly after Queen Anne commenced her reign. She was rebuilt in 1720 and continued in service as a Royal Yacht for a further eighty years, being sold in 1801.

PORTSMOUTH

Built 1674 at Woolwich.		Surveyor Phineas Pett.	
Length on gundeck	–	Length by the keel	57 feet
Beam	20 feet 6 inches	Depth in hold	7 feet 4 inches
Tons burden	133	Crew	30
Guns	8 three-pounders		

Named after Charles II's mistress, the Duchess of Portsmouth.
1688 converted to a bomb-vessel of 143 tons.
1703 wrecked at the Nore in the great gale of 27 November.

Phineas Pett was kept busy in 1674, for as well as the KATHERINE II he was also building the PORTSMOUTH at Woolwich. The warrant from the King and Pepys, dated 10 January 1674, directed the Navy Board 'to cause our new yacht to be carved and gilded in the same manner as our yacht the CLEVELAND'.[16] However, only £26 was allowed for her carved work, which is very low compared to the £300 allocated to the FUBBS, and perhaps indicates she was not intended as a principal Royal Yacht. She was sometimes used to accommodate the King in person, and often named among those in attendance when the King embarked on a principal yacht.

The PORTSMOUTH was named after Louise de Kéroualle, who had been deliberately introduced to Charles's court by Louis XIV as a 'Trojan Horse'. Charles, however, took the bait without swallowing the hook. Her rise was rapid, and in February 1673, less than eighteen months from her seduction – if such a pre-planned event could be called that – she was created Duchess of Portsmouth, Countess of Fareham and Lady Petersfield; a year later the PORTSMOUTH yacht was so named in her honour.[17]

For her services to France Louise had already been granted the Dukedom of Aubigny by Louis XIV in 1672, which her son by Charles – the Duke of Richmond (and later Lennox) – and his heirs owned until the early 1800s. Clearly, courtesanship was both pleasurable and profitable.

Louise, however, was much disliked by the mob, not only for her Catholicism but also her airs and graces. One day, mistaking Nell Gwynn's coach for that of Louise, the mob started battering the sides and hurling insults. Nell popped her head out of the window and entreated, 'Good people you are mistaken, for this is the Protestant whore!'[18]

Poor Nell received neither title nor yacht named after her, but her ready wit and earthiness surely deserved reward at least equal to the rest of the King's rapacious mistresses.

The PORTSMOUTH yacht was made a bomb-vessel in 1688, and wrecked at the Nore in the great gale of 27 November 1703.

There is no doubt Charles loved the sea for, as Arlington wrote, 'He would steal away upon any pretext and board his fleet at Sheerness for a cruise to Plymouth or other ports on the south coast.' Pepys commented, somewhat ruefully, that the King 'possessed a transcendent mastery of all maritime knowledge, and two leagues travel by sea was more pleasure to him than twenty by land'.

CHARLES II

Built 1675 at Rotherhithe.		Surveyor Sir Anthony Deane.	
Length on gundeck	–	Length by the keel	54 feet
Beam	20 feet 6 inches	Depth in hold	7 feet 9 inches
Tons burden	120	Crew	30
Guns	8 three-pounders		

Named after Charles II.
1678 cast away on the coast of Holland in November.

The first CHARLES, a small yacht of 38 tons burden, had been exchanged with the Board of Ordnance in 1688, so the name was available for the second yacht built in 1675 by Sir Anthony Deane. On 13 September that year the King went to see her building at Rotherhithe, yet another example of his keen interest in ships and the navy.

Her career was short. She was in the fleet of yachts that accompanied William of Orange and Princess Mary on their honeymoon voyage in 1677, but in November of the following year she was cast away on the coast of Holland. She was the last Royal Yacht of that name.

CHARLES II, 1675

Drawing by Van de Velde the Elder.

CHARLOT

Built 1677 at Woolwich.		Surveyor Thomas Shish.	
Length on gundeck	–	Length by the keel	61 feet 9 inches
Beam	20 feet 6½ inches	Depth in hold	9 feet
Tons burden	143	Crew	30
Guns	8 three-pounders		

Named after the second daughter of Barbara Villiers by Charles II.
1701-1709 Dublin station.
1710 rebuilt at Deptford.

Private Collection

CHARLOT, 1677

Oil by Willem Van de Velde – 'Two yachts getting underway.' The nearest is probably the CHARLOT. *Painted to a large extent by the Younger c.1685, the yacht in the foreground is identified as the* CHARLOT *from a drawing at the National Maritime Museum. She is seen here getting underway in a very light air, her topsail set but not sheeted home. The small Royal Yacht astern of the* CHARLOT *has not been identified.*

Two years were to elapse before Charles ordered another yacht, and then in 1677 he built two, the CHARLOT and the MARY II.

The new yachts were immediately pressed into service, for Princess Mary travelled to Holland on the CHARLOT following her marriage to Prince William of Orange on 4 November that year. Her husband travelled on the MARY II, so presumably neither yacht was large enough to accommodate the royal entourages. (For details of the voyage see MARY II.)

On 1 May 1689 her Captain was Andrew Cotton, who received orders to make prizes of what ships and vessels he met with belonging to the French King. On 17 May he had just carried the Lieutenant Governor back to Guernsey and was anchored in the Roads off St Peter's Port:

> The wind at E.N.E. this morning I weighed for Jersey with Sir Edward Carteret on board about 4 leagues from Guernsey I espied a small vessel so I stood to speak with her and fired to bring her by the lee; but she being a French privateer made the best of her way to get clear I chased her about 3 hours and fired about 50 guns at her and plying my small shot smartly, they left the deck and the Captain called for Quarter. I found on board her 22 men 4 periers (small guns firing stones) and small arms so I carried her into Jersey Roads and landed Sir Edward.[19]

Between 1701-1709 she was allocated to the Lord Lieutenant of Ireland for service on the Dublin station. (For details see chapter 9.)

The CHARLOT is shown as being among the eight yachts on service at the accession of William and Mary, and was rebuilt in 1710.

MARY II

Built 1677 at Chatham.		Surveyor Sir Phineas Pett.	
Length on gundeck	–	Length by the keel	66 feet 4 inches
Beam	21 feet 6 inches	Depth in hold	8 feet 9 inches
Tons burden	155	Crew	30
Guns	8 three-pounders		

Named after Mary, daughter of the Duke of York.
1727 rebuilt.

The second MARY took the name of her predecessor lost at sea, but was probably named after the Duke of York's daughter, recently affianced to William of Orange, (afterwards King William and Queen Mary). The MARY was built in 1677 at Chatham by the recently knighted Sir Phineas Pett and apart from HENRIETTA II was the largest yacht Charles built.

Her first official duty was to carry the newly married William and Mary on their honeymoon voyage back to Holland, in company with several other Royal Yachts. The couple were married on the 4 November 1677, and two weeks later they left Whitehall accompanied by the King, the Duke of York and many of the nobility in barges. The fleet of yachts, consisting of the MARY II, CHARLOT, KATHERINE II, CHARLES II, PORTSMOUTH, ANNE and NAVY was waiting at Erith, along with the GREYHOUND and SOLDIER ketches. William and Mary embarked in the MARY on Monday 19 November; Van de Velde recorded the scene in a series of drawings, and commented, 'We had remained at anchor a little near Erith owing to the calm, and getting some wind we hoist sails.'

MARY II, 1677

Willem Van de Velde the Younger – 'The departure of William of Orange and Princess Mary for Holland 29 November 1677.' In the centre is the MARY, *at her masthead the special orange standard designed for the occasion. In the left middle distance is the* CHARLOT, *to which William later transferred; his standard is furled at the masthead.*

Down river they sailed, being saluted by Sheerness Castle, then anchoring off Margate before crossing to Holland. In fact, William travelled in the MARY, and Princess Mary in the CHARLOT.[20]

Eleven years later Admiral Herbert was despatched in the MARY to bring Princess Mary back to England as Queen, her father James II having abdicated and fled. She landed at Greenwich on 12 February 1689. The MARY continued in service as a Royal Yacht, and is shown as such at the accession of Queen Anne, before being rebuilt in 1727.

HENRIETTA II

Built 1679 at Woolwich.		Surveyor Thomas Shish.	
Length on gundeck	–	Length by the keel	65 feet
Beam	21 feet 8 inches	Depth in hold	8 feet 3 inches
Tons burden	162	Crew	30
Guns	8 three-pounders		

Named after yacht of same name, sunk in 1673.
1720 sold.

The first HENRIETTA, of whom 'the King has more affection than all the rest', was sunk during the Third Dutch Wars, and a replacement was built six years later, in 1679. The new yacht at 162 tons burden was the largest yacht built by Charles II, but surprisingly little is recorded of her use.

She is shown as among the yachts in service at the accessions of both William and Mary and Queen Anne, being sold in 1720.

The model illustrated overleaf, almost certainly the HENRIETTA II, has a fascinating history. It was originally acquired by Charles Sergison, Clerk of the Acts of the Navy Board from 1689-1719. This and the 13 other ship models he collected remained at his home, Cuckfield Park, in Sussex, until 1922, when the whole collection was purchased by Colonel Henry Rogers of Long Island, New York.

The monochrome illustration (from Commander Gavin's collection) shows the HENRIETTA II shortly after restoration at Greenwich by Dr R.C. Anderson about 1919. It originally carried several furled sails, but they, along with the masts, spars and rigging were quite dilapidated. Dr Anderson was able to knot and splice together a good deal of the old line, but could not save the sails.

Colonel Rogers turned the model over to his restorer, Mr Henry Culver, and although his craftsmanship is of the highest order, sadly he replaced the original masts and rigging, and added a good deal of rigging not in the original version.

When Colonel Rogers died in 1935 he bequeathed his entire collection to the U.S. Naval Academy in Annapolis, which now has one of the finest collections of ship models in the world. For many years it was thought to be of the NAVY yacht, but Major Grant Walker of the Annapolis Museum states the model is almost certainly the second HENRIETTA of 1679.

From paintings and drawings, primarily at Greenwich, he has assembled 'a very strong body of evidence that the model cannot represent the NAVY yacht (which was quite different from the model)'. His measurements of the model's length-to-breadth ratio compare most closely to the HENRIETTA as built. The monogram 'C R' is carved in relief on the inside of the model's taffrail. Only two other of Charles' yachts fit the length-to-breadth ratio: the MARY of 1677 and the ISABELLA of 1682. The MARY clearly had an equestrian figurehead; ISABELLA was ketch-rigged.[21]

HENRIETTA II, 1682

The 'Sergison' model, now at the U.S. Naval Academy, Annapolis.

FUBBS

Built 1682 at Greenwich.		Surveyor Sir Phineas Pett.	
Length on gundeck	73 feet 6 inches	Length by the keel	63 feet
Beam	21 feet	Depth in hold	9 feet 6 inches
Tons burden	148	Crew	30
Guns	12 three-pounders	Ketch-rigged	

Named after Charles II's mistress, Louise de Kéroualle.
1701 rebuilt.

'The King pleases himself mightily with a design he is now going upon building, a yacht the size of the KATHERINE that shall go with a ketch's sail.'[22] In fact the FUBBS was longer than the KATHERINE, slightly narrower, and a foot deeper in the hold, giving a tonnage of 148 tons burden. Her appearance and sailing qualities are legendary, and Charles considered her the finest of his ships for sailing, and,

Left: *FUBBS, 1682*

From Sutherland's 'Ship-building Unveil'd 1717' probably of the FUBBS.

indeed, a design that could hardly be equalled. Her main mast was made of a 22-inch Norway stick, which indicates her superior speed was due to both good hull design and a large sail area.

Charles claimed to have invented ketch-rig, but there are drawings at least a century earlier of ketch-rigged hoys, and it would be more accurate to say Charles introduced it to Royal Yachts. Ketch-rig at this time was the original yacht rig with the addition of a mizzen-mast, on which was set a lateen sail and square topsail, with possibly an additional headsail – a flying jib.[23]

The FUBBS was named after Louise de Kéroualle, Charles II's mistress, who already had one yacht named after her, the PORTSMOUTH, in 1674. Her portrait shows a baby face with fat cheeks surrounded by a halo of curls, which led the King to nickname her Fubbs (for chubby). Although mercenary, haughty to her social inferiors, and at times tiresomely hysterical, Louise possessed an excellent instinct where the King was concerned. Charles was at an age when a good salon, with agreeable company and excellent food, possessed at least as much attraction as a voluptuous bedroom.

But he was not too averse to comfortable beds, for the royal cabin on the FUBBS, situated aft, included a great four-poster bed resplendent with gold brocades and costly silks. Entered from a richly decorated ante room, the cabin was panelled in carved oak, with an inlaid floor. By attending to all Charles' interests Louise retained her status until the King's death, and her son by Charles was created Duke of Richmond and Hereditary High Admiral of Scotland.[24] Louise outlived both Charles and her yacht namesakes, and died in France, aged eighty-five, 'very old, very penitent, very poor'.

There is an interesting series of letters from Phineas Pett concerning the final fitting out and launching of the FUBBS;[25] anyone who has had dealings with HM Dockyards will recognise the concern and anxiety for last-minute stores and fittings expressed over three centuries ago by Pett.

ISABELLA[26]

Built 1683 at Greenwich.		Surveyor Sir Phineas Pett.	
Length on gundeck	–	Length by the keel	60 feet
Beam	18 feet 11 inches	Depth in hold	8 feet 11 inches
Tons burden	114	Crew	30
Guns	8 three-pounders	Ketch-rigged	

Probably named after the Duke of York's daughter, born in 1676.
1702 broken up, and a new ISABELLA built 1703.

The last Royal Yacht in Charles II's reign, was built in 1683. On 23 December 1682 the Admiralty instructed the Navy Board to 'make a contract with Sir Phineas Pett for building a new yacht at Greenwich with a flush deck, according to the dimensions etc. of the enclosed agreement; and to present an estimate of the charge. ...in consideration thereof Pett to have delivered to him the ISABELLA (formerly ISABELLA BEZAN) and £600.'[27]

The yacht was to have flush decks for ketch sails, to be five feet longer aloft and two and a half feet broader then the ISABELLA BEZAN; her rigging, mast, sails, carving, painting and gilding to be a charge against His Majesty. As previously mentioned, Pett was not happy with the bargain, as 'the ANN yacht I had of His Majesty is still upon my hands, to my great cost, being not yet disposed of...'[27a]

This ISABELLA was to be a fine vessel, drawing on over twenty years of Royal Yacht design. With a lofty mainmast and large spread of canvas it is likely she was as good a sailer as the FUBBS.

In 1687 the ISABELLA was part of a small squadron sent to Lisbon by James II to convoy the daughter of the Prince Palatine, Maria Sophia of Neuberg, for her marriage to Pedro II. The squadron was commanded by Henry Fitzroy, Duke of Grafton, Charles II's illegitimate son by Barbara Villiers, Duchess of Cleveland; and consisted of the flagship ANNE (third-rate), three fourth-rates, two fifth-rates, and the ISABELLA yacht. They left Plymouth on 25 July, arriving in Lisbon on 1 August, a remarkably fast passage.[28]

An interesting footnote is provided in 1688 when James II, deserted by Parliament, the Army, and even by his daughter Anne, prepared to flee the throne and England. On 30 November he wrote, 'Order the ISABELLA and ANNE yachts to fall down to Erith tomorrow. J.R.'[29]

He did not, in fact, use either yacht, and the captain's log for the ISABELLA[30] shows he was ordered from Greenwich to 'Eareff' to embark the Count de Louzon. He was delayed by weather, ending up off 'Margett' in December, where the yacht was seized by anti-James factions, which he calls a 'rabble', and is in turn called a 'dog'. The captain was placed ashore under arrest, but eventually freed and ordered to return to Greenwich in January; later he embarked the Right Hon. Arthur Herbert from 'ye MARY' and landed him at Brill Haven (Brighton?).

The ISABELLA is shown on the list of Royal Yachts in service at the accessions of both William and Mary and Queen Anne; she was broken up in 1702 and a new ISABELLA built the following year.

Facing: *ISABELLA, 1683*

Oil by Peter Monamy. For many years thought to have been painted by Van de Velde the Younger, it is now accepted to be a copy by Monamy, c.1705. The original Van de Velde was destroyed in Berlin during the war. The ISABELLA *is shown flying the Royal Standard from the main mast, and firing a gun salute to port.*

THE INFLUENCE OF CHARLES II ON YACHTING

Although Charles fully indulged his passion for yacht building, the 24 yachts built between 1660 and 1688 were also employed on State and naval services. They were always placed at the disposal of the navy on occasions of emergency; when laid up or not required for immediate use the crews of Royal Yachts were lent to other ships, which must have been a jolt from their relatively comfortable billets.

The principal yachts were reserved for the use of the King and those of the Court in attendance on him; but many others were used by dockyard officials, the Governor of the Isle of Wight, the Lords Lieutenant of Ireland, and for ambassadorial duties.
Others were lost or disposed of:

CHARLES, 1668 exchanged with the Office of Ordnance.
KATHERINE, 1673 captured by the Dutch.
ROYAL ESCAPE, 1673 to general service.
HENRIETTA, 1673 sunk in action.

SAUDADOES, 1673 rebuilt as sixth-rate.
MARY, 1675 wrecked off Holyhead.
CHARLES II, 1678 wrecked on the coast of Holland.
ISABELLA BEZAN, 1683 sold to Sir Phineas Pett.

The King and the Duke of York did much to popularise yachting with their public enjoyment of the sport in the small yachts on the upper reaches of the Thames. Indeed by 1663 Christopher Pett demanded an extra gratuity for building pleasure-boats, because of all the people he had to entertain. With their light fore and aft rigs, keen underwater lines and luxurious accommodation, the Royal Yachts were ideally suited to cruising and racing, and were much used by the royal brothers.

The science of mathematics was increasingly having an effect on ship design, and the King's interest in this, as well as navigation and astronomy, led to him paying keen attention to all his yachts and ships. Charles 'understood navigation well; but above all he knew the architecture of ships so perfectly, that in that respect he was exact rather more than became a prince.'[31] His yachts clearly gave him much pleasure, but they also served as experimental ship designs.

In 1678 Charles suggested that 'for the settling a breed of pilots' the boys from his new Royal Mathematical School at Christ's Hospital might be 'constantly borne upon (the) yachts and there kept to that particular practice of observing the depths of water in all places the yachts are employed in and passed through with the shifting of the sands, and what else appertains to the perfecting of a good pilot.' However, it seems unlikely this was acted upon.[32]

Charles enjoyed many pleasant cruises in the FUBBS, and he once made up a party to sail down the Thames and around the coast of Kent. Among those on board was the Rev. John Gostling, a sub-dean at the Chapel Royal, who possessed an exceptionally fine deep bass voice with a wide range. The King was a fair tenor and often enjoyed singing with his clerical friend; he once presented him with a silver egg filled with golden guineas, remarking that eggs were good for the voice. The FUBBS had reached the North Foreland when suddenly 'the sea breeze began to pipe' and 'the King and the Duke of York were necessitated, in order to preserve the vessel, to handle the sails like common seamen, but by good providence they escaped to land'.[33]

The Reverend Gostling was so thankful for his deliverance that on his return to London he selected words from Psalm 107, verses 23-32, and got his friend Henry Purcell to compose an anthem, 'They that go Down to the Sea in Ships'.[34]

They that go down to the sea in ships, these men see
  the works of the Lord and his wonders in the deep.
For at his word the stormy wind ariseth, which lifteth
  up the waves thereof.
They are carried up to heaven and down again to the
  deep; their soul melteth away because of trouble.
They reel to and fro, and stagger like a drunken man,
  and are at their wit's end.
So when they cry unto the Lord in their trouble, he
  delivereth them out of their distress.
For he maketh the storm to cease, so that the waves
  thereof are still.
Then they are glad because they are at rest; and so he
  bringeth them to the haven where they would be.
O that men would therefore praise the Lord, and declare

the wonders that he doth for the children of men,
that they would exalt him also in the congregation of
the people, and praise him in the seat of the elders.

(Chorus) O praise the Lord for his goodness, and declare
the wonders that he doth for the children of men.

Stirring stuff indeed, as any yachtsman who has made shelter after a rough passage will know all too well!

With the death of Charles II yachting lost a kindly royal patron until the foundation a century later of the Cumberland Club (now the Royal Thames Yacht Club) under the personal interest of Admiral the Duke of Cumberland.

Royal Yachts continued to play an important practical role in the lives of succeeding monarchs, but for over a century their use for pleasure died with Charles.

THE SECONDARY, SURVEYING AND DOCKYARD YACHTS OF CHARLES II

THE SECONDARY YACHTS

The size of his Court as well as State duties necessitated several secondary and smaller yachts, and Charles indulged his passion for naval architecture by building some nine secondary yachts in addition to the eleven successive principal ones.

By any standards Stuart Royal Yachts were expensive, but by making them available for general service in the Royal Navy, Charles avoided the need to meet most of their costs from the Privy Purse – not that Charles ever let the question of mere money concern him. The building and crew costs of two Stuart yachts can be seen from those below:

	ANNE			CHARLES		
Tons burden	100			38		
Length on the keel	52 feet			36 feet		
Beam	19 feet			14 feet 2 inches		
Number of guns	8			6		
	£	s	d	£	s	d
Hull	1815	2	4	722	1	5
Masts & Rigging	240	12	0	147	2	0
Lead for ballast	324	0	0	159	13	7
Guns (three-pounders)	186	9	10	120	0	0
Flags & Colours				128	13	6
	2566	4	2	1277	10	6
Cost per ton	25	13	0	33	13	0

For comparison, a man-of-war, ready for sea, would have cost £15/ton, whilst a merchant ship would have been £8/ton.[1]

The cost of flags was high because they were large, numerous and of silk. Large both because the vessel was a Royal Yacht, and to aid identification at a distance; numerous because the more important you were the more flags you flew; and of silk because they were Royal Yachts.

'From the truck flies a silk streamer which in calm hangs down to the water, and it is on all sides proudly decked with flags.'[2] A full set would consist of a Union flag, Standard, Admiralty flag, Ensign and Pennants, and each yacht would have at least two sets.

If the costs of building were high, wages at least were low. The pay roll for the ANNE on 19 April 1661 shows the 12 crew drew an average of 60s per month, compared to an able seaman in the navy who was paid 24s per month.[3] Thus royal yachtsmen were considerably better off financially, as well as having superior conditions of service and the inevitable perks of that age. They were not however immune to the perils of sea and battle, as shown by the loss of the MARY, KATHERINE and HENRIETTA.

ROYAL ESCAPE

Built	–.	Surveyor	–
Length on gundeck	–	Length by the keel	30 feet 6 inches
Beam	14 feet 3 inches	Depth in hold	7 feet
Tons burden	34	Crew	–
Guns	–		

1660 bought by Charles II.
1673 transferred to the navy.
1714 rebuilt.

ROYAL ESCAPE, 1660

Oil by Van de Velde the Younger. Following his defeat at the Battle of Worcester in 1651 Charles II escaped to France in the smack SURPRISE. *At his restoration he bought the vessel, converted her to a Royal Yacht, and renamed her* ROYAL ESCAPE. *She is seen here close-hauled on the port track with half-brailed mainsail.*

One of the first yachts Charles added to his fleet was a humble coasting smack[4], called the SURPRISE. After his fortunes failed at the Battle of Worcester in 1651 Charles fled overland, travelling by a circuitous route to the George Inn at Brighthelmstone (Brighton), where he met Captain Nicholas Tattersall, owner of the SURPRISE. About two in the morning of 15 October he went on board, and the Captain explained to the crew that the passengers were merchants who had suffered losses and were in debt. Offered money, the crew were soon persuaded to divert from their normal route, cross the Channel, and land their royal passenger, albeit unknowingly, at Fecamp.

On his Restoration Charles bought the vessel from Captain Tattersall, renamed her ROYAL ESCAPE, and converted her to a yacht. She was moored off Whitehall Palace where the King could see her, and was used as a houseboat or showboat for royal visitors. In 1672, for one of the King's visits to the fleet the Great Wardrobe supplied to: '…the ROYALL ESCAPE – viz.

> One dozen of Turkey worke chairs, one dozen of Turkey worke Cushions, Four Quilted Bedds, Two small Feather Bedds, Six feather Pillows, Six Covered Quilts, Six pairs of White Blankets, Two small Turkey worke Carpetts, Two small curtacices, Four Pewter Candlesticks, Two Pewter Chamberpotts, and Two pair of Snuffers.[5]

In the following year, 1673, she was handed over to the navy, where she lasted a further forty years before being rebuilt in 1714.

Nearly three centuries later, in 1953, Charles's descendant Queen Elizabeth II reviewed the fleet from on board the frigate HMS SURPRISE, temporarily converted as a Royal Yacht whilst HMY BRITANNIA was building.

The King and the Duke of York did much to popularise yachting with their public enjoyment of the sport in the small yachts (BEZAN, JAMIE, CHARLES) on the upper reaches of the Thames, and in the larger yachts in the estuary and at sea. Indeed by 1663 Christopher Pett demanded an extra gratuity for building pleasure-boats, because of all the people he had to entertain.[6] With their light fore and aft rigs, keen underwater lines and luxurious accommodation the Royal Yachts were ideally suited to cruising and racing, and were much used by the royal brothers.

ANNE

Built 1661 at Woolwich for the Duke of York. Surveyor Christopher Pett.

Length on gundeck	–	Length by the keel	52 feet
Beam	19 feet	Depth in hold	7 feet
Tons burden	100	Crew	30
Guns	8 three-pounders		

Named after Anne, Duchess of York.
1686 sold, shortly after the Duke of York became James II, and for many years she was used by the London Customs House.

At the same time as Commissioner Peter Pett was building the KATHERINE at Deptford for the King, Pett's younger brother Christopher was building a yacht at Woolwich for the Duke of York, now Lord High Admiral, and as keen a sailor as his brother the King. The yacht was to be called ANNE, after the Duchess of York, and at 100 tons burden she was three feet longer than the KATHERINE, and like her based largely on the MARY.

On 9 December 1660 Christopher Pett complained to the Navy Board that he had no timber for His Highness's pleasure-yacht, and again on 29 December that he wanted planks, and suggested that the purveyor should be quickened. On 4 February 1661 he ordered: 'Holland Duck is the best canvas for sails for the Duke of York's pleasure-yacht now building, the same as is to be bought for the King's new yacht at Deptford.'[7]

Pepys's Diary, 21 May 1661:

> So took barge again and was overtaken by the King in his barge, he having been down the river with his yacht (KATHERINE) this day for pleasure to try it, and as I hear, Commissioner Pett's do prove better than the Dutch one (MARY), and that that his brother built.' (ANNE)

ANNE, 1661

'The Anne yacht under sail off Greenwich' painted perhaps by Isaac Salmaher c.1694, with detail on the stern showing the monograms WR and MR (for William and Mary). As the ANNE *was sold by James II shortly after he ascended the throne, it is possible that William and Mary bought back the yacht. As Prince of Orange, William had many interests there requiring his attention and yachts were required to transport officials to and from the Netherlands.*

On 1 October that year the diarist John Evelyn recorded:

> I sailed this morning with His Majesty… on a wager between his other new pleasure boat (KATHERINE), built frigate like, and one of the Duke of York's (ANNE), the wager £100, the race from Greenwich to Gravesend and back. The King lost it going, the wind being contrary, but saved stakes in returning… His Majesty steering himselfe…'[8]

In 1668, on 5 July, the three-year-old Princess Anne (later Queen Anne) with her small entourage landed at Dieppe from the ANNE yacht on the way to stay with her grandmother. The yacht continued in the service of the Duke of York until being sold in 1686, shortly after he became James II; for many years she was used by the London Customs House.

BEZAN

Built 1661 in Holland.		Surveyor	–
Length on gundeck	–	Length by the keel	34 feet
Beam	14 feet	Depth in hold	7 feet
Tons burden	35	Crew	–
Guns	–	Draught	3 feet 6 inches

1686 sold (Gavin).
Broken up at Deptford 1687 (Cowburn).

In the summer of 1661, keen to promote favourable trading conditions, the Dutch gave Charles a second yacht, the BEZAN. Bezaan in Dutch means mizzen-sail, but the yacht had only a single mast, with a large mainsail, very short gaff and long boom, with one or two headsails. Commander Gavin suggests the rig was close to that of the modern Bermudan rig;[9] certainly the BEZAN had the reputation of being a very fast sailer.

Pepys's Diary, 12 September 1661:

> In my way upon the Thames I saw the King's new pleasure-boat (BEZAN) that is come now for the King to take pleasure in above bridge (London Bridge).

This emphasises how the King much enjoyed sailing on Lambeth and Chelsea reaches.

As his importance advanced Pepys seems to have increasingly appropriated the BEZAN for his own use; doubtless by then the King's interest had moved to another new yacht.

On 3 September 1663 Pepys was accompanied by Sir William and Lady Batten, the latter a poor sailor. 'The winde very fresh, and I believe they will all be sicke enough, besides she is mighty troublesome on the water.' Pepys's forecast proved accurate, and poor Lady Batten, 'mighty troublesome on the water', was put ashore at Queenborough, on the Isle of Sheppey, vowing she would never go to sea again.

1 October 1665:

> Embarked on board the BEZAN and come to the fleete about 2 of the clock. My Lord received me mighty kindly;… After supper (went) on board the BEZAN, and there to cards for a while, and so to sleep. But Lord! The mirth which it caused me, to be waked in the night by their snoring round me; I did laugh till I was ready to burst…'

In November of that year Pepys visited Lord Sandwich on board the ROYAL JAMES at Queenborough; by now he was positively proprietorial, over the yacht:

> I left him, and so away to *my* BEZAN againe… So, after supper, to sleep, and sailed all night, and come to Erith before break of day.

BEZAN, 1661

Oil by B.C. Kleenecht

A year later he was again with his patron and took the BEZAN back 'and with a brave gale, and the tide, reached up that night to the Hope taking great pleasure in learning the seamen's manner of singing when they sound the depths...'

After the Great Fire of 1666 had subsided, Pepys went on 13 September to Deptford, whence he had sent his goods for safety. '...and there did, to my content, ship off in the BEZAN all the rest of my goods, saving my pictures and fine things, that I will bring home in wherrys, when the house is fit to receive them.'

The BEZAN was finally broken up at Deptford in 1687.

CHARLES

Built 1662 at Woolwich.		Surveyor Christopher Pett.	
Length on gundeck	–	Length by the keel	36 feet
Beam	14 feet 2 inches	Depth in hold	7 feet
Tons burden	38	Crew	10
Guns	6 three-pounders		

Named after Charles II.
1686 exchanged with the Office of Ordnance.

During 1662 two more small yachts were added, probably to rival the excellent sailing qualities of the Dutch-built BEZAN, and for sailing in the Chelsea and Lambeth reaches of the Thames above Tower Bridge. The CHARLES was the larger, naturally, at 38 tons, but she does not seem to have been very successful, for she was exchanged in 1668 for the TOWER smack from the Office of Ordnance. Her cost of building, £1277 10s 6d, is shown by comparison with the entry for the ANNE yacht. Sir Robert Howard, sergeant painter to the King, estimated £450 for painting and decorating the interior of the CHARLES, a mighty sum for the times – whether he got the job is not known.

JAMIE OR JEMMY

Built 1662 at Lambeth.		Surveyor Commissioner Pett.	
Length on gundeck	–	Length by the keel	31 feet
Beam	12 feet 6 inches	Depth in hold	6 feet
Tons burden	27	Crew	4
Guns	4		

Named after James, Duke of Monmouth, the King's favourite son by Lucy Walter. Or possibly James, Duke of York.
1721 broken up after nearly sixty years' service.

Pepys's Diary, 13 August 1662:

> To Lambeth; and there saw the little pleasure-boat in building by the King, my Lord Brounckner, and the Virtuosoes of the town, according to new lines, which Mr Pett cries up mightily; but how it will prove we shall soon see.

Pepys did indeed soon see, for on 5 September he wrote:

> By water to Woolwich; in my way saw the yacht... set out from Greenwich with the little Dutch bezan to try for mastery; and before they go to Woolwich the Dutch boat beat them half-a-mile; and hear that in coming home it got above three miles, which all our people are glad of.

This curious pleasure at the beating of the English yacht by the Dutch one displays a petty rivalry; for Pepys and his staff were somewhat averse to the 'Vituosoes' designing a yacht and muscling in on their department!

Pepys had obviously caught the sailing bug from his royal master, for a year later, on 2 March 1663, he took the JEMMY 'down to Woolwich and then to the yacht again and went down four or five miles with extraordinary pleasure, it being a fine day and a brave gale of wind'.

SAUDADOES

Built 1670 at Portsmouth.		Surveyor Sir Anthony Deane.	
Length on gundeck	–	Length by the keel	50 feet
Beam	18 feet	Depth in hold	8 feet
Tons burden	86	Crew	40
Guns	8 three-pounders		

1673 rebuilt as sixth-rate.

Queen Katherine's Little Ship, as she was sometimes known, was built in 1670 for excursions on the river by the Queen and ladies of her Court. She was christened at Deptford on 14 April that year, where the 'Queen gave her a Portuguese name and fired a gun.' The name translates from the Portuguese as 'good luck' or 'good wishes', but more accurately as 'intense longing'. The man in the street, as usual, made free with her name, and she was known variously as SUNDADES, SANDANDOS or SODALIS. An eyewitness wrote:

> Her Majesty gives life to all by frequent divertisement upon the river in her new vessel the SODALIS. They undertake long voyages, and, falling short of provisions, victual themselves sometimes at Vauxhall and sometimes at Lambeth Palace.[10a]

Captain James Jenifer was given command of this yacht by the Queen in her personal service; he appears to have neglected to formally register this with the Admiralty, who took four years to appreciate it. 'The King is surprised to find that Jenifer never had any commission for the command of his ship, which for any act of hostility he may have done exposes him to be condemned as a pirate.' A commission was enclosed with the letter, and the King later indemnified Jenifer 'in what he has done by the Queen's directions'.[10b]

Katherine was the daughter of King John IV of Portugal, so it was natural she should wish to have first-hand knowledge of her native country, and Captain Jenifer was twice despatched in the SAUDADOES to Portugal.

Whether it was the need for more warships during the Dutch Wars, or the expense of maintaining a yacht solely for the Queen and her ladies is unknown, but Queen Katherine enjoyed the use of the SAUDADOES for barely three years before the yacht was rebuilt in 1673 and enlarged as a sixth-rate man-of-war of 180 tons.[11]

Captain Jenifer continued in command, and on 20 August 1674, during the Third Dutch War, he was despatched for service under Sir John Narborough in the Channel. Captain Jenifer continued to fly his special flag, presumably the Queen's standard, and so made himself independent of Sir John, much to the latter's annoyance. The dispute was referred to Pepys, who replied, 'You will have no more trouble given you by Captain Jenifer's flag, the King having by special order commanded him to forebear wearing any.'[12]

The SAUDADOES was present at the Battle of Bantry Bay when James II invaded Ireland in a vain attempt to regain his throne, and was eventually captured by a French man-of-war off Cape Barfleur in 1696.

KITCHEN

Built 1670 at Rotherhithe.		Surveyor William Castle.	
Length on gundeck	–	Length by the keel	51 feet
Beam	19 feet 4 inches	Depth in hold	9 feet 7 inches*
Tons burden	101	Crew	–
Guns	6 three-pounders (8 in war)		

* by calculation
Built to accommodate the royal cooks.
1692 converted to a bomb-vessel.
1698 sold.

KITCHEN, 1670

Drawing by Willem Van de Velde the Elder.

When King Charles left Breda at the Restoration he was accompanied by a small fleet of 13 yachts crammed with those nobles who had followed him into the weary years of exile, as well as those who had recently decided it was now politic to support his cause. Adrian Vlackett, writing in 1660 commented:

> Each yacht had her own steward, cooks and officers who were in charge of the pantry, kitchen and wines, and those yachts which had not suitable kitchens on board were accompanied by other vessels, wherein stoves for the kitchen had been provided, also ovens for baking, and there had been made great provision of so great a quantity of all kinds of food, game, confitures and wines, and all the tables were so fully served, that the stewards of the English lords, though accustomed to abundance, were astonished thereat, and confessed that they could not conceive by what means 20 or 25 great dishes for each table could be prepared on board the yachts and with the motion of the water.[13]

Charles adopted the concept of the kitchen boat from the Dutch, and pressed into service the ketch ROE, renamed ROE KITCHEN. John Evelyn recorded in his diary on 1 October 1661:

> There were divers noble persons and lords on board, His Majesty sometimes steering himselfe. His barge and kitchen boate attended. I brake fast this morning with the King in his smaller vessel, he being pleased to take me and onely four more, who were noblemen, with him; but dined in his yacht (KATHERINE), where we all eate together with His Majesty.

Some years later, in 1670, Charles built a highly decorated yacht carrying six guns in peace and eight in war, but her name, KITCHEN, gave away her true purpose, that of kitchen boat to the other Royal Yachts. Her log is at the PRO. The KITCHEN, sometimes KITCHIN, was converted to a bomb-vessel – i.e. a ship strengthened and fitted with mortars for shore bombardment – in 1692, and sold in 1698.

NAVY

Built 1673[14] at Portsmouth.		Surveyor Sir Anthony Deane.	
Length on gundeck	–	Length by the keel	48 feet
Beam	17 feet 6 inches	Depth in hold	7 feet 7 inches
Tons burden	74	Crew	35
Guns	8 three-pounders		

1698 sold 14 April.

Little is known to me of her use, but she accompanied Princess Mary and Prince William of Orange on their honeymoon voyage to Holland in 1677. From 1689-1693 she was allocated to the Lord Lieutenant of Ireland on the Dublin station, and her use is detailed in Chapter 9. She is also illustrated there.

ISABELLA BEZAN[15]

Built 1680 at Chatham.		Surveyor Sir Phineas Pett.	
Length on gundeck	–	Length by the keel	46 feet
Beam	16 feet	Depth in hold	–
Tons burden	52	Crew	–
Guns	–		

Possibly named after the Duke of York's daughter.
1683 ordered to be sold to Sir Phineas Pett.

On 8 June 1681 the Admiralty ordered the BIZAN to be paid off and handed over to the Vice-Admiral of England, the Duke of Grafton, adding that henceforth she was to be called the ISABELLA.[16]

That November a Navy Board letter requested 'an estimate of the charges of altering the ISABELLA yacht and making her fit for a ketch like the FUBBS.' The estimate was for £608 12s 0d; it was proposed not only to re-rig her, but virtually to rebuild her hull above water to be flush-decked, as apparently a ketch ought to be.[17]

Clearly this estimate was not acceptable, for on 23 December the Admiralty instructed the Navy Board to make a contract with Sir Phineas Pett for building a new ketch. (ISABELLA). As for the old ISABELLA (ex ISABELLA BEZAN), she was obviously only lent to the Duke of Grafton, for in April 1683 she was 'ordered to be sold to Sir Phineas Pett' as part-payment for the building of the new ISABELLA. What happened to the ISABELLA BEZAN is not clear, but she was probably renamed ANN to release her name for the new ISABELLA. Pett states, 'the ANN yacht I had of His Majesty is still upon my hands, to my great cost, being not yet disposed of, and ask permission to lay her in mast dock at Deptford this winter.' It is not certain if this is the ISABELLA BEZAN, but it is likely, as the ANNE, built for the Duke of York, was still in the royal service.[18]

YACHTS ASSIGNED TO THE ROYAL DOCKYARDS OR SURVEYING DUTIES

'King Charles was also frequently found in the dockyards, visiting his magazines, giving directions concerning ships upon the stocks, for improving certain of their sailing or accommodation, having an extraordinary genius for naval architecture, whereof he was no uncommon judge; and to show his inclinations for its encouragement, he knighted some of its most eminent builders.'[19]

His deep interest in the sciences, including naval architecture, led Charles to promote the cause not just of the navy but the dockyards which supplied it. He appreciated full well the importance of encouraging men of talent to enter his service, and if he could not always pay them, at least he could honour them. One way was to allocate Royal Yachts to dockyard service, and although much smaller than his own yachts, they carried an undoubted prestige.

The Thames in those days was a major highway, and as many of the dockyards were close to London, Pepys availed himself of every opportunity to make trips in the yachts; '...the wind blowing hard (in the Downs) I made use of the JEMMY yacht and returned to the Tower in her.'[20]

SURVEYING YACHTS

Although seamen went unpaid and their families starved in 1666, funds were still found for the building of two new yachts at Rotherhithe,[21] the MERLIN and the MONMOUTH. Both yachts were later to be employed in the first major survey of the British coastline. Charles was to the forefront in promoting navigation, and allocated the two yachts for the seven-year survey to Captain Greenville Collins. In his preface to the publication Collins wrote:

> His Most Excellent Majesty, King Charles II, who was a great lover of the noble art of navigation, finding that there were no Sea-Charts or Maps of these kingdoms but what were Dutch, and Copies from them, and those very erroneous, His Majesty out of his great Zeal for the better improvement of navigation, was pleased in the year 1682, to give me the command of a Yacht for the making of this Survey; in which Service I spent Seven Years time.[22]

MERLIN

Built 1666 at Rotherhithe.		Surveyor Jonas Shish.	
Length on gundeck	–	Length by the keel	53 feet
Beam	19 feet 6 inches	Depth in hold	6 feet
Tons burden	109	Crew	30
Guns	8 three-pounders	Rigged as a galliot.	
1698 sold.			

For a Royal Yacht the MERLIN was unusually rigged as a galliot i.e. she had a hoy's mainsail with square topsail, one or two foresails, and a lateen-mizzen.[23]

In 1671 she was sent to bring Lady Temple to England, and on her return voyage passed through the Dutch fleet. The captain of the MERLIN demanded the Dutch ships should strike their topmasts in recognition of England's claim to sovereignty over these waters. The Dutch, not unnaturally, refused, but this was only one of the many frictions leading to the Third Dutch War (1672-1674).

The MERLIN was commanded by Captain Greenville Collins in 1681 and 1682 when he commenced his survey of the British coastline. During this he produced 120 harbour and shore plans, 48 of which appeared in *Great Britains Coasting Pilot*. Published in 1693, the year of his death, the atlas was a major aid to coastal navigation, and ran for 12 editions during the next one hundred years.

Collins was well qualified for the task, as he had been Master of the SWEEPSTAKES under Sir John Narborough on his voyage round the Horn to the west coast of South America from 1669 to 1671.[22a] His work was far in advance of his predecessors, and paved the way for the charting of the world by the Hydrographic Department in the eighteenth and nineteenth centuries.

MONMOUTH

Built 1666 at Rotherhithe.		Surveyor William Castle.	
Length on gundeck	–	Length by the keel	52 feet
Beam	19 feet 6 inches	Depth in hold	8 feet
Tons burden	103	Crew	40
Guns	8 three-pounders		

Named after the Duke of Monmouth, Charles II's favourite son by Lucy Walter.
25 November 1698 sold.

The MONMOUTH was employed for most of her career on despatch service between England and Ireland, and for details of her usage see Chapter 9. She was, however, commanded by Captain Greenville Collins for the five years between 1683-1688 when he continued his survey of the British coastline.

QUINBOROW

Commander Gavin includes in his list of Royal Yachts the QUINBOROW of 1671. I have used the name QUINBOROW for this particular yacht, as opposed to the often noted QUEENBOROUGH, as both yachts were in commission at the same time, overlapping by eighteen years.

Built 1671 at Chatham.		Surveyor Phineas Pett.	
Length on gundeck	–	Length by the keel	30 feet
Beam	13 feet 4 inches	Depth in hold	6 feet 6 inches
Tons burden	29	Crew	6
Guns	4 three-pounders		

Named after a village on the Isle of Sheppey.
Sold 1719.

The name comes from the village of Queenborough on the Isle of Sheppey, and from her size she was clearly built as a tender to the principal yachts, or for royal service in general rather than accommodating the King himself. As her replacements of the same name were used for surveying the constantly changing Thames estuary, it is not unreasonable to suppose she was similarly employed.

She was obviously a handy small vessel, for she gave nearly fifty years' service before being sold in 1719.

DOCKYARD YACHTS

In spite of being embroiled in the Third Dutch War, Charles ordered the building of two new yachts in 1673. To be fair, the DEALE and the ISLE OF WIGHT were small yachts, intended not for the personal use of the King, but on his service.

It is probable the DEALE was allocated to Chatham and/or Sheerness dockyards, and that the Isle of Wight was in the service of the Governor of the Island.

DEALE

Built 1673 at Woolwich.		Surveyor Phineas Pett.	
Length on gundeck	–	Length by the keel	32 feet
Beam	13 feet	Depth in hold	6 feet
Tons burden	28	Crew	4
Guns	4 three-pounders		

Probably Chatham or Sheerness Dockyard yacht.
1688 sold.

ISLE OF WIGHT

Built 1673 at Portsmouth.		Surveyor Mr Furze.	
Length on gundeck	–	Length by the keel	33 feet
Beam	12 feet 6 inches	Depth in hold	6 feet
Tons burden	30	Crew	6
Guns	4 three-pounders		

Probably allocated to the Governor of the Isle of Wight.
1701 rebuilt.

THE LATER STUARTS

JAMES II (1685-1688)

James II ascended the English throne on the death of his brother Charles in February 1685, and his reign began auspiciously enough. However, he estranged Parliament and the nation by his determination to overthrow the constitution and the Church, and his reign was spent in discord.

At his accession there were 18 yachts available to the King, made up as follows:

Nine principal yachts:
ANNE, CLEVELAND, KATHERINE II, PORTSMOUTH, CHARLOT, MARY II,
HENRIETTA II, FUBBS, ISABELLA

Four large yachts:
MERLIN, MONMOUTH, NAVY, KITCHEN

Five small yachts:
BEZAN, JAMIE, QUINBOROW, DEALE, ISLE OF WIGHT

James built no new yachts, but disposed of four during his short reign. The ANNE and BEZAN were sold in 1686; in 1688 the DEALE was sold and the PORTSMOUTH converted to a bomb-vessel.

James so alienated the nation with his advocacy of the Roman Catholic faith, his suspension of the Test Act and numerous arbitrary decisions, that the indignation of the people was finally roused. In the autumn of 1688 seven leading politicians formally solicited the interposition of William, Prince of Orange, married to James' daughter Mary. (In the normal event of that period for convoluted royal marriages, William was also nephew to James; the latter's sister, also Mary, having married William II of Orange.)

James, as Duke of York, had for many years worked closely with Samuel Pepys, Secretary to the Admiralty, in building and improving the ships of the navy; it was now that this fleet must be ready and able to prevent William's landing. Pepys made Herculean efforts to man and victual the fleet at a time of year thought not wise to prosecute a war at sea; but having forged the weapon, Pepys was to see it fail to perform the very task for which it was created. The Admiral, Lord Dartmouth, prevaricated over sailing until the fleet was fully equipped, although James and Pepys urged on him the necessity of intercepting William.

Dartmouth admitted, 'it was as fine a winter fleet as ever had been', but having delayed over the equipping of his ships, he now found them trapped at the mouth of the Thames with contrary winds. By the time he had extricated himself from the sands, the English fleet was unable to intercept William, and he landed without opposition at Brixham on 5 November 1688 at the head of 15 000 Dutch and English troops.

James prepared to flee, and on 30 November wrote: 'Order the ISABELLA and ANNE yachts to fall down to Erith tomorrow. J.R.'[1] In the event he used neither yacht, but finally abdicated on 11 December and fled to France. England lost a King who had commanded the fleet in two sea-battles, and yachting one of its strongest royal advocates.

MARY II, 1677

Oil by Van de Velde the Younger – 'His Majesty's Yacht Mary arriving with Princess Mary at Gravesend 12 February 1689.' In this splendidly crowded scene of ships, yachts and boats, the MARY II *is in the centre, proceeding up the Thames preparatory to anchoring. Flying at her masthead is the special white standard of the Revolution bearing the legend 'For the Protestant Religion and the Liberty of England'.*

WILLIAM AND MARY (1688-1702)

William III landed without opposition from the frigate BRIEL at Brixham, and James II abdicated five weeks later. Thus was the Glorious Revolution inaugurated without a blow being struck. But it was not until the following spring that Admiral Herbert was sent in command of the fleet and several yachts to fetch Queen Mary. She crossed from Holland in the MARY II, the yacht which had carried her husband William on their honeymoon voyage. Queen Mary landed at Greenwich on 12 February 1689 on her way to London and her father's throne.

In an attempt to regain this throne James II had set up court in Dublin, and whilst he and his army were in Ireland William and Mary were insecure in London. Although victory for William at the Battle of the Boyne effectively ended any hopes of James achieving success, Mary was often inwardly uncertain. When she prudishly refused to acknowledge James's one-time mistress, Catherine Sedley, she received the full blast of her famously sharp tongue. 'Why so haughty, madam?' Catherine demanded. 'I have not sinned more notoriously in breaking the seventh commandment with your father, than you have done in breaking the fifth against him.' At their accession William and Mary inherited a total of 14 yachts large and small, of which eight principal yachts are shown at the time as being on service, as follows:[2]

	Men
CHARLOT	30
FUBBS	40
HENRIETTA	30
KITCHEN	30
KATHERINE	30
MERLIN	30
MARY	30
ISABELLA	30

Being in all 250 men at £4 per man per month.
The total cost of the up-keep of the personnel
was £13 008 18s 6d

In addition to these William bought, in 1692, the SOESDYKE yacht (allocated to the Lord Lieutenant of Ireland – see Chapter 9); built the WILLIAM & MARY in 1694; bought the PEREGRINE GALLEY in 1700; and built several small yachts throughout the reign. He made much use of his yachts, for as Prince of Orange his interests were as much in Holland as in England. But it was not until 9 February 1693 that the Navy Office ordered: 'An estimate of the charge of building a new yacht for Their Majesties of ye Dimensions of the MARY yacht and of furnishing her with rigging and sea stores £2060.'[2a] This yacht was to be the WILLIAM & MARY, the principal yacht of the reign, and built in the following year.

WILLIAM & MARY

Built 1694 at Chatham. Surveyor R Lee.

Length on gundeck	76 feet 6 inches	Length by the keel	61 feet 5¼ inches
Beam	21 feet 7 inches	Depth in hold	9 feet 6 inches
Tons burden	152	Crew	40
Guns	8 three-pounders	Ketch-rigged	

Named after the reigning monarchs.
1737 great repairs effected. 1746 great repairs.
1765 rebuilt.

WILLIAM & MARY, 1694

The Earl of Sandwich model. This fine model was in the possession of the Earls of Sandwich for nearly three hundred years until sold in 1996 for £260 000 – a then world record. This photograph by Paymaster Commander Gavin about 1932 contains guns at the starboard side; they had disappeared by the time of the sale. Opinion is divided as to whether the model represents the WILLIAM & MARY *or the* FUBBS II *of 1701. I think it is the latter, but for my detailed reasoning see the entry for* FUBBS II.

I doubt if the estimate of £2060 was the total expenditure; by comparison, the ANNE yacht ready for sea cost £25/ton, giving a true outlay for the WILLIAM & MARY of £3800.

She was one of the earliest yachts to be built ketch-rigged, and there were obviously planning difficulties with this comparatively new rig, for the Captain's log read:

> 20th November 1694 – Took out mizen-mast, it being too short. 30th November 1694 – I sett new mizen-mast and rigged it.

The WILLIAM & MARY was much used by William, for constant troubles in the United Provinces required his personal attention. The yacht's log shows regular journeying between the Continent and England, not only with the King but also his high officers of State and ranking military officers. WILLIAM & MARY often sailed in company with the FUBBS, which accommodated the many personages who invariably attended the King; the FUBBS never sailed alone – if she missed the convoy she always waited for the next one.

In January 1698 King William despatched HMS YORKE with an Admiral in command to fetch Tsar Peter the Great from Holland, where he had been studying shipbuilding. In the teeth of a winter storm the YORKE beat her way across Channel, the Tsar relishing the elements, and even climbing the rigging in the icy spray. When he invited the Admiral to join him, the latter replied he was now too fat for that sort of antic.

At the mouth of the Thames the Tsar transferred to the WILLIAM & MARY, and escorted by two more yachts he proceeded up river to London Bridge and a State reception. Peter, however, was bored by affairs of State, and as he had come to England expressly to learn about shipbuilding, he moved to Sayes Court near Deptford, the home of John Evelyn.

Tsar Peter much preferred to be in the dockyard at Deptford learning the skills he needed to develop his navy in Russia. Whilst he was there, the yard was building a ship for him, a present from William keen to obtain trade concessions from Russia. She was to be called ROYAL TRANSPORT, and after witnessing a mock fight of naval vessels in the Solent, Tsar Peter set sail for Holland in May. [2b]

PEREGRINE GALLEY

Built 1700 at Sheerness by R. Lee designed by Peregrine, Lord Danby as a sixth-rate.

Length on gundeck	86 feet 10 inches	Length by the keel	72 feet 8 inches
Beam	22 feet 6 inches	Depth in hold	10 feet 7 inches
Tons burden	197	Crew	–
Guns	20 cannon, 12 swivel guns		

1716 refitted as Royal Yacht and renamed CAROLINA.
1733 rebuilt and renamed ROYAL CAROLINE.
1749 converted to a sloop and renamed PEREGRINE SLOOP.
1762 lost in the Bay of Biscay with all hands.

The building of the PEREGRINE GALLEY was a direct result of the gift of the ROYAL TRANSPORT to the Tsar, for the latter had been designed by Peregrine, Lord Danby (later the Marquess of Carmarthen).[3] Lord Danby had become the boon friend and drinking companion of Tsar Peter, and responsible to a large extent for the success of the Anglo-Soviet trade negotiations. The ROYAL TRANSPORT was one of the fastest ships of her time, and Lord Danby persuaded William III to allow him to design and build a replacement, which was named after him – the PEREGRINE GALLEY.

PEREGRINE GALLEY, 1700

This 1:84 scale model of the PEREGRINE GALLEY *was formerly in the superb collection on board the training ship* MERCURY *at Hamble. Two feet long, the model has a figurehead of a lion, on her escutcheon being a full-length portrait of Queen Anne surrounded by cupids. In one of the panels is the royal monogram, A.R., and the date 1708. The model is remarkable in that the upperdeck contains two falls, and is fitted for three masts.*

She was taken into naval service by William following her launching in 1700, but not specifically classed as a Royal Yacht until her refit and renaming as CAROLINA in 1716. However, her log shows she was often to be found on the Royal Yacht moorings at Deptford and Greenwich, and she was certainly used as a Royal Yacht during the reign of Queen Anne. This is thus an appropriate place to introduce her.

Neither the shipyard nor the Admiralty much appreciated an amateur muscling in on their domain, but the PEREGRINE was exceptionally successful. She had an interesting bell-shaped keel, which would have offered greater resistance to lateral movement, and hence counter any tendency to drift down-wind (See CAROLINA). The hull lines were to be the basis for warship design which spanned nearly two centuries, and is detailed under the entry for ROYAL CAROLINE II.

Following the death of Mary from smallpox in 1694, William reigned alone for six years. His relationship with his heir, Mary's younger sister Anne, had at times been acrimonious, but both sides made a thin attempt in later years to hide their feelings, at least in public.

While out hunting in Richmond Park on 21 February 1702 the King's horse stumbled over a molehill, William fell and broke his collarbone. This lead to the Jacobite toast to 'the little gentleman in the velvet waistcoat'. Two weeks later William was dead, and for Princess Anne – now Queen Anne – this was the moment for which she had waited all her adult life.

SECONDARY YACHTS OF WILLIAM AND MARY

Three small yachts were built during the reign; SQUIRREL for Chatham Dockyard; SCOUT for Portsmouth Dockyard; and QUEENBOROUGH as a surveying vessel based at Sheerness. The ISLE OF WIGHT was rebuilt at Portsmouth for the Governor of the island. The FUBBS was rebuilt 2 feet shorter; her beam, however was increased by a foot, which made the FUBBS II 157 tons burden (cp. 148 tons).

SQUIRREL /SQUIRILL

Built 1694 at Chatham.		Surveyor R. Lee.	
Length on gundeck	47 feet	Length by the keel	36 feet
Beam	14 feet	Depth in hold	6 feet
Tons burden	37	Crew	4
Guns	4 two-pounders		

Chatham Yard yacht.
1714 sold.

SCOUT

Built 1695 at Portsmouth.		Surveyor R. Stigant.	
Length on gundeck	–	Length by the keel	38 feet 6 inches
Beam	13 feet 8 inches	Depth in hold	6 feet 4 inches
Tons burden	38	Crew	6
Guns	4 (two-pounders?)		

Portsmouth Yard yacht.
1703 sold.

QUEENBOROUGH

No dimensions known, other than 44 tons burden.
Built 1701 at Deptford by N. Lee.
Named after the village on the Isle of Sheppey.
Probably used as surveying vessel, based at Sheerness.
1718 rebuilt.

ISLE OF WIGHT II

Rebuilt 1701 at Portsmouth.		Surveyor Mr Wasse.	
Length on gundeck	46 feet 8 inches	Length by the keel	36 feet 9 inches
Beam	14 feet	Depth in hold	6 feet 10 inches
Tons burden	38	Crew	6
Guns	4 three-pounders		

For use of the Governor of the Isle of Wight.
1712 sold.

In time of war Royal Yachts were often used in the fleet, and so it was with the ISLE OF WIGHT, for in 1709 she was used for Channel service. Her armament was increased to eight three-pounder guns, and to man them her crew increased to 30.

FUBBS II

Rebuilt 1701 at Woolwich.		Surveyor N. Lee.	
Length on gundeck	–	Length by the keel	61 feet
Beam	22 feet	Depth in hold	9 feet 8 inches
Tons burden	157	Crew	40
Guns	12 three-pounders	Ketch-rigged	

1724 rebuilt.

The fine model shown on page 58 depicts either the WILLIAM & MARY of 1694 or the FUBBS II as rebuilt in 1701. The model was in the possession of the Earls of Sandwich until sold in 1996 for £260 000 – a then world record. Opinion is divided as to whether the model represents the WILLIAM & MARY or the FUBBS II. In 1998, Simon Stephens, the Curator of Ship Models at Greenwich inclined to the former; as did Sir Geoffrey Callender, a previous Director of the N.M.M. However, Dr R.C. Anderson was convinced the model represented a design for the FUBBS rebuilding/redecorating of 1690, or as rebuilt in 1701 as FUBBS II.

Simon Stephens took detailed measurements of the model, which compares best in length-to-breadth ratio for the WILLIAM & MARY. Callender based his decision on the iconography of the double figurehead (King William & Queen Mary), the coat of arms, and the cypher on the stern; Stephens agrees with Callender on this. However, I am inclined to agree with Dr Anderson that the model represents the FUBBS II of 1701. Both yachts were ketch-rigged; this model shows 12 guns (indicating the FUBBS); the WILLIAM & MARY carried only eight. Moreover, the shields above the stern-windows show the three buckles of the Dukedom of Aubigny, granted to Louise de Kéroualle by Louis XIV in 1672, the year before she became Duchess of Portsmouth. Louise was a mistress of Charles II, and the FUBBS was named after his nickname for her.

Aubigny included the chateau at La Verrerie, and Louise lived there from about 1672-1734, and spent the last years of her life in Aubigny. However, the Compte de Vogüé (the present owner) tells me the three buckles are the coat of arms of the Stuarts, who owned Aubigny before the Duke of Lennox and Gordon, Louise's son by Charles II. Louise de Kéroualle was a fascinating character, who had two Royal Yachts named after her (PORTSMOUTH and FUBBS). She also managed to extract a Dukedom each from the Kings of England and France for her services to both, and retired to her estates a wealthy woman. She is reputed to have died 'very old, very penitent, very poor'.

William and Mary disposed of four yachts during their reign, for the aptly-named KITCHEN was made into a bomb-vessel in 1692, before being sold in 1698 along with the MERLIN, MONMOUTH and NAVY.

QUEEN ANNE (1702-1714)

At the tender age of three and a half the Princess Anne, with her small entourage, landed at Dieppe from the Royal Yacht ANNE on 5 July 1668. She was on her way to stay with her grandmother, the Dowager Queen Henrietta Maria, and this is the first recorded use of a Royal Yacht by her; and apart from possibly using one to join her parents in Holland and later Scotland, it also seems to be the last. Queen Anne was a chronic invalid by the age of thirty-five, so it is highly unlikely she wished to add seasickness to the morning-sickness of her eighteen pregnancies.

She inherited nine principal yachts at her accession: the CLEVELAND, KATHERINE II, CHARLOT, MARY II, HENRIETTA II, WILLIAM & MARY, FUBBS II, SOESDYKE and PEREGRINE GALLEY. There were also six small yachts: the JAMIE, QUINBOROW, SQUIRREL, SCOUT, QUEENBOROUGH and ISLE OF WIGHT II.

One of the first acts of her reign had been to create her consort, Prince George of Denmark, Lord High Admiral in May 1702. In reality it was Marlborough's younger brother, George Churchill, who effectively ran the Royal Navy, for one must bear in mind Charles II's quip on Prince George, 'I have tried him drunk and I have tried him sober, and there is nothing in him.'

In 1703 the new Lord High Admiral wrote:

> Her Majesty takeing notice that Shee is at a great charge in the frequent furnishing Her yachts occasion'd, as is supposed, by the captains takeing away the old furniture from time to time as Fees or Perquisites belonging to themselves, You are therefore required and directed, when Her Majesty's Service will allow fit, to repair to Towne and give the Rt. Honourable the Lord Chamberlaine of Her Majesty's Household a particular account of such goods or furniture on board the vessell you Command as have been at any time issued to her from Her Majesty's Wardrobe and to charge yourself therewith, and you are to take perticular care not to take away or dispose of any of the said goods or furniture which you shall receive from time to time from the Wardrobe for the service of the vessell under your Command, but to be accountable for the same as ye Officers of Her Majesties Removeing Wardrobe, notwithstanding any former Custom as you will answer the contrary at your Perill.
>
> To: Capt. Desbrough, Commr. of the CLEAVELAND yacht.
> Capt. Hanway, Commr. of the SOESDIKE yacht.
> Capt. Mellison, Commr. of the KATHERINE yacht.
> Capt. Guy, Commr. of the MARY yacht.
> Capt. Moses, Commr. of the HENRIETTA yacht.
> Capt. Byron, Commr. of the FUBBS yacht.
> Capt. Robinson, Commr. of the WILLIAM & MARY yacht.[4]

The CHARLOT is missing from this list, possibly as she was not in commission at the time.

From the end of the seventeenth century all Royal Yachts built or rebuilt were rigged as ketches except for a few rigged as ships. Gone was the yacht-rig of the Stuarts, for as England's importance as a maritime power grew, so too did the size of the yachts and the frequency of their use throughout the year.

From the start of the eighteenth century, yachts began to be classed as 'large' or 'small'. 'Large' for the principal yachts used by the monarch, 'small' for those engaged on State duties – such as the Commissioners of Royal Dockyard yachts.

Two more principal ('large') yachts were built during Queen Anne's reign, the ISABELLA II and the CHARLOT II (rebuilt).

ISABELLA II

Built 1703 at Deptford.		Surveyor Mr Harding.	
Length on gundeck	–	Length by the keel	–
Beam	–	Depth in hold	–
Tons burden	104	Crew	30
Guns	8 three-pounders		

1715 sold.

CHARLOT II

The first CHARLOT, built for Charles II in 1677, was beginning to show her age, and in 1710 she was re-built. Although some four feet shorter by the keel, she was broader and deeper than her predecessor, giving a tonnage of 155 tons burden (cp. 142 tons). She was yacht-rigged, and her complement increased by ten.

Rebuilt 1710 at Deptford.		Surveyor Joshua Allin (Senior).	
Length on gundeck	73 feet 8 inches	Length by the keel	57 feet 7½ inches
Beam	22 feet 6¼ inches	Depth in hold	9 feet 6 inches
Tons burden	155	Crew	40
GunS	8 three-pounders		

1736 rigged as a ketch.
1747 lengthened to 79 feet 5 inches.
1761 renamed AUGUSTA.
Original dimensions under entry for Charles II.

CHARLOT II, 1710

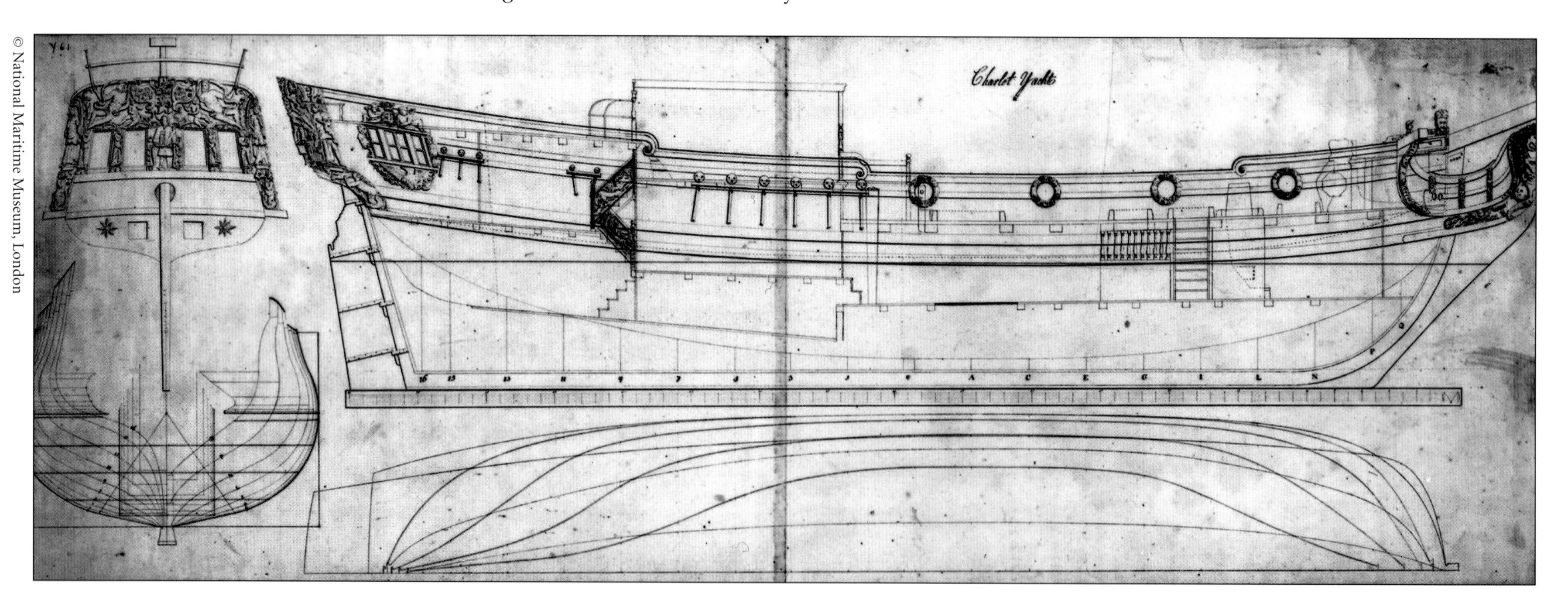

Courtesy of The Corporation of The Hull Trinity House

A Royal Yacht, probably of Queen Anne's reign, but not yet identified. Sometimes called – erroneously – the BETSY CAIRNS. *Photographed here by Paymaster Commander Gavin about 1932 at The Corporation of The Hull Trinity House, where it remains. The model was presented to them in 1844 by R.W. Humphreys.*

SECONDARY YACHTS OF QUEEN ANNE

Queen Anne's reign saw the start of building yachts for the specific duties of Officers of State, rather than vessels being allocated ad hoc when no longer required for royal duty. Thus the original MARY had been assigned to the Lord Lieutenant of Ireland until her wreck in 1675. Her duties were largely replaced by the MONMOUTH from 1675-1678, and again from 1689 until her sale in 1698; by the PORTSMOUTH from 1679-1687; the NAVY from 1689-1693 and by the SOESDYKE from 1693 until replaced by the CHARLOT in 1701, who remained on station until 1709.

To replace these yachts the DUBLIN was built in 1709.

DUBLIN

Built 1709 at Deptford.		Surveyor Joshua Allin.	
Length on gundeck	73 feet 2 inches	Length by the keel	59 feet 8 inches
Beam	21 feet 7½ inches	Depth in hold	–
Tons burden	148	Crew	45 (1709). 40 (1713). 50 (1737).
Guns	10 three-pounders	Ketch-rigged	

1732 fitted with three masts.
1752 taken to pieces.
Lord Lieutenant of Ireland's yacht to replace the MONMOUTH.
(For details of the DUBLIN's use, see Chapter 9.)

Nor were the Commissioners of the Dockyards forgotten, with the PORTSMOUTH II allocated to the Commissioner of Portsmouth Dockyard and the DRAKE to Plymouth Dockyard.

PORTSMOUTH II

Built 1702 at Portsmouth.		Surveyor Thomas Podd.	
Length on gundeck	52 feet 10 inches	Length by the keel	42 feet 10 inches
Beam	17 feet	Depth in hold	8 feet 6¼ inches
Tons burden	66	Crew	14
Guns	6 two-pounders		

1741 renamed OLD PORTSMOUTH.
1752 fitted for the 'use of the young gentlemen of the (naval) Academy (at Portsmouth)'.
1772 she had great repairs, was fitted for the Governor of the Isle of Wight, and renamed MEDINA.
1832 taken to pieces after one hundred and thirty years' service.

DRAKE

Built 1705 at Plymouth.		Surveyor Mr Locke.	
Length on gundeck	–	Length by the keel	34 feet 9 inches
Beam	16 feet 6 inches	Depth in hold	8 feet 11½ inches
Tons burden	50	Crew	4/17
Guns	6 three-pounders (?)		

1727 rebuilt (Lyon) and 1729 (Gavin).
Commissioner's yacht for Devonport.

For much of the eighteenth century the Dukes of Bolton were hereditary Governors of the Isle of Wight and Lords Lieutenant of Hampshire. With stunning originality the Governor's yacht was named after him.

BOLTON

Built 1709 at Portsmouth.		Surveyor Thomas Podd.	
Length on gundeck	53 feet 2 inches	Length by the keel	38 feet
Beam	14 feet 6 inches	Depth in hold	7 feet 6½ inches
Tons burden	42	Crew	12
Guns	6 two-pounders		

1763 found to be 'entirely decayed' and rebuilt unofficially.
1773 fitted for the use of the 'young gentlemen of the Academy' in lieu of the OLD PORTSMOUTH.
1817 taken to pieces.

BOLTON, 1709

A contemporary model with a scale of 1:32. The style and workmanship suggest that it was considerably later than the building of the actual vessel in 1709; probably 1763 when the yacht was extensively rebuilt.

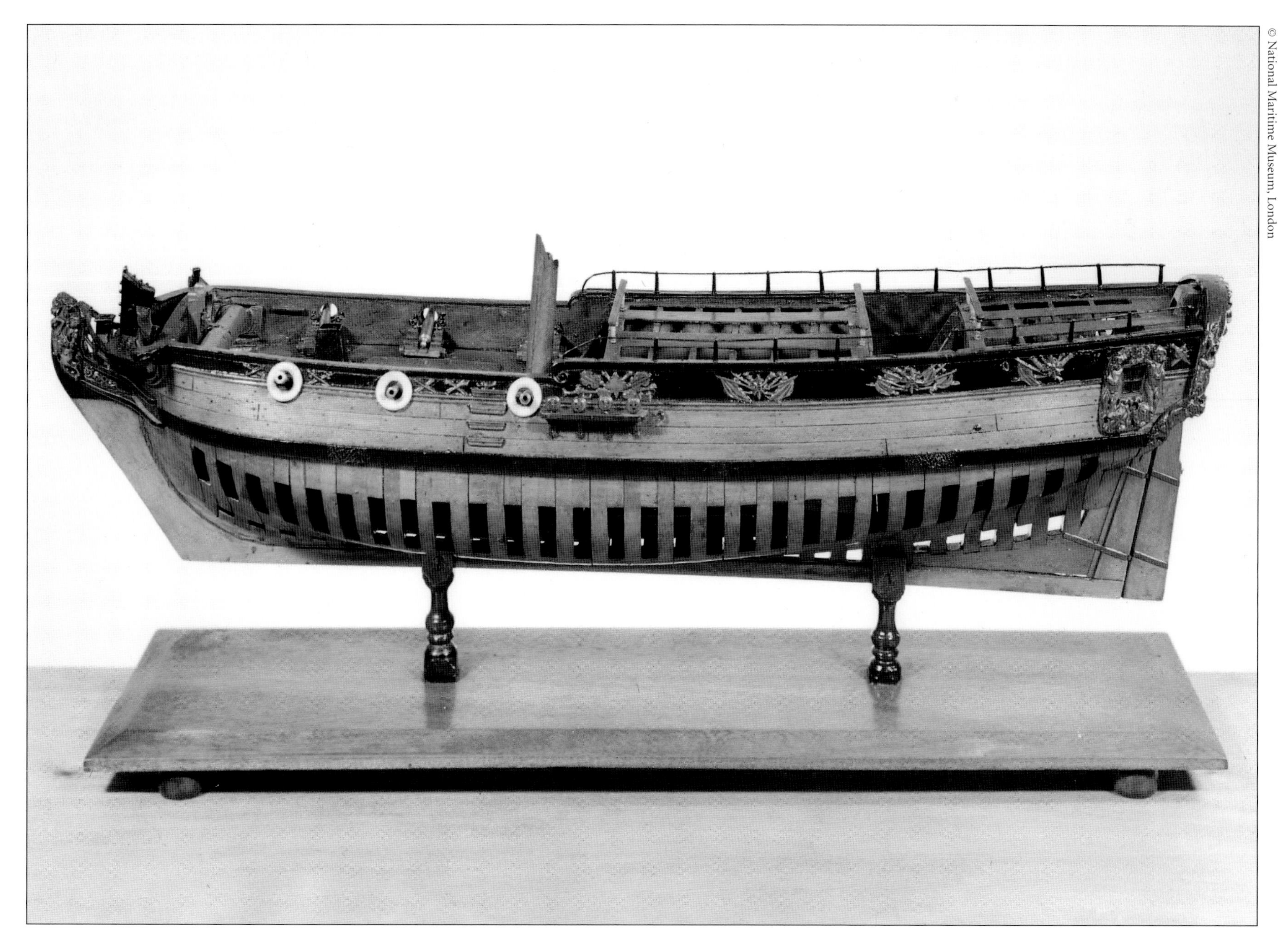

YACHTS DISPOSED OF DURING QUEEN ANNE'S REIGN

SCOUT, sold in 1703 (eight years' service)
ISLE OF WIGHT II, sold in 1712 (eleven years)
SOESDYKE, sold in 1713 (twenty-one years)
SQUIRREL, sold in 1714 (twenty years)

Shortly before eight in the morning on Sunday, 1 August 1714, Queen Anne died aged forty-nine. 'To those who knew her best, her relief from emotional and physical suffering came as a blessing.'

GEORGE I (1714-1727)

Later on the morning of Sunday 1 August, at St John's, Oxford, the Whig head of college ordered prayers to be said for 'King George' in morning worship, when it was objected that the Queen might not yet be dead. 'Dead,' says he, 'she is as dead as Julius Caesar.' In spite of her 18 pregnancies, none of Queen Anne's children survived infancy, and the throne thus descended to the great-grandson of James VI & I, George Louis, Elector of Hanover.

George I inherited a fleet of nine principal, five secondary and two small yachts. If this appears excessive, it should be remembered that four of the principal yachts were built for Charles II, (CLEVELAND, KATHERINE II, MARY II, HENRIETTA II) and were becoming positively elderly; all four in fact were either rebuilt or sold during George's reign. The secondary yachts (QUEENBOROUGH, PORTSMOUTH II, DRAKE, DUBLIN, BOLTON) were allocated to Officers of State, and not available for personal use of the sovereign.

The honour of conveying George I from Oranienpolder in Holland to Greenwich on his accession to the throne in 1714 fell to the PEREGRINE GALLEY. Her Captain was William Sanderson, and his log is at the National Maritime Museum:

> Thursday 16th September. …at noon the King came on board in our boat from Orange Powlder… at his coming on board hoisted the standard at main-topmasthead Lord High Admiral's flag at the fore-topmasthead and the union at the mizzen-topmasthead and fired guns at 5 got out over the Maze at 6 joined the men-of-war which were 13 British and a sloop: commanded by Lord Bartlett[1] Vice-Admiral of the Red and 5 Dutch under a Rear-Admiral they all saluted twice I answered them then we made sail…
>
> Friday 17th September. …we ran up the King's Channel on the back of the Shipwash with all the sails we could make at 6 at night got to the Nore the men-of-war saluted us and anchored my Lord Bartlett hollowed (hailed or cheered) us in a sloop: a Barking smack ran on board us but did no damage at 12 anchored in the lower end of the Hope. Thick fog.
>
> Saturday 18th September. …at flood we weighed and turned up by Gravesend at 4 afternoon the King went in his barge in Long Reach we struck the flag and fired 11 guns at 7 we anchored in the upper end of Erith Reach it being high water.
>
> Sunday 19th September. This morning at 1 weighed and turned up to Greenwich at 7 got to our moorings at Greenwich and put aboard all our colours the King being at Greenwich squalls of wind and rain all day the King's baggage went ashore.

Captain Sanderson modestly forbore to enter that for his services he was knighted on board the yacht that day before the King went ashore! Sir William later was appointed Gentleman-Usher of the Black Rod and created a baronet.[2]

PEREGRINE GALLEY, 1700

Oil by Jan Griffier the Elder – 'The Peregrine and other ships off Greenwich c.1715'.

CAROLINA

CAROLINA built 1700 as PEREGRINE GALLEY, renamed 1716

1700 built at Sheerness by R. Lee designed by Peregrine, Lord Danby as a sixth-rate, the PEREGRINE GALLEY.

Length on gundeck	86 feet 10 inches	Length by the keel	72 feet 8 inches
Beam	22 feet 6 inches	Depth in hold	10 feet 7 inches
Tons burden	197	Crew	–
Guns	20 cannon, 12 swivel guns		

1716 refitted as a Royal Yacht and renamed CAROLINA.
1733 rebuilt and renamed ROYAL CAROLINE.

Oil by L. de Mann – 'His Majesty's Yacht Carolina.' This was the first Royal Yacht to be ship-rigged. The Hanoverian Kings were required to spend time there as well as in England, so Royal Yachts became progressively larger and more comfortable.

Although not originally classed as a Royal Yacht, it is clear from her journals that the PEREGRINE GALLEY continued to perform such duties, and in 1716 she was specifically refitted as a Royal Yacht at Deptford and Woolwich; this did not involve the hull, but only the upperworks and accommodation. She was renamed CAROLINA, in honour of the Princess of Wales, and George II's future Queen, Caroline of Anspach. Quite why it is difficult to understand, for George I's dislike of his daughter-in-law was a public scandal – 'cette diablesse Madame la Princesse'.

Her Captain from 1716 to 1720 was Galfridus Walpole, whose sword Lord Nelson had on first going to sea.

George I's heart remained in Hanover, and as Elector he was obliged to be there for a certain amount of time. CAROLINA was his principal yacht and during his reign he made six crossings to his beloved Herrenhausen. The following description is typical.

London Gazette, 10 July 1716:

> On 7th July 1716, between 8 and 9 o'clock in the morning, His Majesty, with His Royal Highness the Prince, set out from St James's Palace. They embarked in a Royal Barge at the Tower steps, and reached Gravesend about two in the afternoon, where His Majesty went on board the CAROLINA yacht for Holland. His Royal Highness returned to London by land that night.

The King remained on the Continent until 17 January 1717, when he embarked at Helvoetsluys for England. The escorting squadron and yachts were under the command of Admiral Aylmer, who despatched the ROYAL ANNE galley to 'make the best of her way to Margate, or any other part of Great Britain which she could soonest reach'. On arrival she was to despatch a message to His Royal Highness that His Majesty was on his passage, and if the wind stayed fair, ''tis judged His Majesty will be at Margate in six or seven hours time.' Not much warning after an absence of six months! The wind did continue fair, for the King landed the next day and disembarked for London.

London Gazette, 18 January 1717:

> Canterbury, Jan. 18, at six in the evening. His Majesty having landed at Margate about three o'clock, is just now come hither (God be thanked) in perfect good health.

George repeated the crossing in January 1726, but this time it took three days during a violent storm, in which he was in great danger.

With the constant journeying to Hanover the yachts were no longer handed over to the navy for general service. Greenwich became 'the chief harbour for the King's Yachts', with the yachts kept in commission throughout the year; the yachts' companies were idle a great part of the year, with sudden bursts of activity. Sometimes members of the crew were lent to other yachts, or to ships short of men. One can just imagine the reaction of yachtsmen being pitched from their relatively comfortable berths on board one of the yachts to the extreme discomfort, and danger, of a man-of-war.

No principal new yachts were built, but three of Charles II's yachts all previously rebuilt, were rebuilt again: the KATHERINE II, the FUBBS II and the MARY II.

KATHERINE III

Rebuilt 1720 at Deptford.		Surveyor R. Stacey.	
Length on gundeck	76 feet 6 inches	Length by the keel	61 feet 6 inches
Beam	22 feet 4 inches	Depth in hold	9 feet 6 inches
Tons burden	161	Crew	40
Guns	8 (later 6) three-pounders		

Launched 16 January 1721.
1736 fitted as a ketch.
1801 sold.

The KATHERINE III, with the flag of Admiral Keppel flying, took Princess Carolina Matilda to Holland on her way to Denmark for her marriage to King Christian VII. Having landed the Princess, Admiral Keppel returned to England, leaving the WILLIAM & MARY to bring back the suite and attendants who had accompanied the future Queen.

FUBBS III

Rebuilt 1724 at Deptford.		Surveyor R. Stacey.	
Length on gundeck	76 feet 9 inches	Length by the keel	61 feet 5¼ inches
Beam	21 feet 6 inches	Depth in hold	9 feet
Tons burden	152	Crew	40
Guns	8 three-pounders		

Launched 22 October 1724.
1749 ordered 'to have her deck raised as much as conveniently may be.'
1781 taken to pieces.

Over £370 of additional carving was added to that saved from the previous yacht; 85 panes of glass were added to her windows, and £40 spent on gilded leather skins to embellish the fittings in the cabins.

FUBBS III, 1724 (rebuilt)

Contemporary model on a scale of 1:48. The decoration suggests it may be a design for the rebuilding of the FUBBS III in 1724. The shields above the quarter-windows show the three buckles of the dukedom of Aubigny, granted by Louis XIV to Louise de Kéroualle, Duchess of Portsmouth – the original FUBBS *of 1674 was named after her.* FUBBS III *was actually four feet longer than the vessel represented by the model.*

On 4 March 1734, Anne, the Princess Royal, daughter of George II, was married to the Prince of Orange, Stadtholder of the United Provinces. On 22 April the Prince and his bride left London in carriages, accompanied by many persons of distinction. At Greenwich they embarked on the FUBBS for Holland, but the wind being unfavourable they spent two nights at the house of a Dr Holker before finally crossing on 24 April.

MARY III

Rebuilt 1727 at Deptford.		Surveyor R. Stacey.	
Length on gundeck	76 feet 6 inches	Length by the keel	61 feet 6 inches
Beam	22 feet 4 inches	Depth in hold	9 feet 8 inches
Tons burden	164	Crew	40
Guns	8 three-pounders, 10 swivel-guns		

1735 'to mast and rig her as a ketch.'
1783 large repair. Rerigged as a ship.
1816 taken to pieces.

MARY III, 1727 (rebuilt)

Oil by L. de Mann – 'A Royal Yacht, possibly the Mary.' Although rebuilt to new dimensions in 1727, the MARY III *was not rigged as a ketch until 1735. The painter L. de Mann flourished about the time of the yacht's rebuilding, so it is likely that this is* MARY III. *Her decks are crowded with people – as are the boats – whilst the yacht fires a salute.*

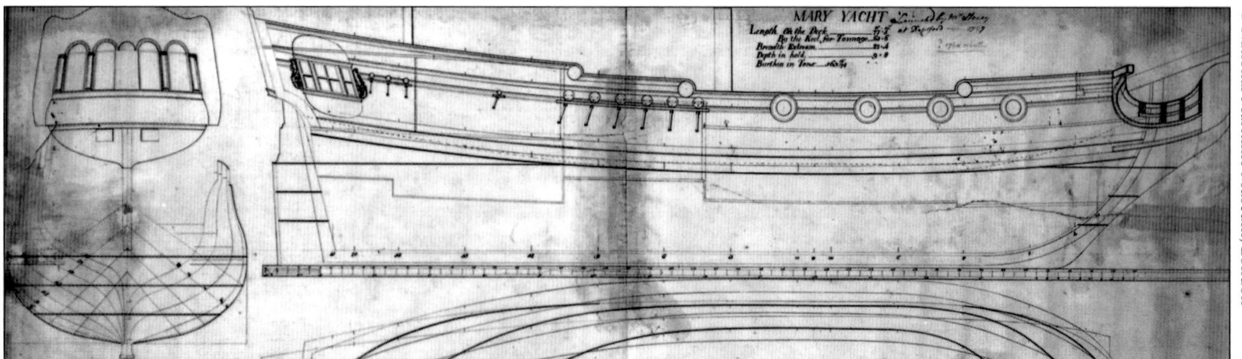

Three principal yachts were disposed of, two having given several decades of service:

CLEVELAND, sold in 1716 (forty-five years' service)
HENRIETTA II, sold in 1720 (forty-one years' service)
ISABELLA II, sold in 1715 (thirteen years' service)

THE SECONDARY YACHTS OF GEORGE I

The CHATHAM, of 60 tons, was built in 1716 for the use of the Commissioner of Chatham Dockyard, and two years later the QUEENBOROUGH was rebuilt as a surveying vessel.

CHATHAM

Built 1716 at Chatham.

Surveyor Mr Rosewell.

Length on gundeck	56 feet	Length by the keel	44 feet 6 inches
Beam	16 feet	Depth in hold	7 feet 6 inches
Tons burden	60	Crew	6
Guns	4 two-pounders		

Launched 27 June 1716.
1742/3 sold.

QUEENBOROUGH II

Rebuilt 1718 at Sheerness.

Surveyor John Ward.

Length on gundeck	51 feet 6 inches	Length by the keel	37 feet 3 inches
Beam	15 feet 2 inches	Depth in hold	6 feet 7 inches
Tons burden	46	Crew	7 (13 when surveying)
Guns	6 two-pounders		

1718-1775 for the Commissioners of Sheerness Dockyard.
1775 fitted as a survey ship (classed as a sloop).
1777 sold.

Two secondary yachts were disposed of, both having given several decades of service:

JAMIE, broken up in 1721 (aged fifty-nine years)
QUINBOROW, sold in 1719 (forty-eight years' service)

George I's final voyage was in the autumn of 1727 journeying to Hanover, for he died in his coach on the way. He had taken little interest in the government of Britain, nor in the navy and his yachts, other than as transport across the sea to Hanover, his first love. 'An amiable blockhead' was one opinion of him; a man of more human faculty 'chiefly of an inarticulate kind' was another. Certainly he was not mourned by his subjects, and his son, already in England at Richmond, succeeded him as George II.

QUEENBOROUGH II, 1718

Small yacht used by the Commissioners of Sheerness Dockyard 1718-1775, then on surveying duties until sold in 1777. Contemporary model on a scale of 1:48, shown as rebuilt in 1718. She is fitted with a large hatchway and capstan amidships for carriage and handling of stores. The windlass forward, which was turned by handspikes, was used for anchor and mooring work.

GEORGE II (1727-1760)

At his accession George inherited six principal yachts, the WILLIAM & MARY, CAROLINA (renamed ROYAL CAROLINE in 1733), CHARLOT II, KATHERINE III, FUBBS III and the MARY III.

Like his father before him, George II was deeply attached to the country of his birth, and the dictates of his heart and the conduct of its affairs involved frequent journeys to Hanover. The voyages were invariably made by the King in the WILLIAM & MARY or the ROYAL CAROLINE, whilst other yachts accompanied him with members of his entourage.

London Gazette, Whitehall, 22 May 1729:

> On Saturday the 17th inst. His Majesty went on board the CAROLINE (CAROLINA) yacht at Greenwich, about one in the afternoon, and set sail with a fair wind; about eight at night came to anchor in the Swyn below the Shooe Beason; and the next morning between two and three, His Majesty got out to sea. On Wednesday evening a Messenger bought the welcome news that His Majesty arrived at Helvoetsluys on Tuesday at six in the morning. God be praised in perfect health.

The King remained on the Continent all summer, returning on board the WILLIAM & MARY in September.

The Admiralty placed much importance on the safe passage of the King or members of the Royal Family, as is shown by the rank of those entrusted in command. The Earl of Berkeley, Viscount Torrington, Lord Anson and Lord Aylmer were all Admirals of the Fleet at the time of their service.

Rear-Admiral Byng (the ill-fated Byng) wrote from Berkeley Square to the Secretary of the Admiralty on the 13 August 1745:

> I request payment of wages for the time I hoisted my Broad pennant when I had the honour of conveying His Royal Highness the Duke of Cumberland over to Holland, which was from the 25th March, 1745, to the 17th April following.

Lord Anson wrote on 2 May 1748:

> I have received Their Lordships' orders of 30th past to take under my command… the Royal Yachts ROYAL CAROLINA (ROYAL CAROLINE), WILLIAM & MARY, KATHERINE, CHARLOTTE, FUBBS, MARY, with such others as may be at the Nore, in order to attend His Majesty to Holland. The HAMPSHIRE and HASTINGS are ordered the Gunfleet, the others of the escort to lay constantly upon the warp and weigh the moment the yachts come in sight. After a tedious passage we arrived at Helvoetsluys, where at five o'clock in the morning I went on shore with His Majesty, who is in perfect health.

CAROLINA, 1716

By Peter Monamy – 'A calm with a Royal Yacht firing a salute.' Probably representing the return of George II from Hanover in 1727.

In October the Admiral took command of the yachts ROYAL CAROLINE, WILLIAM & MARY, KATHERINE and CHARLOTTE, plus three escorts. A month later the King embarked on the WILLIAM & MARY, and landed at King Gate, near Margate.

In later years the King usually embarked at the Nore or at Harwich, and Lord Anson was usually in command. He would conclude his despatch in the manner customary at the time: 'I am this moment stepping into my boat to attend His Majesty on shore, who, thank God, is in perfect health.'

By 1733 the CAROLINA (ex-PEREGRINE GALLEY, built in 1700 and refitted and renamed in 1716) was becoming elderly, and in that year she was rebuilt and renamed – again.

ROYAL CAROLINE

Rebuilt 1733 (ex-CAROLINA) at Deptford.		Surveyor Mr Stacey.	
Length on gundeck	86 feet 6 inches	Length by the keel	70 feet 6 inches
Beam	24 feet	Depth in hold	10 feet 6 inches
Tons burden	216	Crew	70 (100 as a sloop)
Guns	10 three-pounders (16 as a sloop)		

Launched 5 February 1734.
1749 converted to a sloop and renamed PEREGRINE SLOOP.

The Captain's Journal of the first ROYAL CAROLINE is in the National Maritime Museum, and gives a good insight into the long periods of idleness broken by frenetic activity which was the pattern of Royal Yachts at that time. For 1736 her Captain was Sir Charles Hardy, and he noted 'Greenwich at our moorings' for

ROYAL CAROLINE, rebuilt 1733

A contemporary model at the Science Museum, 2 feet 2 inches long, 6 inches high and 6 inches wide: probably the ROYAL CAROLINE.

January, February and March; punctuated only by firing an 11-gun salute for Her Majesty's birthday on 1 March, and paying the crew – but only up to the end of 1735.

In April the yacht fitted out at Deptford.

22 May 1736, at Gravesend:

> Fresh gales, the pm... at 10 this evening the Rt Hon. Sir Charles Wager hoisted his flag on board the WILLIAM & MARY, at past 4 am the yachts saluted the Admiral with 7 guns each, and Tilbury Fort with 9; the signal being made unmoored and hove short; at 7 His Majesty embarked when… the Admiral with the other yachts saluted with 7 guns each as did Tilbury Fort with 21 thrice repeated…

Contrary winds meant the King did not land at Helvoetsluys until 26 May, where 'he was saluted by the yachts with 7 guns, and the garrison with 14 more; which was repeated at the yacht going out of town.' The King, and others, must have been deafened by all this saluting.

The yachts returned to Greenwich, where they remained, apart from a short voyage to Deptford, where the Prince and Princess of Wales dined on board.

In August the yacht went into the wet dock at Deptford: 'unrigged our topmasts in order to fit the new topmast shrouds, but finding the main and fore tops decayed, got them off, and sent them ashore, they were found unserviceable.'

5 October: 'This day I received a new commission from the Rt Hon. the Lords Commissioners of the Admiralty appointing me Captain of His Majesty's Ship ROYAL CAROLINE, before, a Yacht.' This, of course meant an increase in status and pay.

On 28 November the squadron set sail for Helvoetsluys, and although on 9 December they 'took in the King's baggage,' it was not until the 20th that the King himself came on board; but then fierce gales held them up until the year's end.

Thus ended the year of 1736 for the ROYAL CAROLINE, no longer a yacht but a ship. True, they were stormbound in Holland, attempting in the depth of winter to carry the King to England, but as they had done barely three weeks' sea-time all year there was little to complain about.

ROYAL CAROLINE II

Built 1749* at Deptford.		Designed by J. Allin.	
Length on gundeck	90 feet 1 inch	Length by the keel	72 feet 2 inches
Beam	24 feet 7 inches	Depth in hold	11 feet
Tons burden	232	Crew	70
Guns	10 three-pounders, 8 half-pounder swivels		

*Launched 29 January 1750 as a sixth-rate, rigged as a ship, the largest Royal Yacht to date.
1761 renamed ROYAL CHARLOTTE.
1820 taken to pieces.

In spite of having been rebuilt in 1733, and thus being a relatively new vessel, by 1748 things were going wrong for the ROYAL CAROLINE. In March of that year the King commented to Captain Molloy that the ship was not exactly in tip-top condition, and it was reported to Lord Anson that the hull was in need of urgent repairs. The Admiralty decided to build a new yacht, and the old ROYAL CAROLINE was converted to a sloop and renamed PEREGRINE SLOOP.[1]

ROYAL CAROLINE II, built 1749

Oil by John Cleevely the Elder, 1750 – 'His Majesty's Yacht Royal Caroline.'

In a letter dated 26 June 1749 the Master Shipwrights of various yards, and the Surveyor of the Navy in person, were asked to prepare plans for approval by the Admiralty for a new Royal Yacht. The new ROYAL CAROLINE was to be of the same draught and capacity as her predecessor, and to be built in the shortest possible time, as the old yacht was no longer available for the King's use.

Under a month later, on 22 August, Surveyor Joshua Allin's plans were accepted, and building commenced immediately at Deptford, for the Admiralty had specified 'that the whole be completed in less than five months'.[2]

But although the Lords of the Admiralty had ordered the new ship, the Navy Board had not budgeted for her, and there began a lengthy and niggling correspondence between the two. A proportion of the fittings from the old ROYAL CAROLINE were to be used, but even so it was not until October, well into building, that an estimate of the cost was presented.

Hull, mast and spars	£6137
Furnishings & fittings	£1360
Sculptures	£ 906
Gilding	£1507
total	£9910

An impressive sum, given that a new sloop of similar size was barely £2000, and that the total cost of a three-decked, 80-gun ship of the line was £38 000 – fitted out, stored for eight months and ready to sail.[3]

The Navy Board and the yard exchanged countless letters over the stream of high bills for the yacht: £1100 11s 0d for carving from Mr Thomas Burroughs; over £200 for curtains and panels of silk, damask, finest linens, cushions, upholstery ribbons, braids and embroidery from Messrs Bladwell & Reaver; £18 for the stern lanterns from the Widow May's company – this at a time when a seaman's pay was £12 per annum, if he received it.

Mrs Rosamund Turner's company 'laid on with gold size, 120 000 leaves of gold on HMS the ROYAL CAROLINE in gilding her head, stern and all the frieze and weatherwork fore and aft etc. and being the greatest part which is to be gilt for which am humbly of the opinion she deserves to be paid at the rate of 15s for 100 leaves including gold size and workmanship.' But this meant £900, and the Navy Board issued a curt order to the yard that all gilding and painting was to stop. It was only completed six months later, after the yacht's first voyage with the King, and at a further cost of £267. The final bill for the yacht was £12 390, of which £1100 was for the carvings and £1521 for gilding.[4]

ROYAL CAROLINE II was launched on 29 January 1750 at one o'clock, and taken the same day to the hulks for masting. In February and March she spent a fortnight undergoing sailing trials in the Straits of Dover with the WILLIAM & MARY and the FUBBS III, the latter having been specially cleaned for the trials. Sadly, the results have not survived, but on 8 March the yacht anchored at Deptford. There the Duke of Cumberland, second son of George II, inspected the ship and effectively took possession of her for the King.

George II first used the ROYAL CAROLINE II on 17 April 1750, when he embarked at Harwich for Holland, the first of many crossings in his and succeeding reigns. The ports of departure were usually Greenwich, Harwich or Gravesend, and Helvoetsluys was the principal destination, from which the King and his entourage proceeded overland to Hanover. On the return voyage the King usually landed at Harwich, or occasionally Margate, the crossing taking one or two days.

There was always more than one yacht, to house the King's entourage and baggage, and an escort of up to four frigates depending on the political situation. This was necessary protection against privateers, first French, then Spaniards, Algerians and even Americans during and after the War of Independence.

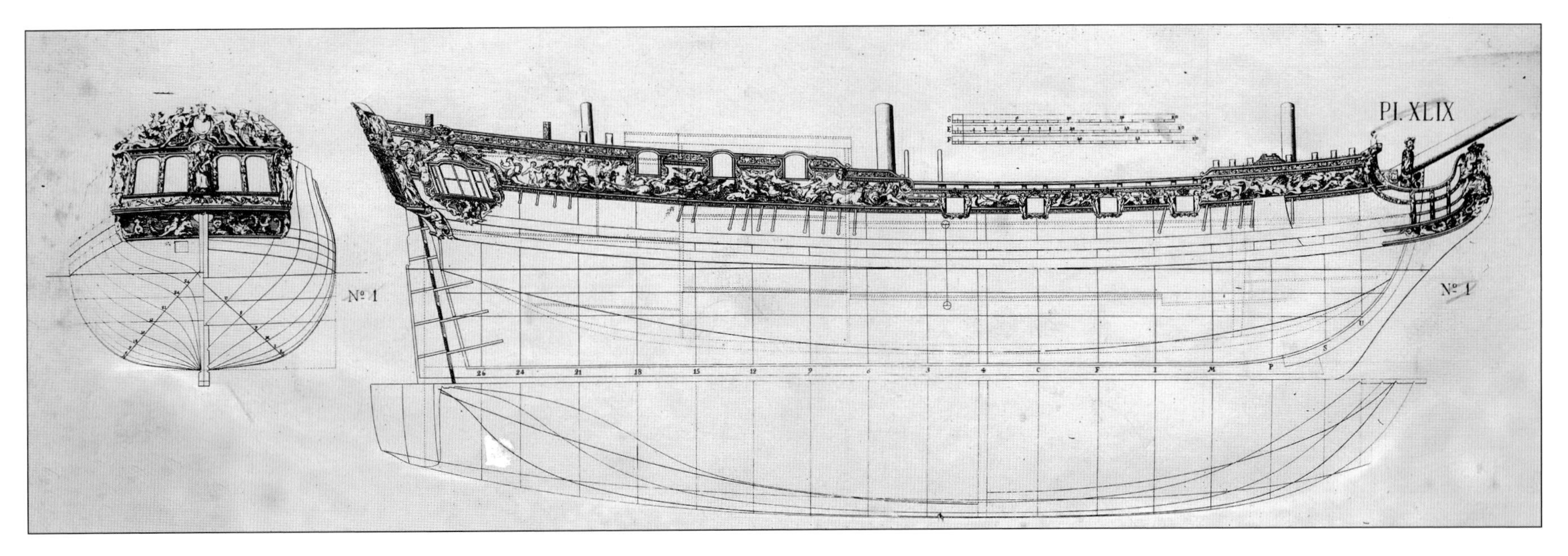

ROYAL CAROLINE II, built 1749

Captain Sir Charles Molloy, the previous yacht's captain, transferred his command to the ROYAL CAROLINE II, and had under him a master, gunner, surgeon and two midshipmen. The boatswain and carpenter, as petty officers, enjoyed the unusual privilege of a cabin each, albeit tiny. The six gunner's mates and three sailing master's mates shared three small cabins, whilst the Captain's six servants, a steward and a clerk all lodged at the far end of the stern. 36 seamen shared 18 bunks, an unusual change from hammocks, and possibly not one much appreciated by seamen used to the comfort of a hammock at sea.

In all there were 70 men, and the paybook[5] from launching on 29 January to 30 June 1750 shows the following rates of pay for those five months:

Captain Molloy	£45 3s 9d
Surgeon	just less than £27
Master	just over £21
Midshipmen	about £8
Able seamen	about £6

The introduction of Dutch yachts in the 1660s had stimulated the rivalry of English shipwrights to improve on and adapt the designs, and they gained much valuable experience from the building of Royal Yachts in the construction of lightweight vessels and rigging. Similarly in the early-eighteenth century the French schools of mathematics and applied physics were engaged in the study of the optimum shape of hulls; their results, if not brilliant, were certainly a positive contribution.

The Admiralty and the dockyards were somewhat hidebound by tradition, but not totally averse to experimentation and change. Although the results of the sailing trials for the ROYAL CAROLINE II have not survived, she must have been a very successful ship, for in 1753 the Admiralty ordered two experimental sixth-rate, 20-gun ships to be built. One hull was the SEAFORD, and given the urgency of designing and building the ROYAL CAROLINE II it is probable that Surveyor Allin lifted the lines from those of her predecessor, ROYAL CAROLINE, ex-CAROLINA, ex-PEREGRINE GALLEY.

The SEAFORD led to a long line of ships: DEAL CASTLE and SQUIRREL in 1754, GLASGOW and ROSE in 1756. And although some three times the tonnage of the yacht, the 32-gun frigates of the RICHMOND class were based upon the same lines. Built between 1757 and 1763 these included the RICHMOND, JUNO,

THAMES, BOSTON, LARKE and JASON. Nor is that the end of the story, for in 1804 the Admiralty ordered new 32-gun frigates, again based on the RICHMOND class, and these included the CIRCE, PALLAS, JASON, HEBE, THAMES, MINERVA and ALEXANDRA.

So a hull designed in 1699 by an amateur, Peregrine, Lord Danby, boon friend and drinking companion of Tsar Peter; adapted in haste by the Surveyor of the Navy, Joshua Allin, in 1749 to a Royal Yacht; further adapted through experimentation in 1753 for a class of 20-gun ships; was lifted for the lines of highly successful 32-gun frigates in 1757; and was finally used for a further class in 1804. Lord Danby was either highly gifted or highly lucky.[6]

SECONDARY YACHTS OF GEORGE II

During his reign George II built new yachts for the main royal dockyards – Portsmouth, Plymouth and Chatham – thus ensuring all three Dockyard Commissioners had yachts appropriate to their need and rank.

Nor was the Lord Lieutenant of Ireland forgotten, as the DORSET was built in 1753 to replace the forty-one-year-old DUBLIN, taken to pieces the previous year.

DRAKE II

Rebuilt 1729 at Plymouth.		Designed by P. Locke.	
Length on gundeck	55 feet 6 inches	Length by the keel	45 feet
Beam	–	Depth in hold	–
Tons burden	68	Crew	–
Guns	6 two-pounders		

Commissioner's yacht Plymouth Dockyard.
1749 decayed and sold.
(Replaced by the PLYMOUTH 1755.)

DRAKE II, 1729

CHATHAM II

Built 1741 at Chatham.
Length on gundeck 59 feet 6 inches
Beam 17 feet 3 inches
Tons burden 74
Guns 6 two-pounders
Commissioner's yacht Chatham Dockyard.
1765 large repairs.
1793 rebuilt.

Designed by John Ward.
Length by the keel 47 feet
Depth in hold 7 feet 6 inches
Crew 9

CHATHAM II, 1741

Contemporary model on the scale of 1:32.

PORTSMOUTH II

Built in 1702 she was renamed OLD PORTSMOUTH in 1741. In 1752 she was fitted for the 'use of the young gentlemen of the (Naval) Academy (at Portsmouth)'.

PORTSMOUTH III

Built 1742 at Portsmouth.		Designed by P. Locke.	
Length on gundeck	59 feet 6 inches	Length by the keel	48 feet 5 inches
Beam	18 feet	Depth in hold	8 feet 6 inches
Tons burden	83	Crew	10
Guns	6 two-pounders		

Built in place of 1702 yacht of same name (renamed OLD PORTSMOUTH) for the Commissioner of Portsmouth Dockyard.
1794 rebuilt.

DORSET

Built 1753 at Deptford.		Designed by Sir T. Slade.	
Length on gundeck	78 feet	Length by the keel	64 feet 10¼ inches
Beam	21 feet 11 inches	Depth in hold	10 feet 10 inches
Tons burden	164	Crew	50
Guns	6 two pounders and 14 half-pounder swivels. (Shown in the *Naval Chronicle* of 1801 as having 10 guns.)		

Replacement for the DUBLIN (Lord Lieutenant of Ireland).
Originally ketch-rigged, later fitted with three masts.
1815 sold for breaking up.

Naval Chronicle 1801.

> This yacht undergoes a thorough repair at Plymouth every three years, being the nearest dockyard to Dublin, where she is stationed and belongs to the Lord Lieutenant of Ireland. She is beautifully ornamented about the head; and over her stern is the Harp on a green field, with much elegant carved work and painting. Sir A. Schomberg, Knt. (is captain). Has been refitted this last year and is just returned to Dublin.[7]

For details of her employment on the Dublin station, see Chapter 9.

PLYMOUTH

Built 1755 at Plymouth.		Designed by Thomas Bucknoll.	
Length on gundeck	64 feet 6 inches	Length by the keel	52 feet 6 inches
Beam	17 feet 10 inches	Depth in hold	10 feet
Tons burden	88	Crew	10
Guns	6 two-pounders		

Replaced the DRAKE at Plymouth.
Dockyard yacht.
1793 taken to pieces.
(Replaced by PLYMOUTH II in 1796.)

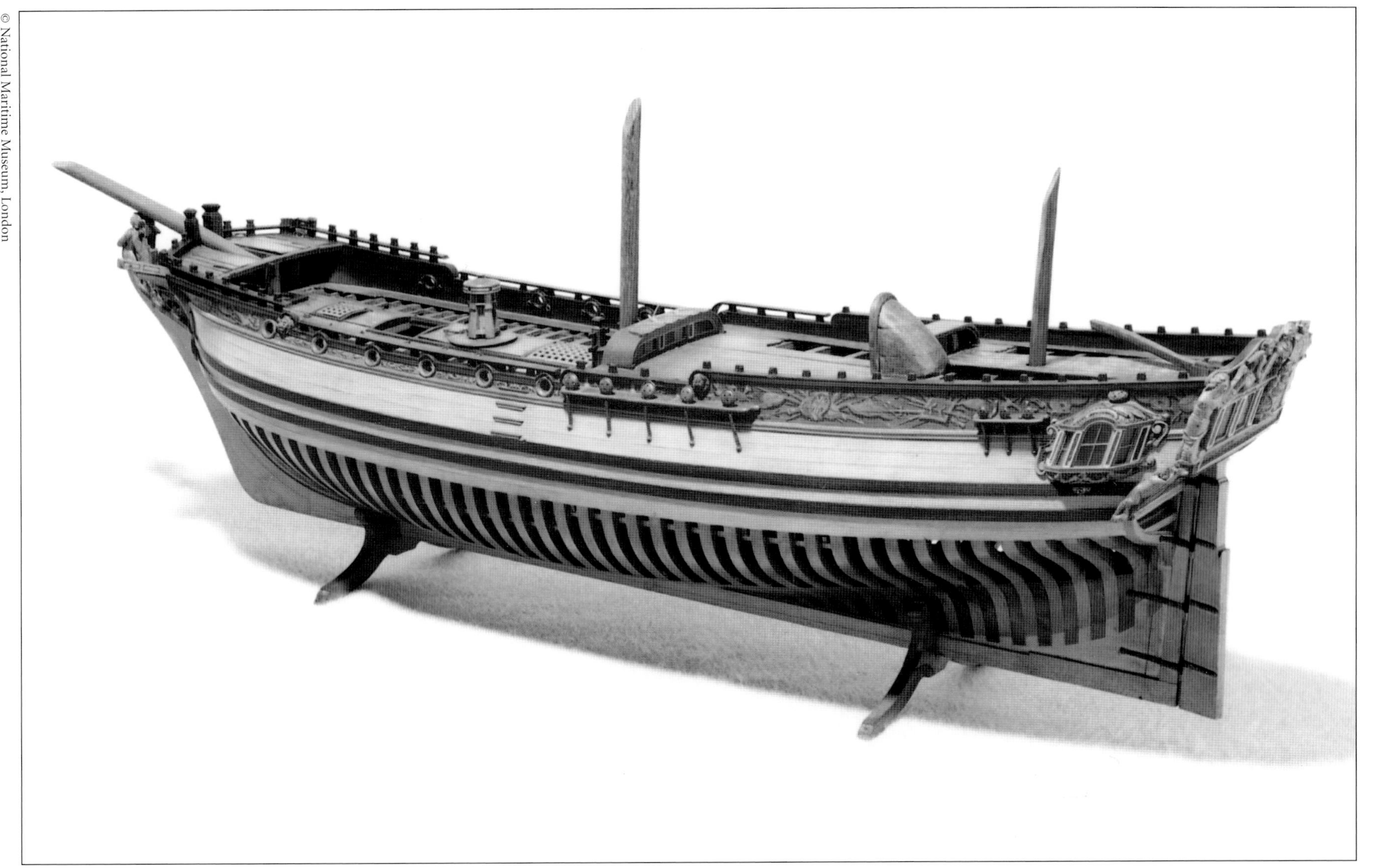

PLYMOUTH, 1755

A contemporary model, although the after decking, companionway and stump-masts are modern replacements.

Three secondary yachts were disposed of during the reign:

CHATHAM, sold in 1742 (twenty-six years' service)
DRAKE II, sold in 1749 (twenty years)
DUBLIN, taken to pieces in 1752 (aged forty-three years)

George II died suddenly at Kensington in 1860, aged seventy-seven. He had no obvious virtues; his worst vice was that common with his father, a propensity for mistresses. During his thirty-three-year reign Britain had prospered and had made notable territorial advances in Canada and India. He is perhaps best remembered by schoolboys as the last British monarch to command an army in the field. His son, Frederick Louis, Prince of Wales, having predeceased him in 1751, he was succeeded by his grandson, George III.

GEORGE III (1760-1820)

George III inherited the throne at the age of twenty-two from his grandfather, his own father having died in 1751. At his accession there were six main yachts, of which the principal and largest at 232 tons was the ROYAL CAROLINE II, built in 1749, and renamed ROYAL CHARLOTTE in 1761.

The other five large yachts were the WILLIAM & MARY (1694), 152 tons; the CHARLOT II (1710), 155 tons; the KATHERINE III (1720), 161 tons; the FUBBS III (1724), 152 tons; and the MARY III (1727), 164 tons.

The KATHERINE II, FUBBS III and MARY III had been rebuilt in 1720, 1724 and 1727 respectively, and although they remained in commission, they were very much relegated to secondary duties. The WILLIAM & MARY was by now sixty-six years old, and was rebuilt to new dimensions in 1764/5.

The CHARLOT II had been built in 1710, and so was half a century old; soon after ascending the throne George III renamed her AUGUSTA, after his sister.

Only one Royal Yacht was (re)built during the first forty years of George III's reign, the AUGUSTA II, (later PRINCESS AUGUSTA) in 1771. Thus for most of George III's long reign only the ROYAL CHARLOTTE and PRINCESS AUGUSTA were serviceable as principal Royal Yachts. The use of the former declined when the ROYAL SOVEREIGN was built in 1804, and the construction of the ROYAL GEORGE in 1817 brought to an end the ROYAL CHARLOTTE's career; she was taken to pieces three years later.

Now that he was King, George III had to consider marriage, and he settled on the Princess Charlotte of Mecklenburg-Strelitz. On 27 July 1761 the ROYAL CAROLINE II was renamed the ROYAL CHARLOTTE, in honour of his bride. There being already a yacht named CHARLOT II, the latter was renamed AUGUSTA – after the King's sister – to free the name for the ROYAL CHARLOTTE.

A squadron of five yachts and six warships was assembled at Harwich to collect the new Queen, and on 7 August 1761 Lord Anson hoisted his flag in the ROYAL CHARLOTTE as Admiral of the Fleet for the last time, and took the squadron to Cuxhaven.[1] The ROYAL CHARLOTTE was fitted out magnificently for the occasion, and three distinguished ladies, the Duchess of Hamilton, the Duchess of Ancaster and Lady Effingham were appointed as Ladies of the Bedchamber to the young Princess. Charlotte, however, seemed slightly overwhelmed by the reception, salutes, firing of cannon and ringing of bells as she embarked at Stade. 'And am I worthy of all these honours?' she asked. The return voyage was appalling, for the yacht was driven north to Norway by two successive gales. However, they finally reached Harwich safely on 6 September, and the Princess landed the next day for the final stage of her journey to London.

ROYAL CHARLOTTE, renamed 1761, (centre)
Oil by Richard Wright – 'Queen Charlotte's Passage to England.' A view of the storm when the Queen was on her passage to England, painted from a sketch drawn on board the FUBBS *yacht.*

AUGUSTA II/PRINCESS AUGUSTA

Rebuilt 1771 at Deptford.		Surveyor	–
Length on gundeck	80 feet 6 inches	Length by the keel	64 feet 11 inches
Beam	23 feet 1¼ inches	Depth in hold	10 feet 11 inches
Tons burden	184	Crew	40
Guns	8 three-pounders	Ship-rigged	–

Principal yacht of George III.
1773 renamed PRINCESS AUGUSTA and rated a ship.
13 August 1818, sold to a Mr Sedger for £650.

AUGUSTA II, 1771 (rebuilt)
Renamed PRINCESS AUGUSTA, 1773.

Dominic Serres – 'The Royal Visit to the Fleet 22-26 June 1773, with King George III on board the Augusta yacht.'

In 1771 the AUGUSTA (ex-CHARLOT II, 1710) was rebuilt to completely new dimensions, and so I have classified her as AUGUSTA II. Her tonnage increased by 20 per cent, and the yacht was ship-rigged, as opposed to her previous rig as a ketch.

From 22-26 June 1773 she was present at the review of the fleet at Portsmouth, and the King used the yacht every day. In honour of the occasion he ordered her name to be changed to PRINCESS AUGUSTA, and to be rated a ship, not a yacht. The Master's Log records for 21 July 1773: 'rec'd an order to alter the name of the yatch (sic) to the Princess Augusta.'[2] The PRINCESS AUGUSTA remained the principal and favourite yacht of George III throughout most of his reign.

In the spring of 1778, King George lived on board the PRINCESS AUGUSTA whilst on a visit to the fleet at the Nore, and went on board the VICTORY (104 guns), then on her first commission. Later that spring the King and Queen Charlotte inspected the fleet at Spithead, followed by a levee on board the flagship, PRINCE GEORGE.

Naval reviews, pageants and processions of boats were frequently organised, and not just for display, for the decade leading to Trafalgar saw the pre-eminence of the Royal Navy. After lengthy and exhausting periods at sea the morale of the fleet, and its esteem with the nation, were raised by the interest and presence of the King at such reviews.

The importance attached to the command of the principal Royal Yacht is shown by the number of ROYAL CHARLOTTE's captains who achieved flag rank.[3] The practice of having the King escorted personally by the highest rank in the Admiralty was invariably kept up.[4]

It was in the summer of 1789 that George III started his 'Aquatic Excursions' as the press called them, for the King, the Queen and the Princesses went to Weymouth in July to stay at the residence of his brother, the Duke of Gloucester. That year the 5th-rate SOUTHAMPTON was used as a Royal Yacht, escorted by the MAGNIFICENT (32 guns), and a number of men-of-war and cutters sent round from Portsmouth to attend upon Their Majesties.

In the following years these Aquatic Excursions followed a set pattern, and outings in Weymouth Bay were much enjoyed by the King, Queen Charlotte and the Princesses.

On 28 March 1795 the Princess Caroline of Brunswick-Wolfenbüttel (daughter of King George III's eldest sister Augusta) sailed from the River Elbe in the frigate HMS JUPITER for marriage to her cousin, afterwards George IV. At Gravesend she transferred by the Royal Barge to the PRINCESS AUGUSTA, and landed at Greenwich on 8 April; had she but known how disastrous her marriage was to be, Caroline would never have left Brunswick.[5]

PRINCESS AUGUSTA, 1773

'The arrival at Greenwich on 8 April 1795 of Princess Caroline of Brunswick' (for marriage to her cousin, later George IV).

After the battle of Camperdown in 1797 George III attempted to visit the fleet at the Nore to thank personally the officers and crews who had won such a splendid victory over the Dutch. The King embarked at Gravesend in the ROYAL CHARLOTTE, escorted by the PRINCESS AUGUSTA, MARY III and two armed brigs. But it was by now early November, contrary strong winds held them back, and the King was forced to return to Greenwich and to London.

At the beginning of the nineteenth century the following yachts appeared in the Navy List:

1. ROYAL CHARLOTTE, 232 tons, built Deptford 1749
2. PRINCESS AUGUSTA, 184 tons, built Deptford 1771
3. WILLIAM & MARY II, 172 tons, rebuilt Deptford 1764
4. KATHERINE III, 166 tons, rebuilt Deptford 1720
5. MARY III, 164 tons, rebuilt Deptford 1727
6. DORSET, 164 tons, built Deptford 1753
7. PORTSMOUTH III, 83 tons, built Portsmouth 1742
8. PLYMOUTH II, 88 tons, built Plymouth 1755
9. MEDINA, 66 tons, built Portsmouth 1702

The first five were for the use of the Royal Family, and of these only the ROYAL CHARLOTTE and PRINCESS AUGUSTA were fit for active service. This lack of use made the older yachts suitable commands for senior officers who had been wounded and were not fit to return to full employment.

The principal yachts were seldom used for some years, partly due to the King's illness, and partly on account of the war. The yachts were generally to be found at Deptford, but were in the habit of lending ratings to ships after refitting at Deptford and going down the Thames to Chatham, Portsmouth or Plymouth, where they would receive their full complement.

George III revived his holidays at Weymouth in 1801, but the PRINCESS AUGUSTA, not having been used for some time, was unavailable for the King's use. Still being at war with France, two frigates were detailed off to guard against surprise attack from the enemy, much to the chagrin of the warship's officers: 'I perceive that the officers considered this an expensive and unprofitable service; full dress every day and no prize money to be made.'[6] The holiday lasted three months, and at the end of it Captain The Honourable Charles Paget of the escorting frigate HYDRA gave a ball on board for the Royal Family and the nobility and gentry of Weymouth. In the middle of dinner – when the Royal Family were observed 'to eat and drink very much like other people' – a piper concealed on staging over the ship's side struck up with God save the King; 'Everyone seemed delighted from the King downwards.'[7]

ROYAL SOVEREIGN

Built 1804 at Deptford.

Length on gundeck	96 feet	Length by the keel	80 feet 5 inches
Beam	25 feet 8 inches	Depth in hold	10 feet 6 inches
Tons burden	278	Crew	67
Guns	8 three-pounders		

Designed by Sir John Henslow.

Launched 12 May 1804.
1832 became a depot ship at Pembroke.
1850 broken up.

By 1800 the ROYAL CHARLOTTE was over fifty years old, and it was decided to replace her with a larger vessel. Plans for the ROYAL SOVEREIGN were drawn at Deptford in November 1801, but she was not

ROYAL SOVEREIGN, 1804

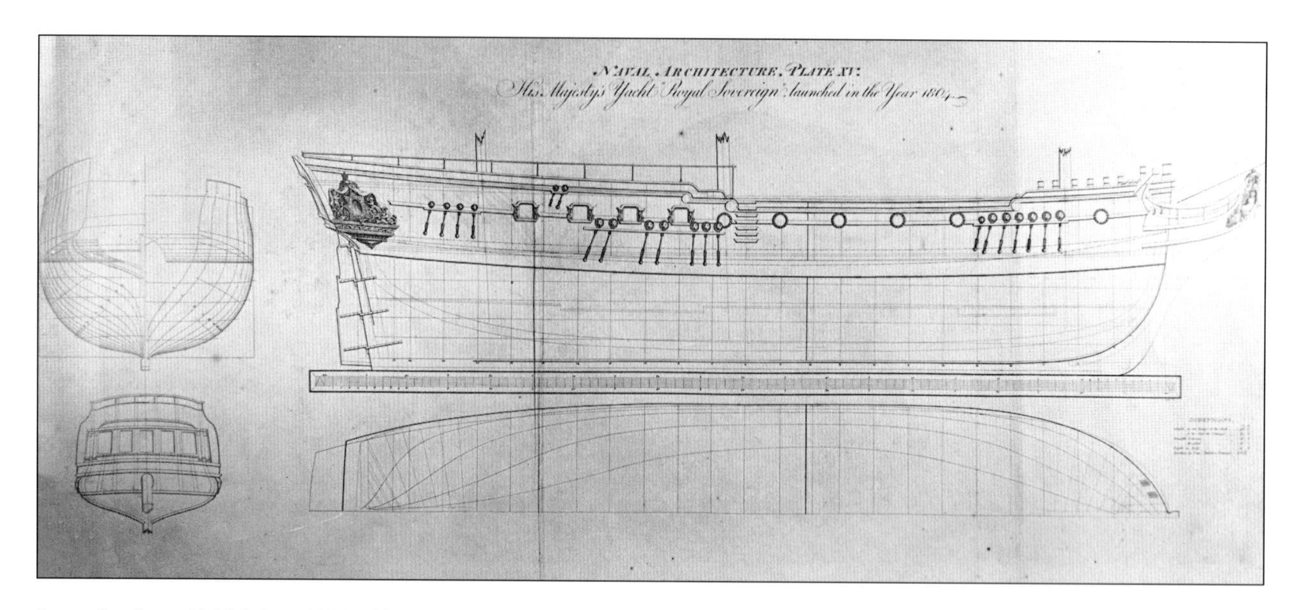

launched until 12 May 1804. She was to be the largest and grandest yacht to date, six feet longer and 46 tons larger than her predecessor.

Naval Chronicle 1804:

> At a quarter before three o'clock on Saturday, May 12th, 1804, the new yacht built on purpose for His Majesty was launched from the King's Dock Yard at Deptford. She is a very neat but small ship. In her present trim she draws about 9 feet forward and 10 feet abaft. She is completely copper bottomed, as above that a streak of yellow and then another of blue, ornamented with medallions representing the four cardinal virtues, as female figures, in gilt frames. Over them is a rich ornament of leaves entwined together, highly gilt. The figurehead is a representation of Her Majesty with the Imperial Crown over her head. This is encompassed by an iron railing to prevent any injury. The stern is decorated with the figure of Neptune in his Car, with his Trident in his hand, and the Sea underneath and Dolphins playing around. Over the cabin windows and under the taffrail are placed the figures of the Four Quarters of the world all over. The accommodation ladder and the differing gratings are painted yellow, with very rich mouldings of carved work highly gilt. Upon the whole, as the sailors term it, there is an abundance of gingerbread work. The apartments laid out for the Royal Family, as might be expected, are most sumptuous. The woodwork is chiefly mahogany or cedar, with satin curtains, velvet seats etc. The whole reflects the highest credit on the taste of Sir J. Henslow, the designer, and Mr Tippet, the Master-shipwright.[8]

The Times was equally effusive:

> The after cabin is elegantly inlaid with damask panels ornamented with gold borders on mahogany; at the head of which is a grand looking-glass having above it the King's coat of arms in gold, and beneath a rich dressing-table designed for Her Majesty. The other royal apartments are embellished in like manner. The two staircases are rich beyond conception, the balustrades are of mahogany, richly carved and ornamented with gold. The apartments below are suited to those above.[9]

The ROYAL SOVEREIGN was commissioned that summer at Weymouth under the command of Captain Sir Harry Neale, who had previously been Captain of the ROYAL CHARLOTTE; he remained in command of the new yacht until promoted to flag rank on 31 July 1810. The ROYAL SOVEREIGN proved a fast sailer:

> Upon one fine morning, in the summer of 1804, when His Majesty was on board, this yacht left Weymouth Roads and proceeded on a cruise, accompanied by the ROYAL CHARLOTTE and PRINCESS AUGUSTA yachts and a frigate. The new yacht excelled her companions so much in point of sailing as to drop anchor in the Roads upon her return at six in the evening; while the ROYAL CHARLOTTE did not arrive until

> ten o'clock that night, and the frigate midnight, and the PRINCESS AUGUSTA until six o'clock the next morning – an unquestionable proof of the very great superiority of the ROYAL SOVEREIGN, a superiority which gives her the eminent distinction, beyond controversy, the best sailer of the British Navy.[10]

Hardly a fair trial against two yachts both over thirty years old, but then the King was delighted!

George III made his last excursion from Weymouth in the ROYAL SOVEREIGN in 1805, and abandoned his sea holidays the following year; he was after all seventy-one, and beginning to appreciate his own bed at nights.

In 1801 the *Naval Chronicle* stated that:

> Of the 10 oldest ships in the Royal Navy, 7 were Royal Yachts, viz: the WILLIAM & MARY (1694), the MEDINA (1702), the PRINCESS AUGUSTA (1710), the CATHERINE (1720), the NAVY (1727), the PORTSMOUTH (1742) and the ROYAL CHARLOTTE (1749).[11]

However, this was not completely accurate, for the WILLIAM & MARY had been rebuilt in 1764/5; the PRINCESS AUGUSTA (ex-AUGUSTA II) in 1771 and the PORTSMOUTH in 1794.

The three warships shown were the second-rate ROYAL WILLIAM, 84 guns of 1719, guardship at Portsmouth; the third-rate YARMOUTH, 64 guns, 1715, receiving ship at Plymouth; and the second-rate CAMBRIDGE, 80 guns, 1755, guardship at Plymouth.

However, *British Warship Names* shows the ROYAL WILLIAM (ex-ROYAL PRINCE), was laid down in 1670, renamed in 1692, and broken up in 1813 and that the YARMOUTH was built in 1745, and broken up in 1811. Without further research these anomalies remain.

For most of his reign George III had two principal yachts which were disposed of in his final years:

PRINCESS AUGUSTA, sold in 1818 for £850 (aged forty-eight years)
ROYAL CHARLOTTE, taken to pieces in 1820 (aged seventy-one years)

SECONDARY YACHTS OF GEORGE III

The King also inherited seven secondary, or 'State' yachts, and there was much cox-and-boxing of their duties. The BOLTON for instance, 42 tons, and built in 1709, had been giving sterling service as the Governor of the Isle of Wight's yacht, but by 1763 she was found to be 'entirely decayed', and was rebuilt, albeit unofficially. Ten years later she was fitted for the use of 'the young gentlemen of the [naval] Academy [at Portsmouth]' in lieu of the OLD PORTSMOUTH, and was finally taken to pieces in 1817.

The original WILLIAM & MARY had been built in 1694, had 'great repairs' in 1737 and 1746, and was then rebuilt to new dimensions in 1764/5.[12]

WILLIAM & MARY II

Rebuilt 1765 at Deptford.		Surveyor A. Hayes.	
Length on gundeck	76 feet 5 inches	Length by the keel	62 feet 10¼ inches
Beam	22 feet 8 inches	Depth in hold	10 feet 1 inch
Tons burden	172	Crew	40
Guns	8 three-pounders	Rigged as a ketch	

1783 'a very large repair', at Deptford and proposed to be rigged as a ship.
1801 sold.

The OLD PORTSMOUTH, 66 tons, built in 1702 as the PORTSMOUTH II, had since 1752 been fitted for the use of the Naval Academy. She underwent 'Great Repairs' in 1772, was renamed MEDINA, and allocated to the Governor of the Isle of Wight in place of the BOLTON.

MEDINA

Built 1702 at Portsmouth as PORTSMOUTH II.		Surveyor Thomas Podd.	
Length on gundeck	52 feet 10 inches	Length by the keel	42 feet 10 inches
Beam	17 feet	Depth in hold	8 feet 6¼ inches
Tons burden	66	Crew	14
Guns	6 two-pounders		

1741 renamed OLD PORTSMOUTH.
1752 fitted for the 'use of the young gentlemen of the (naval) Academy (at Portsmouth)'.
1772 she had great repairs, was fitted for the Governor of the Isle of Wight, and renamed MEDINA.
1832 taken to pieces after one hundred and thirty years' service.

The PORTSMOUTH III was built in 1742, 83 tons, and was rebuilt at Portsmouth in 1794 after fifty-two years' service.

There was something about the longevity of Commissioner's yachts, for the CHATHAM II, 74 tons, gave fifty-two years' service. She had been built in 1741, underwent large repairs in 1765, and was finally rebuilt in 1793 as the CHATHAM III of 90 tons.

CHATHAM III

[13]Rebuilt 1793 at Chatham.		Surveyor	–
Length on gundeck	59 feet 6 inches	Length by the keel	48 feet 5¼ inches
Beam	18 feet 7 inches	Depth in hold	9 feet 8 inches
Tons burden	93	Crew	–
Guns	–		

Chatham Dockyard yacht.
1867 broken up.
(Lyon gives alternative beams of 19 feet or 18 feet 7 inches. The latter most closely computes to a tonnage of 93 tons.)

The yacht played a brief part in history, as is recorded below:

> In 1805 the CHATHAM III was in service as the Commissioner of Sheerness Dockyard's yacht, he being the Honourable George Grey. After the Battle of Trafalgar on 25 October the VICTORY was towed into Gibraltar for repairs by the NEPTUNE, arriving there on the 28th; 'having on board, preserved in spirits, the body of the late lamented hero (Nelson), whose flag she had so long borne, and which was then flying on board of her, but in a melancholy position, at half-mast.'[14]

The log of the VICTORY for 23 December records:

> At 1.40 shortened sail and anchored with The Small Bower in 12 fm… in The Swin. Moored ship. Came alongside Commissioner Grey's Yacht from Sheerness, and rec'd the remains of the late Lord Viscount Nelson K.B. and Vice Admiral of the White. Got a pilot on board to take the ship to Chatham.

The CHATHAM III had been despatched by the Board of Admiralty to receive Lord Nelson's body and convey it to Greenwich.

CHATHAM III, 1793

The body was removed into the coffin made from a part of the wreck of the ORIENT, burnt at the Battle of the Nile, and presented to Lord Nelson by Captain Hallowell of the SWIFTSURE, in 1799. This coffin with its contents was placed within a leaden coffin. The latter was then soldered, and never afterwards opened. On the coffin's being lowered into the yacht, the VICTORY struck, for the last time, Lord Nelson's flag at the fore, and the same was hoisted half-mast high on the yacht.

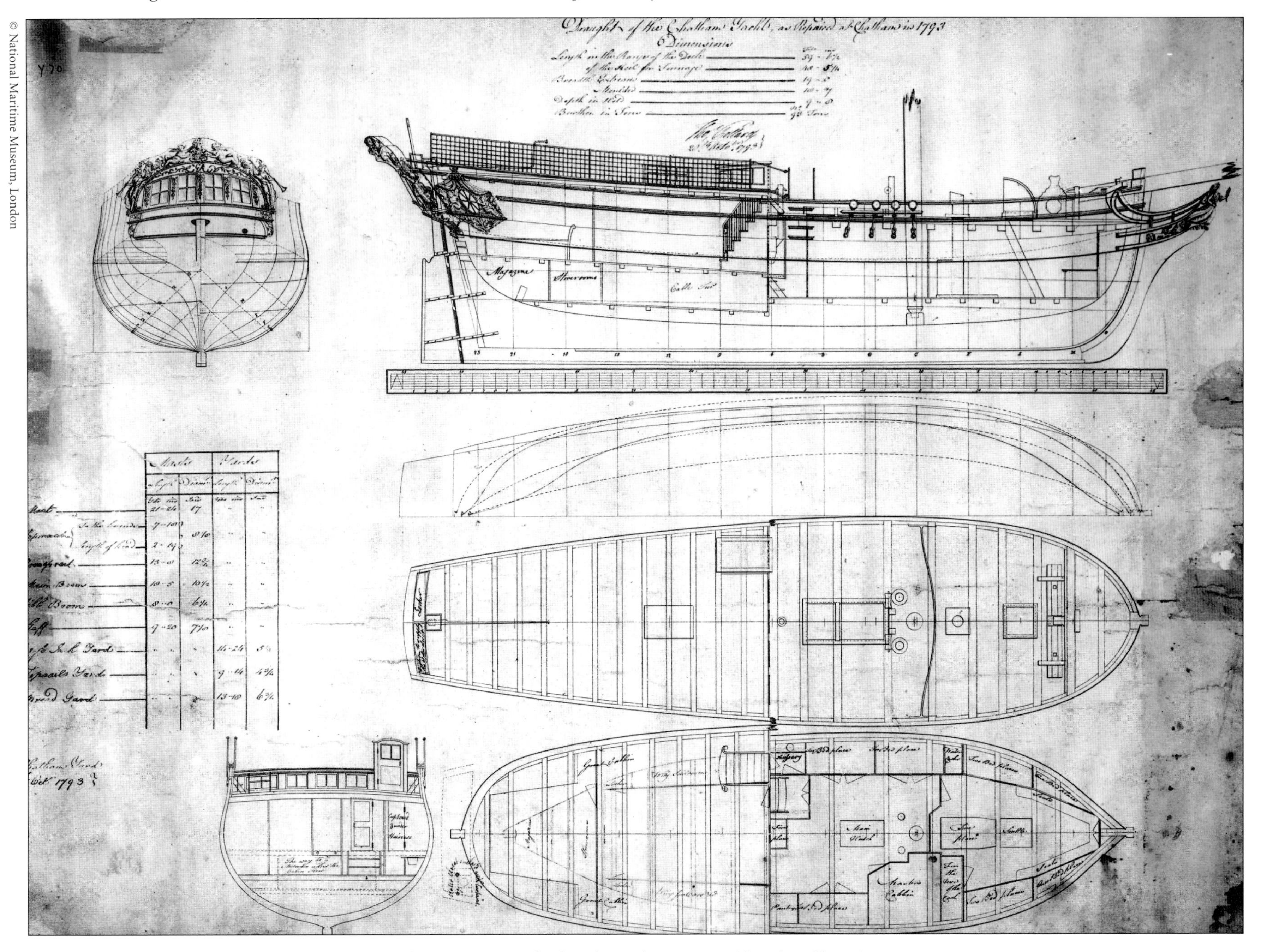

On the 24th, at 2pm, the yacht, having in the passage up had military honours paid to her illustrious charge on both sides of the river, anchored off Greenwich; and at 7pm the body was landed at the centre gate of the Royal Hospital, amidst an immense crowd of spectators. The awful and imposing ceremony which subsequently took place having been minutely detailed by other publications, we shall content ourselves with stating, that on the 9th January 1806, this first of naval captains was buried at St Paul's Cathedral, with all the pomp and solemnity befitting the occasion.[14a]

PORTSMOUTH IV

Rebuilt 1794 at Portsmouth.		Surveyor P. Locke.	
Length on gundeck	70 feet 4 inches	Length by the keel	53 feet 9 inches
Beam	18 feet 11 inches	Depth in hold	11 feet 8 inches
Tons Burden	–	Crew	–
Guns	6 two-pounders		

Portsmouth Dockyard yacht.
1869 taken to pieces.
Plan Y94 is at the National Maritime Museum.

The PLYMOUTH, 88 tons, had been built in 1755 to replace DRAKE II as the Devonport Dockyard Commissioner's yacht; she was taken to pieces in 1793, to be replaced by PLYMOUTH II, 96 tons, three years later.

PLYMOUTH II

[15] Built 1796 at Plymouth.		Surveyor Sir John Henslow.	
Length on gundeck	64 feet ½ inch	Length by the keel	52 feet 7¼ inches
Beam	18 feet 6 inches	Depth in hold	11 feet 8 inches
Tons burden	102	Crew	–
Guns	–		

Launched 2 November 1796.
Plymouth Dockyard yacht.
1830 broken up.

PLYMOUTH II, 1796

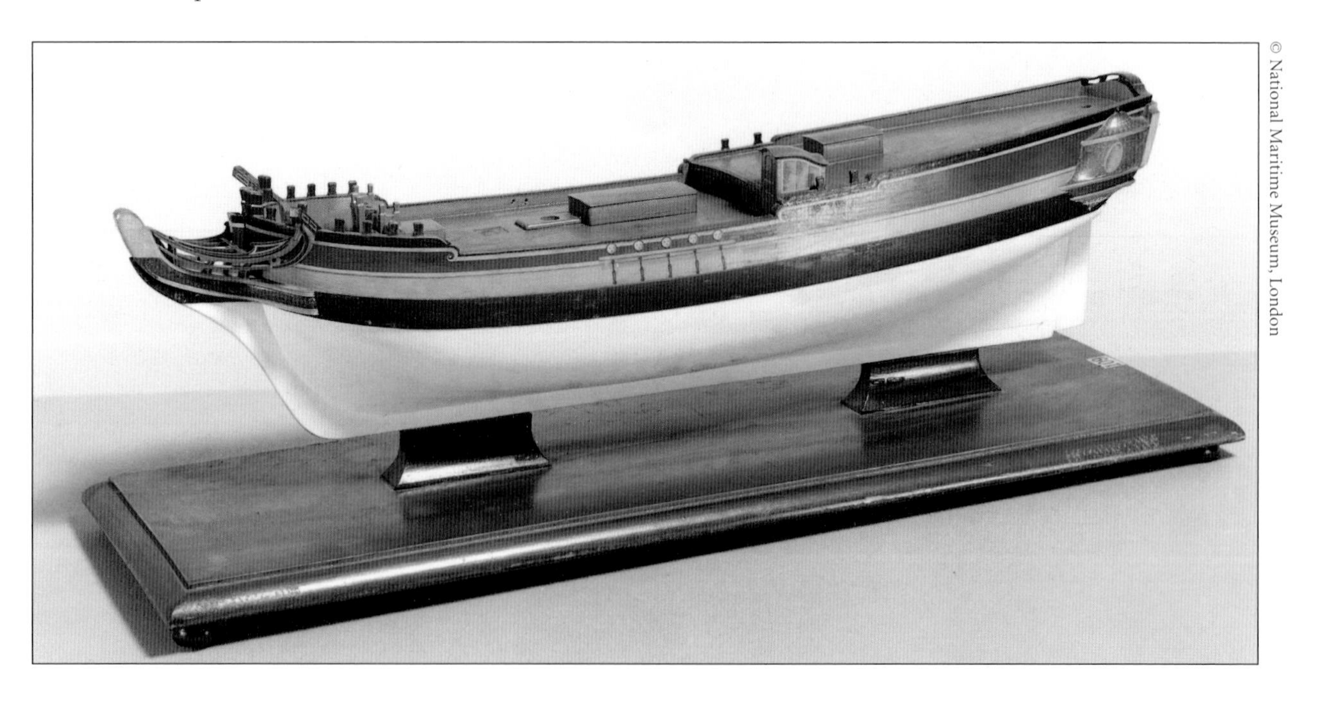

King George was to build another yacht in 1807, the WILLIAM & MARY III. At 199 tons she was considerably larger than her predecessor; after service on the Dublin station she eventually became a depot ship at Woolwich in 1832 following the radical MP Joseph Hume querying the need for five Royal Yachts.

WILLIAM & MARY III

Rebuilt 1807 at Deptford.		Surveyor Sir John Henslow.	
Length on gundeck	85 feet ½ inch	Length by the keel	70 feet 3½ inches
Beam	23 feet ½ inch	Depth in hold	11 feet 1 inch
Tons burden	199	Crew	–
Guns	–		

Named after her predecessor.
Launched 14 November 1807.
1813-1827 as the Lord Lieutenant of Ireland's yacht.
1932 depot ship at Woolwich.
1849 taken to pieces.
(Lyon says beam 23 feet 2 inches)

The DORSET, 164 tons, remained in the service of the Lord Lieutenant of Ireland from 1753-1813, and was sold in 1815. She was replaced by the WILLIAM & MARY III, on station from 1813-1827.

WILLIAM & MARY III, 1807

Plan of stern detail.

The following yachts were disposed of – their length of service is in brackets.

QUEENBOROUGH II, sold in 1777 (fifty-nine years)
FUBBS III, taken to pieces in 1781 (fifty-seven years)
PLYMOUTH, taken to pieces in 1793 (thirty-eight years)
WILLIAM & MARY II, sold in 1801 (thirty-six years)
KATHERINE III, sold in 1801 (eighty-one years)

During the Regency from 1811.

DORSET, sold in 1815 (sixty-two years)
MARY III, taken to pieces in 1816 (eighty-nine years)
BOLTON II, taken to pieces in 1817 (fifty-four years)
PRINCESS AUGUSTA, sold in 1818 for £850 (forty-eight years)
ROYAL CHARLOTTE, taken to pieces in 1820 (seventy-one years)

George III was well-meaning, intensely patriotic, pious and a pattern of the domestic virtues. During his long reign great battles were fought and won on land and at sea; gigantic strides were made in trade and commerce, laying the foundations for nineteenth-century world dominance. He took a keen and knowledgeable interest in the navy and his yachts, and the 'Aquatic Excursions' of the Royal Family gave them a much greater understanding of navy affairs than their European counterparts. His insanity during the final ten years of his life led to the Regency, and the building of the last two yachts of his reign, the ROYAL GEORGE and the PRINCE REGENT. George III never personally used these two yachts, and so they are described under George IV as Regent and King.

Blind, often constrained, and greatly emaciated, King George III died in his eighty-second year 'at 32 minutes past 8 o'clock pm, 29 January 1820.'[16] At the age of fifty-seven the Prince Regent was King himself – at last.

GEORGE IV – REGENT AND KING

REGENT 1811-1820 KING 1820-1830

On 5 February 1811, George, Prince of Wales, was declared Prince Regent and for the next nine years was effectively to be King, followed by ten years as crowned monarch.

At the start of the Regency the principal Royal Yacht was the ROYAL SOVEREIGN, built for George III in 1804, supported by the WILLIAM & MARY III, built in 1807. The two largest yachts were thus relatively new, but the WILLIAM & MARY III was allocated to the Lord Lieutenant of Ireland in 1813.

Four older yachts were disposed of during the Regency; the DORSET in 1815; MARY III in 1816; BOLTON in 1817; PRINCESS AUGUSTA in 1818; and when King the ROYAL CHARLOTTE in 1820.

Four 'small' yachts served the various officers of State viz the MEDINA for the Governor of the Isle of Wight, and the CHATHAM III, PORTSMOUTH IV and PLYMOUTH II for the respective dockyards.

For the first time therefore the fleet of Royal Yachts began to assume a manageable size – but not for long. The Regent was an inveterate builder on land, and he soon turned his attention to the sea, with the ROYAL GEORGE being laid down in 1814, the PRINCE REGENT in 1815, and the ROYAL CHARLOTTE II in 1820. All three yachts were, however, not to be launched for some years after their laying down.

In 1814 Napoleon was forced into exile, and on the very day that he left for Elba, King Louis XVIII, who had spent his own long exile in Buckinghamshire, made a triumphal entry into London. The Regent, whether his people wanted him to or not, took a major part in the victory celebrations. 'Our Prince Regent is never so happy as in show and state' commented Lady Vernon, 'and there he shines incomparably.'[1]

Having invested Louis with the Order of the Garter, the Regent bade him farewell from Dover on 24 April, bowing at the end of the pier as the ROYAL SOVEREIGN carried the new French King across the Channel. Escorting Louis were the JASON (32 guns) and the French frigate POLONAIS, and a few hours later he landed at Calais en route to Paris and his throne.

In June the ROYAL SOVEREIGN and the other yachts, under the command of the Duke of Clarence, returned to England with the Allied monarchs, Tsar Alexander I and King Frederick William III of Prussia. Together with Prince Metternich, representing the Emperor of Austria, they were to visit London for the victory celebrations, but the visit was not a total success. The Tsar and his bossy sister, the Grand Duchess Catherine of Oldenburg were unpopular with host and Government alike. 'When folks don't know how to behave,' Lord Liverpool muttered, 'they would do better to stay at home.'[1a]

ROYAL GEORGE

Built 1817 at Deptford.		Surveyor Sir Henry Peake.	
Length on gundeck	103 feet	Length by the keel	88 feet 4½ inches
Beam	26 feet 6 inches	Depth in hold	11 feet 6 inches
Tons burden	330	Crew	–
Guns	8 brass swivel one-pounders		

Ship-rigged, classed as a second-rate.
Laid down May 1814. Launched 17 August 1817.
1821 registered as a third-rate.
1843 accommodation ship for officers and men of Royal Yachts.
1902 paid off by order of King Edward, who directed that officers and men should live on board their own vessels.
1905 broken up.

Named after the Prince Regent, not King George III, the ROYAL GEORGE bore all the hallmarks of the Regent's flamboyant taste. 'The vessel is the most elegant ever seen. The cabin doors are mahogany, with gilt mouldings, and the windows of plate-glass. Ornamental devices in abundance are placed in various parts, all highly gilt, and producing superb appearance.'[2] As a second-rate she classed with three-deckers of from 80-110 guns, such as the 'fighting TEMERAIRE'. Sir Edward Berry Bt, Nelson's old captain, was the first commander of the ROYAL GEORGE, later to be replaced by Sir Michael Seymour. The ROYAL GEORGE was a fine sailer, and the Regent enjoyed many cruises in her off Brighton, using the Pavilion as his shore base. At the time of his first cruise in her, great crowds had assembled for the occasion, and the yacht-warming on board, like much the Prince Regent organised, was of some magnitude. When finally the yacht put to sea the weather was inclement, and the royal party soon returned to Brighton. This led to some wag composing a neo-heroic poem, 'Address to the ROYAL GEORGE Yacht', of which the first and last couplets give the gist:

> Hail, gaudy Ship, what wonders thou hast done,
> To tempt to Sea our Monarch's eldest son!
> To keep the Sea at such a time were vain –
> You therefore brought the Regent back again.

In the year of her launching the Prince Regent joined the Yacht Club, as the present Royal Yacht Squadron was then known. He took a 'cottage' on the sea-front at Cowes, and in 1821 – as King – returned to visit the town. The ROYAL GEORGE, accompanied by the ROYAL SOVEREIGN, a suitable escort of men-of-war, and private yachts from the Yacht Club, sailed past Cowes in the early afternoon. 'The ships of war as they passed manned their rigging, and the loud huzzas of the sailors as their different ships moved by were acknowledged by His Majesty, who took off his cap in the most condescending manner. The steamboat from Southampton passed very close to His Majesty and the ladies on board were quite delighted with a very near view of his person; they waved their handkerchiefs and absolutely hung over the sides of the vessel that they might see His Majesty as near as possible'.[3]

The Prince Regent had been coerced into marriage in 1795 both as a means of settling his debts and also settling the succession. It seemed as if he chose his first cousin, Princess Caroline of Brunswick, as a peevish protest at having to marry at all, and almost from the first meeting the marriage slipped into antipathy and then hatred. In spite of the public's support for her, and its dislike of the Regent, by the summer of 1814 the Princess of Wales was a lonely and dispirited woman. She determined to live abroad, and in the first week of August arrived in Worthing with a following of ill-assorted attendants (including a doctor 'unfit to attend a sick cat'), servants, stewards and couriers. No Royal Yacht was put at her disposal, so she boarded the fifth-rate frigate JASON, 32 guns, (the same ship had accompanied Louis XVIII to Calais) under the assumed name of the Countess of Wolfenbüttel. The game was given away, however, by a metal case on which was

ROYAL GEORGE, 1817

Oil by John Thomas Serres – 'George IV on board entering Portsmouth Harbour.'

painted in large white letters, 'Her Royal Highness the Princess of Wales, to be always with her'. As the JASON sailed out to sea and to her self-imposed exile, it was noticed the Princess was crying.[4]

Whilst in exile Princess Caroline so alienated various naval captains with her behaviour that they refused to embark her in their frigates. She then chartered a three-masted polacca, the INDUSTRIA, 'stained from its travels to Africa and Asia with cargoes of olives and currants and wine'.[5] Caroline fitted out the polacca to her own requirements, and considered her a Royal Yacht, even naming the refurbished vessel ROYAL CHARLOTTE. She appointed as captain one Lieutenant John Flynn, who had previously commanded a gunboat in the Royal Neapolitan Navy. Together with her motley crowd of attendants the Princess embarked on a ten-month voyage of wanderings around the eastern Mediterranean, gathering into her menage horses, 'Turks, Arabs and Negroes'.[6]

Not until the death of her uncle, George III, six years later, was Princess Caroline to return to England, and then she did so as a Queen, for her husband had succeeded to the throne. Her demand for a Royal Yacht to convey her across the Channel having been ignored, she arrived at Dover on 5 June 1820 on the ordinary packet, the PRINCE LEOPOLD; her baggage and carriages followed on the LADY JANE.[7] Dover Castle fired a royal salute, and 'This brave woman,' as *The Times* commented, was welcomed rapturously by the public. However, as one gentleman observed, 'Hardly a well-dressed person was to be seen in the crowd. Two or three men on horseback assumed a rather more respectable appearance, but one of these was my bankrupt cousin.'[8]

Following the death of his father in 1820, and his own magnificent coronation on 19 July the following year, George IV decided to visit Ireland and Hanover, for he was as proud of being a Hanoverian as he was of being English. Queen Caroline had been turned away from the doors of the Abbey at his coronation, and there is little doubt this act finally broke her spirit, for she became fatally ill immediately afterwards.

On the day of her death, 8 August 1821, the King arrived off Holyhead on board the ROYAL GEORGE, bound for Ireland. His Majesty had been 'in the best health and spirits during the whole passage' from Portsmouth, for the sea air agreed with him, and he was looking forward to the visit. News came of the Queen's illness, and he decided not to proceed directly to Dublin Bay, but to await further bulletins. Word of her sudden death reached the yacht, and 'though it would be absurd to think he was afflicted, he certainly was affected… He walked about the cabin the greater part of the night. He had all the (top) masts of the squadron lowered as a sign of mourning'.[9]

Four days later, on his fifty-ninth birthday, George IV crossed to Ireland in the steam ship TALBOT.

> The passage to Dublin was occupied in eating goose-pie and drinking whiskey in which His Majesty took most abundantly, singing many joyous songs, and being in a state, on his arrival, to double in number even the number of his gracious subjects assembled on the pier to receive him. The fact was that they were in the last stages of intoxification.[10]

Yet the King managed to disguise his drunkenness from his subjects, and the visit was a great success. The return voyage was, however, an ordeal for once out in the Irish Sea a howling storm tossed the yacht relentlessly.

> Most even of our crew and company were sick – wrote the King – but the very worst of all was my poor self; and I am now on 10th September for the first time, since we are at anchor again in smooth water, (Milford Haven) risen from my bed, and not without considerable exertion… I am… completely shattered and torn to pieces.[11]

The wind having dropped, and the roads through Wales and the West Country being so bad, it was decided to round Land's End for Portsmouth. Hardly had they sailed than 'a violent hurricane and tempest suddenly arose' – not uncommon close to the equinox. The King recorded:

> The most dreadful of nights and of scenes ensued, the sea breaking everywhere over the ship. We lost the tiller, and the vessel was for some minutes down on her beam-ends; and nothing, I believe, but the undaunted presence of mind, perseverance, experience and courage of Paget (Captain the Hon. Sir Charles Paget, commander of the ROYAL GEORGE) preserved us from a watery grave. The oldest and most experienced of our sailors were petrified and paralysed; you may judge, then, of what was the state of most of the passengers; every one almost flew up in their shirts upon deck in terrors that are not to be described.[11a]

The King finally arrived home in London on 16 September, but within eight days was off again, this time to Hanover. He spent the night before sailing from Ramsgate with Sir William Curtis, a rich sea-biscuit manufacturer, banker and Tory MP, on board whose lavishly fitted yacht -- DIE JONGE VROW REBECCA MARIA – the King was a frequent guest. Hanover greeted the King rapturously, where he was received with a salute of one hundred and one guns, and the people cheered him as though a hero. He might not be popular in England, but in this, his second kingdom, he most certainly was. By December he was back at Brighton, 'cheerful and happy and good humoured with all the world.'[12]

With the launching of the ROYAL GEORGE in 1817 the ROYAL SOVEREIGN was relegated to secondary duties, and a good description of Royal Yacht life was given in 1822 by Lieutenant John H Boteler:[13]

> Early in June I received an unexpected order to join HM Yacht ROYAL SOVEREIGN, fitting for sea at Deptford Dockyard, taking with me three midshipmen… We found the yacht in the basin, being regilded and painted, the hull purple, the royal colour. She was a beautiful ship richly gilt, with a family head, as it is termed, the King, Queen and two or three children in a group. Her ports were all circular, with carved figures round them, the size of a two-year-old child; her stern was covered with figures.
>
> The crew of sixty-seven consisted of dockyard riggers, all old men-of-war's men, thorough seamen, of good character, and mostly married men. Our proper captain was Charles Adams, commonly called Charlie Adams, more like a midshipman than a staid post-captain…
>
> In two or three days I was sent for to the Admiralty… about our mess arrangements. 'You will keep a gentlemanly table, your fish, soup, joint, and occasional game, and for wine, port and sherry; and if you have a friend at table, a little champagne and claret will do no harm.' I told him I perfectly understood him, and would allow no extravagance.'
>
> When moored in the river they had several visitors, one of whom fell into the water. 'What's all this Franklin?' I asked. 'I couldn't help it sir; he began to abuse the King, and I hustled him to the gangway meaning to kick him into his boat, but she had dropped astern and overboard he went.' And there he was, his bald head above water, paddling and splashing like a dog. A wherry took him up, and he would be landed. …they were not gentry.
>
> They embarked the Duke and Duchess of Clarence and party, but 'it turned out an ugly night, blowing hard, with many squalls of rain; and there was much sea on. The Duke, Sir Edward (Owen, a noted pilot), and our captain were on deck all night, and of course I could never go below. The yacht had the character of being, and was, a most excellent sea-boat, but she did kick and roll about famously'. (In fact the crossing was so rough that the Duke's two daughters were pitched out of George III's four-poster bed, and 'found in the lee scuppers, rolling over each other'. No harm was done, and the party was safely landed at Antwerp.)
>
> The ROYAL SOVEREIGN returned to the Thames, expecting to be laid up, instead of which they 'were off for Dover Roads, and in a day or so embarked the Crown Prince of Denmark and suite for Calais. On their leaving the yacht a diamond ring was presented to the Captain and 100 sovereigns to me for the ship's crew, and which I gave the purser to be distributed among them as prize money'.

ROYAL SOVEREIGN, 1804

> We returned to England and were ordered to Sheerness to be in readiness to join the ROYAL GEORGE yacht, about taking the King to Scotland. It was blowing very strong, and we had to beat from the Nore into Sheerness Harbour; the yacht worked like a top, tack and tack without a fault.

In July 1822 George IV determined to visit Scotland, the first monarch since Charles II so to do. He ordered several Highland outfits, including 61 yards of royal satin plaid, 31 yards of royal plaid velvet, a fine basket hilt Highland sword and a pair of fine polished steel Highland pistols. The total cost was £1354 18s; twice the annual pay of the ROYAL GEORGE's captain.

On 10 August the King embarked at Greenwich in the ROYAL GEORGE, which was towed down river to Gravesend by the steam packet COMET, accompanied by the Lord Mayor's barge drawn by another steam boat. Lieutenant Charles Boteler again:[14]

> I took command of our tender, the SEAGULL, a cutter of fifty tons only, a good sea-boat, but very wet in the winter months. My first movement was to the Nore, and there… to wait for the ROYAL GEORGE yacht, with the King on board, coming down the Thames in tow of a steamer. It was a dark and very still night, and the measured strokes of the paddle-wheels were a new and most peculiar sound to us. Steam then was in its very infancy.

Four days later, about two in the afternoon, and in pouring rain, the ROYAL GEORGE moored off Leith, having been towed in by two steam-packets, the COMET and the JAMES WATT. Numerous boats sailed round the ROYAL GEORGE, their passengers ignoring the rain and waving at the King, who appeared occasionally under the dripping quarter-deck awning, bowing and smiling.

Due to the appalling weather the decision was taken to delay the King's landing until the next day. Luckily, the 15th dawned with a clear blue sky, and the King descended into his barge shortly before noon. It was

ROYAL GEORGE, 1817

Oil by William Anderson – 'The Royal George at Greenwich with King George IV disembarking on his return from Scotland.'

manned by 16 seamen in blue frock coats and black velvet hats, and Commodore Sir Charles Paget himself was at the helm. Entering Leith inner harbour, King George stepped ashore to a tumultuous reception on to a crimson carpet strewn with summer flowers.

The visit was a tremendous success, both politically and socially – by the end of it the King was exhausted, but remained as affable as ever. After a farewell breakfast for 300 at Hopetoun House, the King drove to Port Edgar, in pouring rain driven by an east wind. Here, in the afternoon, he made his brief farewells on the new stone pier before embarking for the ROYAL GEORGE, anchored one mile out in the Forth. 'This is a vile day,' wrote Sir Walter Scott, 'but it is right Scotland should weep when parting with her good King.'[15]

In spite of the weather numerous boats and yachts followed the ROYAL GEORGE, under tow from the JAMES WATT, and the King gazed with rapt interest at a small boat. In the bows was a piper, held upright by three men clasping his legs; he must, commented the King, have been 'making too free with the Glenlivet' (the King's favourite whisky).[16]

The return voyage took three days, and the ROYAL GEORGE was towed upstream to Greenwich before anchoring at half past four, twenty-two days after she had left her moorings. An exhausted but exhilarated King George landed amongst crowds of well-wishers, and sank back into the carriage cushions for the last leg of the journey to London and home. As for the ROYAL GEORGE, she was towed upstream to moorings at Deptford, her holds laden with gifts from the King's Scottish subjects.

SECONDARY YACHTS OF GEORGE IV

The Prince Regent inherited from his father four relatively new yachts – and one over one hundred years old – allocated to officers of State. As King he saw no necessity to build new ones and, apart from the PLYMOUTH II, they lasted into Queen Victoria's reign. These yachts were:

CHATHAM III, 1793	(taken to pieces 1867)
PORTSMOUTH IV, 1794	(taken to pieces 1869)
PLYMOUTH II, 1796	(taken to pieces 1830)
WILLIAM & MARY III, 1807	(taken to pieces 1849)
MEDINA, 1702	(taken to pieces 1832)

The WILLIAM & MARY III remained as the Lord Lieutenant of Ireland's yacht until 1827, before being replaced by the ROYAL CHARLOTTE II from 1827-1832.

ROYAL CHARLOTTE II

Built 1824* at Woolwich.		Surveyor R. Seppings.	
Length on gundeck	85 feet 8 inches	Length by the keel	72 feet 8⅜ inches
Beam	22 feet 10½ inches	Depth in hold	8 feet 2 inches
Tons burden	202	Crew	–
Guns	8 one-pounder swivels		

(Lyon says beam 23 feet)
*Laid down April 1820. Launched 22 November 1824.
Named after the Prince Regent's only child.
1832 taken to pieces at Pembroke.

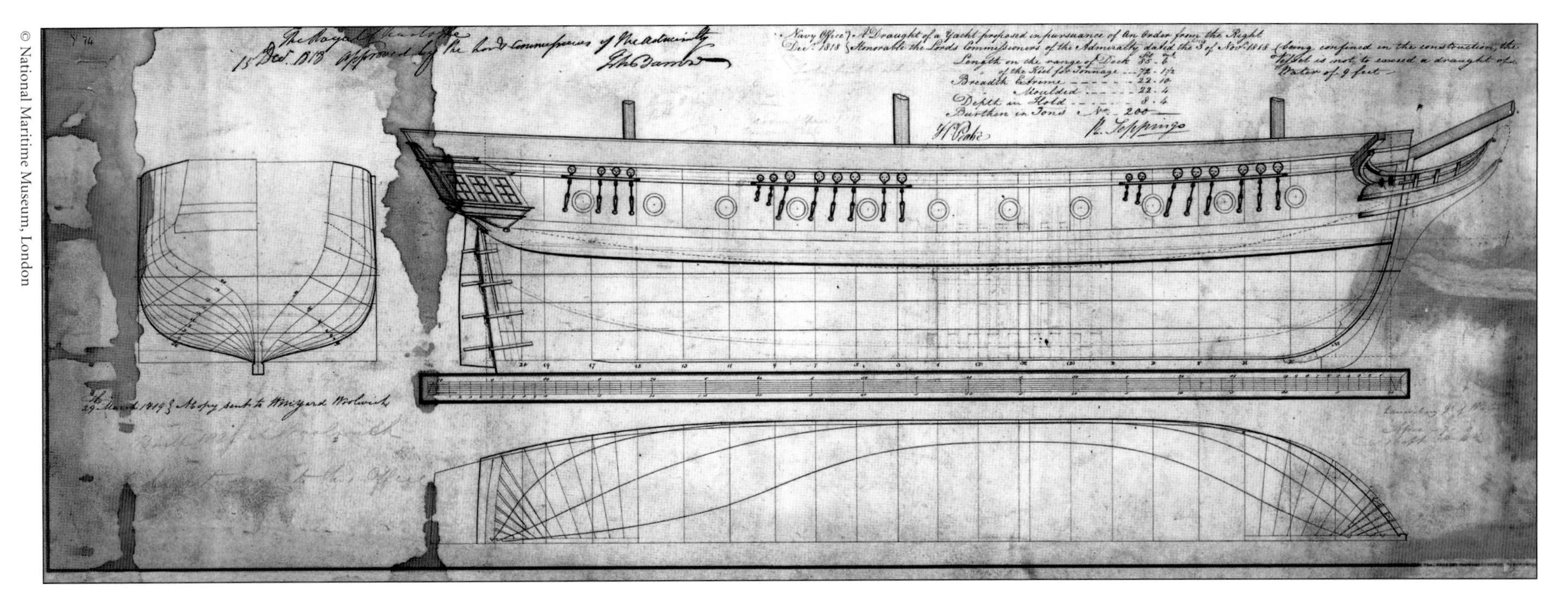

ROYAL CHARLOTTE II, 1824

Plan showing sheer and profile.

The first ROYAL CHARLOTTE (ex-ROYAL CAROLINE, 1749) was taken to pieces in July 1820, but already, in April, a start had been made on building a replacement. Although the plans show engines and paddle-wheels, the Admiralty must have had second thoughts, for she was built with sails only, at a cost of £12 821. She was not launched until 22 November 1824, and was then towed by steam-boat to Deptford for fitting out.

The yacht was finally commissioned in May 1826 for the Lord Lieutenant of Ireland, and she remained in his service until taken to pieces at Pembroke in 1832. The ROYAL CHARLOTTE was not replaced, since from 1820 the Irish steam-packet boat services were much improved, and it was considered no longer necessary for a yacht to be at the disposal of the Lord Lieutenant. Indeed, as early as 1817 the WILLIAM & MARY III had spent nine months at her moorings in Dublin; one officer wrote that apart from attending his Excellency, as part of his suite, I have literally nothing in the world to do.'[17]

(For further details of this yacht's time on the Dublin station, see Chapter 9.)

PRINCE REGENT

Built 1820 at Portsmouth.		Portsmouth Academy design.	
Length on gundeck	96 feet 0 inches	Length by the keel	81 feet 3 inches
Beam	25 feet 6 inches	Depth in hold	10 feet
Tons burden	282	Crew	–
Guns	–		

Laid down September 1815 and temporarily housed over on the stocks. Launched 12 June 1820.
1836 refitted at Deptford, and presented to Iman of Muscat.
Possibly 1847 was broken up.
(Lyon says beam 25 feet 8¼ inches)

One other yacht was built during George IV's reign, the PRINCE REGENT, to a design of the Portsmouth Academy. Although laid down in September 1815, she was temporarily housed over on the stocks until completed five years later, and was finally launched on 12 June 1820. Little is known (to me) of her use, but in 1836 she was refitted at Deptford and presented to the Iman of Muscat. There is, however, some doubt that she was actually delivered, and she may have been broken up in 1847.

PRINCE REGENT, 1820

Plan Y52 at the National Maritime Museum.

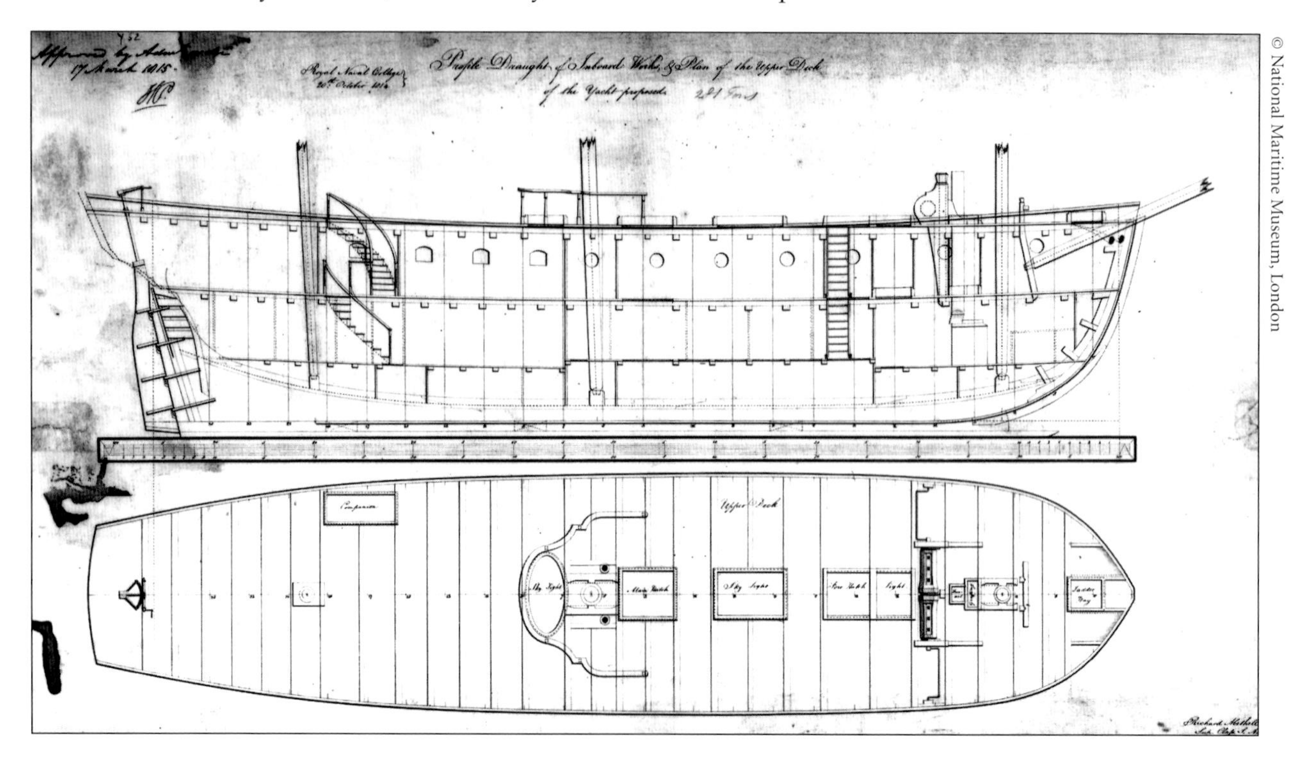

Four older yachts were disposed of during the Regency (from 1811), and one when King; their length of service is in brackets:

DORSET, sold in 1815 (sixty-two years)
MARY III, taken to pieces in 1816 (eighty-nine years)
BOLTON II, taken to pieces in 1817 (fifty-two years)
PRINCESS AUGUSTA, sold in 1818 for £850 (forty-eight years)
ROYAL CHARLOTTE, taken to pieces in 1820 (seventy-one years)
PLYMOUTH II, taken to pieces in 1830 (thirty-four years)

George IV was ill for several months in the spring of 1830, and 'expired exactly as the clock struck quarter after three (am), June 26'.[18] His close companions mourned the passing of a kind and generous friend, but during the funeral at Windsor *The Times* correspondent 'could see not a single mark of sympathy among the congregation'.

After two hours of the service King William could stand no more of it, thanked the Earl Marshal for the arrangements, and left St George's Chapel. With his brother, the new King, absent, and with the minute guns booming in the Long Walk, George IV was lowered into his grave.

WILLIAM IV (1830-1837)

AS DUKE OF CLARENCE

With two elder brothers it was considered unlikely that William would inherit the throne, and so he was sent to sea as a midshipman at the age of thirteen. As a junior officer he was regarded by Nelson as an excellent seaman and a highly competent officer. Yet Byam Martin commented, 'He was deficient in almost all the qualities necessary for a person in high command,'[1] a remark that was to come prophetically true when the Duke was Lord High Admiral.

No doubt William was a capable junior officer, but his elevation to the peerage at the age of twenty-three effectively marked the end of his naval career. As a royal duke he would not have been content with command of a frigate, and the King and the Admiralty were strongly opposed to him having control of a fleet.

There were to be a few small compensations, such as when Louis XVIII returned to France in the ROYAL SOVEREIGN after the downfall of Napoleon. The Duke hoisted his standard in the fifth-rate JASON (32 guns), and proudly escorted the French King across the Channel. Better was to follow, for the Duke transferred his standard to the second-rate IMPREGNABLE, from whence he wrote:

> ...to my great joy and satisfaction the Emperor of Russia and the King of Prussia embark with me in this ship; their suites are large but with activity and regularity I shall arrange everything.[2]

William remained with the IMPREGNABLE at Portsmouth for the return journey, and as he was greeting the Emperor, the King of Prussia and the Prince Regent, he noticed something wrong with the topgallant yards. A torrent of oaths was directed at the hapless sailors responsible, and the Emperor winced. The Regent, however, found the right phrase: 'What an excellent officer William is!' he remarked benignly.[3]

With the death of the Prince Regent's only legitimate child, Princess Charlotte, in 1817, and then of Frederick, Duke of York, in 1827, William suddenly found himself heir presumptive. And in February of that year, for political reasons, he was appointed Lord High Admiral, a post last held in the early-eighteenth century by the Earl of Pembroke. Later that year William hoisted his flag in the ROYAL SOVEREIGN and took a squadron of ships briefly to sea, content at last with a command.

However it was not to be a successful appointment, for William found himself at constant loggerheads with the Admiralty Council. One instance arose from his being appalled at the low standard of naval gunnery,

Oil by Nicholas Pocock – 'The Royal Sovereign yacht taking King Louis XVIII to France 24 April 1814.'

and he set up a standing commission of naval officers to look into the matter. The Admiralty objected that he was exceeding his brief, so in July 1828 William promptly hoisted his flag in the ROYAL SOVEREIGN and summoned the commission to Portsmouth.

A temporary truce was patched up, but on the last day of July William made another break for freedom. 'I think our Lord High Admiral is getting into another scrape,' wrote Lord Aberdeen. 'He has gone to sea without any of his Council, and has sent some extraordinary orders to the Admiralty…'[4]

In fact William had disappeared to sea for ten days from Plymouth, and for all that time no one knew where the Lord High Admiral was. Even George IV, fond of his younger brother though he was, could not countenance this behaviour, and William was forced to resign. He had been Lord High Admiral for barely eighteen months, but as a professional seaman he instigated several much needed reforms. Perhaps his best claim to far-sightedness was commissioning the LIGHTNING, the first steam vessel on the naval list, and he urged the construction of many more.

AS KING

At 6am on 26 June 1830, William was woken to learn that his brother, George IV, was dead, and that he was now King. Within a few hours he was on his way to Windsor, 'grinning and nodding to everybody as he whirled along'.[5] It was, of course, sad about poor George, but the best job in the world had at last fallen to his lot, and he found it impossible to hide the fact that he was an exceedingly happy man.

At his accession he inherited five large Royal Yachts, of which the principal was the ROYAL GEORGE, barely thirteen years old; the others being the ROYAL SOVEREIGN, WILLIAM & MARY III, PRINCE REGENT and ROYAL CHARLOTTE II. In addition there were three small yachts for officers of state, the elderly MEDINA for the Governor of the Isle of Wight, and the CHATHAM III and PORTSMOUTH IV for their respective Dockyard Commissioners. The PLYMOUTH II, the Devonport Dockyard Commissioner's yacht, taken to pieces that year, does not appear to have been replaced.

However, in 1831 the radical politician Joseph Hume questioned 'the extravagant waste of the public money in keeping afloat no less than five Royal Yachts, as well as one for the Commissioners of the Navy, and one for the Lord Lieutenant of Ireland'. The First Lord of the Admiralty, Sir James Graham, argued that none of the five yachts was perfectly manned, the expense was small, and this was about the only patronage the Admiralty had to keep old veteran officers on full pay. Hume won his point though, for the following year the ROYAL SOVEREIGN and WILLIAM & MARY III were converted to depot ships at Pembroke and Woolwich respectively, and the ROYAL CHARLOTTE II, barely eight years old, was taken to pieces.

The Governor of the Isle of Wight suffered in this cut-back too, for his yacht, the MEDINA, was taken to pieces the same year – at one-hundred-and-thirty years old!

The Sailor King thus remained with but one principal yacht, the ROYAL GEORGE, the smallest number since his ancestor Charles II made popular their use one hundred and seventy years previously.

SECONDARY YACHTS OF WILLIAM IV

King William inherited one yacht from Queen Anne's reign, in the previous century. This was the Governor of the Isle of Wight's yacht, MEDINA, originally built as the PORTSMOUTH II; in view of her exceptionally long service, it is worth reviewing the history of this small yacht of 66 tons.

MEDINA

Built 1702 as PORTSMOUTH II at Portsmouth.		Surveyor Thomas Podd.	
Length on gundeck	52 feet 10 inches	Length by the keel	42 feet 10 inches
Beam	17 feet	Depth in hold	8 feet 6¼ inches
Tons burden	66	Crew	14
Guns	6 two-pounders		

1741 renamed OLD PORTSMOUTH.
1752 fitted for the 'use of the young gentlemen of the (naval) Academy (at Portsmouth)'.
1772 she had great repairs, was fitted for the Governor of the Isle of Wight, and renamed MEDINA.
1832 taken to pieces after one hundred and thirty years' service.

From George III's reign William inherited three further secondary yachts:

CHATHAM III, 1793 Dockyard yacht; taken to pieces 1867.
PORTSMOUTH IV, 1794 Dockyard yacht; taken to pieces 1869.
(Plymouth dockyard does not appear to have had a yacht following the breaking up of the PLYMOUTH II in 1830.)
WILLIAM & MARY III, 1807. This yacht had been on the Dublin station from 1813-1827, but in 1832 was made into a depot ship at Woolwich following the radical MP Joseph Hume querying the need for five Royal Yachts. Although the Admiralty contended this was their only form of patronage for elderly or sick senior officers, they lost the argument.

The Lord Lieutenant of Ireland was served by the ROYAL CHARLOTTE from 1827–1832, but with the increasing regularity of the steam-packet services to Ireland, she was not replaced.

William IV loved his illegitimate children by Mrs Jordan and, in spite of her frequent miscarriages, so did Queen Adelaide. Windsor often spilled over with children and grandchildren, and for the latter the King built his only yacht, and named her after his childless Queen.

ROYAL ADELAIDE

Built 1833 at Sheerness.		Surveyor Sir William Symonds.	
Length on gundeck	50 feet	Length by the keel	42 feet 8¼ inches
Beam	15 feet	Depth in hold	8 feet
Tons burden	50	Crew	–
Guns	22 one-pounder brass guns		

She was completed in December 1833, taken to pieces and transported to Virginia Water, where she was assembled, and launched on the lake on 13 May 1834. She was a complete miniature frigate with a coppered bottom, and was sailed upon the lake for the amusement of the Royal Family. She was broken up in 1877, having given pleasure to Queen Victoria's children as well as the numerous FitzClarences. Her guns went to the Royal Yacht Squadron at Cowes.

Five yachts were disposed of during the reign:

ROYAL CHARLOTTE II, taken to pieces 1832 – (aged eight years)
MEDINA, taken to pieces 1832 – (aged one hundred and thirty years)

ROYAL ADELAIDE, 1834

Contemporary model at the National Maritime Museum.

ROYAL SOVEREIGN, converted to a depot ship 1832 – (aged forty-six years)
WILLIAM & MARY III, converted to a depot ship 1832 – (aged twenty-five years)
PRINCE REGENT, refitted and presented to the Iman of Muscat 1836.

By April of 1837 King William was gravely ill. He struggled on until 24 May, when his niece and heir Princess Victoria came of age, buoyed by the realisation that her abhorred mother, the Duchess of Kent, would not now become Regent. By the middle of June he survived by sheer will power alone; 'The King dies like an old lion,' wrote Disraeli.[6]

At 2.20am on the morning of Tuesday, 20 June, what little of life left to him flickered out. The last Hanoverian King of England was dead.

THE LORDS LIEUTENANT OF IRELAND'S YACHTS

In the sixteenth century a small warship was stationed in Irish waters, known as 'Her Majesty's Irish Galley'. In 1576 Lord Deputy Sidney asked for 'one of Her Majesty's ships to lie upon the Irish coast for the safe conduct of treasure', and was allocated the 90 ton HANDMAID.[1] Replacement vessels included the POPINJAY in 1587, TREMONTANA in 1601 and the curiously named FIFTH WHELP and NINTH WHELP from 1627.[2]

These naval ships were primarily defensive, to deal with privateers and escort merchant ships in convoys, but they were also at the disposal of the Lord Lieutenant. With the Restoration and the general introduction of yachts into the navy, the Lord Lieutenant was allocated a Royal Yacht for his personal use. They were particularly suited for short passages across the Irish Channel, being light, fast sailers, and ideal for conveying despatches, money and passengers of rank to and from Ireland.

Warrants were issued for permission to use the yacht officially, and the names of warrant-holders were entered in the muster roll for each voyage. They were carried as supernumeraries, i.e. extra to the ship's company, and entitled to passage and board, but not pay. Spare capacity could be filled by private arrangement with the commander of the yacht; the DUBLIN was known to have carried 200 passengers on one occasion in 1738, so the perks were considerable.

The commander of the yacht was invariably a senior captain in the navy – in two instances the most senior on the captain's list. On entering the Lord Lieutenant's service they generally retired from the active list, although remaining on the captain's list. The duties were not onerous, particularly in the later years, but the responsibility could be heavy; conditions in the Irish Channel could often be treacherous, and the yachts were not large vessels. Occasionally a midshipman was carried, but no other commissioned officer.

The sailing-master, or pilot, commanded the yacht in the captain's absence, and was generally responsible for the navigation and technical running of the vessel. For much of the eighteenth century the Lords Lieutenant of Ireland were in the country only a few months on alternate years for the Parliamentary sessions. From 1767 to 1800 they were resident almost continuously. In their absence the Lords Justices held office – the Primate of all Ireland, the Archbishop of Armagh; the Chancellor; and the Speaker of the House of Commons – although others could be appointed.

With the Act of Union in 1800 Dublin lost its cachet as a capital city; Irish MPs preferred to be at Westminster, and the use of the Royal Yacht diminished. The introduction of steam ferries in the 1820s meant the yacht's days were numbered, and when the ROYAL CHARLOTTE II was broken up in 1832 she was not replaced.

MARY

Length on gundeck	–	Length by the keel	52 feet
Beam	19 feet	Depth in hold	7 feet 7 inches
Tons burden	100	Crew	20 peace (30 war)
Guns	8 three-pounders		

Draught 10 feet with leeboards down; actual draught about 3 feet.
(For full details of this yacht see Chapter 2 – Section 1.)

The first Royal Yacht to be allocated in 1661 to the Dublin station was the MARY, presented the previous year to Charles II by the City of Amsterdam. The King, however, had rapidly ordered a new yacht, the KATHERINE, and the MARY was handed over to the navy for general service. Her build and sea-worthiness made her ideal for the short seas of the Irish Channel, 'for the sea is so short and broken that Holland-built ships are found the fittest for that passage'.[3]

Her normal destination from Dublin was Dawlpool on the Dee Estuary, or Holyhead. The MARY, like her successors, was employed carrying despatches, passengers and money – £11 700 on one voyage in 1666. Yet in spite of transporting this fortune, the crew were often much in arrears with their pay – fifty-two weeks in 1667, and forty-six months in 1674.

During the 1660s and the turbulent years of the Dutch Wars she was usually accompanied by the ketch-rigged HARP frigate of 10 guns. The MARY's war complement was increased from 20 to 30, determined as follows:[4]

	No. of men
2 men per gun	16
to carry powder and shot for the guns	2
To fill and hand powder to the guns	1
Carpenter	1
Men for the small shot	4
Men to stand by the sails	6
Chirurgeon (when borne)	1
Total	31

The MARY (commanded by William Burstow) was wrecked on the foggy night of 4 April 1675 [25 March Julian calendar] when, at about 2am, she struck a rock near the present Skerries lighthouse, seven miles from Holyhead. She carried a crew of 28 and 46 passengers, including the Earl of Ardglass, the Earl of Meath and his son Lord Ardee. As she settled she listed heavily, and her mast touched the rocks of the Skerries, enabling 39 of those on board the overcrowded vessel to scramble ashore. However, 35 were lost, including the Captain, Boatswain and the Earl of Meath; those on the rocks were rescued after two days by a Wicklow vessel.[5]

At the time of her wreck the MARY carried two Dutch bronze four-pound cannon, probably as bow chasers, six bronze English three-pound cannon, and one, possibly two, bronze one-and-a-half pound cannon, probably as stern-chasers. The two Dutch cannon were almost certainly part of her original armament from Holland, the rest possibly having been moved to the KATHERINE when she was built, and the MARY transferred to general service in 1661.[6]

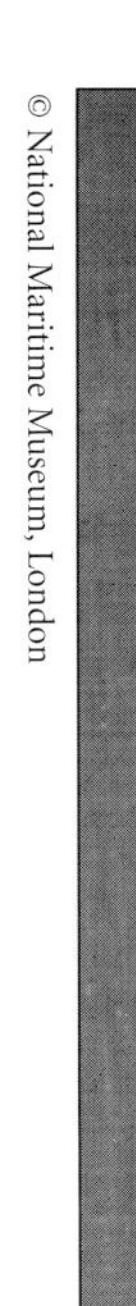

MARY, 1660

A reconstruction model made in 1949, based on contemporary drawings and plans.

MONMOUTH

Built 1666 at Rotherhithe.		Surveyor William Castle.	
Length on gundeck	–	Length by the keel	52 feet
Beam	19 feet 6 inches	Depth in hold	8 feet
Tons burden	103	Crew	40
Guns	8 three-pounders		

Named after the Duke of Monmouth, Charles II's favourite son by Lucy Walter.
1675-1678 Dublin station.
1678-1683 English Channel station.
1683-1688 Greenville Collins' hydrographic survey.
1689-1698 Dublin station.
1698 sold, 25 November.

Yachts crossing from Dublin to Holyhead or the Dee Estuary had to take the ground at the latter places when the tide was low. The MARY with her leeboards was ideal, but with her loss Pepys, as Secretary for the Navy, was faced with finding a suitable replacement yacht, for men-of-war were becoming too large for the shallow Dee Estuary.

The MONMOUTH yacht (commander Morgan Kempthorne) was appointed to the station in 1675. The yacht had made one previous voyage to Dublin, in 1669, when she had carried the Earl of Orrerey from Milford. Her commander, Captain William Fazeby, had written: 'If this yacht stays upon the coast she will be quite spoiled as she will not take the ground.'[7] With a keel length of only 52 feet and a beam of 19 feet 6 inches – i.e. the rough dimensions of a Thames barge – it is difficult to see how the MONMOUTH would not take the ground admirably.

She remained on station until 1678, when Pepys wrote: 'The Monmouth yacht be laid up as soon as she shall be brought back from the coast of Ireland, where she has long been.'[8] After her refit the MONMOUTH was employed in the English Channel before being commanded by Captain Greenville Collins from 1683-1688 when he continued his survey of the British coastline. He had started in the MERLIN yacht, but possibly found, as Pepys had commented, that she was unsuited to taking the ground in the remote harbours and anchorages of his seven-year survey.

Following completion of the survey MONMOUTH returned to Irish waters in July 1689 as part of the invasion fleet, for the deposed James II held court in Dublin. Her commander was William Wright, and on 10 August he wrote in the log: 'This day the Army began to imbarque for Ireland. God prosper their proceedings.'[9]

The MONMOUTH was employed in the passage of the army that year, and of the King in 1690. On one occasion she carried 120 passengers; on another 50 chests of money; on another prisoners bound for Chester Castle. However, once William had defeated James II at the Boyne and the throne was secure, the MONMOUTH's duties returned to normal. Parkgate, also on the River Dee, became the normal port for passengers, for the anchorage allowed graving, caulking and minor repairs to be effected.

Her last duty on 2 July 1698 was to land the Earl of Athlone at Parkgate. There she had her hull washed, and proceeded to Deptford and sale on 25 November.

PORTSMOUTH

Built 1674 at Woolwich.		Surveyor Phineas Pett.	
Length on gundeck	–	Length by the keel	57 feet
Beam	20 feet 6 inches	Depth in hold	7 feet 4 inches
Tons burden	133	Crew	30
Guns	8 three-pounders.		

1679-1687 on Dublin station.
1688 converted to a bomb-vessel of 143 tons.
1703 wrecked at the Nore in the great gale of 27 November.

Whilst the MONMOUTH was on surveying duties, her place on station was taken by the PORTSMOUTH yacht. (Further details of the latter are in Chapter 2 – Section 1.) She had been built in 1674, and named after the King's mistress, Louise de Kéroualle, who had been created Duchess of Portsmouth, Countess of Fareham and Lady Petersfield the previous year.

Captain William Wright, the PORTSMOUTH's commander, was 'remarkable for having never, through a long service of nearly thirty years' continuance, commanded any vessel except a yacht'.[10] He had previously served in the BEZAN and in the KITCHEN yachts before assuming command of the PORTSMOUTH on the English Channel station and bringing her to Dublin.

At that period the officer in charge of a ship may not have been a professional seaman, and often relied on his sailing-master for navigation and the technical conduct of the vessel. Charles II, however, encouraged the formation of career naval officers from whom commanders of ships would increasingly be drawn. Royal Yachts though, in view of the importance of their passengers and cargoes, tended to be commanded from the first by professional seamen who were also expert navigators and ship handlers. A prime example is Greenville Collins, chosen to conduct the first full hydrographic survey of the British coast from 1681-1688.

The Captain's journal from March 1686 to September 1687[11] shows the PORTSMOUTH made 21 voyages to 'Chester Way' – the Dee Estuary – using variously Holyhead, Parkgate, Beerhouse hole and Dawlpool to land passengers. Beerhouse hole was a mile down-river from Parkgate, but the latter had graving ways to allow ships to dry out and clean their hull bottoms, as the PORTSMOUTH did on 14 May 1687: 'Made an end of graveing, hal'd off the wayes and fell down to the Beerhouse hole.'[12]

In October the same year Captain Wright sailed the yacht to London, and left her for his new command, the MONMOUTH yacht. As for the PORTSMOUTH, she was made into a bomb-vessel[13] in 1688, and subsequently wrecked at the Nore in the great gale of 27 November 1703.

NAVY

Built 1673 at Portsmouth.[14]		Surveyor Sir Anthony Deane.	
Length on gundeck	–	Length by the keel	48 feet
Beam	17 feet 6 inches	Depth in hold	7 feet 7 inches
Tons burden	74	Crew	35
Guns	8 three-pounders		

1689-1693 Dublin station.
1698 sold 14 April.

The NAVY yacht had accompanied Princess Mary and Prince William of Orange on their honeymoon voyage to Holland in 1677. A decade later, commanded by Phineas Pett, she was on the Dublin station; for the first four years the MONMOUTH was also there. Relatively little work was found for her, and she spent long periods at Liverpool, spasmodically taking passengers between Dublin and Holyhead or Parkgate.[15] In June 1693 Captain Pett took command of a new yacht, the SOESDYKE, purchased by the navy the previous year. Five years later, on 14 April 1698, the NAVY was sold.

In 1691 James Vickers of Holyhead had been granted the contract to carry mail to Ireland, and his ships also carried passengers. He clearly resented the fact that the nobility and gentry preferred to travel in the Royal Yacht, for in 1696 he complained that 'the yachts which are ordered to attend to His Majesty's service between Dublin, Holyhead and Chester do convey passengers, which were used to be conveyed in the packet boats, whereby he (Vickers) is a great sufferer.'[16]

The Lord Lieutenant – or in his absence the Lords Justices – would issue warrants for the official use of the yacht, but there was often spare capacity on each voyage, enabling a private agreement to be reached with the captain. This was a most lucrative arrangement for the commander, and in later years was to be the subject of official disapproval.

Not only was there a social cachet to travelling in a Royal Yacht, but they were more comfortable, better equipped and better manned than the packet boats. Nor did the nobility and gentry have to rub shoulders with the common folk travelling to and from Ireland.

The yacht's captain was sometimes given direct orders: 'The yacht is to call at Holyhead to bring over the Rt Hon. Sir Thomas Prendergast and his lady; and will immediately go to Parkgate for Cooly Westley Esq and his family.'[17] Sometimes he was given general orders: 'to sayle to Chester water, there to attend such further orders as he shall from time to time receive from us.'[17a] The end effect for the yacht and her crew was, however, the same.

SOESDYKE

Built 1692 at Wapping.		Surveyor Mr Freame.[18]	
Length on gundeck	63 feet 2 inches	Length by the keel	58 feet 9 inches
Beam	19 feet 10 inches	Depth in hold	9 feet 1½ inches
Tons burden	116	Crew	35/30/12
Guns	8 three-pounders, 6 swivel-guns		

Named after a royal palace near Soest, east of Hilversum, Netherlands; in modern Dutch 'Soestdijk'.
1692 'bought of ye Earl of Monmouth.'
1693-1701 Dublin station.
1702/3 rebuilt (or large repair) at Deptford.
1713 sold 13 July for £315.

The SOESDYKE was built in 1692, and 'bought of ye Earl of Monmouth', so we can assume she was built at his order. This nobleman, as so many of the period, had a fascinating life. He was captain of his own ship-of-war in 1681; the LOYALL MORDAUNT, a 46-gun fourth rate, built by him at Deptford, and taken into the navy in 1683. King Charles II dined on board with Lord Mordaunt on 10 November 1681.

As Viscount Mordaunt he served as a volunteer against the Algerines and at Tangier 1678-80, where he and other 'gentlemen… did dishonour to the service… committing villanies of all sorts and debauching the poor seamen.'[19]

Created (third) Earl of Monmouth 9 April 1689 in recognition of his support for William and Mary, he succeeded to the Earldom of Peterborough on the death of his uncle, 19 June 1697; and on the death of his cousin Mary, (the divorced Duchess of Devonshire) he became Baron Mordaunt on 17 November 1705.

He was appointed Governor of Jamaica in 1702, but did not go there. His military reputation was established in April 1705, when he was appointed as General of the Allied Forces in Spain, and Joint Admiral and Chief Commander of the Fleet on behalf of the Archduke Charles.

He married, secondly, Anastasia, a celebrated singer. Lord Peterborough died 'Of a Flux, by eating Grapes', on his yacht off Lisbon, on 25 October 1735, at the ripe old age of seventy-seven.[19a]

As for the SOESDYKE, her logs[20] show that from June 1693 she was based in Dublin, at moorings in 'Clantarfe Poole'. She was commanded by Captain Phineas Pett (ex-NAVY) until 1694, then by George Breholt until 1701. The first full year of Breholt's command, 1695, he visited Dublin twelve times, Parkgate ten times, Holyhead twice and Liverpool once. This pattern continued to the end of the century.

The SOESDYKE's new commander, Thomas Marks (or Marke), delivered her to Deptford in March 1702, where the List of the Navy records 'R' (rebuilt?), and underneath 'or great repair'. The yard wrote to the Admiralty on 19 August that year: 'being about to fit her with a new mast (the old being unserviceable) I humbly propose the making of it two feet shorter and three quarters of an inch less than the old one.'[21] Her new captain, Jonas Hannay, completed the refit in January 1703, and thereafter the SOESDYKE was based at Deptford moorings. She remained in service a scant ten years before being sold on 11 July 1713 for £315; this low price would indicate she was in poor condition.

CHARLOT

Built 1677 at Woolwich.		Surveyor Thomas Shish.	
Length on gundeck	–	Length by the keel	61 feet 9 inches
Beam	20 feet 6½ inches	Depth in hold	9 feet
Tons burden	143	Crew	30
Guns	8 three-pounders		

Named after second daughter of Barbara Villiers by Charles II.
1701-1709 Dublin station.
1710 rebuilt at Deptford.

Charles II built the CHARLOT in 1677 as one of his succession of principal yachts. That same year her first royal duty was to convey Princess Mary to Holland following her marriage to Prince William of Orange (later King William and Queen Mary). Her husband travelled on the MARY II, so presumably neither Royal Yacht was large enough to accommodate their entourages – for details of the voyage see MARY II.

CHARLOT joined the Dublin station in 1701 when she sailed from Deptford under command of Captain Thomas Marke. At Dublin he exchanged commands with Captain George Breholt of the SOESDYKE, and returned with the latter to Deptford for refit.

Chester at that time depended greatly on its trade by sea, particularly to Dublin and other parts of Ireland. In addition to the normal dangers of travelling by sea were added the risk of privateers, especially in time of war.'... the Irish Channel is greatly infested with privateers, invited thither by the prospect of intercepting the coal fleetes, and other ships with persons of great quality and very valuable goods.'[22]

Convoys were frequently necessary, and in time of war the Royal Yacht, with her meagre eight guns, did not sail alone. In 1703 Mary Lovett wrote from Chester that she hoped to:

> take shipping if we can get room, for they say it was never known the ships to be so full; there is 6 Ladys of Quality and a Lord gone down to wait there, ready for the ships to go off, with abundance more passengers; it is said their goods are worth at least £30 000.[23]

CHARLOT, 1677

William Van de Velde the Elder.

Rich pickings, indeed, for any privateer. In the event, Mary Lovett journeyed overland to Holyhead where she joined the CHARLOT and travelled safely to Dublin under convoy. That same year the Lord Lieutenant was petitioned that there was a ship at Chester '...very richly loaden with Merchants goods for Dublin, worth several thousand pounds, and dare not venture her to go without a convoy'.[24] The response was to send the 24-gun HMS SEAFORD, and the following year she patrolled with the Royal Yacht, 40 soldiers being embarked on the CHARLOT; they found a French privateer and the SEAFORD gave chase.

The problem continued, however, for in 1707 Mrs Elizabeth Freke wrote in her diary:

> My cosin John Freke landed saffe at Dublin after he had bin fower days att sea in a packett boatt from Chester. Whilst he was crossing the sea, were eleven ships taken by privateers from Holly head.'[25]

Captain Breholt was still in command of the CHARLOT when he 'went for London' in 1709 to collect his new command, the Royal Yacht DUBLIN, the first to be purpose built for the Lord Lieutenant of Ireland.[26]

DUBLIN

Built 1709 at Deptford.		Surveyor Mr Allin.	
Length on gundeck	73 feet 2 inches	Length by the keel	59 feet 8 inches
Beam	21 feet 7½ inches	Depth in hold	–
Tons burden	148	Crew	45 (1709). 40 (1713). 50 (1737)
Guns	10 three-pounders	Ketch-rigged	–

Named after the city. Lord Lieutenant of Ireland's yacht.
1709-1752 Dublin station. 1732 fitted with three masts.
1752 taken to pieces.
Plan Y54 is at the National Maritime Museum.

Captain Greenville Collins's chart of Carlingford Lough. From the Admiralty Collection.

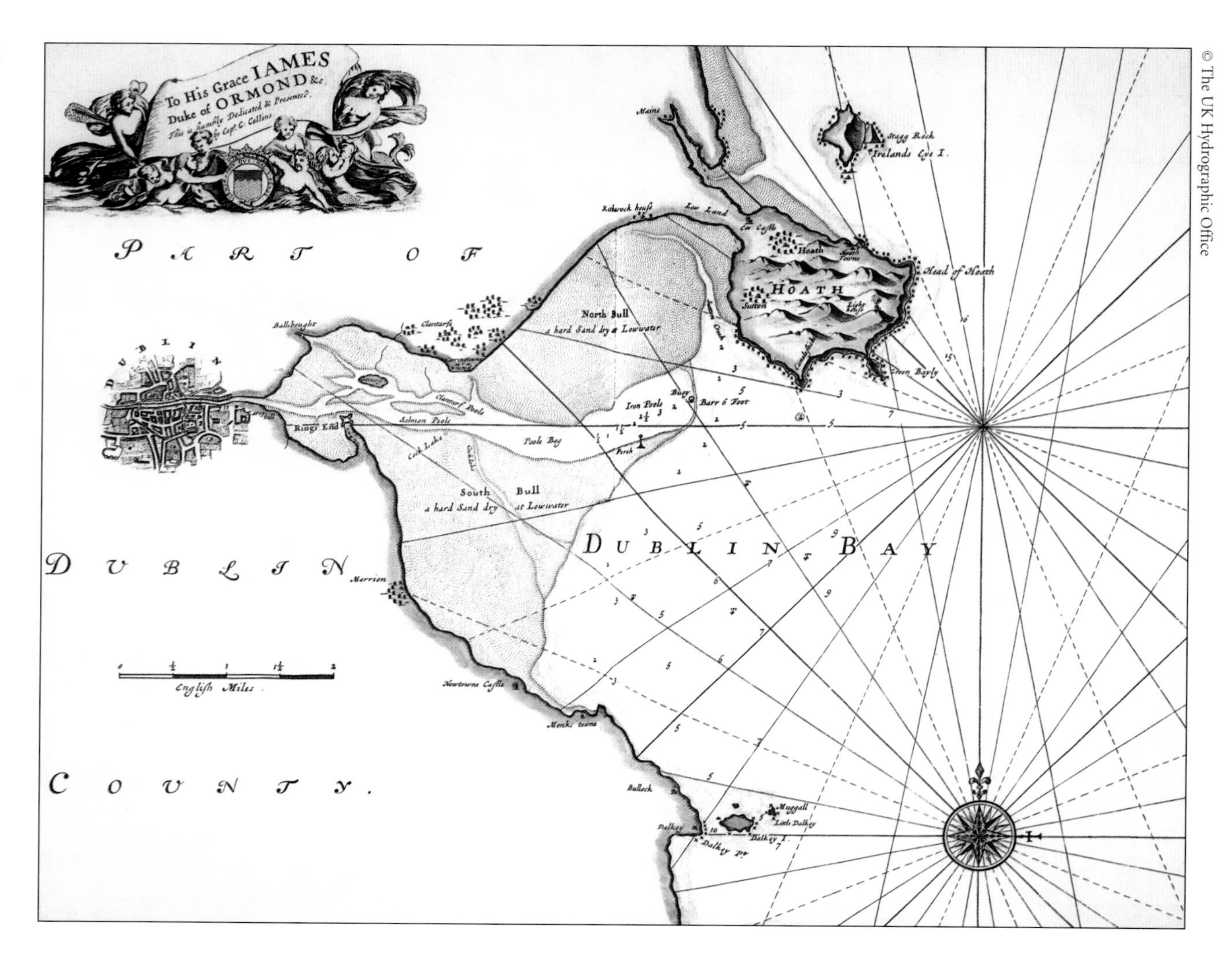

Captain Greenville Collins's chart of Dublin Bay. From the Admiralty Collection.

Up to this period Royal Yachts had been allocated to the Lord Lieutenant of Ireland when the King had tired of them, or from general service in the navy. Queen Anne, however, was to build a yacht specifically for the Dublin station, and this vessel was to spend her entire life allocated to the Lord Lieutenant. She was to be the ketch-rigged DUBLIN yacht, launched in 1709, and about the same size as her predecessor.

Captain George Breholt had delivered the CHARLOT to Deptford for her refit. He remained there to assume his new command when, on 13 August 1709, 'the Dublin Yacht was launcht into the wet dock not being near completed'.[27] (A phrase familiar to many a naval officer before and since!) By October she was completed, and sailed for Milford in convoy with HMS SOUTHAMPTON; shots were exchanged with several enemy ships off Penzance. By January 1710 she had reached Dublin, and took up the normal pattern of duties; carrying persons of importance, despatches and money.

The DUBLIN's slightly larger size enabled the guns to be increased to ten from the eight in preceding yachts. The crew was originally increased to 45 – partly to man the extra guns – but four years later reduced to 40 men. The complement was increased to 50 in 1737, five years after the yacht was rerigged with three masts as a ship.

In 1738 the DUBLIN made 15 voyages with an average of seven warrant passengers each trip. Often the passengers were noblemen, sometimes senior military officers, more often gentry and the quality. But in

March that year the Duke of Devonshire, as Lord Lieutenant, embarked with his retinue of 38; the Duke, Duchess and two children, two ADCs, two secretaries and a gentleman of the bedchamber, two chaplains, four pages, four gentlemen for His Grace, Her Grace's four women, a steward, a cook and thirteen footmen.[28]

We have seen how the carrying of passengers in addition to the warrant-holders provided a lucrative perquisite for the commander of the yacht; perhaps because of this they tended to retain command for many years. Captain Breholt was replaced in April 1711 by Captain Henry Lawson, who died at sea in April 1734, still in command twenty-three years later. Lawson's replacement was Captain John Weller, who took command the following month: 'an experienced commander, a well-bred gentleman and a sincere friend…'[29] He resigned command during 1751 in favour of his son, also John Weller; the latter took the DUBLIN to be broken up the following year, and commissioned her successor, the DORSET yacht in 1753.

DORSET

Built 1753 at Deptford.		Designed by Sir T. Slade.	
Length on gundeck	78 feet	Length by the keel	64 feet 10¼ inches
Beam	21 feet 11 inches	Depth in hold	10 feet 10 inches
Tons burden	164	Crew	50
Guns	14 half-pounder swivels		

Lord Lieutenant of Ireland's yacht.
1753-1813 Dublin station. 1815 sold for breaking up.

Built to replace the forty-one-year-old DUBLIN, taken to pieces the previous year, the DORSET was 6 feet longer and thus slightly larger than her predecessor. Her armament was numerically greater, but carried a lighter charge, perhaps an acceptance that Royal Yachts invariably sailed in convoy.

The DORSET was 'beautifully ornamented about the head, and over her stern is the Harp on a green field with much elegant carved work and painting'.[30] Below decks she was equally elegant:

> The cabin of the yacht is red velvet with silk flowers, very grand indeed… a few steps into a cabin where there was two or three nursery beds for the children and their nurse, there was two doors out of this, one of which led into a closet where the captain slept, and the other into the state cabin which has two beds in it, one for the Lord Lieutenant and Lady it is a crimson silk bed and the other for someone else I don't know who… Each man has a small cabin and bed to himself. The crew (50 men) is half English and half Irish, when she is at Dublin the Irish stay ashore and when she is here the English stay ashore.[31]

The number of sailings per year varied greatly, partly due to weather, partly waiting for convoys and partly because the yacht was refitted triennially at Plymouth; but the average in the early 1780s was 27 times a year. However, in 1787 the Parkgate Packet Company began regular sailings with ships that offered increased and more comfortable accommodation. The yacht was used less and less; average sailings fell to 16 a year, and then to 13 in the period 1800-1810.[32]

In the first year of the DORSET's duties, the average number of warrant-holders per voyage was 12; in 1758 it was ten. Thus the scope for private arrangements with the commander to carry passengers was considerable, as were the resultant perks. The First Lord of the Admiralty objected to the appointment of Captain Alexander Schomberg in 1771 as he did 'not think the carrying of passengers for emolument… a proper school for a person that is to command a fleet'.[33]

Captain John Weller was succeeded in command of the yacht by Captain Hugh Bonfoy. It had become the practice for commanding officers to retire from the active list when they entered the Lord Lieutenant's

DORSET, 1753

Basically a contemporary model, but heavily restored and repainted in the 1930s.

service, although they remained on the captain's list; Captain Bonfoy died in 1762, still in command of the DORSET. His successor, Captain William Williamson, also died while still in command, in 1771; as did his successor, Captain Alexander Schomberg, in 1804 at the grand age of eighty-four. His sailing master, Thomas Simmons, did not retire until nearly ninety! Schomberg was succeeded by the most senior captain in the navy, Lambert Brabazon, who too died whilst still in command in 1811, probably in his seventies.

WILLIAM & MARY III

Built (not rebuilt) 1807 at Deptford. Surveyor Sir John Henslow.

Length on gundeck	85 feet ½ inch	Length by the keel	70 feet 3½ inches
Beam[34]	23 feet ½ inch	Depth in hold	11 feet 1 inch
Tons burden	199	Crew	–
Guns	–		

Named after her predecessor, sold in 1801.
1807 launched 14 November.
1813-1827 Dublin station.
1832 depot ship at Woolwich 1832.[35]
1849 taken to pieces.

By the turn of the century the DORSET yacht was showing her age and required increasingly extensive, and expensive, refits. Four months in 1802; six months in 1805; and a further three months the following year. Improvements to the roads in north Wales, more frequent and comfortable packet boats combined with the Act of Union in 1800 meant a reducing demand for the services of the Royal Yacht. She spent long periods at anchor in Dublin Bay; seven months in 1800; five months in 1801; four months in 1803; nine months in 1807 and six months in 1811.[36] Two years later she sailed to Deptford, and after a lengthy period in dock was sold in 1815 for breaking up.

Her commander, Captain Andrew Sproule, took over the six-year-old WILLIAM & MARY III yacht,[37] but there was little for him to do. At nearly 200 tons the yacht was too large for the Dee Estuary and Parkgate, and she called at Holyhead on the rare occasions the yacht was used.

The economy of Parkgate had been much bound up with the conveyance of passengers to Ireland, and those voyaging on the Royal Yachts were nobility, gentry and quality, and thus big spenders. Halfway between Chester and Parkgate was an inn, which in 1757 was advertised to let as, 'the Half-way House, commonly known by the sign of the Dublin Yacht'. Ten years later, 'James Philips (late horsebreaker of Chester) has taken the Dorsetshire Yacht… on the Parkgate Road. He will continue to break horses.'[38] After nearly one hundred and fifty years of using the Dee Estuary, the change of port to Holyhead for the Royal Yachts must have had a severe effect on Parkgate's income.

Like her predecessor, the WILLIAM & MARY lay idle at anchor for many months in Dublin Bay, particularly after the introduction of a steam ferry service between Holyhead and Liverpool to Dublin about 1820. William Burnaby Green joined the yacht as a junior officer in 1823, and described his full court dress of garter blue coat richly embroidered about the chest, collars and cuff with sprigs of shamrock, white breeches with gold garters, hat and feathers, sword. His undress uniform was a brown coat with shamrock buttons, buff waistcoat and breeches; but apart from attending His Excellency as part of his suite, 'I have literally nothing in the world to do.'[39]

ROYAL CHARLOTTE II

Built 1824* at Woolwich.		Surveyor R. Seppings.	
Length on gundeck	85 feet 8 inches	Length by the keel	72 feet 8⅜ inches
Beam[40]	22 feet 10½ inches	Depth in hold	8 feet 2 inches
Tons burden	202	Crew	–
Guns	8 one-pounder swivels		

*Laid down April 1820. Launched 22 November 1824. See plan, page 109.
1827-1832 Dublin station. 1832 taken to pieces at Pembroke.

The first ROYAL CHARLOTTE (ex-ROYAL CAROLINE, 1749) was taken to pieces in July 1820, but already, in April, a start had been made on building a replacement. Although the plans show engines and paddle-wheels, the Admiralty must have had second thoughts, for she was built with sails only, at a cost of £12 821. She was not launched until 22 November 1824, and was then towed by steamboat to Deptford for fitting out.[41]

The ROYAL CHARLOTTE II was named after the Prince Regent's only child by the Princess of Wales. Princess Charlotte had married Prince Leopold of Saxe Coburg-Saalfeld (later King Leopold of the Belgians), and died on 5 November 1817 after giving birth to a still-born boy.

The yacht was finally commissioned in May 1826 for the Lord Lieutenant of Ireland, and she remained in his service for six years, until 1832. But with Britain heavily in debt from the Napoleonic wars, the extravagance of keeping five Royal Yachts afloat had in 1831 been challenged by radical reformer Joseph Hume.[42] First Lord of the Admiralty Sir James Graham countered by saying that of the five Royal Yachts, not one was perfectly manned; their expenditure was small; and this was the only patronage left to the Admiralty to keep old veteran officers on full pay. As to the Lord Lieutenant of Ireland, as His Majesty's representative, it was only fitting that when at sea he should appear with the paraphernalia of royalty. Mr Warburton, for the Opposition, countered that His Majesty could use a man-of-war when he wished to go to sea; and that it was not proper to maintain these vessels, painted and gilded like gingerbread, for that purpose.

Whether on account of this debate or not, as we have seen in Chapter 8, the following year the WILLIAM & MARY and ROYAL SOVEREIGN went as depot ships to Woolwich and Pembroke respectively. The ROYAL CHARLOTTE, still in service as the Lord Lieutenant of Ireland's yacht, was taken to pieces at Pembroke and not replaced. She was barely six years in commission; whether rot had set in during her extended building, or whether she was not a successful design is not known.

For over two centuries a vessel had been at the disposal of the Lords Lieutenant of Ireland; initially a man-of-war, but for most of that time ten successive Royal Yachts carried out the duties. With the withdrawal of the ROYAL CHARLOTTE a long tradition ended.

PART TWO

THE STEAM YACHTS

QUEEN VICTORIA (1837-1901)

VICTORIA & ALBERT

William IV and Princess Victoria's mother, the Duchess of Kent, were at permanent loggerheads, and no doubt this was the reason the Royal Yacht (although lying idle at Portsmouth) was not put at their disposal for visits to North Wales in 1832 and Plymouth in 1833. Instead the EMERALD cutter, tender to the ROYAL GEORGE was used, and seems to have been most successful: 'the dear EMERALD and her excellent crew', as the Princess confided to her diary.[1]

After her accession in 1837 five years were to elapse before the young Queen Victoria made any use of the Royal Yachts, and then it was to visit Scotland. She had inspected the ROYAL GEORGE on 28 February 1842 during a visit to the fleet at Portsmouth, and like her uncle, George IV, it was in the ROYAL GEORGE that she and Prince Albert travelled to Scotland. This time, however, the yacht was towed by two steam-ships, much to the Queen's distaste, as she recorded in her Journal:

> Monday 29 August 1842:
> At five o'clock in the morning we left Windsor… and arrived at Woolwich before seven… There was a large crowd to see us embark (and) I annex a list of our squadron.
> 1. The ship PIQUE, 36 guns.
> 2. The sloop DAPHNE, 18 guns.
> 3. The steam vessel SALAMANDER (with the carriages on board).
> 4. The steam vessel RHADAMANTHUS (Lord Liverpool and Lord Merton on board).
> 5. The steam vessel MONKEY, a tender, which has towed us till nine o'clock.
> 6. The steam vessel SHEARWATER, which is now towing us.
> 7. The steam vessel BLACK EAGLE (which has the ladies on board and which tows us in front of the SHEARWATER).
> 8. The steam vessel LIGHTNING… in front, which has gone to take our barge on board from the PIQUE.
> 9. The steam vessel FEARLESS (for survey).
> This comprises our squadron, besides which the Trinity House steamer (VESTAL) goes with us, and, also, a packet. Innumerable little pleasure steamboats have been following us covered with people.
> 30 August: We heard, to our great distress, (the Queen had been seasick) that we had only gone 58 miles since eight o'clock last night. How annoying and provoking this is! We remained on deck all day, lying on sofas; the sea very rough towards evening and I was very ill.
> 31 August: We heard, to our great vexation, that we had only been going three knots an hour during the night.

However, the sea became calmer, and the Queen wrote:

> The men begged leave to dance, which they did so to the sound of a violin played by a little sailor-boy; they also sang… We felt most thankful and happy that we are near our journey's end.

'The Principal Steam Yachts and the Racing Cutter Britannia' by Tony Gault.

The voyage had taken nearly three days, covering the 404 miles in sixty-six hours at an average speed of six knots. The Queen was so annoyed at being constantly overtaken by steam vessels that the paddle-steamer TRIDENT was chartered for the return journey. Quite what the young Queen said to her Prime Minister is not recorded, but Sir Robert was clearly still smarting when he wrote from Whitehall;
22 September 1842:

> Sir Robert Peel presents his humble duty to Your Majesty, and begs leave, with reference to Your Majesty's note of yesterday, to state to Your Majesty, that the first act of Sir Robert Peel on his return from Scotland was to write to Lord Haddington and strongly urge upon the Admiralty the necessity of providing a steam yacht for Your Majesty's accommodation. Sir Robert Peel trusts that Your Majesty may entirely depend upon being enabled to make any excursions next summer in a steam vessel belonging to Your Majesty, and suitable in every way for Your Majesty's accommodation... The Admiralty is now building a large vessel to be worked by steam-power, applied by means of a revolving screw instead of paddles... Sir Robert will leave nothing undone to ensure Your Majesty's comfort in any further excursions that Your Majesty may be pleased to make.[2]

Sir Robert stated the new yacht was 'building', whereas I assume he meant 'planning', for the keel was not laid until 9 November 1842, the first anniversary of the birth of the Prince of Wales. What a contrast to the 1996 prevarications over a replacement for BRITANNIA, when the Government seemed unable to make a

ROYAL GEORGE visit to Scotland, 1842

Watercolour by Algernon Yockney – 'The Royal George under tow off North Berwick with headsails set.' Presented to Queen Victoria 14 August 1897 by the officers of the VICTORIA & ALBERT II *for the Golden Jubilee. Painted on 1 July 1897 by Paymaster Algernon Yockney (1843-1912).*

sensible, if any, decision. Compare this to Sir Robert Peel; within a month of the Queen's visit to Scotland he had instructed the Admiralty to prepare plans for a new yacht, within three months the keel was laid, and in under ten months she was in commission.

In spite of declaring the yacht was to be driven by the new-fangled screw propellers, the Admiralty played safe, (as they did with the VICTORIA & ALBERT II twelve years later) and chose the well proven paddle-wheels. The comfort and safety of the Queen were to be paramount, for the Queen was laid low by rough weather, and Prince Albert was reputed to grow 'pale and queasy the moment he spied a ship'.[3]

Given all the considerations it might have been too much to expect the Admiralty to accept both a steam-yacht and propellers both at the same time.

VICTORIA & ALBERT I

Paddle-wheel yacht with sails, one funnel and two masts.
Wooden hull, of Danzig oak on the diagonal with an outer horizontal planking of Italian larch.

Laid down:	at Pembroke, 9 November 1842.
Designer/builder:	Rear-Admiral Sir William Symonds.
Launched:	26 April 1843 by the Countess of Cawdor.
Commissioned:	1 July 1843, under the command of Captain Lord Adolphus FitzClarence.
Tons displacement:	1034
Speed:	11.5 knots
Length (extreme):	225 feet
Length (between perpendiculars):	200 feet 1 inch
Beam:	Hull 33 feet, outside paddle-boxes 59 feet
Draught:	14 feet
Engines & I.H.P.:	Double-cylinder ('Siamese') engines, direct-acting by Messrs Maudslay & Son, giving 420 I.H.P. (nominal)
Coal stowage:	170 tons
Complement:	–
Disposal:	Name changed to OSBORNE in 1855 when VICTORIA & ALBERT II launched; paid off in 1859 and broken up in 1868
Remarks:	The brig NAUTILUS was tender from 1843 to 1845, thereafter the FAIRY

The VICTORIA & ALBERT was over 100 feet longer than the ROYAL GEORGE, and her two engines drove paddle-wheels to give a maximum speed of 11 knots. At her launch a copper box – containing coins of the realm – and a brass plate with an inscription were sunk into a groove let into the forepart of the sternpost.

Prince Albert, accompanied by the Lords of the Admiralty, inspected her in the Thames on 17 June and she was commissioned on 1 July 1843 under the command of Captain Lord Adolphus FitzClarence. Lord Adolphus was an illegitimate son of King William IV, and had been appointed in command of the ROYAL GEORGE a few weeks after his father ascended the throne in 1830. Although the Duchess of Kent took great pains that her daughter should not mix with the King's bastards, Victoria, when Queen, took a more tolerant view, and confirmed her illegitimate cousin in his appointment.

Queen Victoria paid her first visit to the new yacht when she was being painted at Deptford, and recorded in her journal for 8 August 1843: 'We drove from Woolwich to the Deptford Dockyard, where we inspected the VICTORIA & ALBERT, which is a beautiful vessel, with splendid accommodation.'

VICTORIA & ALBERT, 1843

Oil by G.W. Atkinson – 'HM Queen Victoria's first visit to Ireland – Cork Harbour 3 August 1849.'

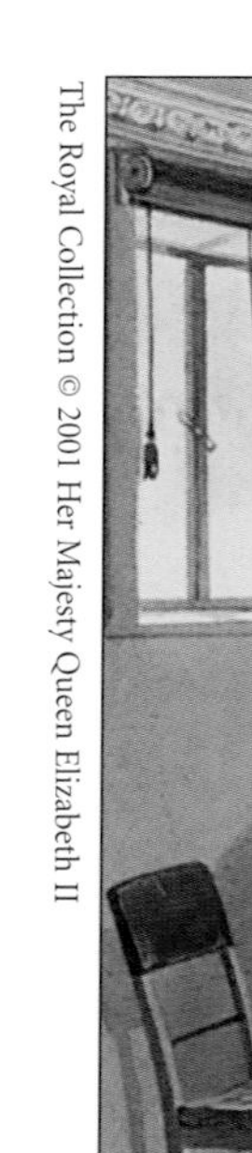

Watercolour by F.X. Winterhalter – 'The royal visit to Louis-Philippe, 7 September 1843. The leave-taking on board Victoria & Albert.'

In keeping with normal practice the State apartments were aft of the engine-room; forward were those of the yacht's officers and crew, plus the Queen's suite. The Queen's bedroom, with Prince Albert's dressing room adjacent, was on the starboard side, together with cabins for the royal servants. Opposite on the port side was the drawing-room, 25 feet long by 13 feet wide, painted a lilac colour, bordered with gold beading. Right aft was the reception room, with leather sofas curving round the stern of the yacht. Not everyone was content with the new yacht, for as one politician dourly commented, 'The royal apartments are luxurious but the ship's company was crammed into wretched dog holes with not enough room to move.'[4]

For her maiden voyage from Southampton the weather was not propitious, for as reported in the *Illustrated London News* of 28 August 1843, '(it) did not augur a very promising appearance, being dark and lowering, with the Scotch mist falling, that would wet an Englishman to the skin.' The VICTORIA & ALBERT left Southampton and crossed to Ryde on the Isle of Wight, where, as the Queen was leaving the yacht, the mate, Mr Warren, fell overboard. He had been in attendance on the accommodation ladder, and was luckily pulled back on board without injury, except presumably to his pride.

Inveterate correspondent that she was, Victoria wrote the very next day to her uncle, King Leopold of the Belgians:

> The yacht is quite delightful, as to accommodation and hitherto we have not even thought of being sick. Mais aujourd'hui nous verrons.

The Queen's apprehension was correct, for she recorded in her journal:

> ...towards one, it got very rough and we both began to feel very uncomfortable so we went below. Considering how rough the sea was, I must say the ship was very steady.

On the 29th the cruise continued along the coast of Devon and Cornwall, calling at Weymouth, Dartmouth and Plymouth. At the latter the log for 31 August contains the entry, on one line: '3.00 Her Majesty, Prince Albert, Lords etc, etc, left the ship. Lost overboard scrapers, two in number.'[5]

Watercolour of 3 September 1846 at Victoria Harbour, Plymouth.

At every port the Mayor and Corporation came on board to present a loyal address, while the harbours were crowded with vessels and the shores lined with vast multitudes of spectators. The yacht stopped off at Falmouth, and the Mayor, resplendent in robes and regalia, followed the fashion set by Mr Warren at Ryde and fell overboard. Fortunately he was rescued; unfortunately his mace was not.

From Falmouth they crossed to Treport, arriving about 6pm on 2 September. The French King came off immediately:

> The good kind King was standing on the boat, and so impatient to get out that it was very difficult to prevent him, and to get him to wait till the boat was close enough… His barge is a very fine one, with many oars, and the men in white, with red sashes, and red ribbons round their hats.

Very soon the Royal Families went ashore to the King's Chateau d'Eu, and there was 'the novel spectacle of the Royal Standards of France and England floating side by side over the sovereigns of the two countries as they were rowed ashore in the French royal barge'.[6 & 7] The visit was the first by an English sovereign to France since Henry VIII in 1520 at the Field of the Cloth of Gold, and was made for the express purpose of improving the somewhat strained relations between the two countries. It was a great success, and on 7 September Queen Victoria and Prince Albert took leave of their hosts: 'We set off before nine… and at half past three we got into the barge off Brighton.'[8]

A few days at Brighton to see the royal children, and then the yacht was off again to Ostend for a six-day visit to the King and Queen of the Belgians. The Royal Party finally arrived back at Windsor on 21 September, after a highly successful inaugural cruise, and the yacht was laid up at Portsmouth for the winter. As Prince Albert commented, 'Heaven favoured us with glorious weather,' and this maiden voyage set a pattern for cruises that was to become an annual event.

With the VICTORIA & ALBERT and her successor, the Queen was enabled to visit those parts of her kingdom remote from road and railways, as well as continuing the 'maritime excursions' so beloved of her predecessors. By using the yachts to visit the crowned heads of Europe and her ever-expanding continental relations the Queen did much to advance the cause of British diplomacy, whilst the increasing size of the yachts was a visible sign of the nation's growing international dominance.

The following year, 1844, saw a voyage from Woolwich up the east coast of Scotland, blessed by magnificent weather. In October, Her Majesty inspected a combined British and French fleet assembled at Portsmouth and on 15 October she and Prince Albert crossed to the Isle of Wight, where they had leased Osborne House from Lady Isabella Blatchford. The following year they bought Osborne, thus setting the pattern of use for the Royal Yachts which lasted the rest of the century.

It was 1844 that saw the establishment of a permanent crew for the Royal Yachts, instead of them being borrowed temporarily from other ships. When not on royal duty the yacht's crews were employed as riggers in Portsmouth Dockyard, and often had small businesses ashore as well.

In June 1845 the Queen witnessed the departure of the Experimental Squadron, eight line-of-battleships assembled at Spithead to test the speed and sea-going qualities of ships of various designs. From the steam-powered VICTORIA & ALBERT this was to be the last review of ships powered by sail alone, for even the hidebound Lords of the Admiralty were beginning to realise the advantages of steam. Later that year the yacht conveyed the Queen and Prince Albert to Germany so that Victoria could visit Albert's birthplace and 'the scenes of his youth'. In September they visited again King Louis Phillipe, landing over the beach at Treport with the aid of a bathing-machine drawn up by horses.

So the pattern of use for the VICTORIA & ALBERT developed. Visits across the Channel for the Queen to meet other crowned heads; the conveying of important visitors to Britain; visiting the main home ports, perhaps to lay a foundation-stone here, or to present new colours to a regiment there. And of course the cruises, soon established as an almost annual event – the Channel ports from Weymouth to Plymouth, the Cornish ports from Fowey to Penzance, and the Channel Islands in 1846; Dartmouth, the Scilly Isles, Holyhead and the West Coast of Scotland in 1847; Woolwich to Aberdeen in 1848; Portland, a visit to Ireland, the Scottish cruise in 1849; Ostend in 1850; Liverpool in 1851; the Channel ports as far as Plymouth and Antwerp in 1852; Holyhead and Kingston in 1853; Alderney, Portland and Boulogne in 1854.

FAIRY

Screw iron yacht.

Laid down:	1844 at Blackwall.
Designer/builder:	Messrs Ditchburn & Mare.
Launched:	1845.
Commissioned:	at Portsmouth, 9 July 1845.
Tonnage:	317
Speed:	13.25 knots
Length (extreme):	161 feet
Length (between perpendiculars):	146 feet
Beam:	21 feet
Draught:	7 feet 4 inches
Engines & I.H.P.:	Oscillating, geared engines by Messrs Penn & Sons, giving 128 I.H.P. (nominal)
Coal stowage:	18 tons
Complement:	–
Disposal:	Replaced by the ALBERTA in 1863, and taken to pieces January 1868

It had soon become apparent that the VICTORIA & ALBERT was too large to visit many of the minor ports, and that a steam-tender was needed able to keep up with the larger yacht's 11 knots. So in 1844 the screw

FAIRY, 1844

Watercolour by Lieutenant C.P. Williams, Royal Navy.

iron yacht FAIRY was laid down, and commissioned the following year; it is interesting to note the adoption of the screw in the very year that the Admiralty at last was convinced of its superiority over paddle-wheels following the RATTLER trials.

The FAIRY was not only one-third the tonnage of the VICTORIA & ALBERT, but her great advantage was that at 7 feet draught (cp. 14 feet) she could go into small ports and rivers impassable to the larger yacht, as well as alongside Trinity Pier for Osborne House. Thus in 1845 the FAIRY carried the Royal Party up the Rhine; and in 1846 up the Tamar River, the many people on the Cornish bank begging that the young Duke of Cornwall might be shown to them. The following year, during the Scottish cruise, the FAIRY transited the Caledonian Canal with the Queen, the yacht just squeezing through the locks.

In 1847 the Admiralty authorised the appointment of a Stewardess of the Royal Apartments, and that she should be paid as a petty officer – but not called one! The first Stewardess was Mrs Jane Hooper, and she served for more than thirty years, being recommended for a Long Service Medal in 1881. The Admiralty, however, refused to award it, stating that there was no precedent.[9]

With the establishment of the Queen and her family for so many months of the year at Osborne House, the need for a small yacht arose to act as tender to the VICTORIA & ALBERT, and more importantly to serve Osborne. And so in 1849 the paddle-yacht ELFIN came into service, and carried out these duties for the next fifty-two years.

ELFIN

Paddle-wheel steam yacht, one funnel, two masts. Diagonal planked mahogany hull.

Laid down:	1848 at Chatham.
Designer/builder:	Mr Oliver Lang.
Launched:	8 February 1849.
Commissioned:	at Portsmouth, 1 May 1849.
Tonnage:	98 tons
Speed:	12 knots
Length (extreme):	112 feet 3 inches
Length (between perpendiculars):	103 feet 6 inches
Beam:	13 feet 2 inches
Draught:	4 feet 10 inches
Engines & I.H.P.:	Oscillating, by Messrs H.G. Rennie, giving 40 I.H.P. (nominal)
Coal stowage:	7 tons
Complement:	–
Disposal:	Taken to pieces 1901
Remarks:	Tender to the VICTORIA & ALBERT I and II, but mostly on the 'milk-run' for Osborne House

Although writing in 1878, Staff Captain Watts, temporarily in command of the ELFIN, accurately described her role:

> The duty of the ELFIN was to leave Portsmouth, while the Queen was at Osborne, every weekday about 10 o'clock with the London papers and official letters for Osborne, landing them at Osborne Bay, and then proceeding to Cowes; leave Cowes about 2pm with the Queen's messenger, taking him to Southampton with Government despatches, land him there and embark another, taking him to Cowes and remaining there till 7am the next day, when she proceeded to Portsmouth, to leave again at 10am.

ELFIN, 1848

On Wednesdays and Saturdays she did not remain at Cowes. On Saturdays one Queen's messenger embarked at Gosport at 2pm, and then ELFIN returned with the other, landing him at Gosport.

She was known locally as 'the milk boat', and continued in these duties until 19 March 1901, when she was paid off for breaking up; her masts and certain of the scrollwork were retained in Portsmouth Dockyard by order of Edward VI. Nearly thirty years later, with the Great War intervening, her mainmast was sent to Craigwell House, Bognor in February 1929, and erected as a flagstaff for the Royal Standard during the residence there of King George V.

PRINCE OF WALES

Built 1850 at Chatham.		Surveyor	–
Length on gundeck	38 feet	Length by the keel	37 feet 2 inches
Beam	11 feet 5 inches	Depth in hold	4 feet
Tons burden	25	Crew	–
Guns	–		

Amidst all this building of steam-yachts for the grown-ups the royal children were not forgotten, for in 1850 Chatham Dockyard built the PRINCE OF WALES. She was a 38-foot launch, fitted as a miniature version of a 22-gun corvette, possibly intended for Virginia Water, although there is an illustration of her on the Serpentine. Her fate is unknown.

In 1850 the VICTORIA & ALBERT was sent (without royalty on board) to Lisbon and Gibraltar to test her sea-keeping abilities. Although she made the journey at an average speed of 11.6 knots, she was not to be used for such long journeys again, for her days were numbered.

The next review of the fleet was not until 11 August 1853, when 25 battleships and frigates, all but three powered by steam, were reviewed by the Queen at Spithead from on board the VICTORIA & ALBERT. The yacht then led the fleet to sea for a sham fight before a race back to Spithead for a programme of boat actions. 'No other country ever exhibited a spectacle so grand and so impressive,' eulogised the *Hampshire Telegraph*.

Five weeks later, on being promoted Rear-Admiral, Lord Adolphus FitzClarence retired, after twenty-three years' service as captain of two Royal Yachts. He was born the seventh child and fourth son of the Duke of Clarence (later William IV) and Mrs Jordan; and died, unmarried, a few years after retiring. His naval career spanned from just before Waterloo to the eve of the Crimean War, and by all accounts he was a competent seaman and well liked by his men.

PRINCE OF WALES, 1850

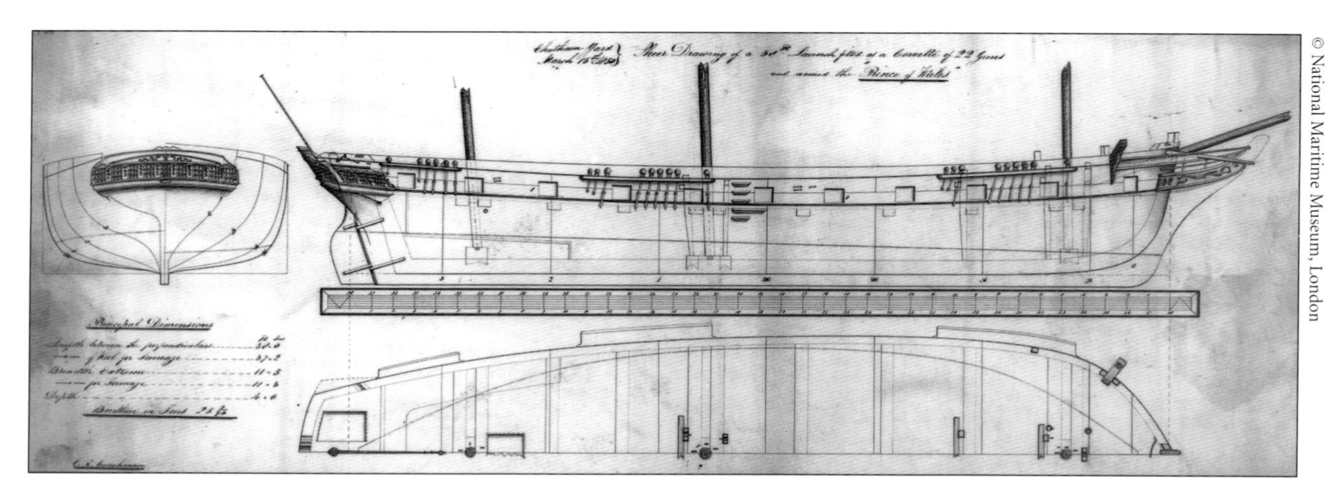

VICTORIA & ALBERT II

THE BUILDING OF THE VICTORIA & ALBERT II

By the early 1850s the growing size of the Queen's family, and her evident liking of a Royal Yacht made a replacement essential. She and Prince Albert had made 20 voyages in the VICTORIA & ALBERT, much extending her knowledge of the kingdom, and giving thousands of her subjects a personal contact with their sovereign. The yacht was ageing, however, and as early as 16 August 1847 the Queen wrote: 'Something had gone wrong with the paddle-wheel – just as happened last year – and it took two full hours to set it right.' But it was to be some years before a replacement yacht, provisionally called the WINDSOR CASTLE, was laid down at Pembroke on 6 February 1854. Her building was suspended for a time owing to the Crimean War and the need for small naval vessels in the Baltic; and four months after the keel was laid the question of screw or paddle-wheel propulsion had still not been decided. Extensive consultation was being carried out, and the report concluded: 'Till further improvements shall have much lessened, or entirely removed the shock and vibration from the Screw itself, a Screw Ship as a Yacht will in that vital and all important point – the personal comfort of Her Majesty – prove a total failure.'[10] Paddle-wheels were eventually chosen for the new yacht, and at her launch the vessel's name was changed to VICTORIA & ALBERT. The old yacht was renamed OSBORNE, and she continued to act as a secondary Royal Yacht until paid off in 1859, and finally broken up nine years later.

VICTORIA & ALBERT II

Wooden paddle-wheel yacht, two funnels, three masts.

Laid down:	as the WINDSOR CASTLE 6 February 1854 at Pembroke.
Designer/builder:	Mr Oliver Lang.
Launched:	by Lady Milford, and name changed 16 January 1855.
Commissioned:	3 March 1855.
Displacement:	2470 tons
Speed:	14.75 knots
Length (between perpendiculars):	300 feet
Beam:	40 feet 3 inches (hull)
Draught:	16 feet 3 inches
Engines & I.H.P.:	Two-cylinder oscillating engines, by Messrs Penn & Sons, giving 2400 I.H.P.
Coal stowage:	350 tons
Complement:	23
Disposal:	Paid off 3 December 1901. Broken up and burnt 1904

The new yacht was 100 feet longer than her predecessor; displacement tonnage was over double; engine horse-power was increased nearly six-fold and coal stowage was doubled.

The hull was of wood and the construction is described in the journal *Naval Architecture*, published in 1894:

> Three thicknesses are employed, the two inside being worked diagonally and the outer one longitudinally. The two diagonal layers are inclined in opposite directions, and the skin thus formed possesses

VICTORIA & ALBERT II, 1855

Her Majesty Queen Victoria embarked. Note the First Lieutenant at attention in the bows.

> such superior strength to the skin of an ordinary wood ship that there need be comparatively little transverse framing above the bilges. The Royal Yacht… with her unusually powerful engines and high speed, although subjected to excessively great sagging moments, has continued on service for forty years with complete exemption from signs of weakness.[11]

On 27 January 1855 the yacht was towed by the DRAGON from Pembroke to Portsmouth, which she reached two days later. There her machinery was installed, and at her sea-trials on 5 July she achieved a maximum speed of 15 knots. Captain Denman reported that his new command was '…decidedly very easy. She is for her length extremely handy and steers much better than the OSBORNE.' (The old VICTORIA & ALBERT.)[12]

In nearly fifty years of service the VICTORIA & ALBERT gave exemplary service, and much credit is due to her designer, Oliver Lang. On her being broken-up in 1904 the Naval and Military Record wrote:

> Built by Oliver Lang, she was from the first a highly successful ship… In beauty of design, in speed, in internal comfort, there was no ship in the world like her. If her success as a ship was due to Oliver Lang, her success as a floating home was due to the Prince Consort, who made himself responsible for the minutest detail in the fitting out of the royal apartments. At a time when the garish and the lurid were considered artistic in domestic ornamentation, the Prince Consort designed the chintz which took the place of the ordinary wallpaper – a moss-rose bud on a white background. At a time when the nouveau riche had set the fashion of heavy gold leaf decoration, he had the royal apartments painted white, with just a suspicion of gold leaf as relieved rather than oppressed the eye. In the furnishing of the royal apartments generally the question of cost was never considered; the governing ideas were comfort, good taste and simplicity. It was a complete revulsion from the inartistic monstrosities of domestic ornamentation of the day, and exactly harmonised with the homely lives led by the Queen and Prince Consort, when they could break away from Court life and spend a holiday en famille on the sea…

VICTORIA & ALBERT II, 1855

Coloured lithograph by T.G. Dutton.

The upper deck of the VICTORIA & ALBERT II was enclosed by bulwarks, and the deck covered with linoleum, which must have been lethal when wet; it was covered by 'red and black granite' carpet when the Queen was on board. On the upper deck were two tea-houses, with the dining pavilion right aft; an armoury, lamp-room, charthouse, royal larder and a number of signal-flag lockers. Two six-pounder guns were carried for signalling purposes. The original lighting was by candle-power, but in 1888, much against the Queen's wishes, electric lighting was provided from 42 accumulators.

On the main or State deck, passages ran port and starboard under the shafts of the paddle-wheels connecting the royal apartments aft to the cabins for the suite and the ship's officers forward. The royal apartments were entered by double swing-doors leading to a wide central corridor, from which a spacious staircase mounted to the dining-room lobby. Cabins on the starboard side, from forward to aft, ran as follows: the Queen's wardrobe room, the Queen's bedroom, Prince Albert's dressing-room then cabins for the Princess Royal, the governess and dresser. Right aft came the breakfast room with square stern and side ports. On the port side, from forward to aft, ran the drawing room, the cabins of the Prince of Wales and his tutor, valet's cabin, bathroom and royal pantry. All the royal apartments had the floors covered with red and black Brussels carpets, and the walls were hung with rosebud chintz, box-pleated. The doors, of birds-eye maple, had ivory handles and electroplated fittings.

Forward of the engine room was accommodation for the Household, the ship's officers and crew. The cabins for the ladies-in-waiting were on the starboard side, and those for the lords-in-waiting on the port side; the lords' and ladies' dining room was also forward, decorated in white and gold. There were 12 cabins for the Queen's servants, six of them fitted with two berths. In addition there were numerous offices, a dispensary, the officers' cabins and accommodation for the crew, numbering 240 in all. The Queen had never hidden her distaste for the decoration of the ROYAL GEORGE, and together with Prince Albert she stamped her own taste firmly on the new yacht.

Oil by Claudius Jacquard – 'Queen Victoria and Prince Albert disembarking at Boulogne to visit Emperor Louis Napoleon III, 18 July 1855.'

VICTORIA & ALBERT II came into service on 12 July 1855, when the Royal Party cruised round the Isle of Wight, and the Queen wrote: '…it is indeed a most magnificent and enormous vessel. One feels quite lost in her!'[13] The yacht was later taken to sea again to try her in a seaway under steam and canvas. In a strong breeze of gale force, and in a high sea, the ship was very easy, rolling from five to fifteen degrees.

Five days later, on 17 July, the Queen and Prince Albert spent their first night on board, prior to crossing to Boulogne on a State visit to the Emperor of the French, Louis Napoleon. They were anchored off Osborne, and the Queen wrote: '…this splendid ship, with a lovely view of my dear Osborne from the windows of my sitting cabin'. Next day she continued: 'Could not sleep at all for a long time, though the Yacht is most comfortable. At 5 we got underway. From the rapidity at which she goes, there is a good deal of vibration.'[14]

The following year, 1856, the yacht was sent to Madeira and thence to Cork, to test her sea-keeping qualities and coal consumption. The passage from Cork to Portsmouth was carried out at full speed, at an average speed of 15.4 knots, and the ship proved an excellent seaboat.

During the years of the Crimean War (1854-1856) the yacht was in frequent use for reviews and inspection of ships, and following the peace a great review of the English fleet was held on 23 April 1856. Assembled at Spithead were 254 ships in total, manned by over 50 000 men and carrying 1132 guns; 8 Royal Yachts and tenders were in the fleet and it must have been a magnificent sight. Due credit should be given to the change of heart at the Admiralty from sail to steam, albeit belatedly.

That year, too, the Queen and Prince Albert visited Dartmouth and Plymouth again. The following year, 1857, the newly created Prince Consort visited Antwerp without the Queen; and together they cruised to Cherbourg and Alderney.

In 1858 the yacht conveyed the Princess Royal from the Thames to Antwerp on the occasion of her marriage to Prince Frederick William of Prussia. It was 2 February, cold, with snow falling, but a vast crowd assembled on the shore to wish the Princess well. On the passage across the VICTORIA & ALBERT II collided with a brig, damaging a paddle-box; history does not relate the damage to the brig! Later in the year members of the Royal Family made a total of four more voyages, none of them any great distance.

1859 saw the Prince Consort, on his own, visiting Portland and, together with the Queen, the Channel Islands. Service on the Royal Yacht could hardly be called taxing.

In November 1860 the VICTORIA & ALBERT, accompanied by the OSBORNE (ex-VICTORIA & ALBERT I) was lent to the Empress of Austria for a cruise to Madeira; but it was late in the year, and the weather was decidedly unkind. One of her companions wrote:

> our dreadful voyage has come to a happy termination; what we have all suffered on the ship it is not in my power to describe. …the storm rose with such violence that even some of the officers and crew were ill; the ship groaned and cracked in her innermost parts, she rose and tossed about and struggled with the foaming and furious waves, but when we reached the insidious Bay of Biscay, it seemed as if all the evil water sprites had combined with the elements to destroy us.[15]

The Empress remained on Madeira for the winter, then in the spring of 1861 the yacht was again lent to her for a cruise from the island by way of Gibraltar to Trieste. This was the only time the VICTORIA & ALBERT II entered the Mediterranean, although the OSBORNE II was to make many voyages there in the 1870s, '80s and '90s with the Prince and Princess of Wales.

Later in 1861 the Queen and Prince Consort visited Holyhead and Dublin. The latter's death, probably from typhoid, at Windsor on 14 December that year, shattered the Queen, and totally altered her own usage of the yacht. In the next five years the VICTORIA & ALBERT II was used by the Queen only three times, and barely a dozen times by her family. However, as she slowly emerged from seclusion, Queen Victoria allowed many members of her extended family to make frequent use of the yacht. But much as she loved the ship and all its associations with Albert, for the rest of her reign Queen Victoria used the yacht – with very few exceptions – mainly as a cross-Channel ferry.

The breakfast room.

The dining saloon.

Watercolour by Anton Penley.

Clockwise (from top left):
Queen's bedroom.
Prince Consort's dressing room.
The Queen's drawing room.
State corridor and staircase.

VICTORIA & ALBERT II, 1854

ALBERTA

Wooden paddle-wheel yacht, two funnels, three masts.

Laid down:	1863 at Pembroke.
Designer/builder:	Controller's Department, Admiralty.
Launched:	3 October 1863.
Commissioned:	at Portsmouth, 30 November 1863.
Displacement:	370 tons
Speed:	14 knots
Length (between perpendiculars):	160 feet
Beam:	22 feet 8 inches
Draught:	7 feet 9 inches
Engines & I.H.P.:	Oscillating, by Messrs Penn & Sons, giving 1000 I.H.P.
Coal stowage:	33 tons
Complement:	47
Disposal:	Paid off 30 March 1912. Broken up in 1913

With the Queen immured at Osborne so much of the year it became essential for her to have a yacht smaller than the VICTORIA & ALBERT II, but more comfortable than the elderly FAIRY. The question of paddle versus screw was raised again. Speed was important to keep up with the VICTORIA & ALBERT II and to enhance the Queen's dignity. Shallow draught was required to go alongside Trinity Pier at Cowes (for Osborne) at all states of the tide, which thus limited the draught to eight feet. And a reduced draught enabled the tender to enter rivers and harbours too shallow for the main yacht. Speed combined with shallow draught meant rolling, particularly in a screw vessel; yet a low, fast paddle-yacht would be wet much of the time. 'Lack of motion is all important, as Her Majesty takes days to recover. Speed is to be

ALBERTA, 1863

sacrificed if necessary.' The decision to choose paddle-wheels was made, and in October 1863 the ALBERTA was launched and came into commission a scant eight weeks later.

The new yacht became a great favourite with the Queen, yet the captain of the VICTORIA & ALBERT II described her as 'the greatest beast ever floated', and alleged the engines were too powerful, 'shaking so bad that HM would have been frightened.' Minor alterations were made, and she then proceeded to give exemplary service for the next forty-nine years.

The new yacht took over the duties of the FAIRY, that is conveying the Queen to and from Osborne House, and for making short sea excursions with members of the Royal Family on board. As planned, her shallow draught enabled her to go alongside Trinity Pier, East Cowes, from where the Royal Family could land on their way to Osborne House. No longer required, the FAIRY was broken up four years later.

In 1875 the ALBERTA was involved in a collision with the schooner MISTLETOE, which resulted in the death of the master and two passengers from the latter vessel. The Queen and her two younger children, Prince Leopold and Princess Beatrice, were on board, but were not harmed.[16]

The Queen slowly emerged from seclusion, and in 1867 she opened Parliament in person. On 17 July that year she held a great naval review at Spithead in the presence of the Sultan of Turkey and the Viceroy of Egypt. The weather was very squally, the Sultan was not a good sailor, and as the Queen recorded in her journal:

> he went below, followed by the rest of his suite, and did not appear on deck until we were halfway through the line. He was constantly retiring below and can have seen very little.

The Sultan had set his heart on receiving the Order of the Garter, and:

> The little ceremony took place just outside the entrance to the (dining) saloon, and the Sultan was very

VICTORIA & ALBERT II

Oil by George Housman Thomas – 'The Investiture of the Sultan of Turkey 17 July 1867, at Cowes Roads.'

> much pleased. Everyone, Princes, Princesses and the whole suite were assembled outside to witness the ceremony. We sat down sixteen to luncheon in the deck saloon (only royal personages).

For the rest of the time the Sultan remained below:

> not feeling very comfortable, but he came on deck as we stopped off at Osborne, and I took leave of him with many mutual expressions of good-will and gratitude on his part.[17]

Such are the travails of diplomatic niceties!

The following year, 1868, the VICTORIA & ALBERT II was lent to the Princess of Leiningen for a cruise to the Norwegian fjords. The same year the OSBORNE (ex-VICTORIA & ALBERT I) was finally broken up; she had been paid off nine years earlier, but the Queen could not bear to part with the many happy memories of some 20 voyages with Prince Albert.

That winter of 1868 the VICTORIA & ALBERT underwent a thorough overhaul, during which the midship section was found to be very rotten, and the yacht had to be completely cleared. The cost of the repairs was £52 000, a staggering sum at the time.

In November that year a new OSBORNE was laid down, a smaller version of the VICTORIA & ALBERT II, and the yacht destined to be principally used by the Prince and Princess of Wales. Denied by his mother any form of training for his role as future King, it is not surprising that the Prince of Wales turned to a life of pleasure, in which yachting was a major part. He regularly attended Cowes Regatta during August on board the OSBORNE, and the Prince owned and raced a series of yachts, culminating in the most famous of all, the Racing Cutter BRITANNIA. Although the OSBORNE was laid down in 1868, she was not launched until two years later, and finally commissioned three years after that. Regard for the Royal Family was at its lowest since George IV's attempted divorce from Queen Caroline over fifty years earlier, and given the £52 000 repair bill to the VICTORIA & ALBERT, it was considered impolitic to proceed with another Royal Yacht.

The turning-point in the public's affection for the Royal Family came when the Prince of Wales nearly died from typhoid in the winter of 1871. And with Disraeli's return as Prime Minister in 1874 the Queen's re-entry into political life was made much easier. Two years later she was created Empress of India, a title she much desired, and for the rest of her reign she could do little wrong in the eyes of her subjects.

OSBORNE II

Wooden paddle-wheel yacht, two funnels, three masts. The last of the paddle-wheel Royal Yachts.

Laid down:	30 November 1868 at Pembroke.
Designer/builder:	Mr E.J. Reed.
Launched:	19 December 1870.
Commissioned:	12 June 1874.
Displacement:	1850 tons
Speed:	15 knots
Length (extreme):	278 feet
Length (between perpendiculars):	250 feet
Breadth:	36 feet 2 inches
Breadth over paddleboxes:	62 feet 6 inches
Draught:	15 feet 1 inch

OSBORNE II, 1870

Lithograph by T.G. Dutton.

Engines & I.H.P.:	Oscillating, by Messrs Maudslay & Sons Ltd, giving 3000 I.H.P.
Coal stowage:	200 tons
Complement:	120, afterwards 147
Disposal:	Sold 1908

See chapter notes[18] for more details

The OSBORNE was 50 feet shorter than the VICTORIA & ALBERT II, and about three-quarters of her tonnage. She was a comfortable sea-boat, and in the 1870s, '80s and '90s the Prince and Princess of Wales made many cruises in her, especially to the Mediterranean.

The OSBORNE was cruising off Sicily in 1877 when at 5pm on 2 June Captain Pearson reported the sighting of a sea-serpent. He 'distinctly saw the seal-shaped head of immense size, large flappers and part of a huge body'. Two other officers had good sightings; 'a head, two flappers and about thirty feet of an animal's shoulders. The head was about six feet thick, the neck narrower, about four to five feet; the shoulders about fifteen feet across, the flappers about fifteen feet in length'.[19] Fantasy? Hardly, with three experienced officers observing the creature through telescopes at four hundred yards range.

The OSBORNE was only kept in commission for a few months each year, but several cruises were made to Denmark for shooting parties. Commander (later Admiral) Lord Charles Beresford was in command from 1879 to 1891, and recounts how on one occasion, 'I was the only person present who was not either a King actual or King prospective. There was the King of Denmark, the King of Norway and Sweden (then one country) and the King of Greece, the Prince of Wales, the Cesarewitch, the Crown Princes of Denmark, Norway and Sweden and Greece.'[19a]

On the return journey a gale sprang up, and the starboard paddle-wheel was damaged on some wreckage. They saw a small craft being driven on a lee shore, and so the OSBORNE anchored both to repair her damage and to render assistance to the craft. The yacht prepared to veer a boat astern on a hawser down to the stricken vessel, but before they could help the ship was wrecked, although the crew of four reached shore safely in their own boat. It was then the custom for officers to remain a long time in the Royal Yachts; one had been fourteen years in the OSBORNE. Lord Charles Beresford suggested to the Prince of Wales that they should serve for only two years, so that the Prince might meet more officers from the fleet. The Prince adopted the suggestion, but Queen Victoria was not at all keen to do so on her yacht. 'I am an old woman now and I like to see faces I know about me, and not have to begin again with new faces.'

The Prince of Wales paid an official visit to India in 1875, embarking at Brindisi on 11 October in the Indian trooper SERAPIS, which had been fitted out as a Royal Yacht. The OSBORNE had sailed out from England to accompany the Prince, and in the Suez Canal he transferred to her in order to visit the Khedive at Ismailiya. Bombay was reached on 8 November, and the Prince spent four months travelling round India before re-embarking at Bombay on 13 March. At Gibraltar the Prince embarked in the OSBORNE to visit the Kings of Spain and Portugal, re-embarking in the SERAPIS at Lisbon for England.

HMS SERAPIS, *used for the Prince of Wales' visit to India in 1875/6.*

In 1884 the OSBORNE, her gilt work draped in black cloth, went to Cherbourg to bring home the remains of Prince Leopold, the Queen's fourth son, who had died at Cannes.

On 8 September 1886 the OSBORNE was suddenly ordered to Copenhagen. As normal she had been laid up for the winter, and the officers and crew were living on board the hulk BELVEDERE. The captain and second lieutenant were on leave; the senior lieutenant was in charge, but his mother being taken suddenly ill he had set off for London, having arranged for the navigating lieutenant to sleep on board that night. A lieutenant was borrowed from another ship, the crew hunted up and telegrams sent to the officers that the yacht would call at Dover to collect them. She sailed at daylight, and Lieutenant the Hon. Gerald Digby recalled, 'I was out cub-hunting when I received the telegram, so I rode straight to the station and went to London by the first train, and was aghast to see my opposite number catching the same train to Dover.' Awaiting the arrival of the OSBORNE at Dover they dined at the Lord Warden Hotel, where before long Captain Fawkes appeared. He was much amused to see one of his lieutenants in hunting kit, but much less amused to see the other, whom he had supposed in charge of the yacht.[20]

The OSBORNE was used by the Prince and Princess of Wales regularly at Cowes Regatta, where she had a buoy mooring inboard of the VICTORIA & ALBERT. By the time the Prince of Wales succeeded to the throne as Edward VII the OSBORNE was elderly and she was finally sold in 1908.

Service on the Royal Yacht was keenly sought after. For the officers it meant automatic promotion on leaving, and a relaxed and pleasant lifestyle when serving, with the cachet that inevitably comes with service in royal circles. For the men it was a pleasant interim between active service and retirement, and many of them had small businesses ashore in addition to their dockyard employment as riggers when the yacht was laid up. And for both officers and men it was a chance to serve their monarch and to rub shoulders with the Royal Family, however distantly.

The appointment of officers was through influence leading to a personal recommendation to the sovereign, and although we deprecate this system now, it was the norm then. Many distinguished senior officers had at one time served in the Royal Yachts, so the methods of selection must have accounted for ability as well. After all, no one was going to recommend someone useless, for short shrift was given by monarchs who were not served efficiently. There are several accounts from officers of their time in various Royal Yachts, but a rare insight from another viewpoint is given by Lady Poore in her autobiography.[21]

As a daughter of the Bishop of Limerick she confessed 'to pulling several strings with my own hand' when it was suggested her husband be appointed to the yacht, 'but I need not have troubled, for Captain J.R. Fullerton, Captain of the Queen's Yachts, personally recommended my husband to Queen Victoria'. She and her husband had no income other than his naval pay, and the couple were hard pushed to maintain the standard expected of his appointment. Commander Poore joined the VICTORIA & ALBERT II as Commander in May 1887 on his return from service in the West Indies, and:

> ...for the first month there was so much to do, bewilderingly much for me... Among other things I had to be presented at Court, to take a house (at Southsea) and to find servants, and I was so painfully inexperienced that I made mistakes enough... to fill a chapter. The rent of our furnished house was out of all proportions to our modest income, so was my presentation gown, and so, it presently appeared, was everything, and I no longer contemplated my account-book with the pride and satisfaction it had given me... We did not appear to be extravagant, but our scale of living was at fault, and only when we let our house for... July and August did I breathe freely. For this period the Yacht was at Cowes, and I found rooms, unfashionable, of course, but quite suitable, at East Cowes.
>
> Unless there have been drastic changes in the last five and twenty years a Royal Yacht is unlike any other ship, and, to say the truth, she is far less interesting, viewed from a naval standpoint. There is no

> mingling of rough and smooth, 'good boys' and bad characters, in her ship's company. They are all good, blameless, and often smugly self-satisfied, and I could not detect any signs of that esprit de corps which animates the officers and crew of a ship in general service, for there was no competition and none of the effervescence or keenness which is always found in a 'smart' ship or one ambitious of becoming smart. The men of the V. & A. were not unlike the sailors in HMS PINAFORE, and most of her officers were pausing for a rest after a period of strenuous service, or merely revelling in the social opportunities which their position afforded. The navigator was a very live man, since his responsibilities were great when the yacht was at sea, and so, of course, was the captain, but the commander had not nearly enough to do, while the three subs. were only appointed for the six weeks which ensured their promotion, and these six weeks were spent at Cowes!
>
> Apart from July and August and an occasional trip across the Channel the V. & A.'s officers lived on board the little old yacht ROYAL GEORGE lying perpetually at anchor in Portsmouth Harbour, half-way between the dockyard and Gosport. There were two lieutenants who put in two years for promotion, and if they were young men of means they had an excellent time ashore, turn and turn about. Neither watch-keeping nor navigation, torpedo nor gunnery vexed their souls. But when Queen Victoria was on board officers and crew were every button on duty, for nothing short of perfection in dress and 'deportment' as well as intelligence and aptitude would satisfy the Greatest Lady in the Land…

Mrs Poore enjoyed the two months at Cowes, but 'I was naturally more an onlooker than an actor at Cowes, for I did not belong to the society which can afford to take its pleasures handsomely'. Although she was amused at 'the spectacle offered by the crowds of smart folk on the lawn of the Yacht Squadron… merely looking at people to whose monde one does not belong soon palls, and I enjoyed our games of tennis at Northwood and the outings in the Commander's blue galley more than the occasional doses of grape-seed which punctuated Cowes week'. One evening she was summoned at short notice to attend a small informal dance on the Yacht, where the Crown Princess of Germany had been dining; and on another occasion dined as the only guest with the Crown Princess at Norris Castle, so her visit to Cowes had its highlights.

> The rest of our time at Portsmouth was uneventful. We were not rich enough to take advantage of the many possibilities such an appointment affords to people better endowed… One day we discovered that even our modest way of living was costing more than we could afford, so we let the small house we had furnished (our second venture), my husband took up his quarters on board the GEORGE, and I, with Roger (her son) and the faithful and accommodating nurse… departed for Brittany.

The cost of living on the Continent, particularly in France, was then much less than in England, and after two months in a 'little thin-walled furnished villa' Mrs Poore was again able to peruse her account-book with joy. For the rest of that summer she rented a:

> truly delightful chateau… sparsely furnished… but habitable, and here my husband was with me for a good part of the time… In October, 1889, we returned to Portsmouth lighter of heart and easier of pocket and fully determined to cut our coat henceforth according to our cloth. It was hardly a coat – something more like a monkey-jacket indeed – but it sufficed, and we never seriously regretted the exchange of a whole house with servants… for five sunny rooms on the third and fourth floor at No. 11, Southsea Terrace. There we lived till our three years at Portsmouth were up…

In May 1890 Commander Poore's time on the Royal Yacht came to an end, and he was promoted Captain, albeit on half-pay. The family decided to return to France in order to economise, and for Captain Poore to continue his French studies. For two years they struggled on half-pay in France, Switzerland and Italy until Captain Poore was appointed to a new ship, eventually being promoted to Rear-Admiral in 1903.[21a]

Queen Victoria never again used the VICTORIA & ALBERT II for cruising as she had done with the Prince Consort. Of the 125 voyages made after his death in 1861, the Queen was on board a mere 32 times, nearly always restricted to crossing the Channel. The yacht made just four longer cruises in all that time, but she was much used fetching and carrying the Queen's innumerable continental relations. The list of her passengers reads straight from the Almanack de Gotha.

In 1878 the VICTORIA & ALBERT II conveyed the Duke of Connaught, (Queen Victoria's third son) to Heligoland (then a British possession) for a tour of inspection, and then on to Hamburg to visit the German Emperor.

During the summer of 1879 an incident occurred at Cowes which shows an amusing side of the Queen's character. An excursion had been arranged, and the Duke and Duchess of Edinburgh, the Duke and Duchess of Connaught, Prince Leopold, Princess Beatrice and a few others all came on board the yacht about 11am. The Duke of Edinburgh informed the Captain that they were ready to leave, but the latter replied he could not do so without the Queen's permission. So they all looked at each other, and one said, 'Did you not ask Mother?' 'No, I did not.' 'Thought you did,' and so on, and it appeared that no one had asked. So the Duke of Connaught was sent to ask Mother, who had known all about the excursion, for permission, which was duly granted.[22]

Later in that year Queen Victoria and her daughter Princess Beatrice crossed to Cherbourg in the yacht en route for Italy. The passage was rather rough, with snow falling, and the Queen's servant John Brown repeatedly asked the Navigator if the weather would improve. For, as he put it, 'the puir boddie downstairs does not feel at all well'. On being told they would get shelter from the French coast he said brightly, 'That will cheer her up, I will tell her.'

In 1883 the yacht underwent a thorough refit, which lasted nearly two years. The cross-Channel trips were made in the OSBORNE, and after the second the Queen gave orders that the VICTORIA & ALBERT II should be ready by the time she next embarked on a sea-passage. Queen Victoria did not like change.

And so the years rolled by. In 1885 the yacht conveyed wedding guests for the marriage of the Queen's daughter Princess Beatrice to Prince Henry of Battenberg. In 1886 it was a great review of the fleet at Spithead on the occasion of the Colonial and Indian Exhibition. 1887 saw a review at Spithead in honour of the Sultan of Turkey, accompanied by Queen Victoria and the Viceroy of Egypt. For the first time the White Ensign flew on every ship, for gone were the old red, white and blue squadrons.

In 1896 the Duke and Duchess of Connaught visited St Petersburg for the Tsar's coronation, the yacht mooring close to the Nicholas Bridge in the heart of the city. At the 1897 Diamond Jubilee review the fleet consisted of 21 battleships, 12 first-class cruisers, 27 second-class cruisers and many destroyers and other craft – 173 British warships in all, arranged in four lines about five miles long each. Sir Charles Parsons slightly stole the show by racing through the lines at 32 knots in his turbine driven ship TURBINIA.

A good picture of life as an officer on the Royal Yacht is given by Captain The Hon. Sir Seymour Fortescue, KCVO, CMG, RN, then a lieutenant aged thirty-two.

> I joined the Royal Yacht in the autumn of 1888… In those days the VICTORIA & ALBERT was only inhabited by a small party of caretakers except when she was actually on some cruise, or when the Queen was paying her summer visit to Osborne. During… the greater part of the year the officers lived on board the ROYAL GEORGE… and all communication with Cowes was carried on either by the tenders ALBERTA and ELFIN, or by packet-boat. I loved the old hulk. We were very comfortable, as the officers messed in what had been the royal apartments.
>
> During the Queen's winter residence at Osborne no leave was given, as it was never known when we might be required, and when the Royal Yacht lay at Cowes, in the summer, the officers were not allowed

'The Diamond Jubilee Review 1897.'

ashore until it had been finally ascertained that Her Majesty had no further commands that day; but when the Court was not at Osborne we had a very easy time. The two lieutenants used to take it in turn to go on leave, one of them having to live on board the ROYAL GEORGE, but as soon as Morning Prayers had been read there was little or nothing more to do, and there was no trouble about attending such Race Meetings as Sandown and Kempton...

And so the time passed agreeably enough, conveying the Queen across the Channel in March 1889 en route to Cimiez, and back again in April. At the end of June... we were sent to Antwerp to embark the Shah... (who)... had an enormous retinue of Persians for us to embark. Some of them... were no doubt very distinguished men; but the tail end of the suite seemed to me to consist principally of what the Bluejackets used to call 'scallawags'.

In the middle of July the Queen went, as usual, to Osborne, and that season the Kaiser made his first descent on Cowes... with his usual arrogance, or perhaps to save himself from paying their board in Germany while he was in England, he brought over an immense and entirely unnecessary suite. Osborne, and all its little dependencies, were strained to the utmost to house this swarm of locusts, and even then an overflow party had to be put up on board the Royal Yacht.

After the German Invasion had come to an end... Cowes became quite a pleasant place. Our duties were not very exacting. There were occasional return trips to Southampton and Portsmouth to bring over or take back the Queen's visitors in one of the tenders, and every other day it was my duty to walk up to Osborne, take luncheon with the Household and ascertain whether Her Majesty had any commands.

About the middle of September the Court moved to Balmoral, the Queen crossing as usual in the ALBERTA, and we officers took up our quarters again on board the ROYAL GEORGE, the great bulk of the ship's company, as usual, going back to the dockyard to work as riggers. And so ended my first season at Cowes as a Lieutenant of Her Majesty's Yacht.

ROYAL GEORGE, c.1890

The ROYAL GEORGE *in use as an accommodation ship.*

Lieutenant Fortescue's second year mirrored the first, for the Queen was a woman of strict routine. At the end of August 1890 the Court left for Balmoral, and the following week he ...'was promoted to Commander, on the magnificent half-pay of eight shillings per diem – and a very pleasant time it was.'[23]

Sub-Lieutenant (later Admiral) Roger Keyes joined the VICTORIA & ALBERT II on 21 July 1894 as a Season Officer i.e. just for the six-week summer season. He was presented to Queen Victoria on board the ALBERTA:

> The Queen walked from the train and over the gangway to a chair on the quarterdeck, supported under each elbow by Hindu servants, followed by the Munshi, who was teaching her Hindustani, and preceded by her Highland gillie, one of John Brown's successors, whom we all thought a most unpleasant individual. He put on intolerable side, elbowing everyone out of his way, and behaving as if he alone was responsible for the Queen's comfort and safety. On the way over to Cowes the new officers of the Royal Yachts were presented to the Queen, who I thought was an alarming old lady.[23a]

A few days later the Kaiser arrived for Cowes Week in his great new cruiser yacht, the HOHENZOLLERN. This yacht 'looked overwhelming beside our ancient paddler, but on board gave one the impression of being rather like a flashy modern hotel alongside a quiet, dignified private house'.[24] (An equal impression was given by BRITANNIA.)

In March 1899 the Queen crossed from Folkestone to Boulogne on board the steamer CALAIS-DOUVRE, Her Majesty having been persuaded she would be more comfortable than in the Royal Yacht. A special cabin had been built on deck, fitted with furniture brought from the VICTORIA & ALBERT, and the Queen expressed her satisfaction with the arrangements. But she ordered her own yacht to be ready for the return journey; the old lady, it seemed, preferred to be uncomfortable in familiar surroundings!

The days of the elderly VICTORIA & ALBERT II were however numbered. On 6 May 1899 she proceeded to Pembroke for the launch of the new Royal Yacht by the Duchess of York. Before leaving Cowes at the end of the racing season the VICTORIA & ALBERT II was saluted with 21 guns by the Royal Yacht Squadron. No royalty was on board, but the salute was a final mark of respect to the old yacht in her last summer season at Cowes in attendance upon the Queen.

Pembroke Dockyard Archives

VICTORIA & ALBERT II *at the launch of* VICTORIA & ALBERT III, *9 May 1899.*

Lieutenant Henry Pelly (later Admiral Sir Henry Pelly KCB, CB) joined the Royal Yacht in September 1899, when she was laid up for the winter, the officers living on board the ROYAL GEORGE. His letters and autobiography are fascinating, especially relating to the death of Queen Victoria.[25]

> I was the only bachelor amongst the officers, and generally the only one to sleep on board, so time hung rather heavily on hand, and for the first time in my life I had more leave than I knew what to do with.
>
> All the officers used to assemble on board about ten, and then each would proceed about his work, but they all departed very soon after lunch, and I was left to make my own plans. It was a daily amusement to me to overhear the betting going on in the back regions as to what my movements would be in the evening. If I stayed on board, the cooks and stewards had to remain, and the boat's crews went home to their wives and families. If I arranged to dine ashore, boat's crews had to remain whilst the cooks and stewards went home.

The late Admiral Sir Henry Pelly, KCVD, CB

VICTORIA & ALBERT II (clockwise, from top left)
Looking forward from the quarterdeck.
The forecastle on 'Open Day'.
The bridge.
Looking aft from the mainmast.

VICTORIA & ALBERT II *at Dartmouth on Pretoria Day, 5 June 1900. Flying the standard of Princess Henry of Battenburg.*

Queen Victoria embarking at Holyhead, 1899.

> It was not until December that I first had the honour of being presented to Queen Victoria. I can see her now sitting in her chair on board the ALBERTA as we took her across from Portsmouth to Osborne. So small she looked, but so very terrifying, and I confess to being thoroughly scared when I was being brought along to be presented.
>
> My first trip in the old yacht was to Holyhead, where we embarked the Queen for her visit to Ireland.[26] The arrival at Kingston was... ahead of time, and the yacht was safely moored in the harbour before most people knew it. When Her Majesty came on deck for her drive to Dublin she remarked that she did not appear to be very welcome, for all the people on the pier had their backs to her. This actually was the case, for the crowds had not grasped the fact that the yacht was actually in the harbour. They were all looking out seaward to see the yacht arrive.
>
> The Queen had a great reception and a triumphal drive from Kingston to the Vice-Regal lodge. ... The Queen remained in Dublin for a little over three weeks... then on April 26th Her Majesty, after receiving a wonderful send-off, embarked, and we sailed for Holyhead. This was the last time that the Queen was on board the old VICTORIA & ALBERT.

In early June the VICTORIA & ALBERT II was lent to Princess Henry of Battenberg and her children for a cruise to the West Country and the Scilly Isles. Then in July the Queen crossed to Osborne in the ALBERTA, and the VICTORIA & ALBERT followed, taking up her moorings in Cowes Road for the summer season. At the end of August the Royal Yacht took the Princess Christian and her two daughters on a cruise to the West Coast of Scotland, and it was then back to Portsmouth for the yacht and her usual winter lay-up.

> There was little to do for the rest of the year until December 18, when I was in attendance on board the ALBERTA to receive HM Queen Victoria with a large suite, and convey the party to Cowes for Christmas at Osborne. Little did we think that the Queen was afloat for the last time.
>
> On January 18 (1901) the state of the Queen's health began to cause alarm, and we found ourselves very busily engaged carrying members of the Royal Family to Osborne. On the 21st, the Prince of Wales, accompanied by the German Emperor, were our passengers. ...the following morning we were told that the Queen was 'slowly sinking'.

The log of the VICTORIA & ALBERT II[27] contained the entry for Tuesday 22 January, edged round in thick black lines:

> 6.30 Her Most Gracious Majesty, Queen Victoria,
> departed this life; at Osborne, Isle of Wight;
> aged 81 years, 243 days.

Busy days and long hours followed for the Royal Yachts, transporting the Royal Family and their many relations to and from Cowes. The crew of the VICTORIA & ALBERT II were hastily assembled, and on the 23rd the yacht crossed to Cowes, where she secured to her moorings. At noon that day the cruiser AUSTRALIA began firing 81 minute guns, one for each year of the late Queen's life. On the 25th the Kaiser's yacht HOHENZOLLERN arrived and anchored at Spithead before securing to a buoy at Cowes the following day.

Lieutenant Pelly was placed in charge of conveying the Queen's coffin to the mainland, and every morning, before the household was awake, he held a rehearsal with a dummy coffin. 'Our movements were somewhat hampered by the German Emperor, who was always up and about early, and liked to have a finger in every pie.' The funeral was on 1 February, and:

> through a great crowd of people we marched safely to Trinity Pier, where the coffin was safely carried across and placed on board the ALBERTA. ...I had to hasten to my position in the bows for that memorable run of twelve miles which took nearly two hours. I stood there, a solitary figure, for all that time, and at the end was so stiff from the cold that I had to be lifted down.

> The King and Queen were on board the VICTORIA & ALBERT II, and during the passage the King noticed the Royal Standard was at half-mast. On enquiring why, he was told that the Queen was dead. 'The King of England lives,' he replied, and ordered the Standard to be raised.

> The King was 'well pleased with the way his (Pelly's) men had done their sad and painful task. He then said, 'So will you now accept from me this order which I am conferring on you not so much for my sake, but for the sake of my Beloved Mother whom you have served so well.' He then handed me the Cross of the 4th Class of the Victorian Order. What I said, I know not, I was taken flat aback and quite unable to say what I should like to have done. However, that I fancy did not matter much. Then I went back to the Wardroom to receive the congratulations of all assembled there.

The ALBERTA was berthed alongside the Clarence Yard at Gosport, and a very distinguished general was meant to be in full uniform standing by the bier. When the King checked later that night he found the general sitting there, certainly not in full dress, and smoking his pipe! Luckily the King saw the humorous side of it, and the incident passed off well.

Next day, Saturday 2 February, disaster was only narrowly avoided by Lieutenant Pelly checking the royal train. For he found that not only were the specially built steps too weak to take the weight of the coffin and bearers, and would certainly have collapsed; but they were also higher than the carriage doors, which could thus not be opened. Urgent summons were issued for carpenters to strengthen the steps and to saw four inches off the carriage doors. Lieutenant Pelly just had time to rush back to the ALBERTA where the Royal Family was assembling.

> There followed the last part of my duties. It was a vile morning, rain falling in torrents and half a gale blowing. The walk from the yacht to the train was a long one, and the funeral march, most beautifully played, seemed at that early hour more pathetic than I had ever felt it before. At 8.52 the train with its Royal Burden proceeded to London (and Lieutenant Pelly's) sad but honoured duty to our late Queen was finished.

One cannot but help feeling that mixed with the sadness Lieutenant Pelly felt was relief that his task had been successfully accomplished in the face of several difficulties.

The *Daily Graphic* of 3 March 1904 stated that after the funeral voyage of the VICTORIA & ALBERT II 'through the lines of the fleet at Spithead… her services ceased, and the old ship never after left Portsmouth Dockyard.' However lyrical the prose, it is not quite accurate, for she had one more duty to perform before being superseded by the new yacht, already launched and waiting in the wings.

The Empress Frederick, sister to King Edward VII, lay gravely ill in Berlin. Late on the night of Saturday 23 February the King embarked in the VICTORIA & ALBERT II at Sheerness, attended by only two gentlemen.[28] The yacht sailed early the next morning, and by 3.45pm had entered Flushing Outer Harbour. Whether by accident or design the Dutch pilot totally misjudged the strength of the tide. Lieutenant Pelly was on board:

> From my point of view, standing in the bows, it seemed that we must be dashed against the harbour wall, and I much doubted if that old wooden yacht could withstand such a shock. I saw the pilot throw up his hands and heard him cry, 'The ship is lost!' but our Captain was equal to the occasion, for he promptly took charge, and we scraped safely into harbour.[28a]

At that time the Boer War was still dragging on, and feelings in Holland were very strong against the British. There were many who thought the pilot had deliberately tried to wreck the yacht with the King of England on board. There is no mention of the incident in the ship's log, merely the entry: 'Lost by accdt. thro' fouling tugs propeller 25 fms of 6" hawser.'[29]

The King returned from Berlin a week later, sailing from Flushing on 2 March, and disembarking at Port Victoria, Sheerness, the following afternoon. This was the last crossing that Admiral Sir John Fullerton made

ALBERTA *bearing the coffin of Queen Victoria, with HMS* VICTORY *afloat in the foreground. From the print by Charles de Lacey.*

as Flag Officer Royal Yachts, and the final voyage on royal duty for the VICTORIA & ALBERT II. Admiral Fullerton retired on 1 April 1901, having been Captain and Admiral of the yachts since 1884. He was appointed the first Flag Officer Royal Yachts on his promotion to Rear Admiral on 1 January 1893, but continued to retain personal command of the VICTORIA & ALBERT II. The old yacht returned to Portsmouth to await paying off, and in July of 1901 the VICTORIA & ALBERT III was commissioned. There is a strong note of pathos in the log of the VICTORIA & ALBERT II for Wednesday 29 October 1901:[30]

7.15 Tugs transported Yacht to No 27 Moorings in Fareham Creek. (the breakers yard)
9.00 Took in moorings. Tugs left.
9.30 HMY 'Victoria & Albert' (new) proceeded alongside S.Ry. Jetty.

On 3 December 1901 – along with the ROYAL GEORGE – the old yacht was paid off into the Dockyard Reserve. The King wished to have her brought out for the Coronation Review the following year, and although the Dockyard was instructed to furnish an estimate for refitting her, the cost was too high. Still the King delayed giving the final order, but at last, in 1904, after forty-nine years afloat, the VICTORIA & ALBERT II was broken up and burnt. Mingled with her flames and ashes were the last few vestiges of the Victorian era.

VICTORIA & ALBERT II *at the funeral of Queen Victoria with King Edward VII embarked.*

VICTORIA & ALBERT III

The launch at Pembroke 9 May 1899, by HRH The Duchess of York, accompanied by HRH The Duke of Connaught.

Pembroke Dockyard Archives

Queen Victoria hated change. We have already seen how she preferred the greater physical discomfort in the familiar surroundings of her own yacht to the mental anguish she felt in the luxurious but strange deckhouse built for her on the CALAIS-DOUVRES when crossing to Boulogne. The VICTORIA & ALBERT II was by now forty-four years old, and her shortcomings were apparent, but the Queen regarded her as home and was most loathe to consider a new yacht. Pressure was put upon the old lady however, not least the argument that as the premier maritime nation Britain should visibly display this with the largest Royal Yacht in the world.

The German Kaiser had by 1894 the biggest and most powerful steam yacht in Europe, the HOHENZOLLERN. Yacht was, however, an incongruous word, for the Kaiser had appropriated one of the new German Navy's destroyers for his own use and conversion. The huge sums involved raised objections in the Reichstag, and were only sanctioned on condition that, when needed, the yacht could be available to the navy as a despatch vessel. (In spite of this the HOHENZOLLERN lay idle during the Great War, eventually being sold and scrapped in 1923.)

Within a few short years it was the turn of the Tsar of Russia to boast the biggest and most impressive yacht, for the STANDART was some forty feet longer than the HOHENZOLLERN, although 2 knots slower. Both yachts dwarfed the elderly paddle-yacht VICTORIA & ALBERT II, not only in size but in modern design, and it was these arguments more than anything which swayed Queen Victoria.

As she wrote to Lord Salisbury, her Prime Minister;

> VICTORIA & ALBERT is no longer in accord with our dignity as the head of a great maritime State, and is the subject of continuous comment among our relations on the Continent.[31]

Sir William White, Director of Naval Construction, and his staff at the Admiralty were overwhelmed with work building warships, but it was desired that the new yacht should be designed by him and built in a Royal Dockyard. Early in January 1897 discussions were held between Sir William, Vice-Admiral Sir John Fisher (the Controller) and Vice-Admiral Sir John Fullerton (Flag Officer Royal Yachts) regarding the features required in a new yacht. A model was prepared, and shown to the Queen at Windsor, where Her Majesty had only one comment. She wished the staircase to be high, for when she was being carried up in her chair she felt as if she would bump her head – 'she knew it was impossible, but she had the feeling'.[32] The Queen was assured a lift could be installed.

In August Sir William travelled to Cowes to inspect the existing yacht and discuss with Admiral Fullerton details of accommodation. A few days later he took to Osborne a brass model of the proposed yacht in which the fittings were minutely shown, and it was much admired by the Royal Family. Her Majesty reluctantly gave her consent, and on 15 December 1897 the keel was laid at Pembroke, and provisionally called BALMORAL. Queen Victoria, however, was never to set foot on her great new yacht, although she saw her from Osborne.

VICTORIA & ALBERT III

Twin-screw schooner yacht, two funnels, three masts. Steel hull, sheathed in teak.

Laid down:	15 December 1897 at Pembroke.
Designer/builder:	Sir William White, KCB.
Launched:	9 May 1899, by HRH The Duchess of York, accompanied by HRH The Duke of Connaught.
Commissioned:	at Portsmouth, 23 July 1901.
Displacement:	5500 tons (deep draught)
Speed:	20 knots
Length:	430 feet – overall, 380 feet – between perpendiculars
Beam:	50 feet
Draught:	20 feet 6 inches – extreme
Engines & I.H.P.:	Two vertical triple expansion engines, built by Humphreys & Tennant & Co. Ltd. giving 11 000 I.H.P. Eighteen Belleville boilers
Coal stowage:	714 tons
Range:	2500 miles at 14 knots
Complement:	367, plus 40 royal servants
Disposal:	Broken up 1955
Remarks:	Last used as a Royal Yacht 1939. Accommodation ship at HMS EXCELLENT 1942-45. Refitted 1946, but never again used by the Royal Family

The yacht was of steel construction, clad with teak to maintain a more equable temperature within, and a smarter appearance without. She was 80 feet longer than her predecessor, and over twice the displacement. Engines more than four times as powerful drove the yacht at 20 knots through twin screws. Steam was provided by eighteen Belleville boilers, then at the height of their popularity, but soon to be superseded by improved designs; and so for most of her long life the yacht was to be the only Royal Naval vessel with these boilers. Coal stowage was doubled, and the crew increased by 130 to a complement of 367. Truly she was an impressive vessel.

The VICTORIA & ALBERT III was launched on 9 May 1899 by the Duchess of York (later Queen Mary), accompanied by the Duke of Connaught, Queen Victoria's son. The yacht was then berthed under the sheer-legs at Hobb's Point, where her engines, boilers and masts were fitted. After about six weeks the berth had to be vacated for fitting out the new cruiser HMS SPARTIATE, and there being no other jetty available the yacht was put into dry dock for completion.

Lieutenant Pelly (later Admiral Sir Henry Pelly, KCVO, CB) had joined the VICTORIA & ALBERT II that summer, and left with a party of officers and men to bring the new yacht to Portsmouth. He recounted in his autobiography:[33]

> The programme did not go according to schedule, for when the dock, wherein she was being prepared, was flooded (on 3 January), the yacht quietly began to heel over (to port), until she reached an angle of about twenty-five degrees. This was at about five-thirty in the morning, and the first I knew of it was gently slipping out of my bunk whilst everything in my cabin took charge and went crashing to leeward. Her top hamper had been too much for her stability – so she slipped off the blocks with her side against the dock walls, and in so doing forced the caisson open, which thereafter could not be closed. The result was that as the tide fell the yacht settled down in a very precarious position…
>
> The first idea was to try to keep her waterborne, and to the intense amusement of some of us the fire brigade of the dockyard were set to work to pump water into the dock, hoping thereby to defeat the tide, which was flowing out through the dock entrance. Meanwhile, all hands were set to work to find ballast to place in the yacht's bottom, and we dug up and used pig iron, which was in use as paving in the dockyard. I expect that pig iron is still to be found at the bottom of the yacht.

When the yacht began to list, 'The Marine guard immediately sounded the bugle call' and 'all ports and scuttles were closed'.[33a] It was as well they were, for the coaling-ports and circular side-scuttles of the lower deck were immersed… High tide having passed it was decided unsafe to attempt to move the yacht, and she remained canted in the dock while 105 tons of pig-iron and 200 tons of water were placed in the double bottom as near the keel as possible.

As soon as the incident had occurred the dockyard gates were shut with the hope of keeping things quiet, but of course the London papers had full accounts the next morning. The Queen was furious she had not been told, and then stated that nothing would ever induce her to go on board the new yacht – and of course she never did.

Sir William White was summoned from London, and arrived at 2am on the 4th at 'the bleak dock-side and saw the beautiful thing heeled over with naptha flares burning all round, a host of men climbing all over her and shouting angrily.'[34] He could not fail to sense the hostility in the air, for the incident was bound to damage the professional reputation of the dockyard. But he was generous in his praise for the steps taken, and damage to the yacht was slight; an indentation on either side of the bottom some eight inches deep and 24 feet long.

It was impossible to ballast the yacht in time for the next tide, but by the following morning's tide (on the 4th) the vessel was floated, and righted to about ten degrees. Lieutenant Pelly again:

> For a time the yacht remained on her side against the dock wall, and living on board was a very uncomfortable affair. Eventually weights were adjusted so that she could be got out of the dock and moored in the stream. Even then she had a very considerable and dangerous list. Coal-lighters were brought alongside, and I was left in charge with orders to get the ship on an even keel. That seemed easy enough, but to my horror, when she reached the upright, she started to heel over in the opposite direction. For some seconds it was most alarming, and I was more than thankful when she steadied at about ten degrees. Coal-lighters had to be shifted round to the other side, and further operations got the yacht on an even keel at last.

Pembroke Dockyard Archives

VICTORIA & ALBERT III

After undocking and with tugs holding her upright.

> It was quite obvious the ship was not sea-worthy, and before we could leave for Portsmouth a considerable amount of top-hamper had to be removed. The designers had apparently been aiming to build a Royal Yacht which could be used as a cruiser. The shutters all round the big saloon were of one-inch steel and the doors into it were three-inch – practically armoured doors. Everything had been built on very heavy lines, and one of the weights which had to be removed was a large hand capstan from the fore-castle. It had been built there as it was thought to be picturesque for the cables to be handled in the old-fashioned way.[35] I believe that something like four hundred tons was removed from the upper and main decks before the ship was declared fit to face the open sea. Amidst many prophecies that we should never reach Portsmouth we left Pembroke, and turned the ship over to the dockyard authorities.

During the passage a rough sea was encountered, but the yacht behaved well, and she later turned out to be an excellent and safe sea-boat, albeit with a peculiar motion. The inevitable Committee of Enquiry was set up, and found what was obvious to everyone, that the yacht was top heavy.[36] Sir William's original designs had been excellent, but his pressure of work at the Admiralty, centralised decision making, changes of staff and distance from Pembroke had all allowed the excess weight to creep in without checks.

For the Government, Lord Selborne spoke in defence of Sir William White, praising his 'very great' services to the country. ' ...and it is unfortunate that of the 220 ships... he designed, the only one in which any error in calculation existed was the one most calculated to draw public attention to it'.[37] Sir William would have none of it, and accepted full responsibility. He was formally censured by the Admiralty, and retired a broken man. He left behind the finest navy in the world, and surely one of its most elegant yachts. After carefully rechecking all the weights and following her alterations Sir William was to write in October 1901:

> It may be asserted confidently that there is no safer vessel afloat. Her stability as completed is in all respects most satisfactory.[38]

(A detailed account of this incident is given in *Royal Yachts* pp 297-305.)

There is an old chestnut that the Admiralty borrowed the plans of the Tsar's yacht – the STANDART – for the VICTORIA & ALBERT III; and that one of the reasons for her initial lack of stability was that no one knew if the plans were metric or imperial. Clearly implausible, but there is an almost uncanny similarity between the VICTORIA & ALBERT when first launched and the STANDART. Sir William White certainly was swamped with work, and the British and Russian Royal Families were close. However, I have checked most thoroughly, and can find absolutely no documentary evidence to support the story. I am certain the Admiralty – and especially Queen Victoria – would not have sanctioned such plagiarism of plans at a time when Britain was in intense naval competition with Russia, and the story remains just that – a story.[39]

The Russian Royal Yacht STANDART.

Captain Augustus Agar, VC, served in the VICTORIA & ALBERT III as a Lieutenant Commander in 1924-5, and wrote in his autobiography:[40]

> She had lovely lines, clipper bows with a wooden bow-sprit, a graceful counter beautifully ornamented with scroll work, white upper decks, black hull and three masts with a slight rake on each. Teak planking was fitted to give the hull a good surface for painting, and relieved by two lines of carved gilt roping running round the sides with square ports instead of portholes in between. Our sailors and the dockyard mateys took the greatest pride and delight when carrying out painting and gilding the scroll-work with gold-leaf which was a skilled job. When finished and ready for service the V. & A. looked a picture, whatever may have been her other drawbacks.

The Prince of Wales certainly did not consider the new yacht lovely, for in October 1900 he described her as 'simply hideous, far too large and unwieldy and draws too much water'. A few weeks later, however, he modified his opinion, and stated, 'I believe the new Royal Yacht is perfectly safe and she may be made

VICTORIA & ALBERT III

After lightening and as commissioned.

comfortable but I fear she will always be ugly.' He was later to alter his opinion still further, and was certainly to make great use of her.[41]

The total cost of the VICTORIA & ALBERT was £512 034, including the alterations following the incident at Pembroke. She certainly was comfortable, quiet and luxurious, and proved a safe and sea-worthy vessel. 'There was no possible question of her seaworthiness… (but) …the yacht, like her predecessor the V. & A. II, had a corkscrew motion of her own in a bad sea-way, with an unpleasantly sharp roll.'[41a]

Yet despite Sir William White's assertions as to her stability, it was still considered safer to carry her boats 'outboard' instead of 'inboard' which placed a strict limitation as to the amount of heavy weather the ship could stand without damage being done to the boats. On one occasion in 1925 when on passage from Gibraltar to Genoa the yacht encountered a full gale, and 'to save our boats – beautifully painted with enamel – we had to "heave to" at dead slow speed for two days, during which we made no more than 40 miles distance over the ground (less than one knot).'[41b]

Luxurious she certainly was, as the following descriptions of the State apartments will show. But it was luxury without ostentation, and the good taste displayed by Prince Albert in the previous yacht was carried over to the new one. Queen Victoria had directed that as many as possible of the fittings of the old yacht should be transferred to the new one, and that wherever practical the same arrangements made for the Royal Family and their suite.

Lieutenant Commander Agar again:

> The internal construction and arrangements of the V. & A. naturally centred round the royal apartments. They followed very closely those of her predecessor. The reception rooms and dining saloon were on upper deck level, while the cabins and other private suites and rooms were one deck below. Ample space therefore had to be allowed on the upper deck for receiving guests, making presentations and so on. For this purpose, the upper deck from right aft as far as the bridge of the ship was fitted with carpets. These had to be taken up by sailors whenever it rained and included two strips, one for each side of the ship, 200 feet long, and known by the men as 'the serpents'.[42] Above the upper deck, and on boat deck level, four small sun pavilions known as tea-houses took the place of the boats which would normally have been stowed inboard. These small pavilions trapped all the sun available, and being sheltered from the wind with an all-round view, were very cosy indeed.
>
> The wardroom and officers' cabins were under the bridge. These were most comfortably furnished and upholstered, but following the Victorian tradition there were no bathrooms. I had my bath every morning in a small tin tub brought into my cabin by Watts, my marine servant, with two cans of water; and as far as I can remember everyone else did the same, including most of the royal suite.
>
> The men's quarters were forward of the bridge. They were quite comfortable but rather cramped at sea, because we took on a few extra staff when 'on service', plus the Royal Marine band for which accommodation had to be found. At that time we were the only ship in the navy allowed a 'wet' canteen, i.e., the men were allowed to have their own beer on board and of course never abused the privilege.
>
> There were about thirty Court servants of varying degree, ranging from the sergeant butler to the lesser kitchen staff. Except for a few upper servants their quarters were very cramped, but they never complained, and the discipline they kept amongst themselves was truly fine. Never have I seen servants who knew so exactly what 'service' was and took real pride in their job without presumption or reward.
>
> There were 14 cabins for guests, with a further 7 for their maids and valets. In the stern the original Royal Household dining-room was converted at the command of King Edward into three cabins; one for three servants, one for the Superintendent of Police, and one as a Post Office.[43]

The following photographs date from 1932, but the furnishings and fittings were practically unchanged since the yacht was completed.

On the upper deck was a pavilion containing (from forward) the smoking room, reception lobby and dining room.
Access to the main or State deck was down a splendid staircase to the State corridor, off which opened (going forward on the starboard side):

The King's writing room
The King's dressing and bathrooms
The King's bedroom
The Queen's bedroom
The Queen's dressing and bathrooms
The Queen's dresser's cabin

Smoking room.

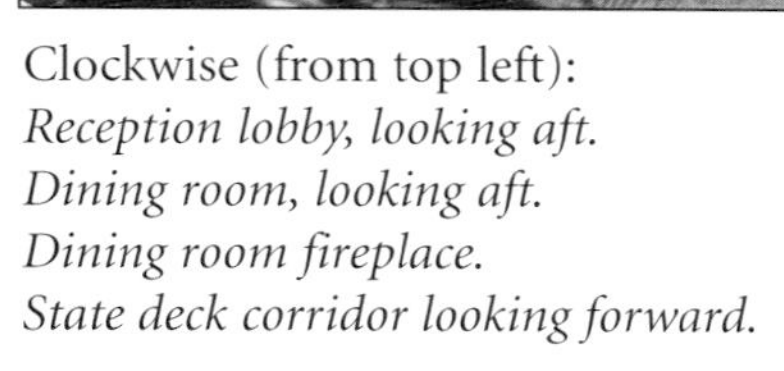

Clockwise (from top left):
Reception lobby, looking aft.
Dining room, looking aft.
Dining room fireplace.
State deck corridor looking forward.

Clockwise (from top left):
State deck corridor looking aft.
King's writing room.
King's bedroom.
King's dressing room.

Clockwise (from top left):
A lady in waiting's bedroom.
Princess's bedroom.
Drawing room.
Queen's bedroom.

Clockwise (from top left):
Sickbay.
Upper-deck staircase.
Hand-steering wheel and binnacles.
Wardroom.

On the port side were the Prince and Princesses bedrooms, the drawing room and dressers'/valets' cabins. Members of the Royal Household were accommodated aft of the entry-ports; royal servants on the deck below that. The yacht's officers and crew were forward of the funnels; conditions for the crew were cramped and basic, and even the officers had to have a tub brought into their cabin for bathing.

TRINITY HOUSE

Trinity House holds the traditional privilege of Royal Escort, in which the TRINITY YACHT, and no other vessel including warships, precedes the sovereign in pilotage waters.

This prescriptive right was founded in 1822 when George IV visited Scotland in the ROYAL GEORGE, but only after an acrimonious row between the Navy Board and Trinity House. Captain William Mingaye, Commander of the ROYAL GEORGE, objected to the level of fees previously charged for pilotage of the yacht, and turned off the ROYAL GEORGE both pilots submitted by Trinity House. A compromise was eventually reached whereby two approved pilots, accompanied by the Elder Brethren, embarked in the TRINITY YACHT and preceded the Royal Yacht to Scotland. The privilege is now only exercised on ceremonial occasions.

The splendid photograph below of three paddle-wheel yachts at speed was clearly not a ceremonial occasion. For it shows the VICTORIA & ALBERT II leading the ALBERTA and IRENE – the Trinity House yacht – from Portsmouth to Cowes, with Queen Victoria embarked in the VICTORIA & ALBERT II. Note the yachts are not in line astern; was this because the paddle-wheels preferred undisturbed water?

TRINITY HOUSE

Three paddle-wheel yachts at speed – The Trinity House Yacht IRENE *(left), together with the Royal Yachts* ALBERTA *and* VICTORIA & ALBERT II.

EDWARD VII (1901-1910)

After so many years of waiting in the wings, Edward was at last King, but he reigned for a brief nine years. He inherited from Queen Victoria a fleet of five yachts, including the largest Royal Yacht in the world, albeit not quite completed. In addition to the VICTORIA & ALBERT III there were the very elderly VICTORIA & ALBERT II, built in 1855; the paddle-yacht OSBORNE II, finally commissioned in 1874; the ALBERTA, built in 1863; and the maid-of-all-work, the ELFIN, built in 1848. The four yachts in commission had a total of one hundred-and-sixty-four years' service to their names, for Queen Victoria, as well as disliking change, expected value-for-money from her yachts. The new King continued this tradition of economy, for he directed the ROYAL GEORGE to be paid off, officers and men henceforth being required to live on their yachts.[1] As Prince of Wales, the King had used the OSBORNE II largely as his own yacht, but his great love, among others, was the Racing Cutter BRITANNIA, and this would appear an appropriate place to recount her story.

It is now more than one hundred years since BRITANNIA was built in 1893, but she remains one of the best remembered and best loved of Royal Yachts. Her building marked not only a transition in yacht design from the 'plank-on-edge' with huge keels and vast clouds of more or less efficient canvas, but revitalised the sport of large cutter racing. The transition did not occur with BRITANNIA alone, but she created the strongest impression on yachtsmen in her first season. She and her contemporaries were built to skim over the waters, not plough through them, and with her advent the old, slow yachts died.

> For King Edward (then Prince of Wales) the great designer Watson produced his masterpiece, for the big cutter BRITANNIA has remained the most noteworthy racing-yacht of her time, and is one of the most graceful ships the world has ever seen.[2]

To those of us accustomed to the loveliness of her lines it comes as a surprise that she and her contemporaries were at first universally condemned as 'hideous machines'. Dixon Kemp, writing in *The Field*, said:

> The feature in the new cutters which made the greatest impression on the spectators was undoubtedly the 'finish off forward'. The general verdict appeared to be that it was gratuitously ugly; and yet, after all, the form of a stem or cutwater is a matter of taste.[3]

The Prince of Wales's interest in yachting was triggered off whilst watching the racing for The Queen's Cup at Cowes from on board the FAIRY in 1864. In the following twenty years he had seven yachts,[4] and when Commodore of the Royal Yacht Squadron in 1892 he commissioned G.L. Watson to design for him a first-rate cutter, with the firm intention of revitalising the sport, which in Britain had been in decline.

King Edward VII, The Prince of Wales (George V) and Prince Edward of Wales (Edward VIII).

THE RACING CUTTER BRITANNIA

Designer:	G.L. Watson.
Builder:	D & W Henderson of Glasgow.
Registered:	19 May 1893.
Tonnage:	159 tons displacement. 221 tons Thames measurement
Length overall:	122 feet 6 inches
Loadwater line:	88 feet
Beam:	23 feet 7 inches
Draught:	16 feet 3 inches
Mast height:	164 feet, deck to truck, Bermudan rig
Boom:	91 feet (1893)
Spinnaker boom:	66 feet (1893)
Sails:	10 384 square feet (1893); sails made throughout her life by Ratsey & Lapthorne
Complement:	30 men, plus captain and sailing master
Cost:	With sails and cabin fittings; under £8000
Disposal:	Sea burial 1936

BRITANNIA was of composite construction; steel frames with pitch-pine and American elm planking, with cedarwood topsides. Although the competition was keen to build light yachts, George Watson did not go too far in the direction of light material or in the reduction of quantity used in her construction. This is borne out by the fact that all her contemporaries were gone by 1922, BRITANNIA being the sole survivor until her sea-burial in 1936.

BRITANNIA sailed her first race, and won, on the Thames on 25 May 1893, with the Prince of Wales on board, and went on to win 20 first prizes from 38 starts that season. Such was her success that she raised widespread excitement in yachtsmen and public alike for her second season in 1894. Starting on the Riviera in March she followed the large cutter 'circuit', handsomely winning most of her races. During Clyde Fortnight in July, crowds lined the shores everywhere, and an immense fleet of steamers and boats followed the races; indeed, the Royal Clyde Yacht Club steamer was 'dangerously crowded'. Over the 50-mile course there was but 67 seconds difference at the finish; VIGILANT, the American larger yacht, crossed the line first, but BRITANNIA won on points.

It was in 1896 that the German Emperor built his cutter METEOR II – British designed, built, crewed and skippered – with the express purpose of beating BRITANNIA. A foot longer than BRITANNIA, METEOR carried an extra 2000 square feet of canvas under the amended Y.R.A. rules. The appearance at Cowes of the German Emperor, with his overbearing manners and open discourtesy to his uncle may well have hastened the Prince's decision to sell BRITANNIA. 'The Regatta used to be a pleasant recreation for me,' he said. 'Since the Kaiser takes command it is a vexation.'[5]

This is not the place to detail the rating changes imposed by the Y.R.A., but they effectively killed large cutter racing. At the end of the 1897 season the Prince of Wales hauled down his racing colours, and his famous yacht was sold.[6]

In 1902 BRITANNIA was sold back (again) to the Prince of Wales, now King Edward VII, and she remained in royal ownership until her end. As King he never raced her, but under reduced rig she continued as a cruiser, and His Majesty seldom missed a day at Cowes. Wearing a panama hat, smoking a cigar, he would sit in a wicker chair by the doghouse, Queen Alexandra by his side.

The VICTORIA & ALBERT was not designed nor intended for ocean passages, and the practice grew of chartering liners and equipping them as Royal Yachts when longer tours were planned. In late 1900 the Duke

The Racing Cutter BRITANNIA

Oil by W.L. Wyllie – 'Britannia wins the Kaiser's Challenge Shield 1893.'

and Duchess of Cornwall and Kent (later George V and Queen Mary) had contemplated a tour of Australia and New Zealand to thank the colonies for their support in the South African War. Queen Victoria's death had obviously delayed the voyage, but in 1901 the steamship OPHIR, of the Orient Line, was chartered and fitted out as a yacht for their Royal Highnesses.

OPHIR

Length:	482 feet
Beam:	52 feet 6 inches
Draught:	37 feet
Register tonnage:	6910 tons
Commissioned at:	Tilbury 26 February 1901

ALBERTA *leads* OPHIR *to sea, 16 March 1901.*

Petty Officer Harry Price, who was on board the whole voyage, wrote an account of the Tour:[7]

> with a complement of 125 bluejackets, 100 marines, 37 bandsmen, 20 boys, 7 engineer officers, 88 stokers, 2 pursers, 50 stewards, 9 cooks and assistant cooks, 3 bakers, 2 butchers, 1 laundryman and wife, 1 printer, 2 barbers. The whole under the command of Commodore A.L. Winsloe and 21 other officers… The ship's complement with the royal suite included would be about 525 all told.
> (2nd March)… took in several hundred tons of best hand picked coal… we were coaled by people from shore, the likes of which I had never seen done in home waters before. (Normally in the Royal Navy all the ship's company and junior officers helped with coaling; a long, hard, dusty process.)
> 11th March the Royal Yacht VICTORIA & ALBERT was berthed alongside the jetty astern of us.[8]
> 15th The King, Queen, Duke, Duchess etc. arrived. The next day the King conferred the Victorian Order on the men forming the guard of honour that rendered such valuable assistance at Windsor at the time of the burial of our late beloved Queen Victoria; (and) distributed medals to men from S. Africa.
> (16th March) About 4.30 in the evening we… proceeded slowly down the harbour, preceded first by the Trinity House yacht, and next by the ALBERTA with the King and Queen on board; eight torpedo boat destroyers in two lines one off each quarter brought up the rear; immense crowds of people lined the

> shores on both sides, and one could see handkerchiefs waving as far as the eye could reach... The ALBERTA still kept right ahead, till well out at Spithead; when she slowed down and dropped abrest (sic) of us. ...(then we) went full speed ahead, and we soon left the ALBERTA far astern.

The OPHIR was away for over six months visiting Australia, New Zealand, South Africa and Canada, doing much for diplomatic relations. On his return the Duke of Cornwall and Kent was created Prince of Wales, and in a speech at the Guildhall he said, 'although we travelled over 45 000 miles (with the exception of Port Said) we never set foot on any land where the Union Jack did not wave'.[9]

Whilst they were away the VICTORIA & ALBERT III was in the hands of Portsmouth Dockyard, finishing eighteen months of completion and alterations to reduce the top-hamper. Finally, she was commissioned at Portsmouth on 23 July 1901, and the very first entry in her log[10] is for that day, and records:

> 9am – lit fires in no 4 & 5 boilers.
> 10am – Commodore Hedworth Lambton commissioned ship and broke broad pendant.

Under his command the Commodore – soon to be promoted to Rear Admiral – had 19 officers, 151 petty officers and seamen, 51 marines, 119 engine room ratings and six boys, a total complement of 346. The yacht's first duty was to embark Edward VII when he crossed to Germany for the funeral of his sister the Empress Frederick.

A year before, as Prince of Wales, the King had described the yacht as, 'simply hideous, far too large and unwieldy and draws too much water'. A few weeks later, however, he modified his opinion, and stated, 'I believe the new Royal Yacht is perfectly safe and she may be made comfortable but I fear she will always be ugly.' After the inaugural passage to Flushing the King's Private Secretary reported, 'The King and Queen were very much pleased with the new Royal Yacht when they crossed in her to Flushing the other day. She certainly is most comfortable and luxurious and in these respects she beats the Russian and German yachts. I think too that her outward appearance has improved.'[11]

VICTORIA & ALBERT III

At Portsmouth, riding high after completion, but before loading boats and stores.

The yacht then proceeded to Gibraltar for sea-trials, which included allowing her to lie broadside to waves 25 feet high: 'The rolling was very moderate, mean angle of inclination to the vertical about 7 degrees only; and the maximum angle about 13 degrees.'[12] On board the yacht was the Portuguese Ambassador, who had apparently failed to inform anyone of the yacht's visit, and her arrival in the Tagus caused a considerable stir. The Ambassador hurried ashore to arrange for the King to visit the yacht, which he duly did, but in the meantime the delighted yacht's officers were 'free to go where we liked and how we liked without any official functions'.[13]

The VICTORIA & ALBERT III was affectionately known throughout the fleet as the 'V. & A.', and soon settled down to the pattern of her duties. Before being laid up for the duration of the Great War she made some 60 voyages, two-thirds of them to foreign ports. For in spite of his early misgivings Edward VII soon discovered the combination of speed, comfort and elegance much to his liking, as did Queen Alexandra, who made many cruises on her own.

The yacht was in regular attendance during Cowes Week, where she had her own moorings. She was invariably attended by a guardship and other Royal Yachts, including the racing cutter BRITANNIA.

On her return, the OPHIR was escorted from Land's End by the Channel Squadron of six battleships and six cruisers. On 1 November 1901 she was met at Spithead by the VICTORIA & ALBERT III with the King and Queen embarked, accompanied by the Trinity House yacht IRENE. The sea was too rough for the King and Queen to cross to the OPHIR, so after passing through the fleet anchored in two lines the OPHIR 'hove to for a few minutes to allow the Royal Yachts to enter and get berthed first.'

> In the evening a grand dinner was held on board the King's yacht, the OPHIR's band attending. ...the VICTORY made a unique spectacle for between her for (sic) and mainmast triced high up, like a sky sign, was the words Welcome Home in golden electric lights; a torpedo boat destroyer, berthed alongside of her, supplied the motor power. Out at Spithead the Channel fleet looked grand, clothed with electricity.[14]

In March 1902 the King and Queen, embarked in the VICTORIA & ALBERT, laid the foundation-stone of the new Royal Naval College at Dartmouth, then the King alone visited the West Country and the Scilly Isles. In May the Duke of Connaught sailed in the Royal Yacht to Bilbao, from where he attended the coronation of King Alphonso XIII at Madrid. And later in the year, after his illness which had caused the cancellation of his coronation, King Edward VII cruised round the Isle of Wight whilst convalescing.

The Coronation Review took place on 16 August 1902, the first time a review had been staged for a coronation. Following it the yacht sailed for a cruise to Scotland, calling at Portland, Milford Haven, the Isle of Man, and various places on the west coast of Scotland. Their Majesties disembarked at Invergordon for Balmoral, and the yacht sailed for Queensferry ready to embark Queen Alexandra for her autumn cruise.

In the nine years of his reign Edward VII made extensive use of the VICTORIA & ALBERT as a floating palace, visiting many British and European ports. He much enjoyed entertaining, and was a charming, if demanding, host, for standards were kept as high afloat as they were on shore. The food and wine were of the best, and dinner on board was usually 12 courses. The men dressed in white tie, tails and decorations, while the ladies wore long evening dresses with diamonds and 'every rock in the book'.[15] The King was served first, and being a serious and fast eater, he invariably finished first, when his plate was immediately cleared, as were those of everyone else. Thus the unfortunate guest served last often had time for a scant few mouthfuls before his plate was removed! The King took some 30 servants to sea with him, including an Arab boy whose sole task was to provide His Majesty with a constant supply of his favourite coffee. Mountains of luggage also went, for even on a weekend stay the King could take as many as 40 suits and uniforms and 20 pairs of boots and shoes. And of course the King was accompanied everywhere by his favourite fox-terrier Caesar, whose temperament was decidedly unfriendly. Lord Hardinge, who accompanied the King in 1903, recalled:

VICTORIA & ALBERT III & OPHIR

Oil by Eduardo de Martino – 'Victoria & Albert and Ophir in the Solent, 1 November 1901.'

> Whenever I went into the King's cabin, this dog always went for my trousers and worried them, much to the King's delight. I used not to take the slightest notice and went on talking all the time to the King, which I think amused His Majesty even more.[15a]

Some of the present Queen's corgis have similar tendencies, and, as with everything else connected with Royal Yachts, one is reminded of the continuity over the centuries. For it was a courtier of Charles II who on being bitten by one of the King's spaniels exploded, 'God bless Your Majesty, but God damn your dogs!'

As Prince and Princess of Wales, Their Majesties had regularly cruised the Mediterranean each spring on board the OSBORNE II, and they now continued this pattern in the VICTORIA & ALBERT III. The goal was Corfu or Athens, where Her Majesty would meet her brother, the King of the Hellenes. Summer duties invariably included Cowes, and usually ended with an autumn cruise with Queen Alexandra to Christiana, where she visited her daughter, the Queen of Norway, and then on to Copenhagen to call on her relations in Denmark. Incidentally, the Mediterranean cruises involved an escort of two cruisers for the King, but only one when the Queen alone was embarked; this also applied to her Norwegian cruises. In addition the King was escorted by two to four destroyers, mostly connected with His Majesty's mails and the King's messengers.

At the end of March 1903 the Royal Yacht took the King to Lisbon, where, on 2 April, King Don Carlos I of Portugal came on board, being conveyed in the State barge, said to be 100 feet in length. It was built in the eighteenth century, with a Braganza dragon as figurehead, and was 'rowed by eighty bargemen dressed in picturesque red shirts with antiquated red-and-gold bonnets'.[16] The cruise continued to Gibraltar, Algiers and Malta, where the King reviewed 8000 men from the Mediterranean Fleet, including 1500 Marines, ashore at the Marsa. HMS BACCANTE's ship's company was led by its pet donkey, and midshipmen on bicycles acted as orderlies. Next day the VICTORIA & ALBERT was escorted to sea by eight battleships, six cruisers and four destroyers; the cruise continued to Surcease and Rome, from where the King returned home overland.

In 1904 a visit was made to Germany, the yacht entering the Kiel Canal on 24 July. A squadron of cavalry escorted the yacht, the detachments being changed about every 12 miles; much amusement was given to sailors on the yacht when some of the cavalry became bogged down in soft ground, the riders tumbling over their horses' heads. Following the visit to Germany the VICTORIA & ALBERT was at Cowes; then in September Queen Alexandra made a cruise to the Norwegian fjords, and on to Copenhagen.

Although the old VICTORIA & ALBERT II had been paid off in December 1901, and most of her fittings transferred to the new yacht, King Edward delayed issuing the order for her final demise. Finally, in 1904, he gave it, and the old yacht was broken up and burnt, half a century after she was laid down.

The following year, 1905, the King reviewed the English and French fleets at Spithead, for His Majesty had done much to promote the Entente Cordiale between the two countries. That same year the ROYAL GEORGE was finally broken up, the King instructing that the wood-carving and all ornamental work should be stored pending his decision on its distribution.[17] The yacht had given eighty-eight years' service under five monarchs; true, she had been an accommodation hulk for officers and men of the Royal Yachts since 1843, but she had remained in commission all that time.

An extended spring cruise was made in 1906, the King and Queen embarking at Marseilles, from where they sailed to Sicily. At Messina the destroyer sent to Naples for mails returned empty-handed owing to the severe eruption of Vesuvius, and the yacht continued to Corfu. There, in April, they met with the battleship RENOWN, flying the standard of the Prince of Wales, recently returned from his Indian tour.

That summer the yacht took the Prince and Princess of Wales to Norway for the coronation of King Haakon VII and Queen Maude (daughter of Edward VII). And of course there was always Cowes.

VICTORIA & ALBERT III *transiting the Kiel Canal 24 June 1904, escorted by a squadron of cavalry.*

King Edward VII in Cowes rig.

ROYAL GEORGE, *1817, being broken up in 1905.*

By 1906 the OSBORNE II was nearly forty years old, and a paddle-wheeler to boot, but a smaller yacht would always be needed for short passages. And so the ALEXANDRA was laid down, designed along the lines of the VICTORIA & ALBERT, but about one third her size.

ALEXANDRA

Twin-screw yacht, two funnels, three masts.

Laid down:	March 1906 at Glasgow – Messrs A. & J. Inglis' Shipyard.
Designer:	Sir Philip Watts, Director of Naval Construction.
Launched:	30 May 1907, by HRH The Princess Louise, Duchess of Argyll.
Commissioned:	at Portsmouth, 7 May 1908.
Tonnage:	2050 tons
Speed:	18.86 knots
Length:	275 feet (between perpendiculars)
Breadth:	40 feet
Draught:	13 feet
Engines & I.H.P.:	Two turbines, by Messrs Parsons Three boilers by Messrs Yarrow 4500 I.H.P.
Coal stowage:	250 tons
Complement:	172
Disposal:	Paid off at Portsmouth 9 June 1922. Sold 1925. Sunk 1940

ALEXANDRA, 1907

Leaving Portsmouth, Royal Standard flying.

The ALEXANDRA was named after King Edward VII's wife, Queen Alexandra, daughter of the King of Denmark. The yacht made numerous cross-Channel passages as well as further afield.

The ALEXANDRA's first duty in 1908 was to accompany the VICTORIA & ALBERT III on a visit to the Emperor of Russia at Reval, and as the *Penny Illustrated Paper* commented:

> The police supervision of the harbour has been very severe, and the fisherfolk are grumbling at the interference with their livelihood. Every craft in the harbour, from open boats to merchant steamers, was practically seized by the authorities. No vessel could enter or leave the port without the most rigid scrutiny. At night the coast was illuminated for miles by means of tar barrels placed on lofty posts along the cliffs. …hotel accommodation was at a premium, and many new-comers had to sleep in the corridors.

During the Great War her crew – along with that of the VICTORIA & ALBERT III – were used to commission the battleship AGINCOURT; on conclusion of hostilities the men returned to their yachts. For reasons of economy ALEXANDRA was laid up in 1922,[18] her last duty being to take King George and Queen Mary across the Channel on a State visit to the King and Queen of the Belgians. The ALEXANDRA was sold to the Norwegian Shipping Company of Trondheim in 1925, converted to a cruise liner and renamed the PRINCE OLAF. She was sunk during the German invasion of Norway in 1940.

Sport in general and yachting in particular owed much to Edward VII when Prince of Wales, and we have seen how he revitalised large yacht-racing with his cutter BRITANNIA. As King he did much to dispel national animosities by visiting many European capitals, and with his regular Mediterranean cruises the Royal Yacht played an important part.

We tend to forget how much influence the reigning monarchs had in the pre-Great War years, and Edward VII had very firm ideas as to how he should rule. He was not just a pleasure-seeking monarch, but strove to influence European and world affairs through his influence and wide network of crowned relations. There were of course the formal occasions, like fleet reviews, when the monarchs vied with each other displaying their yachts and warships. But there were also the informal occasions, such as Cowes, and we shall never know how far these monarchs shaped events, for the whole essence of their meetings was informality. Court protocol was then remarkably formal, and it was only on their yachts or at shooting parties that the monarchs could escape the rigid protocol. At Cowes there were no ministers or private secretaries hovering, albeit discreetly, and thus we have no records of these essentially private conversations. But the proverbial fly on the wall may well have heard an exchange between the Kaiser and King Edward: 'Uncle Bertie, what are you going to do about this Serbian situation? We can't let it go on as it is.' 'I know Willie, but I'm having trouble with my Foreign Secretary at the moment and just need to jolly him along for a bit.'
Or with the King of Spain: 'Look here Bertie, my chaps are wanting Gibraltar back – can't you and I sort something out?' 'Next race due to start soon Alphonso – must get aboard BRITANNIA. Why don't we chat after dinner?'
Nor must one underestimate the power of the queens, particularly Queen Alexandra, who did much behind the scene lobbying, and who had wide influence throughout Europe. On many of these occasions, formal State or informal, Cowes or cruises, the VICTORIA & ALBERT played a part.

The familiar pattern of spring cruise, Cowes and the autumn cruise followed in 1909, interspersed with a review on 31 July, the first at which battle-cruisers appeared. On 2 August the King again reviewed the fleet, this time accompanied by Tsar Nicholas of Russia.

In the spring of 1910 Queen Alexandra embarked for a Mediterranean cruise and a visit to her brother in Greece. The Queen returned overland from Venice, and a few days later, whilst the yacht was on passage to England, came news of the King's death on 6 May 1910.

Group photo on board VICTORIA & ALBERT III, *August 1909.*

Sitting:
The Hon. Charlotte Knollys
The Countess of Derby
The Princess Mary
The Prince of Wales (George V)
Queen Alexandra
King Edward VII (his fox terrier Caesar in front)
The Princess of Wales
The Prince Edward of Wales (Edward VIII)
The Princess Victoria

Standing:
The Chevalier Edward de Martino (marine artist)
Rear Admiral Sir Colin Keppel
The Marquis de Soveral
Lord Knollys
The Hon. Harry Stonor
Captain The Hon. Seymour Fortescue RN
Commander Sir Charles Cust Bt RN
Colonel F. Ponsonby

Right: *HMS RENOWN, 1895*

At Corfu, April 1906, flying the Standard of the Prince of Wales.

HM Yacht VICTORIA & ALBERT III

Above left: *Reval, 1908. King Edward VII and the Tsar of Russia.*
Above centre: *Cowes, 1908. King Edward VII and Prince Edward of Wales (Edward VIII) and, of course, Caesar.*
Above right: *'On board our yacht* BRITANNIA*'.*

All four images were taken by Queen Alexandra and sold as an album in aid of the Red Cross.

Group photo on board HM Yacht VICTORIA & ALBERT III, *c.1909.*

KING GEORGE V (1910-1936)

Although as keen a sailor as his father, whom he succeeded on 6 May 1910, George V's reign was so marked by momentous changes and the Great War that affairs of State often kept him from the sea. He inherited the yachts VICTORIA & ALBERT III, known throughout the navy as the 'V. & A.'; the three-year-old ALEXANDRA; the elderly ALBERTA and the yacht he loved best of all – BRITANNIA. In October 1900 King Edward VII had sold BRITANNIA to Sir Richard Bulkeley, Bt; two years later Sir Richard sold the yacht back to the King, but no bill of sale was produced, and it was never registered. In December 1910 Sir Richard wrote to the Registrar in Glasgow, for the Mercantile Navy List showed him still the owner, whereas she was now the property of His Majesty King George V. Steps were taken and BRITANNIA was registered in the new King's name on 11 March 1911.

Before the Great War the use of the 'V. & A.' settled into the familiar routine enjoyed by the new King's parents. His mother was certainly not one to have the precedents of so many years overturned – thus in that autumn Queen Alexandra sailed from Dundee on 19 September for her usual cruise to Copenhagen. In the spring of 1911 the VICTORIA & ALBERT took Queen Alexandra for her last cruise in the Mediterranean, visiting Corfu to meet the King of Greece and the German Emperor. The autumn cruise included Christiana as well as Copenhagen, as did that of 1912, but in 1913 Queen Alexandra only visited Copenhagen.

The first occasion King George V used the VICTORIA & ALBERT was to review the fleet at Torbay on 26 July 1910. The fleet then was an impressive 36 battleships, 34 cruisers, four scouts, 48 destroyers, seven submarines and six auxiliaries – 135 ships in all, manned by about 3140 officers and 52 000 men. 1910 was to prove a busy year for the VICTORIA & ALBERT; in October came the revolution in Portugal, and King Manuel fled to Gibraltar in his yacht AMELIA III. The VICTORIA & ALBERT was sent at speed to Gibraltar to embark the deposed King and his family, and bring them to exile in England.

The procedure of chartering ships for longer tours was continued later that year when the Union Castle liner BALMORAL CASTLE took the Duke and Duchess of Connaught to open the first Parliament of the Union of South Africa.

Then on 24 June 1911 it was the Coronation Review at Spithead:

> Early in the afternoon the VICTORIA & ALBERT cast off from the jetty. Preceded by the Trinity House yacht IRENE, and followed by the Royal Yacht ALEXANDRA, the Admiralty yacht ENCHANTRESS and the Commander-in-Chief's yacht FIREQUEEN, the Royal Yacht proceeded to Spithead, where the King reviewed the fleet assembled there under the command of Admiral Sir Francis Bridgeman. There were in all 167 ships of the British Navy, and, in addition, 18 foreign warships, representing all the important

King George V, Queen Mary, the Duke and Duchess of York (later King George VI and Queen Elizabeth).

maritime nations of the world. Unlike some earlier reviews none of the ships present had been specially commissioned or brought forward from reserve. The official programme stated that the 'naval estimates 1910-1911 total £40 603 700 – a prodigious sum it may appear for preserving the integrity of the Empire'.[1]

After the review the King and Queen visited Ireland, the Home Fleet acting as escort, which must have been an impressive sight; then it was on to Caernarvon for the Investiture of the Prince of Wales.

That summer saw the King, Queen Mary, Prince Edward and Prince George all on board BRITANNIA, cruising in the Solent. Queen Mary took great delight in sailing (if the sea was calm), and as the young princes were destined for naval careers, what better training ground than BRITANNIA. 'By the end of the season the two young princes were going up the rigging by the ratlines and down by the backstays, and shinning out to the gaff-end, so that they were soon as confident and secure aloft as they were on deck.'[2]

In the autumn of 1911 the P & O liner MEDINA left Portsmouth (11 November) with the King and Queen, bound for India. The ship transited the Suez Canal, where for the first time the three flags flown by a Royal Yacht were seen east of Suez. On the return journey a hawser fouled a screw at Malta, causing a delay of three days whilst the MEDINA was docked. Spithead was reached on 4 February 1912. (MEDINA was later torpedoed and sunk off Start Point, Devon, 28 April 1917.)

MEDINA

An etching by W.L. Wyllie – 'King George V and Queen Mary leaving Portsmouth, 11 November 1911, for the Indian Durbar, on board the P & O liner MEDINA, *chartered as a Royal Yacht.'*

In May of 1912 the King visited the fleet at Portland, where he watched many exercises, took a short trip in the submarine D4, and viewed several aeroplane flights, then in their infancy. In June Their Majesties visited Cardiff, and lived on board the Royal Yacht. And as always, there was Cowes.

This year marked the passing of the last of Queen Victoria's yachts, for the paddle-yacht ALBERTA, laid down in 1863 and employed on royal service ever since, was paid off on 30 March; she was broken up the following year.[3]

By 1913 big-class yacht racing had become prohibitively expensive, and the new Handicap Class became increasingly popular. King George V lent his weight to this class, and in the summer of 1913 BRITANNIA made her first appearance as a Handicap racer at Cowes and the South Coast Regattas; with BRITANNIA in the class it became immensely popular.

In 1914 BRITANNIA attended the Welsh, Irish and Scottish Regattas in June and July, taking eight first prizes in 13 starts, but affairs of State prevented the King sailing in her. That year there was to be no cruising for the VICTORIA & ALBERT, for the clouds of war were gathering. A test mobilisation of over 200 ships of the Home Fleet was held in July, the King informally reviewing the fleet on the 19th, and leading the ships to sea on the 20th on board VICTORIA & ALBERT. The war clouds broke when Britain declared war against Germany on 4 August. The VICTORIA & ALBERT III and ALEXANDRA were laid up under the care of the Keeper and Steward of the Royal Apartments, together with a small party of ship-keepers. The crews of the yachts were used to commission the AGINCOURT, one of two battle-ships completing for the Turkish Navy but which the Admiralty had commandeered. The crew did not change during those four years, and on the conclusion of hostilities the men returned to their yachts. The AGINCOURT served in the Grand Fleet throughout the war, and was present at the Battle of Jutland; she was sold in 1922.

BRITANNIA was laid up in a mud berth on the Medina; she was one of the lucky ones, for so many large yachts were left derelict, or never recommissioned.

Peace came in 1918, but for some eight million people it was too late – they would never see another sunrise. Gone also were two great yachts; for the Tsar of Russia's STANDART had become a minelayer, and the German Kaiser's HOHENZOLLERN lay idle from war's outbreak until scrapped in 1923. The VICTORIA & ALBERT remained as the only large Royal Yacht in Europe. She had steamed 100 791 nautical miles from her launching to the outbreak of the Great War, making more than 60 passages. The yacht was recommissioned in 1919, but apart from her almost annual presence at Cowes, she was used a scant 13 times in the next twenty years. It was as if the Great War had destroyed the desire to use such a large yacht, along with so many other things.

The following year, 1919, the battlecruiser RENOWN was fitted out as a yacht to carry the Prince of Wales to thank the Canadian people for their support in the Great War.[4] In 1920 the Prince sailed, again in the RENOWN, to Australia and New Zealand on a similar mission.[5] The ship was clearly a success as a Royal Yacht, for the Prince of Wales used her again in 1921/22 to visit India, returning to England via Japan and the Pacific.[6]

One area where the King was as enthusiastic as ever was his beloved BRITANNIA. In the post-war years yachting naturally had to take its place at the tail of more pressing priorities, but it was given just the stimulus required when the King decided to fit her out for the 1920 season.

The King and Queen made visits that year in the VICTORIA & ALBERT to the west coast of England and the Clyde ports, and on 12 July they transferred to the royal cutter for the first race of the Clyde Fortnight. In a stiff breeze BRITANNIA won that race, and went on at Cowes and the South Coast Regattas to beat such modern yachts as TERPSICHORE, MOONBEAM, WESTWARD and WHITE HEATHER in the Big Handicap Class. She took seven first prizes and five other prizes in 23 starts; a remarkable feat at twenty-seven years of age, and a great tribute to her designer. BRITANNIA's rig had been reduced for cruising by Sir Richard Bulkeley in 1900, and in this rig she was like a reefed yacht. And so in 1920 her mast was heightened by seven feet, increasing the sail plan back to almost its original area, but with important changes in the shape of the plan for both sails and rigging. The result of the alterations was a complete success, and she was driven in strong winds like the very devil, and never carried anything away; so much so that a good breeze and heavy seas became known as 'BRITANNIA's weather'.

The Prince of Wales leaving Portsmouth, 19 March 1920, on board the battlecruiser HMS RENOWN, *fitted as a Royal Yacht, en route to visit Australia and New Zealand.*

In 1921 the 'V. & A.' was used only three times,[7] and in 1922 but twice.[8] That same year was to be the last for ALEXANDRA, and she also was only used twice; her final duty being to carry King George and Queen Mary from Dover to Calais for a State visit to Belgium. For reasons of economy this elegant yacht was paid off at Portsmouth on 9 June 1922, and laid up until being disposed of three years later. The ALEXANDRA was sold to the Norwegian Shipping Company of Trondheim as a cruise ship in 1925, renamed the PRINCE OLAF, and sunk during the German invasion of Norway in 1940.

BRITANNIA was not in commission in 1922, for the previous year's rerigging and increase in mast height had been hard on the old vessel. Beyond renewing copper, and replacing the odd deck plank worn by scrubbing and scraping, nothing had been done to her hull since she was built; and so during that winter and the spring of 1923 she underwent a thorough refit at Cowes.[9]

In 1923 the VICTORIA & ALBERT only attended Cowes and the East Coast Regattas. No wonder one yacht officer wrote:

> My service in the Royal Yacht could not by any stretch of imagination be called 'arduous'.[10] It was in the same year that the King decided to end the system of 'Yacht promotions', whereby officers were automatically promoted out of the Royal Yacht, thus jumping the promotion queue. From then on the Admiralty submitted a short-list of officers, all of whom had been selected for promotion, to the King, who then made his own choice from the list. It was, like everything else that monarch did, a most wise and fair decision...[11]

Queen Mary only enjoyed sailing with the King in calm weather, but during the Clyde Regattas of 1923 there was a sudden gale, and the Queen remained below while King George helped on deck, for BRITANNIA's jib-topsail sheet had run out. The wire itself thrashed around the mast, beating a tattoo on deck and

King George V and Queen Mary embarking in the Royal Barge from VICTORIA & ALBERT III *at Cowes, 1928.*

threatening to injure anyone who got in its way. When at last all was secure the King sent a seaman below to enquire after the Queen.
'Well, how is Her Majesty?' asked the King.
The sailor doffed his sou'wester, but seemed at a loss for words.
'Well, what did she say?' shouted the King. 'Speak up!'
'Her Majesty said – "Never again, she's damned if she will!"' the sailor stammered, to the huge delight of his master.[12]
It must have been after this event that the Queen recorded in her diary one August:

> The BRITANNIA has just passed us by, and I saw the King looking very wet and uncomfortable in oil-skins. What a way to enjoy oneself.[13]

Lieutenant Commander Augustus Agar (later Captain Agar, VC) joined the yacht in January 1924:

> Once the highlight of Cowes Week was over the 'V. & A.' returned to Portsmouth to lay up for the winter or until required for her next service. Her crew of 22 officers and 367 men might be classed as being on the high side, but all ships which burned coal had to carry additional men to stoke the boilers, run the boats and so on. It was suggested that a conversion should be carried out to fuel oil, but King George refused to sanction the expense.
>
> The Royal Yacht had special customs and a special routine of its own. When the 'Royals' (as the Royal Family were termed) were on board, all officers and men were on duty, and took the greatest pride in the appearance of the ship, the boats and everything that had to be done. No noise of any sort was allowed and orders were given as far as possible by sign if they were necessary at all. It needed no order for the carpets to be taken up when it rained, or decks swept of coal smuts immediately on any shift of wind; men just appeared and did these things. Dozens of willing hands and eyes were always on watch to be of some service to the monarch when he was on board; and I am sure Queen Mary knew it for she had a most discerning eye for detail and service.
>
> Everyone on board loved the Queen. She enjoyed particularly Cowes Week on board the 'V. & A.' as this gave her the opportunity of visiting Princess Beatrice and special friends in the Isle of Wight and Lord Montagu of Beaulieu in Southampton Water while the King was sailing in BRITANNIA. Without in any way relaxing Court rules both King George V, and especially Queen Mary, carried with them a most charming informality when on board which endeared them to everyone.[14]

King George was ill with chest troubles during the winter of 1924/5, and so in mid-February the yacht sailed for Genoa to embark the King and Queen Mary.[15] The King was not at all keen on foreign travel, and had only reluctantly agreed to come on the cruise; he declared Naples to have a harbour 'full of dead dogs' and Malta to be a 'bloody place'. Having visited Naples, Syracuse, Taormina and Palermo, the cruise ended at Genoa six weeks later, on 23 April. Despite his previous misgivings the King kept saying, 'Well, well. Like all good things, one day they must come to an end. But we shall meet again at Cowes.'[16]

For the next six years the VICTORIA & ALBERT was only used for Cowes Week, where the King continued enthusiastically to race BRITANNIA against the other J-class yachts.[17]

In 1927 the battlecruiser HMS RENOWN was again used as a Royal Yacht when she conveyed the Duke and Duchess of York to Australia and New Zealand. The sea was so rough at South Island, New Zealand, that a tug had to be used to ferry the Duke out to the RENOWN, and as the Duchess recorded: 'I was glad to be on board when I saw my husband being thrown (literally) from the bridge of the tug onto our quarterdeck at Bluff. It looked most unpleasant, but he did not seem to mind much.'[18]

On the passage home across the Indian Ocean from Australia a raging fire broke out in RENOWN's boiler room which soon threatened to spread to the ship's main fuel tanks. The situation looked desperate, for the

VICTORIA & ALBERT III *leaving Portsmouth with HMS* VICTORY *in the foreground, 1911.*

sea was heavy, RENOWN was three days sailing from her escort, and her lifeboats had been smashed in a previous storm. Plans were made to abandon ship, but with the flames only feet away from the tanks the situation was controlled. Throughout it all the Duke and Duchess remained calm, and as he afterwards remarked to the King, 'Oil is a very dangerous substance for a fire and it might have been very serious.'[18a]

BRITANNIA had her rig altered for the fourth time for the 1928 season,[19] and by the end of it had sailed a total of 461 races, some 14 000 miles.

The King's illness prevented his attendance at Cowes during 1929, but writing in that year the then Yachting Editor of *The Field* commented:

> There is surely one thing that none of us can estimate. That is the beneficial influence upon the whole sport of yacht-racing due to the entry of King Edward when Prince of Wales, and King George with the great cutter BRITANNIA. Twice in the history of the sport this vessel has joined in our regattas round the coast. On each occasion in the year previous to her joining our beloved maritime sport… was at a low ebb.
>
> In 1892 everybody was saying the industry was declining, and the sport of first-class yacht racing was almost dead. Then in the following year the Prince of Wales built the BRITANNIA and hoisted his racing colours. The effect was electrical, the whole pastime immediately revived.
>
> Again, in 1919, times had changed. The First World War had so affected the whole industry of British yacht building that yachting people who loved the old sport were in despair. Again BRITANNIA came to the rescue '…from the day in 1920 when she began to try her fortunes against modern vessels the sport has revived. There are now so many yachts in commission that it is no easy matter to engage a crew!' (wages were then £3/week).[20]

In 1930 King George V resumed racing and cruising. At Cowes, with His Majesty on board and sailed by Sir Philip Hunloke, BRITANNIA won her 200th victory, a record which no other yacht in her class has equalled.

BRITANNIA's *last race, 1935.*

Beken Maritime Services Ltd

Throughout all the changes to her rig was the King's desire to do the best for the old yacht, for he loved her dearly, and took a keen interest in her. At sea, whenever on a passage to windward, the King would be on deck casting an appraising eye over all, or at the wheel; but when BRITANNIA settled down with the wind astern His Majesty would disappear into the doghouse with *The Times*. The King was also keen to further the sport of big-class yacht racing, as well as to use BRITANNIA as a pace-maker for Mr Sopwith's Americas Cup challenger ENDEAVOUR, much as his father had done for Sir Thomas Lipton's SHAMROCK. And so throughout the early Thirties the great yachts of the J-class[21] became familiar and well-loved sights in the Solent and off the south coast. At their head was BRITANNIA, a slim black hull, her clouds of snowy canvas poised between the sea and the sky.

Although BRITANNIA took part in other regattas, during this period the King usually only attended Cowes Week, living on board the VICTORIA & ALBERT, and joining BRITANNIA under way on racing days. 'She is fitted with a combination of lightness of structure, taste and comfort. The fittings throughout are of polished yellow pine and mahogany, with tapestries and cretonnes above the polished wood dado, the effect being extremely bright, cosy and unostentatious. The hull is black. The interior provides four guests' sleeping cabins, a spacious saloon, a cabin for the captain and sleeping accommodation for her entire racing crew of 30 hands, besides a galley and a pantry.'[22]

In 1932 the King, accompanied by the Prince of Wales and Prince George, visited the fleet assembled at Weymouth, the Princes flying their own aircraft to Portsmouth. The Royal Yacht sailed from Portsmouth on 11 July, and that evening steamed through the lines of the fleet. A royal salute was fired, and HM Ships manned ship and cheered as the yacht passed. The following days were devoted to exercises at sea, and one afternoon His Majesty embarked on the aircraft carrier COURAGEOUS to watch flying practice. Each afternoon there were sailing regattas, and each evening the King entertained flag officers and captains on board the VICTORIA & ALBERT. The Royal Pulling Barge, which had not been used for over twenty years, was used on the 12th to convey His Majesty when he visited the battleship HMS NELSON. On the last day of the visit, Thursday 14th, the Royal Yacht proceeded to sea with the fleet for a series of exercises; destroyer attacks on the battle fleet, submarines diving as a flotilla, smoke screens laid by aircraft and firing at a target were all witnessed by the King before the yacht returned that evening to Portsmouth.

In July the VICTORIA & ALBERT was, as usual, at Cowes with BRITANNIA, and for the next two years this was to be the only use of the yacht. It was about this time that an intriguing glimpse of life at Cowes Week is given. The American Gerard B. Lambert took not one but two yachts to Cowes, the big schooner ATLANTIC on which he and his guests lived, and the J-class YANKEE, which he had brought along to try at the summer regattas. Lambert was duly commanded to dine on board the VICTORIA & ALBERT, and his more Republican and irreverent friends lined up on deck to salute him into his tender. He made his first faux pas by attempting to board the Royal Yacht by the starboard gangway – reserved for the Royal Family only – and was waved off by a 'discreet arm' as he put it. At the entry port on the carpeted port gangway he was met by Sir Philip Hunloke, the sailing master of BRITANNIA, and ushered up the main staircase into the reception room. He and the other guests were shown the dinner-table seating plan by the Master of the Household so that everyone knew where they were sitting.

King George in dinner jacket and Queen Mary in a long gown and magnificent choker moved grandly down the line, shaking hands as their guests bowed and curtsied. Without more ado the Royal couple led the way into the dining-saloon, where Lambert was guest of honour on the Queen's right. On his other side was the wife of his yachting friend, Sir Ralph Gore, who soon put him at ease by promising to alert him whenever Queen Mary turned to speak to him. 'When you see the Queen turning,' said Lambert, 'just say "Lee-ho".' The system worked, reported Lambert, since the Queen, 'slower in stays, would make a more magnificent manoeuvre' than he would.

King George V in the Royal Pulling Barge at the Weymouth Fleet Review, 1932.

VICTORIA & ALBERT III, *with King George V embarked, leading the Home Fleet to sea, 14 July 1932. From left to right His Majesty's Ships* RODNEY *(battleship),* HOOD *and* RENOWN *(battlecruisers).*

The dinner drew to its leisurely conclusion, and the Queen and ladies retired to the drawing room on the deck below. The King and the gentlemen remained for cigars and port, and the King asked Lambert if he could visit the American's two yachts. The next day the King went all through the YANKEE, asking questions about each piece of unfamiliar equipment on the yacht. At one stage a passing vessel erupted in cheers as her passengers recognised the King hanging over the yacht's bows inspecting the forestay.[23]

The Silver Jubilee of King George V occurred in 1935, and His Majesty, accompanied by the Prince of Wales, the Duke of York and the Duke of Kent stayed on board the VICTORIA & ALBERT at Portsmouth from 15-17 July for the Silver Jubilee Naval Review and fleet exercises at Spithead. This was to be the last time the King used the yacht for an official occasion, although he and the Queen, together with the Duke and Duchess of York (soon to be King George VI and Queen Elizabeth), used the yacht during Cowes Week in early August.

Admiral Sir William O'Brien, KCB, DSC

THE SILVER JUBILEE REVIEW 1935

Oil by Rowland Langmaid – 'Victoria & Albert leads to sea the First Battle Squadron of the Mediterranean Fleet.' His Majesty's Ships QUEEN ELIZABETH, ROYAL SOVEREIGN, RAMILLIES, REVENGE *and* RESOLUTION.

During that winter two new masts and two booms were fitted to the VICTORIA & ALBERT, selected from the forests of Vancouver Island. One log was 106 feet long with a 20-inch top, the other was 96 feet long with a 22-inch top. The King was never to see them installed however, for on 20 January 1936 George V died.

The reign of King George V involved momentous change politically and socially, spanning as it did the traumas of the Great War. He saw the Union of South Africa, the Irish Free State settlement, the first Labour governments, the General Strike of 1926, the economic crisis of the Thirties, the statute of Westminster – whereby the Dominions were granted autonomy – and the 1935 Government of India Act, which led to elected Congress ministries in most of the provinces.

With such concern for affairs of State, it is no wonder this considerate and much-loved monarch could find little time to use the VICTORIA & ALBERT to the full. Unlike his father he was not at all fond of travel, and particularly not when it involved 'abroad'; George V much preferred to be by his own hearth. In racing BRITANNIA, however, the King found some short relaxation, and he thought of her to the end, for in his will he directed that if none of his sons wanted the yacht, she was to be given a sea-burial.

Mr Mason, the King's Steward, recounts the event:[24]

> It was at the Jubilee Review of 1935 that BRITANNIA made her farewell to the Solent. The next January the King was dead, but he had not forgotten his beloved yacht, for he left instructions she was to be given a sea-burial.
>
> It was a sad, simple little affair, that last launch from Marvin's yard at Cowes. The yard foreman had gathered a garland of wild flowers and draped them over her stem-head as she lay waiting on the slipway. A handful of schoolboys, brought there by a master with imagination, helped with the warps that guided her down the slipway. For once she seemed reluctant to leave the ways, but gradually she was got off into deep water.
>
> For two days she lay on her old buoy in the Roads, waiting. Her tall mast, her gear, wheel, compass, everything that had been part of her, had been taken from her. Much of it had been sold by auction, the money going to the George V Fund for sailors. £1025 went to the Fund; her 175-foot mast went to Britannia Royal Naval College; the 50-foot boom was erected as a flagstaff at Carisbrooke Castle. She was a slim black hull – nothing more.
>
> At midnight on 9 July they came for her – two destroyers out of Portsmouth Harbour (HM Ships AMAZON and WINCHELSEA). On board of them was a handful of men who had loved and served her. There was Sir Philip Hunloke, the late King's Sailing Master, Captain Turner, her skipper, Mr Fred Mason, the King's steward, and an old pensioner from Portsmouth Dockyard. They towed her round St Catherine's Point into the deep water, and then they pulled her up alongside one of the destroyers. A party went on board and put the explosive down below. They returned to the destroyer, and the two ships backed and waited. It was very early morning, and as the charge went off those on board the destroyers could just see some pieces fly into the air. They watched for a matter of four or five minutes until the entire hull had disappeared beneath the dark water. They turned the searchlight on her, but there was nothing there and the destroyers returned to Portsmouth in the dawn.

'We were,' said Mr Mason, 'a very sad party.'

King George V at the helm of BRITANNIA.

KING GEORGE VI (1936-1952)

EDWARD VIII – 1936

Edward VIII succeeded his father on 20 January 1936, but he reigned less than twelve months and was never crowned, for he abdicated on 11 December the same year.

As King he carried out his first official visit to the Royal Navy at Portsmouth on 30 June. Torrential rain (much needed, due to a drought) caused the cancellation of a parade at the Royal Naval Barracks, but the King much enjoyed a 40-knot trip in Fast Motor Boat, the first of a new class. A successful torpedo firing at HMS AMAZON was somewhat ironic, as she was one of the two escorting destroyers at the sea-burial of BRITANNIA the following month.

The King then landed at Whale Island, the gunnery school, and later inspected the Royal Marines at Eastney Barracks; according to *The Times*, this was the first inspection of the Marines by a reigning monarch. After lunch he inspected the VICTORIA & ALBERT following completion of her refit. Whilst on board he presented a silver cigarette case to Leading Rigger Batchelor, who for eight years had acted as signalman on the BRITANNIA. And from on board he gave the order to 'Splice the Mainbrace' to mark his visit.

The yacht then embarked on 8 July (no royalty embarked) for a short 'shake-down' cruise after her refit, calling at Weymouth Bay, Falmouth and Torbay before returning to Portsmouth on the 16th.

On 10 July, in accordance with the explicit instructions of King George V, the Racing Cutter BRITANNIA was given a sea-burial. (see p 211/2.)

That summer King Edward chartered the yacht NAHLINE (later King Carol of Rumania's LUCEAFARUL) and cruised the Mediterranean with Mrs Simpson.[1]

On 12 November the King visited ships of the fleet at Portland. Before lunch he boarded the NELSON, ORION, COURAGEOUS, ROYAL OAK and CAIRO; after lunch on board HMS NELSON it was the turn of the ROYAL SOVEREIGN, LEANDER, NEPTUNE and GUARDIAN, as well as the shore base, HMS OSPREY. Much climbing of gangways! His Majesty gave a dinner party for officers of the fleet on board the VICTORIA & ALBERT, and afterwards was present at a ship's concert on board HMS COURAGEOUS. He subsequently attended an At Home to officers of the fleet on board HMS NELSON before sleeping (one assumes thankfully) on board the yacht that night – the only time he did so as King.

King Edward VIII abdicated on 11 December 1936, and as the VICTORIA & ALBERT was laid up for the winter he left for exile the following morning in a warship, the destroyer HMS FURY.

GEORGE VI (1936-1952)

As a consequence of the abdication of Edward VIII, King George V's second son – the Duke of York – succeeded to the throne. His Majesty first used the Royal Yacht for his Coronation Review the following year, when he stayed on board her from 19-21 May 1937. The King was accompanied by Queen Elizabeth, Princess Elizabeth (now Queen Elizabeth II), and the Duke and Duchess of Kent (the King's younger brother).

In late July the King and Queen Elizabeth sailed in the VICTORIA & ALBERT from Stranraer to Belfast and back for their coronation visit to Belfast. BRITANNIA having been given a sea-burial, and being much preoccupied with the unexpected burden of the monarchy, King George VI did not attend Cowes Week, and the royal link with the Regatta was broken for almost twenty years.

In 1938 King George and the Duke of Kent stayed on board the Royal Yacht from 20-22 June at Weymouth for fleet exercises, and it was apparent that a new Royal Yacht was urgently needed. Although her engines were sound enough, the 18 Belleville boilers had been rendered obsolescent by improved designs soon after they were installed. Pressure had already been reduced for safety, resulting in curtailed speed, and although she had steamed relatively few miles, the yacht was now nearly forty years old.

Prime Minister Neville Chamberlain's Cabinet met in July, and in spite of the country being deep in recession with three million unemployed, the decision was taken to build a new Royal Yacht which could act as a hospital ship, at a cost of £900 000. Cabinet minutes record:

> In the course of the discussion the importance was emphasised of avoiding any possibility that the King might be exposed to criticism by building the yacht. The kind of argument that might be used for political discussion was that money was not available for the unemployed but could be... found for a Royal Yacht. The King was interested in the new yacht but did not want to press it if there was any risk of interrupting progress with rearmament.[2]

Outline drawings and plans for essential requirements for a new Royal Yacht were sent to leading shipbuilders, but the outbreak of war caused any such plans to be shelved. The following summer (1939) the King and Queen visited Canada and the USA, travelling out in the chartered RMAS EMPRESS OF AUSTRALIA and arriving at Quebec on 17 May. The visit was to elicit support from those two nations in the forthcoming war, and, unknown at the time, the escorting cruisers SOUTHAMPTON and GLASGOW carried a large amount of gold bullion for safe-keeping in Canada. Their Majesties returned in the EMPRESS OF BRITAIN, arriving back at Southampton on 21 June.[3]

Boy Seaman Stevens (later Lt Cdr Stevens, MBE, RN) joined the VICTORIA & ALBERT as one of six messengers for the 'Season' (1 May-1 October) on 1 May 1939. He recounts:[4]

> Our mess was small by any standards. Six lads, three each side of a small table, and when the outboard lads wanted out the rest had to shift. The for'ard mess bulkhead, made of five-ply, was hinged across the centre, and the top was let down so that we could sling our hammocks across the ship's company bathroom. Hardly hygienic, but we only used this mess at sea when 'themselves' were on board. Our harbour mess was a space about 17 feet square edged with small seat lockers. This was the sea mess for the Royal Marine Band and how they all managed to fit into that space I never did find out. They must have eaten and slept in four watches or standing up.
>
> We reported to the stores for an issue of Yachtsman's uniform, Jack Dusty making the point that this was no ordinary purser's kit but had been personally provided and paid for by His Majesty himself. I was

The EMPRESS OF AUSTRALIA *and* EMPRESS OF BRITAIN, *1939 (used as Royal Yachts to visit Canada and the USA before the outbreak of war).*

really chuffed with the shoes with watered silk bows – if Mum could see me now!! Doeskin, serge and white drill was issued in lengths and taken to the Sailmaker to be made up into uniforms. I recollect that he had a tailoring business on the Gosport side because we went to his house for a final fitting. Now, at last, we were dressed for the part and could sally forth like swans amongst the geese.

The ship was on Canteen Messing. We purchased our scran from the cheapest sources and, being good scroungers, always had a welcome rebate from the pusser. There were a couple of anomalies in that meat was ordered from a civilian butcher boy who came aboard once a week to take orders; and that the poor old Chief Cook had to work out in which order to cook the large variety of dishes presented to him each forenoon. To spoil a dish was to invite keel-hauling!! At that time the V. & A. was the only HM Ship with a beer bar for the ship's company. It was forbidden to the boys of course, but most evenings a fanny full of beer appeared on our mess table for medicinal reasons – to help prevent scurvy!!

At colours every day, except at sea, the boys handled the hoisting of the Jack. This involved walking out onto the bowsprit, sitting aside with each foot on a whisker guy, and securing and hoisting the Jack on a small, about eight foot, mast. Sounds good, but you were facing for'ard and if there was a breeze you couldn't hear what was going on behind you. Could provide an embarrassing situation, but we didn't let the side down.

The ship was fitted with a foresail which was hoisted to assist steering. I saw it used only once but I believe that she was quite difficult to handle with the large amount of top hamper that she carried, huge steel masts and funnels etc. I was told that she had more than her share of ballast and I know that she rolled in 'wet grass'. If you watched the bowsprit it would describe three circles and, at the top of the third circle, would give a shudder and go round the opposite way, repeating the process – oops!! She was reputed to achieve 13.5 knots flat out but was never pushed too hard because the boilers were getting thin. The fuel was coal and 'coal ship' was a big evolution conducted with the usual yacht efficiency and minimum of fuss. All hands turned to in a variety of rigs to man the coal lighters which were positioned alongside large access ports in the ship's side. The coal was shovelled into wicker baskets which were manhandled up planks, through the ports and into the coal bunkers. Although this unique method was cleaner than hoisting onto the upper deck the coal dust seemed to penetrate everywhere and, in general, took at least a week to finally clear.

The day's work in harbour started about 8.30 when the ship's company came on board, changed into their working rig and got on with their allotted tasks. No pipes, bugles or divisions, just quiet efficiency. At about 1500 the ship's company went ashore leaving only the duty part of the watch on board. The fire party mustered at 1700 in accordance with Dockyard Regulations and that was the only muster of the day. The Fire Party appeared like magic on the upper deck, were called to attention, reported to the Duty W.O. who ordered them to give the port or starboard gash chute a good wash out thus ensuring the fire main was functioning and avoiding splashing the highly polished paintwork.

I have a special regard for small boats and used to drool over the beautifully maintained gig, galley, the open cutter with a small steam engine in the bows, the steam barge with its brass funnel and brass dolphins, and, of course, the Royal Barge. All of these craft, including the large Royal Barge, used to be hoisted by hand and, to liven the proceedings and give us a step, there was a Ship's Fiddler. Not the Canteen Manager I hasten to add, but a second-class Petty Officer who wore a badge of a crown over a single anchor. He only came aboard when we went to sea – a sort of honorary job, I believe.

The ship's anchoring arrangements were very impressive. Two 3-ton Admiralty pattern anchors were hoisted out on special davits to be suspended from a slip from Clump Cat Heads. They were slipped by using a Commander – a long-handled hammer. There were no navel pipes, the cable running uncovered through the for'ard messdecks and the cry 'Stand clear of the cable' had some meaning.

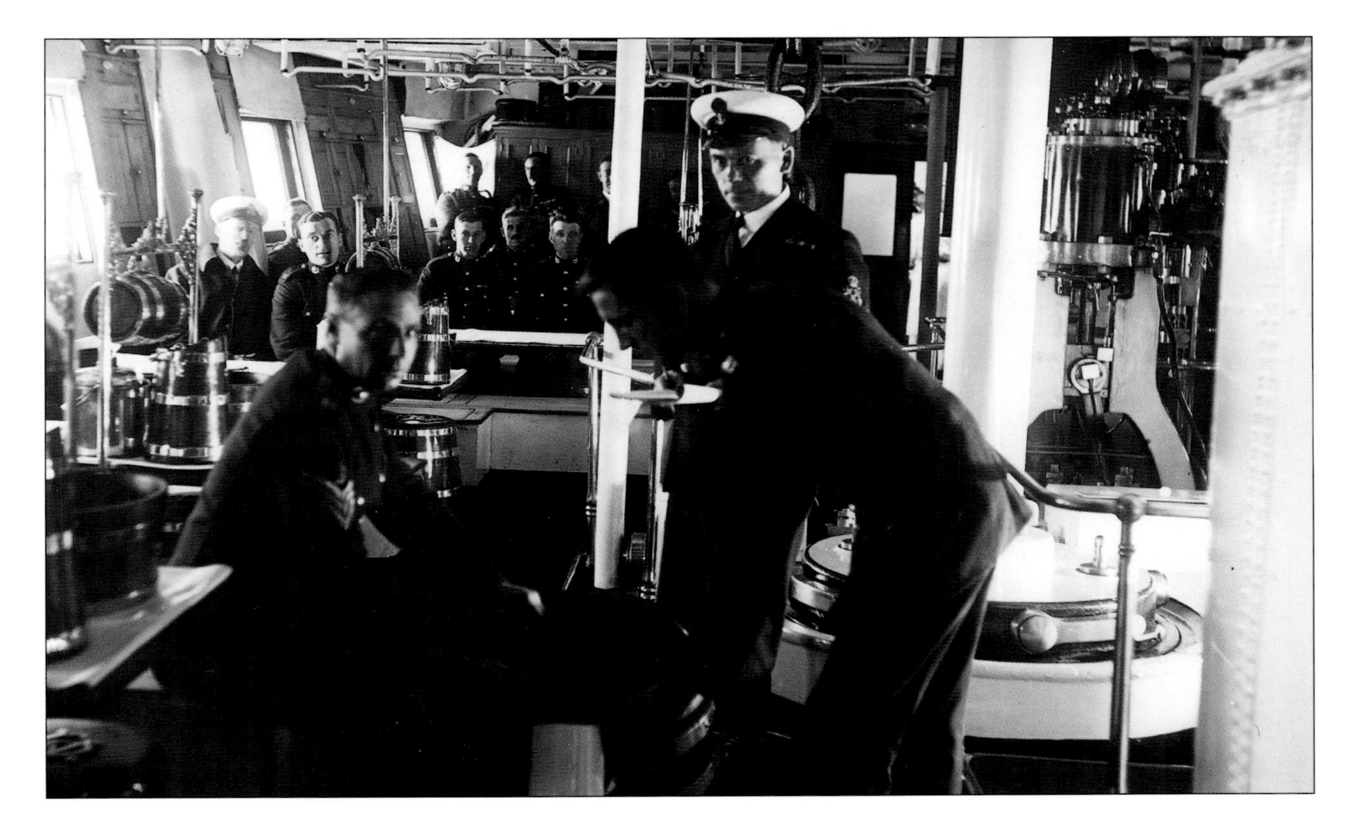

VICTORIA & ALBERT III

'Up spirits' in the forward messdeck. Note the unprotected anchor cable.

> To join the V & A was to take a step back in time. The only modern fittings I can think of were the Royal Barge and some of the boats, the rest being exactly as she was commissioned for Queen Victoria in 1899. The crew, the riggers, were an exceptional body of men. As they walked up the gangway to join the ship they were placed on a promotion roster and advanced as the leaders fell away. A lot of them were or had been outstanding games players, indeed some of international standard. Many, because they were in a world of semi-retirement, had small businesses ashore. The ship went to sea about three times a season, which was from 1 May to 1 October, and during that time the seasonal extras, which included the boy messengers, joined. We were all in love with the Queen – (the present Queen Mother) – for she was and is the most kind, caring and considerate lady. Boy Phillips and myself had our birthdays about the same date in June and were honoured with a special birthday cake from Her Majesty. It was my 18th birthday and so I was rated Ord. Smn. and told that I was the only O.S. to date to have served in the V. & A. Such is fame…
>
> When war was declared the boys joined the training cruiser, but because I was an O.S. I went to join HMS NELSON. A number of riggers went to join HMS ARGUS – the floating ditty box – and some joined a couple of 'Q' ships refitting in the dockyard.

In that last year of peace the Royal Family embarked on a cruise to the West Country, and on 21 July 1939 King George VI, Queen Elizabeth, Princess Elizabeth and Princess Margaret joined the VICTORIA & ALBERT at Weymouth and sailed to Torbay. From 22-23 they were at Dartmouth to visit the Royal Naval College. One of the first functions of the VICTORIA & ALBERT had been to convey Edward VII to Dartmouth in 1902 where the King laid the foundation-stone of the new Naval College. This visit was to be one of the yacht's last.

It was also to be the first recorded meeting between Princess Elizabeth and her future husband, then a cadet at the College. The yacht sailed from Dartmouth on the 24th, escorted to sea by Cadet Philip Mountbatten in a sailing dinghy, until he was waved off and ordered back by the King. His Majesty and his family continued to Cowes in order to visit Osborne, and then left the yacht at Portsmouth.

With war imminent, His Majesty inspected the Reserve Fleet – reinforced by a few vessels from the Active Fleet – at Weymouth Bay on 9 August. This was intended as an inspection rather than a review, and the King went round the fleet in the Royal Barge rather than the yacht. His Majesty boarded and inspected selected ships, most of which never stood down, but went straight on to war. As for the VICTORIA & ALBERT, it was to be the last time the yacht was ever to be used by any of the Royal Family.

War was declared on 3 September, and the majority of the ship's company dispersed to other ships. Vice Admiral Sir Dudley North struck his flag as FORY at sunset on 18 September, and shortly afterwards went as Flag Officer commanding the North Atlantic Station, based on Gibraltar. He was suddenly dismissed in 1940 following the failure to capture Dakar, although it is now accepted he was made a scapegoat.[5]

The VICTORIA & ALBERT was reduced to care and maintenance on 5 December, with Lieutenant W.G.C. Crouch, MVO, DSC, appointed in command of a skeleton crew. For two and a half years she continued idle, then on 5 June 1942 she was moored to the south side of Whale Island, which housed HMS EXCELLENT, the gunnery school. The yacht was connected to the island by a pontoon bridge for foot passengers only, and used as overflow accommodation for officers and men from the school. She was painted battleship-grey, and by 21 July she had six officers and 251 men accommodated on board.[6]

At the war's end the yacht was handed back to the dockyard, and she reverted to her normal colours of black hull and buff funnels. On 19 January 1946 The *Illustrated London News* reported on the sea-trials after the yacht's post-war refit:

> Cabins have been fitted up for Princess Elizabeth and Princess Margaret Rose, and it is hoped that she will be seen this summer lying once more at her special buoy in the roadstead at Cowes.

THE ROYAL FAMILY AT DARTMOUTH: THE "VICTORIA AND ALBERT" AND THE NAVAL COLLEGE.

As referred to in the caption to our front page illustration, the King and Queen, accompanied by Princess Elizabeth and Princess Margaret, visited last week-end the historic Devonshire seaport of Dartmouth. Here his Majesty carried out an inspection of the cadets and buildings of the Royal Naval College, where he himself served as a cadet from 1911 to 1913, and returned for a brief stay as a naval lieutenant in 1919. The visit, in addition to its official and sentimental interest, possessed added significance by virtue of the fact that it was the last voyage of the "Victoria and Albert," the royal yacht which, after some forty years of service, is now due for replacement. The yacht arrived off Dartmouth Castle — a familiar landmark to West Country holiday-makers—on the morning of July 22, where the many local craft had been decked out in honour of the visit of their Majesties. By their express wish, however, there was no civic ceremony on disembarkation at the town steps opposite Kingswear, the royal party being received privately by the [Continued on opposite page.

HER FIRST VISIT TO DARTMOUTH COLLEGE: THE QUEEN PLANTING A GOLDEN BEECH-TREE. (Graphic).

WHERE HE WAS A NAVAL CADET, 1911-13: THE KING PLANTING A PURPLE BEECH-TREE IN THE GROUNDS OF THE ROYAL NAVAL COLLEGE. (Keystone.)

A HEAVY SPADE-FULL: WATCHED BY THE KING, PRINCESS MARGARET AND THE COLLEGE COMMANDER, PRINCESS ELIZABETH PLANTS A WHITE BEAM-TREE.

IN WORKMANLIKE FASHION: PRINCESS MARGARET ALSO PLANTS A TREE IN THE GROUNDS OF THE COLLEGE.

THE LAST VOYAGE OF THE "VICTORIA AND ALBERT": THE FAMOUS OLD ROYAL YACHT, WHICH WAS BUILT IN 1899, ARRIVING AT DARTMOUTH, CARRYING THE KING AND QUEEN AND THEIR DAUGHTERS.

The last use by royalty of the VICTORIA & ALBERT III, at Dartmouth, 29 July 1939.

But it was not to be, for the VICTORIA & ALBERT was never used again; in spite of her refit the old ship was just not seaworthy. Her Belleville boilers, the only ones in the navy, had already had their steam pressure reduced in the 1930s, and after being laid up for the war were probably past safe operation. She returned to Portsmouth, was laid up with a skeleton crew, and only left to be broken up.

On 18 September 1939 Vice Admiral Sir Dudley North, CSI, CMG, CVO, had struck his flag as FORY at sunset. Although dismissed by Churchill for his action (or lack of it depending on your viewpoint) over the Dakar affair, in August 1945 he was appointed Admiral Commanding Royal Yachts at the express command of the King. Admiral North drew up a 'skeleton Royal Yacht service so that the benefit of … long experience was not lost to the Admiralty.'[7] On 16 May 1947 Admiral Sir Dudley North retired as Admiral Commanding Royal Yachts, and the appointment was thereafter in abeyance until 2 February 1953. With the building of BRITANNIA Vice Admiral E.M.C. Abel Smith CB, CVO, was appointed as FORY, with a full complement of officers appointed to the VICTORIA & ALBERT III.[8]

In the winter of 1947 the Royal Family travelled in HMS VANGUARD to South Africa to thank that country for their support during the war. During the cruise King George VI, his health already sapped by war work, first noticed the cramps in his legs that would later require major surgery. The Government felt that a new Royal Yacht, in which the King could cruise in warmer climes, would assist his recovery; but in post-war Britain there were other, more urgent, priorities.

Finally, in October 1951, the Admiralty announced a new Royal Yacht, which could also act as a hospital ship, was to be built. The contract with the renowned Clyde shipbuilders John Brown was signed on 6 February 1952. Sadly, King George VI, who had been ill for some time, died the following day.

On 16 February 1953 FORY transferred his flag from shore offices at Whitehall to the VICTORIA & ALBERT. However, Lieutenant Commander Woodford had been appointed in command on 23 December 1949, and he remained as such until the VICTORIA & ALBERT was broken up in 1955.

In January 1954 the VICTORIA & ALBERT III disappeared from the Navy List after more than half a century; for a hundred and ten years three yachts of that name had faithfully served through four reigns. During that year the yacht was dismantled at Portsmouth, the most valuable pieces being transferred to BRITANNIA or Buckingham Palace. Other pieces and fittings went to the National Maritime Museum and various naval shore establishments.[9]

Gales delayed a start to the final voyage of the 'V. & A.' but on 1 December the old yacht, stripped of her fittings and now little more than a hulk, was towed to the Clyde Estuary. There, at Faslane, she was broken up by the British Iron and Steel Corporation.

The 'V. & A.' was in her time the largest and grandest Royal Yacht in the world, and her breaking-up marked the end of an era. She had out lasted almost all the other Royal Yachts of her day, which had progressively disappeared along with their monarchs.[10] Yet she was but one of a long line of Royal Yachts stretching back through the centuries, and her place had already been taken by the grandest of all Royal Yachts – BRITANNIA.

HMS VANGUARD *entering Portsmouth 12 May 1947 on her return from South Africa with the Royal Family embarked.*

QUEEN ELIZABETH II AND HM YACHT BRITANNIA

BRITANNIA – BUILDING AND HER FIRST YEAR

Prime Minister Neville Chamberlain's Cabinet met in July 1938 and the decision was taken to build a new Royal Yacht which could act as a hospital ship, at a cost of £900 000. Outline drawings and plans for essential requirements were sent to leading shipbuilders in 1939, but the outbreak of war caused any such ideas to be shelved.

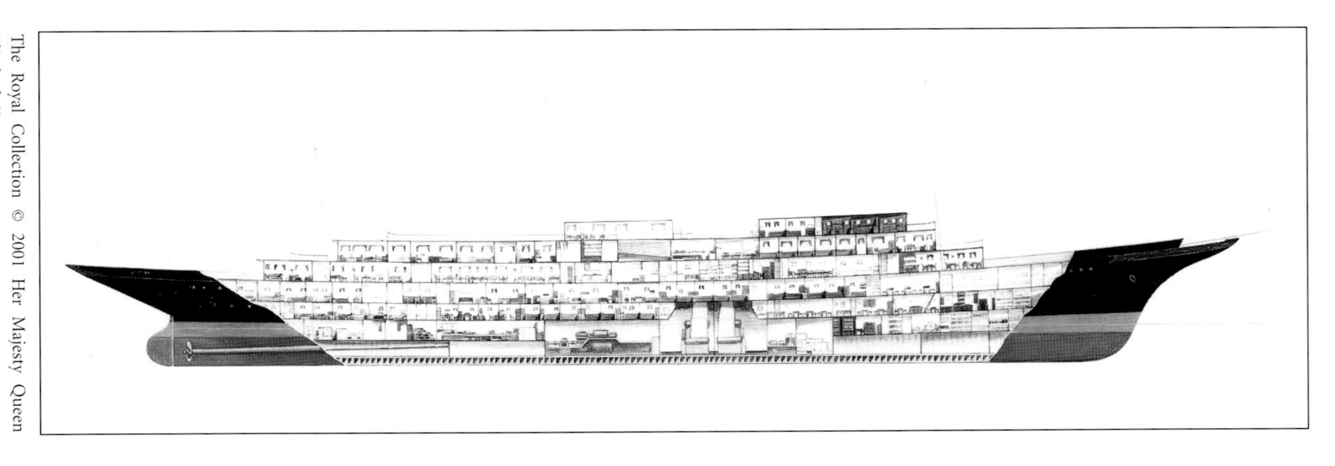

Projected design for a replacement for the VICTORIA & ALBERT *by Thornycroft & Co.*

In the winter of 1947 the King and Queen, accompanied by the two Princesses, travelled on board HMS VANGUARD to South Africa to thank that country for its support during the war. During the cruise King George VI, his health already sapped by war work, first noticed the cramps in his legs that would later require major surgery. As the King's health declined over the next few years there became an increasing need for a new Royal Yacht, in which he could cruise in warmer climates to aid his recovery.

The King was conscious that in austerity post-war Britain lavish expenditure on a new yacht would arouse criticisms, and he emphasised that economy was to be the watchword. Sir Victor Shepheard, Director of Naval Construction, afterwards explained: 'The late King and the Queen both stressed this need for economy and made many suggestions with the object of reducing expenditure. The project was undertaken as a matter of urgency since it was the hope that a yacht in which His Majesty could undertake sea voyages would greatly improve the chances of his recovery to good health.'[1]

In October 1951 the Admiralty announced that a new Royal Yacht, which could also act as a hospital ship, was to be built; the plans were submitted to His Majesty for approval towards the end of that year. Seven firms were invited to make suggestions, and it soon became clear that the renowned Clyde shipbuilders John Brown & Co. Ltd. could best meet the Admiralty's requirements – particularly as to delivery date, for the King's failing health demanded early completion. John Brown & Co. had built the great liners QUEEN ELIZABETH and QUEEN MARY and the contract for the new yacht (number CP8/50839/52/V.91) was signed on 6 February 1952. Sadly, King George VI died the following day. Aged only twenty-six, his elder daughter succeeded to the throne as Queen Elizabeth II.

Admiralty press release of a new Royal Yacht.

HANDOUT

THE ROYAL YACHT

Her Majesty The Queen has seen and approved a model showing the general arrangements of the small hospital ship to be used as a Royal Yacht in peacetime. Photographs of the model, with sea and sky effects added, are available to-day for publication.

To be launched by Her Majesty in April of next year, the ship is expected to complete at the end of 1953.

The keel was laid at the Clydeside yard of Messrs. John Brown and Co. Ltd., in June of this year. Most of the structure below the tank top and many bulkheads and frames are already erected.

The vessel is to Admiralty design and is being built to conform to the rules of Lloyd's Register of Shipping, i.e. merchant ship practice will be followed in her construction.

The Royal and State Apartments are situated in the after part of the ship, while accommodation for the ship's officers and crew is forward. The State Apartments themselves are to be on the upper deck abaft the main mast, with the Royal Apartments on the Shelter Deck.

Arrangements are such that the ship can be converted into a hospital ship with the minimum structural alteration. Should she be required as a hospital ship, the Royal and State Apartments could be converted into hospital wards, operating theatres, etc., for which air conditioning is being fitted. The after end of the Shelter Deck is strong enough to allow a helicopter to land on it with patients.

The load displacement is about 4,000 tons and the maximum draught in any seagoing condition will not exceed 16 feet.

The ship's overall length will be 413 feet; her length at the water line 380 feet; her maximum beam 55 feet, and her moulded depth 32' 6". Single reduction geared steam turbines fed by two boilers will drive twin screws to give her a continuous cruising speed of 21 knots.

She will have a modified cruiser stern and a raked bow. Three masts are to be fitted. The Royal Standard will be worn at the Main, the Flag of the Lord High Admiral at the Fore and the Union Flag at the Mizzen.

The ship will be fitted with a stabiliser to reduce her roll in bad weather. There will be both a Decca Navigator and Navigational Radar to assist her navigation. The ship will be fitted out for voyaging in both cold and tropical waters. The entire above water line structure is to be riveted.

NOTE TO EDITORS AND PICTURE EDITORS:
The pictures of the Royal Yacht model are available through the rota agency, Messrs. Planet News Limited, 3,Johnson's Court, E.C.4., (Telephone: Central 3671).
Facilities for photographing the ship on the stocks cannot be granted.

Admiralty, S.W.1.
20th November, 1952.

One of the first audiences of the new Queen's reign was granted to the Controller of the Navy on 29 February 1952 to discuss the new yacht, and Her Majesty subsequently approved the plans.[2] In June the keel was laid of Ship Number 691, and her name was kept a closely guarded secret until the day of the launch.

The brief to John Brown's was to build a robust vessel with an ocean-going capability, an advertisement for British shipbuilding at its best. The hull was based on designs for two Harwich-Hook of Holland ferries built by John Brown & Co., the ARNHEM and AMSTERDAM, but the hull form was modified to give her extra speed as a hospital ship. Her relatively shallow draught of 17 feet was to enable the ship to enter the smaller harbours and rivers of the Commonwealth, but this led to a reduction in the fuel stowage in the double bottoms. This in turn caused reduced range, so that BRITANNIA was barely able to cross the Atlantic without refuelling; not a factor of great importance in 1952 when Britain had a much larger navy, and hence many tankers available for refuelling ships at sea. The reduced draught also caused a tendency to roll, which was largely counteracted by the fitting of stabilisers. The hull was further modified by the addition of a modern clipper bow and cruiser stern, in place of the more traditional swan bow and counter stern of her predecessors. All these design features gave the Yacht not only a unique sleek shape but an extra half-knot at her speed trials.

The idea of a dual role as hospital ship was not just a sop to public opinion, but a very real solution to the navy's needs at that time, and the Medical Director General of the Navy was involved in the design stage from the outset. Two hundred patients could be accommodated in the royal apartments, with isolation cases in cubicles in the drawing room. Tuberculosis patients requiring 'fresh-air' beds were to be housed in the sun lounge off the verandah deck, which was strengthened to take helicopters landing with casualties. A dental surgery and laboratory, operating theatre, anaesthetic rooms, physiotherapy room, pathology laboratory and X-ray department would be on the main or lower decks. The ship's laundry was expanded beyond that required for a Royal Yacht to cope with the increased demand when in use as a hospital ship. Eight medical and dental officers, five nursing sisters and 47 male ratings would be required to staff the wards. In wartime the ship would sail under the Red Ensign and with a Merchant Navy crew instead of her Royal Navy crew under the White Ensign.

In theory the Yacht could be converted to a hospital ship in 24 hours, but this theory was sorely tested during the Falklands War of 1982. At that time BRITANNIA was almost the only naval ship still burning FFO – furnace fuel oil, a thick black oil much used in earlier steam boilers. The rest of the fleet burnt diesel – either in diesel engines or in steam boilers – or kerosene in ships fitted with gas turbine engines; to use BRITANNIA would have required sending a separate tanker. Given the shortage of tankers this was clearly impractical, and the UGANDA was chartered as a hospital ship. BRITANNIA, with a top speed of 21 knots, would also have had problems keeping up with the main Task Force. Fuel apart, the Government also feared the Yacht would be too small for the projected number of casualties, especially at such a distance.

In fact the idea that BRITANNIA should have a secondary role as a hospital ship was dropped fairly early on as impractical. She was then considered a 'Hospital Carrier,' a role she fully justified in the evacuation of 1300 civilians from Aden in 1986.

HM YACHT BRITANNIA

Twin-screw yacht, one funnel, three masts.

Laid down:	June 1952 at John Brown & Co. Ltd.
Designer/builder:	Sir Victor Shepheard, Director of Naval Construction /John Brown & Co.
Launched:	16 April 1953 by HM Queen Elizabeth II.
Commissioned:	at sea, 11 January 1954.
Displacement:	4961 tons deep draught
Gross tonnage:	5769 tons
Speed:	22.5 knots maximum. 21 knots continuous
Length overall:	412 feet 3 inches
Beam:	55 feet
Draught (extreme):	17 feet
Engines & I.H.P.:	Two geared steam turbines, developing a total of 12 000 shaft horse power. Two main boilers, Foster Wheeler 'D' type; and an auxiliary boiler for harbour requirements.
Fuel stowage:	510 tons of FFO (furnace fuel oil) until 1984. The boilers were then converted to burn diesel fuel (549 cubic meters).
Consumption:	Diesel: 3.87 CUM/hr @ 18 knots. 5.00 CUM/hr @ 20 knots
Range – nautical miles:	2800 (FFO); 2196 (diesel) at 20 knots. 3200 (FFO); 2553 (diesel) at 18 knots. 3675 NM at 14 knots, both FFO and diesel.
Fresh water:	210 tons
Complement:	21 Officers, 256 Royal Yachtsmen
Masthead heights:	Main-mast 139 feet 3 inches (Royal Standard). Fore Mast 133 feet (Lord High Admiral's Flag). Mizzen-mast 118 feet 10 inches (Union Flag).
Remarks:	25 February 1994 – completed 1 000 000 nautical miles
Paid-off:	11 December 1997

HMY BRITANNIA

Oil by Norman Wilkinson – 'The launching of HMY Britannia, 1953.'

'Although economy was still the keynote, it is in many respects its triumph, for BRITANNIA is a clever combination of economy and elegance, careful craftsmanship and cunning design. The design constraints were used to advantage, giving her a smooth sleek exterior, and a simple but stylish interior.'[3] The Queen and Prince Philip took a keen interest in the new Yacht, and as Dr John Brown, John Brown & Co.'s chief architect recalled: 'You had to be on your toes when Prince Philip was on board. He was very keen and peppered us all with questions.'[4]

Sir Hugh Casson, responsible for much of the interior decorations, recalled: 'The Royal couple took a close interest in every aspect of the design. The Queen is a meticulous observer with very strong views; there was no question of showing her a drawing and her saying, "All right, that will do." She had definite views on everything from the door handles to the shape of the lampshades.'[5]

The Queen voiced her own view of the Yacht when she declared at the launch: 'My father felt most strongly, as do I, that a yacht was a necessity, and not a luxury for the head of our great British Commonwealth, between whose countries the sea is no barrier, but the natural and indestructible highway.'[6]

Although economy was the watchword, there were the inevitable carpings from certain Members of Parliament, and of course the press. And chalked on the wall outside John Brown's one day was the message:

TORY GOVERNMENT

FOR THE POOR 4/– INCREASE IN RENT
FOR THE RICH £400 000 FOR THE QUEEN'S YACHT

KICK THE TORIES OUT
C.P. meeting today 1200

However, the First Lord of the Admiralty, JP Thomas, spoke for most of the nation when he said, 'The country wants the Queen to have this yacht and they want it to be worthy of her and her family.' The estimated cost was £1 615 000, including £290 000 profit; in the end the overall cost was £2 098 000, which included the thin line of gold around the hull. This latter item, at a cost of £90 plus £150 for labour to apply the gold leaf, nearly caused one Labour MP to have apoplexy.

The original estimate for the cost of decorating the royal apartments was £55 000–60 000, which reflected the extensive use of furniture and fittings from the VICTORIA & ALBERT. Had the quarters been decorated to normal wardroom standards the cost would have been £25 000; in the end the total bill was £78 000 with another £9000 for carpets – hardly extravagant by any standards.[7]

The royal apartments aside, the standard finish for the forward part of the ship was as per HM Ships – no panelling, rivets showing, 'tin' furniture, metal doors in the wardroom – real 'utility' stuff. As building progressed Admiral Ralph Edwards (Third Sea Lord & Controller) visited us and took the initiative and ordered the wardroom to be panelled and properly finished. But even then the standard forward was far short of what it is today. She was built to Lloyd's Register rules – class A1, and we had two superb Lloyd's Surveyors for Hull and Engineering instead of Admiralty Overseers.'[8]

The Navy List contained an interesting entry for 2 February 1953, for Rear Admiral E.M.C. Abel Smith CB, CVO, was appointed as Flag Officer Royal Yachts (FORY), with a full complement of officers appointed to HMY VICTORIA & ALBERT. This was an administrative move, for the new yacht was not even launched, and the old yacht was at that time laid up at Portsmouth. However, the VICTORIA & ALBERT was still in commission after half a century, with Lieutenant Commander Reggie Woodford in command; he was to remain the Commanding Officer until the old yacht was broken up in 1955.

Stripping the VICTORIA & ALBERT.

584 THE ILLUSTRATED LONDON NEWS OCTOBER 9, 1954

THE END OF AN OLD ROYAL YACHT: STRIPPING H.M.Y. *VICTORIA AND ALBERT.*

STRIPPING THE OLD ROYAL YACHT, *VICTORIA AND ALBERT III.* FOREGROUND, THE ORNATE WHEEL, WHICH WAS IN THE *ROYAL GEORGE* AND ALL THREE *VICTORIA AND ALBERTS.*

THE LAST COMMANDER OF *VICTORIA AND ALBERT*: LIEUT.-COMMANDER R. WOODFORD (RIGHT), LOOKING, WITH LIEUT.-COMMANDER E. J. SAWDY, AT A SOVEREIGN FOUND BENEATH THE FOOTING OF THE FOREMAST.

PANELLING AND HAND-RAILS FROM THE MAIN STAIRCASE OF THE ROYAL APARTMENTS BEING REMOVED. THEY ARE DESTINED FOR H.M.S. *EXCELLENT.*

THE BOWS OF THE FIFTY-THREE-YEAR-OLD ROYAL YACHT *VICTORIA AND ALBERT*, NOW BEING STRIPPED. THE SCROLL-HEAD AND ROYAL ARMS HAVE BEEN ALLOTTED TO THE R.N. BARRACKS, PORTSMOUTH.

THE former Royal yacht, *Victoria and Albert III.*, laid down in 1897 and first commissioned in 1901, is being handed over to the British Iron and Steel Corporation for breaking up. Her most valuable pieces of furniture have been already transferred either to H.M.Y. *Britannia* or to Buckingham Palace; but a number of mementoes are being stripped and presented to various institutions and establishments. To the Maritime Museum go: an anchor, the wardroom stove, a fireplace and surrounds from the Queen's drawing-room, two semi-circular cupboards from the base of the mizzen mast, and the Royal Arms and scroll from the stern. To the R.N. Barracks, Portsmouth, go: panelling and wall-lights from the Royal accommodation, some cannon, a bell and the figurehead (strictly speaking, a scroll-head). The Merchant Taylors Company receive the silver ship's bell, which they originally presented to the ship. To a number of naval barracks and shore establishments are being distributed a quantity of ornamental lanterns of Grecian design; H.M.S. *Excellent* receives the main staircase and doors from the Royal apartments, and H.M.S. *Royal Arthur*, the Petty Officers' School at Corsham, some upper-deck gear, including davits. Under the footings of the three masts have been found various coins placed there as gifts from Queen Victoria, King Edward VII. (when Prince of Wales) and King George V. (when Duke of York).

Commander J.S. Dalglish, known throughout the navy as Fish from his nickname at Dartmouth, was appointed the first commander of the new yacht. On 8 April he joined the ship at John Brown's yard on Clydebank, and his autobiography and official letters provide a contemporary account of her completion. 'The Admiral told us the name the Queen had chosen, and which was still a secret and John Mott (Commander (E)) was suspicious the secret had leaked because of a ship's bell he had seen in John Brown's boardroom where the last three letters were visible "...NIA"; this we found on closer inspection had belonged to AQUITANIA!'[9]

On the day of the launch, 16 April 1953, 'there was a great cheer from the crowd of shipyard workers with their wives and us when the Queen declared, at exactly 2.30, "I name this ship BRITANNIA and God bless all who sail in her." BRITANNIA went down the slip and into the waters of the Clyde where tugs took hold of her and brought her alongside the fitting out berth.'[10] Instead of the traditional champagne the Queen used a bottle of Empire wine for the naming, thus symbolising the new yacht was to be a link with the Commonwealth.

Commander Dalglish and his team had a multitude of details to attend to in planning how the Yacht was to be run, for it was fifteen years since the Royal Family had last used the VICTORIA & ALBERT. In that period had occurred the Second World War, the death of King George VI and the loss of many men from the old yacht. When in Portsmouth BRITANNIA's officers were accommodated on board the VICTORIA & ALBERT, which enabled them to absorb how things used to be done in the old yacht. Lieutenant Commander Woodford was an old shipmate of Fish, and together with his engineer, Lieutenant Ted Sawdy, and the Keeper and Steward of the Royal Apartments, Mr Pardy, he provided invaluable help. Some of the pre-war yachtsmen were to transfer to BRITANNIA, but the vast majority were selected from over 1000 volunteers from the fleet, of which 200 were selected.

'The five commanders – (E), (L), (S), surgeon and myself – formed the interview board and we had sessions at the three home ports (Portsmouth, Plymouth and Chatham) after we had examined all the service certificates and weeded out those we did not think we wanted. We were able to be choosy, avoiding for example those who were not "V.G. Superior". The interview process was intriguing and, with the senior ratings in particular, we had plenty of choice and found ourselves looking for people with unusual interests, such as football referees, concert party experts, those who liked sailing or who played a lot of games or who had distinguished themselves in some way.'[11]

'We also became involved in designing what uniform the yachtsmen were to wear. In the past they had a traditional rig where trousers were worn outside the jumpers and had a silk bow at the back (reputed to have been ordered by Queen Victoria to be worn as a mark of respect when the Prince Consort died in 1861); they also had white rather than red badges and a Royal Yacht flash on both shoulders, and all this was retained.' For working rig 'we chose the Royal Yacht flash they wore on their shoulders and had this placed on the front of both flannel and jersey where it looked very neat'.[12]

The full complement of officers was to be the Flag Officer Royal Yachts, with an Executive Commander (Fish) responsible for the daily routine of the Yacht. Four further commanders headed their respective departments – Navigation, Engineering, Supply and Medical.

The Commander had under him three seaman lieutenant commanders, the Shipwright, the Boatswain and three seaman sub-lieutenants (later lieutenants) as 'season' officers i.e. when the Yacht was on Royal Duty.

Commander (E) had a senior engineer and three warrant engineers. Commander (S) was also the Admiral's Secretary, and had a deputy supply officer.

Mr Pardy, the Keeper and Steward of the Royal Apartments, came from the VICTORIA & ALBERT, and when the Royal Yacht band was embarked the bandmaster was usually a captain RM.

Clockwise (from above):
Ship number 691 – 12 September 1952, keel and first few plates of hull.
Fish placing coins under the mainmast.
Her Majesty The Queen with John Rannie (the Shipyard Manager) and Dr McNeil at the launching of BRITANNIA.

The White Ensign being hoisted on the acceptance of HMY BRITANNIA *from John Brown & Co. Ltd on 11 January 1954.*

There is a long tradition of keeping all noise to the minimum in Royal Yachts, and BRITANNIA was to be no exception, in spite of her size and complexity. 'Everything on deck had to be done in silence, which demands a lot of initiative. I introduced various gimmicks for signalling orders including hand-held wooden pads coloured red one side (for STOP) and green the other (HOIST or LOWER or GO). I made all the seaman officers become proficient in the quick semaphore used by signalmen for the passing of instructions. …Perhaps my craftiest idea was the 'red hot notice board' on which stop-press notices could be displayed, e.g."Muster for anchoring at 1200 instead of 1230." To draw attention to this, coloured discs were located at important points such as near the heads, dining room, messes, rec space etc. and one coloured disc could be replaced by a different one if circumstances changed again. The disc meant, "Go at once to the red hot notice board." Chaps had to be on the ball. We did of course use telephones below deck as well. Incidentally, yachtsmen always wore soft soled shoes on deck and we issued a chamois to each, to be used if doing nothing else for polishing in the vicinity. One forgets how much noise goes on in a ship until one has to stop it! All these plans proved entirely worthwhile as we found out when entering Malta and going up the Thames where verbal orders would never have been heard above the sirens and cheering and fireworks which greeted Her Majesty.'[13]

Her Majesty Queen Elizabeth II was crowned on 2 June 1953, and as the VICTORIA & ALBERT was unseaworthy, the frigate HMS SURPRISE was converted for use as a temporary Royal Yacht for the Coronation

Naval Review at Spithead on 15 June 1953. The twin 4-inch gun mounting in B position was removed to provide an inspecting platform for the Queen.[14] It is probably coincidental, but entirely in keeping with the pattern of continuity in Royal Yachts, that Charles II made his escape after the Battle of Worcester in the brig SURPRISE; at his Restoration he bought the ship, converted her to a yacht, and named her ROYAL ESCAPE.

BRITANNIA, meanwhile, was gradually put together.

> The boilers and the main engines were shipped, then the funnel and the masts. It is a custom when masts are shipped in a vessel to place a coin beneath each, and in wooden ships these coins would get squashed flat by the weight of the mast. In BRITANNIA we had hollow masts, at the base of which the firm welded small containers for the coins. On behalf of all officers then standing by the vessel I placed under the mainmast a Coronation crown, together with a Coronation shilling from myself, and my fellow commanders did the same for the foremast and mizzen when they were shipped.[15]

The coins from under the masts of the VICTORIA & ALBERT III were recovered when she was broken up, and were later displayed on board BRITANNIA.

The Royal Barge arrived by road from the VICTORIA & ALBERT, but all other boats were made for BRITANNIA by the well known yacht-builders, McGruers. There was provision for a Rolls Royce to be hoisted inboard on the Royal Barge's davits, then transferred to a garage on rails set into the deck. However as initially planned there was a scant ¼ inch of clearance between the roof of the car and the ventilation trunking of the garage, and it was decided not to attempt loading the vehicle. After alterations the garage housed a Rolls Royce or Land Rover, and then was later used as the Bosun's store.

'Hugh Casson was the expert concerned with the interior decorations of the royal apartments and we saw a lot of him. I remember his insistence that a beautiful circular mirror in Her Majesty's sitting room should be at such a height that its centre was at the precise height of her eyes.'[16] Sir Hugh Casson was known to the Royal Family, and as he recalled in his diary: 'The design of ship interiors has fascinated me... and working on the royal apartments of BRITANNIA and the public rooms of the P & O flagship CANBERRA were among the most interesting experiences of my professional life.'[17]

In September Commander Dalglish and his wife set up in a bedsit in Helensburgh, and his autobiography almost exactly mirrors that of his contemporary in the VICTORIA & ALBERT II sixty years before, whose wife had to live in France to make ends meet. The Dalglishes had just sent their two children to boarding school: 'We were extremely short of money and our accommodation was no better than it had been in Plymouth when we were first married, in fact it was worse. The room was large with a bed and a dining table and there was a kitchen and a bathroom. It was ridiculous really for the Commander of the Royal Yacht to be slumming it like this but that was how it was.'[18]

In October steam was raised for the first time, followed by basin trials when the ship was secured alongside with extra cables, and the engines run ahead and astern. These were followed in November and December by contractor's sea trials, testing every last item in the ship.

The two geared steam-turbines built by John Brown's were identical to the engines fitted in the ferries ARNHEM and AMSTERDAM, and were fed by two main boilers. The engines developed a total of 12 000 shaft horse power, sufficient to give the Yacht a top speed on sea-trials of 22.5 knots, and a continuous seagoing speed of 21 knots. However, in a strong wind and with her top-hamper the Yacht was to prove underpowered, it being difficult to bring her head to the wind.

On 10 November, whilst BRITANNIA was conducting sea trials, the Shaw Saville liner SS GOTHIC, temporarily converted to a Royal Yacht, sailed at the start of the Queen's Commonwealth Tour. In addition to the conversion costs the Admiralty paid a charter fee of £40 000 a month; they also had to pay for the ship

HMS SURPRISE, 1952

Oil by Norman Wilkinson – 'HMS Surprise at the Coronation Review, 15 June 1952.'

The Queen's sitting room, sketches by Sir Hugh Casson.
Right: *workmen finishing the decoration.*
Opposite: *design for the sitting room.*

to be painted white, the colour decided on for the tour, and for her then to be repainted her original black. The total cost was over 10 per cent of the final cost of the BRITANNIA.[19]

The Queen was to join the GOTHIC later by air from London, but by tradition whenever the monarch is afloat she is accompanied by the Flag Officer Royal Yachts. Admiral Abel Smith was therefore in attendance upon Her Majesty, and Fish was appointed temporarily in command of BRITANNIA with the rank of acting Captain, the only officer ever to hold that rank while serving in BRITANNIA.

The programme was for BRITANNIA to take over from the GOTHIC towards the end of the tour, at Tobruk, and return with the Queen via Malta and Gibraltar to the Pool of London. The Queen's children, Prince Charles and Princess Anne, would join the Yacht for the passage to Tobruk. A myriad of forward planning had to be approved by FORY before his departure, and he had no choice but to leave Fish and his fellow officers with an uncompleted and uncommissioned Yacht in the sure expectation that they would present him with an immaculate ship fully worked up in a brief five months' time.

> My chief memory of the work up period that followed, supplemented as it is by the diary I kept at the time, is that of really foul weather wherever we went. Another memory was that the Yacht was by no means completed, in particular a lot to be done by the firm in the royal apartments, and spaces and decks on board were filthy by the standard we had to set for when we were on Royal Duty. Leading on from these two factors, a certain amount of discontent came to light among my yachtsmen before they settled down to realise how much hard work was needed (whereas I fancy many of them expected a cushy job). There were some who pulled out of it altogether and left the Royal Yacht Service by request.[20]

On 7 January 1954 the Third Sea Lord and Controller, Admiral Sir Ralph Edwards, made his final inspection and signed the form D.448 so that the advance party could embark and formally commission the Yacht. The next day the main body came up from Portsmouth, and 'we left Clydebank on 11th January, being seen off by vast crowds of shipyard workers and their families. They did so in complete

silence, which is a custom dating back to when the departure of a ship from the yard inevitably meant men being laid off work to unemployment. We did the requisite two hours steaming and I myself then signed the form accepting the Royal Yacht from the builders on behalf of the Admiralty, the White Ensign was ceremoniously hoisted, and we came back to anchor at Tail o' Bank off Greenock.'[21]

The Navy List recorded that Vice Admiral Abel Smith (temporarily absent in the SS GOTHIC) had transferred his flag to BRITANNIA, and the VICTORIA & ALBERT III, after more than half a century, disappeared from the List.

Four days later a full gale hit the Clyde, with gusts of 97mph recorded, and the Yacht hit the BBC News:

> The Royal Yacht BRITANNIA, completing off Gourock, dragged both her anchors and was in danger of blowing broadside on to a sandbank. A tug went to her assistance but at the last minute her Captain managed to get her bows into the wind and she went to sea to ride out the gale.

Captain Dalglish had found out, rather sooner than he would have wished, how badly the Yacht yawed from side to side in such conditions (up to seventy degrees). The tug that was sent could only communicate by shouting, and would in any event have been totally inadequate in the Force Nine gale then blowing. Fish took the ship to sea, and spent the night cruising up and down off Arran; next day he tried to anchor once more, but again the Yacht dragged, and the ship returned to sea.

Then followed further trials, especially on the radio equipment with its worldwide capability. The ship had to be run over the measured mile, and her handling qualities assessed, particularly in coming to a buoy or

Oil by Leslie Wilcox. Arrival at Sydney of Queen Elizabeth II, 3 February 1954, on board the SS GOTHIC.

VICTORIA & ALBERT III

Oil by Leslie Wilcox – 'Last voyage to the breakers, 1 December 1954'.

Sketches by Sir Hugh Casson.
Right: *working on the royal apartments.*
Opposite: *design for the ante-room and drawing room.*

berth. 'We lost no opportunity of manoeuvring at sea and all the while the yachtsmen got down to the long task of making the vessel clean.' The Yacht steamed into the Atlantic as far as St Kilda, searching for large swells to test the stabilisers before rounding the north of Scotland to Invergordon and Rosyth. There she hit another gale, and 'for hours we shipped it green over the forecastle, which was good, because it tested our freeing ports (which are important in a ship like that with bulwarks all round)'.[22] The gale was a good test of the ship's capabilities, even though half of the ship's company were seasick, and the paint peeled off the port side. The Royal Barge, ex-VICTORIA & ALBERT, caused problems, for as the Yacht dipped into the heavy seas the barge surged two feet forward and back on its davits. The pads failed to grip the highly polished hull, and speed had to be reduced whilst tackles were rigged to secure the barge.[22a]

At Rosyth the Flag Officer Scotland, Vice Admiral Sir Geoffrey Robson, and Mrs Dalglish deputised for the Queen and Prince Philip in a rehearsal of the reception of royalty on board with full ceremonial. The various Yacht traditions had evolved over the centuries, and many of the routines were firmly established, and recorded, by precedent. But it was fifteen years since the Royal Family had last used the VICTORIA & ALBERT, and few of her ship's company transferred to the new Yacht. Every possible routine and manoeuvre expected in the months ahead had to be practised until it was perfect, for not only would Prince Philip be keeping a critical watch, but every moment would be recorded by the world's press.

Eight days were spent at Portland – the navy's base for working-up ships – practising refuelling at sea, jackstay transfers, dressing ship, coming to buoys and the myriad other essential seamanship and engineering

manoeuvres that a new ship's company has to master. And above all the ceremonial that the Royal Yacht performed so faultlessly, and which was later taken for granted, had to be learnt and perfected.

At Portsmouth in early March the Yacht 'gave two weeks leave to each watch while John Brown's people swarmed on board and finished the ship off, at last'.[23] There was a multitude of faults to be rectified, as is normal with any new ship, and this one was rather exceptional, especially as it was under a year since she had been launched. Portsmouth Dockyard turned to with a will to finish the ship and 60 joiners were allocated to the royal apartments, and a similar number of painters to the Yacht's paintwork. The hull, funnel, masts and upper decks were repainted; it took 50 painters with 44 stages nine hours to do one side, and the hull required two coats of undercoat before the glossy enamel topcoat.

Designed for short North Sea crossings, and not for the continuous cruising of the Yacht, the patent gland on the stern shafts had been overheating and leaking oil. The makers could offer no solution, but after several trials Commander (E) solved the problem by the simple expedient of slacking back on the packing. The awnings on the royal and verandah decks were spread and stretched, in doing which the after stanchion buckled under the strain, and had to be strengthened. Then it was discovered the roof of the verandah was planned to be green and white stripes, whilst the awnings were red and white stripes.

The propeller shafts of the Royal Barge were found to be bent, for the heavy engines of the old boat had to be uncoupled from the shafts each time before hoisting, and this had not been done; it was known in the VICTORIA & ALBERT, but no one had told BRITANNIA! Petty-fogging at the highest level had obstructed much in the supply of stores and equipment; one theory was that Naval Stores did not know whether to classify the Yacht as a destroyer or a minesweeper! Amongst all these greater problems the Admiral Superintendent finally got the Yacht's totally inadequate allocation of 12 chamois leathers increased to 100.

The First Sea Lord, the Controller, and the First Lord all inspected the Yacht; Palace officials checked the arrangements for the royal children; security men examined the ship for possible problems; and there was

Clockwise:
Rear Admiral A.G.V. Hubbard (Admiral Superintendent Portsmouth) and Admiral Sir John Eddstein (Commander-in-Chief Portsmouth) greet Prince Charles and Princess Anne, under the supervision of Her Majesty Queen Elizabeth, The Queen Mother and Princess Margaret.
Her Majesty The Queen embarking for the first time at Tobruk, 1 May 1954.
The First Cruiser Squadron of the Mediterranean Fleet passing the Royal Yacht and cheering on 2 May 1954.

an endless stream of requests to 'look round' the Yacht, all of which had to be politely but firmly refused. The press were particularly cross at not being allowed on board, and even though one man did manage to evade the security by posing as a naval friend of the Commander, he saw only the wardroom. The going rate on offer for a photograph of the Queen's cabin was £500 – a year's wages for many then – but no newspaper obtained the coveted picture.

Even so it was touch and go whether the Yacht would be ready, and Fish recorded: 'God knows how Hampton's will finish the royal apartments by the day after tomorrow... Sir Hugh Casson didn't help matters by lowering the position of the light fittings last week after all were installed.' Half an hour after the final inspection of the royal apartments, 'all the workmen poured back in and continued polishing and even painting in some cases. It all looks very beautiful however and I dearly wish the press and Mr Bence MP (who was vociferous over the cost of the Yacht) could come and see it all in its simplicity and lack of expensive or lavish ornament.'[24]

Yachtsmen, dockyard personnel and contractors all worked very long hours, and finally – almost miraculously – she was ready. The moment which had first been thought about back in 1938, the commencement of the first Royal Duty of a new Royal Yacht, arrived.

On Wednesday 14 April HM Queen Elizabeth the Queen Mother and HRH the Princess Margaret brought Prince Charles and Princess Anne on board. Then at 5pm BRITANNIA sailed from Portsmouth to the cheers of an enormous crowd. The yachtsmen had assembled a range of shipboard playthings for the royal children, including a slide, a sandpit and an inflatable liferaft as a tent. Two seamen and two stokers acted as royal lifeguards, and one was in attendance on each child whenever they were on the upper deck. On coming in to harbour the stokers were always on duty, the seamen being required for berthing, and this led to an upset from the wife of one of the seamen. On leaving Gibraltar there was a prominent picture of the royal children and their (stoker) lifeguards, which led one seaman's wife threatening to leave him as a liar, saying he was the Princess's lifeguard yet he was not in the picture. It took a personal letter from Captain Dalglish to soothe the ruffled feathers!

Two days after sailing was the 16th of April, exactly a year since the ship was launched, during which time a monumental amount of work had been achieved. Much of the acclaim for this achievement must go not only to the builders, but also to Captain Dalglish, his officers and yachtsmen.

On 22 April BRITANNIA entered Grand Harbour, Malta, and watched by vast crowds made the difficult sternboard up Dockyard Creek to secure between two buoys. Six days later Fish removed his acting fourth stripe and handed over command to Rear Admiral Abel Smith; the Yacht sailed that evening, and two days later arrived at Tobruk.

Her Majesty embarked in BRITANNIA for the first time at Tobruk on 1 May 1954, and the Yacht sailed immediately for Malta. 'Next day the Mediterranean Fleet met us and did an astonishingly brilliant steam-past extremely close on both sides of BRITANNIA (thank goodness for our stabilisers!) followed by the jackstay transfer to us of the C-in-C.' (Lord Mountbatten.)

'Our arrival in Grand Harbour was fantastic thanks to the great crowds and cheering, and fireworks in typical Maltese style. The Admiral handled the Yacht beautifully between the two buoys and we got secured as neatly as we had always hoped we would.'[25] The four days that followed were filled with State receptions, banquets, dinners, balls and polo matches. Then it was off to Gibraltar for two days, and, finally, the last leg home to the Pool of London.

The Yacht was met by the Home Fleet as escort, and the Prime Minister, Sir Winston Churchill, travelled to Southampton and joined BRITANNIA off the Needles. And so, on Saturday 15 May, some seven months after she had left, the Queen was conveyed to the heart of her capital on board the largest and most elegant Royal Yacht in the nation's history. Sir Hugh Casson was among the dignitaries on board, and recorded the scene vividly in his diary:

> The Prime Minister in the Admiral's barge, cigar stuck in smile, waving his little taxi-driver hat to the escorting yachts… BRITANNIA looking impossibly tall and heraldic... the fleet reviewed... the excited, sleepless night aboard... the end-of-term atmosphere as we entered the Thames... two men in trilby hats boiling shrimps in a small boat off Gravesend... Tower Bridge and the fur-hatted Lord Mayor in an open boat with upraised oars... BRITANNIA's captain Commander Dalglish (with a broken ankle) hopping agonizedly from one side of the bridge to the other as we moor up determinedly without tugs ('The navy doesn't use tugs')... the lunch party and family reunion... the boatloads disappearing in order of grandeur (Royals... entourage... personal staff... luggage... finally, after a cup of tea, the Admiral, now bowler-hatted, and me).[26]

Fish had broken a bone in his ankle while playing deck-hockey in Malta, and had it set in plaster. He recalls their arrival with as much enthusiasm as Sir Hugh: 'Every bit of land we passed was crowded with people and we must have seen millions that day; hundreds of boats crowded to the gunwales; everyone cheering and waving; sirens hooting and general noise (which made us thankful once more we could do our stuff in silence). The Royal Yacht band played 'Rule BRITANNIA' as we passed under Tower Bridge...(and) we got secured fore and aft, dressed overall, and two ladders down precisely eight minutes after passing Tower Bridge. We had never done it so fast before and that set the seal on everything we had been training for.'[27] Commander Dalglish was promoted to Captain that June.

The Queen knighted Admiral Abel Smith, and the Royal Family disembarked. The following day the press at last were invited on board for a carefully selected tour of the ship. After all the carping over the cost of the Yacht the press were amazed at the restraint in the decor. 'The big surprise was the lack of luxury,' said the *Daily Mail*. Correspondents noted that some of the carpets – saved from the VICTORIA & ALBERT – were wearing thin, and that certain guest cabins... still had bare floorboards.[28] Not so, said Captain John Mott, who stood by BRITANNIA during building.

A few days later the Yacht took up her moorings off Whale Island in Portsmouth Harbour, adjacent to where the VICTORIA & ALBERT had lain during the Second World War, and close to the ROYAL GEORGE's mooring as an accommodation ship for sixty years.

In July and August BRITANNIA sailed to Canada, where she visited Quebec, Montreal and Goose Bay (Labrador) before bringing Prince Philip back to Aberdeen, from where he travelled to Balmoral. Admiral Sir Conolly Abel Smith was a wonderful ship-handler, and somewhat of an eccentric. 'The night we left Aberdeen after dark the dock's pilot... told me to warn the old man of a 'fresh' down the river which could be nasty as we moved into it from the docks. Conolly was having a glass of port after dinner with a guest who was taking passage and did not go up to the bridge to get his eyes accustomed to the dark as I would have done. As soon as he got up there he ordered "Let go forward. Let go aft. Half ahead both" and out we shot safely to sea, disembarking the pilot in his cutter outside.'[29]

Thus finished BRITANNIA's first year in commission, the start of over forty years of service to the Royal Family and the nation, and one which was to set the pattern for those which followed.

HMY BRITANNIA

Oil by Leslie Arthur Wilcox – 'HMY Britannia at Tower Pier 15 May 1954.'

THE LAYOUT OF BRITANNIA

THE ROYAL APARTMENTS

BRITANNIA was an official residence of Her Majesty the Queen, and as such had to carry out many ambassadorial and diplomatic functions abroad. The Yacht thus had to provide not only suitable apartments for State occasions, but accommodation for the Royal Family, their guests, the Household and staff. The tastes of the Queen and Prince Philip were much in evidence throughout the royal apartments, and from the start they had been involved in the designs, as we have seen.

One of the first appointments John Brown & Co. made in 1953 was that of Mr J. Patrick McBride (of the firm of McInnes Gardner & Partners of Glasgow) to oversee the decoration of the royal apartments and suites. Mr McBride was one of the most experienced ship's architects in the world, and had decorated the royal apartments in the SS GOTHIC for the Queen's Commonwealth Tour, as well as much work for John Brown & Co. Mr McBride was to receive a fixed fee of £2400 for his services, and over the year submitted various decorative schemes to the Palace, and discussed them personally with the Queen and Prince Philip. They, however, felt the designs were too grand for a yacht, and the decision was taken to appoint Sir Hugh Casson as consultant architect. Sir Hugh was well known as the architect of the Festival of Britain, and was renowned for his tact. He soon won Mr McBride's confidence, and thereafter the two men worked closely together.

The Admiralty had had their fingers burnt by an extra consultant for the GOTHIC who had several times obtained Palace approval without consulting them, leaving the Admiralty to pay. They were therefore not initially keen on the idea, but on 24 March the Under Secretary for Finance, Mr P.N.N. Synnott, grudgingly minuted: 'In the circumstances, no financial objection is seen to this proposal. If Sir Hugh Casson asks for more than £250 – which it is hoped he will not – we will have to consult the Treasury.' Sir Hugh's final bill amounted to 700 guineas, and his expenses, expected to be no more than £50, totalled £184. But to obtain his cheque he had to provide itemised expense accounts, and even then had to write several times for his money.[30]

In his diary Sir Hugh recalled of Mr McBride's plans: 'The Queen and Prince Philip felt they were too fussy; elaborate interiors do look ridiculous at sea. Simplicity was the keynote – hence for example the grey carpeting which runs throughout the State apartments. I also wanted to show off the quality of light at sea. (For the ante-room and drawing room)… the overall idea was to give the impression of a country house at sea. I think we succeeded. Even today the Yacht looks very striking. She has an attractively old-fashioned air about her.' The Architect's Journal of 1954 commented: 'The architect's restraint has retained an atmosphere of space which could easily have been destroyed.'[31]

Sir Hugh certainly succeeded in his ideas, and over the years many distinguished guests have been deeply impressed by the restrained country-house style of the light and airy rooms.

The following descriptions applied to BRITANNIA when in use as a Royal Yacht; now she is preserved at Leith, some items have obviously changed.

The Keeper and Steward of the Royal Apartments was responsible to the Admiral/Commodore and to the Master of the Royal Household (and through them directly to the Queen) for the efficient running of all the royal apartments and the safety of their priceless contents. The last holder of the office was Lieutenant Commander Barry Llewelyn, appointed on 2 August 1994; under him he had 13 royal stewards drawn from the Yacht's complement. Unlike the other officers the Keeper remained in post for many years, often until he retired. Not only do the Royal Family prefer familiar faces around them, but the Keeper was an invaluable repository of the preferences of the Family, and he ensured BRITANNIA remained the Queen's 'home afloat'.

The royal apartments were entered from the upper deck through pairs of doors port and starboard into the main entrance area. Off the main entrance to starboard was the Queen's sitting room, and opposite to port the Duke of Edinburgh's sitting room. The wide mahogany grand staircase ascended to the shelter deck, where were situated the Queen and Prince Philip's bedroom suites, and bedrooms A and B for important guests. A staircase from the lobby descended to the Household and staff cabins; forward of the lobby was the dining room, and aft was the ante-room. A lift serving the main deck, royal deck and shelter deck was for the use of Her Majesty and the dressers.

Main staircase.

Eric Thorburn © The Glasgow Picture Library

The original plans of BRITANNIA.

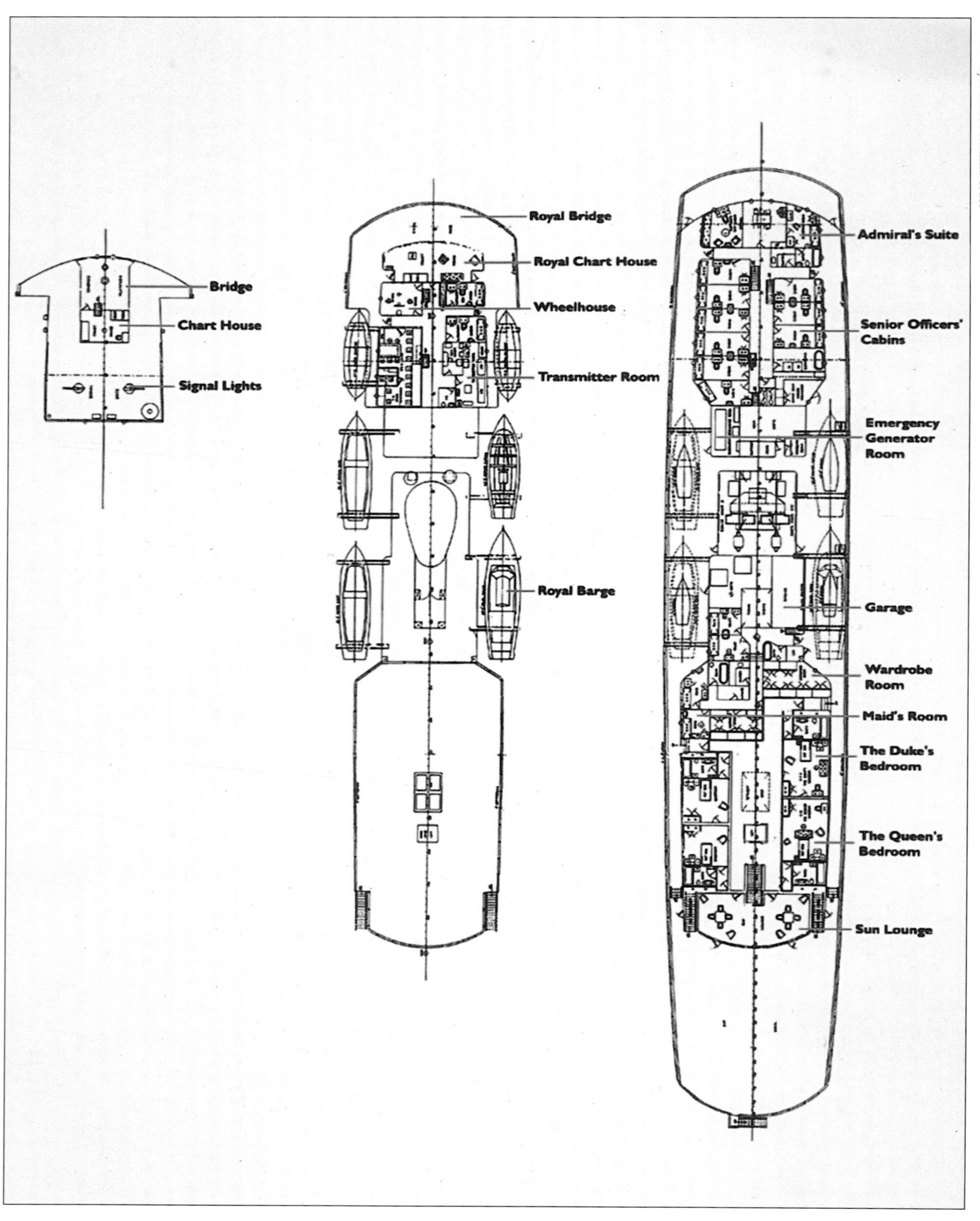

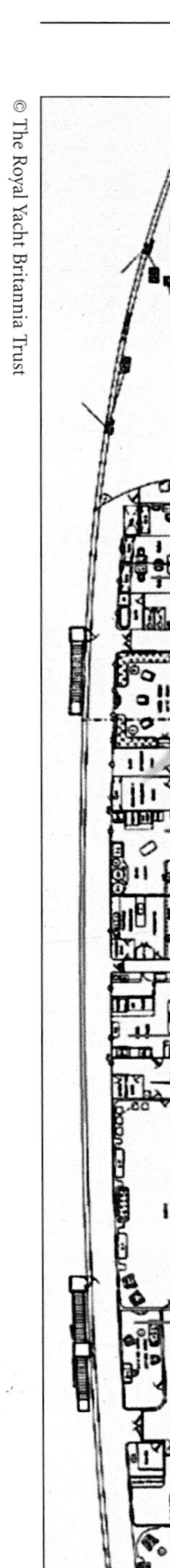
© The Royal Yacht Britannia Trust

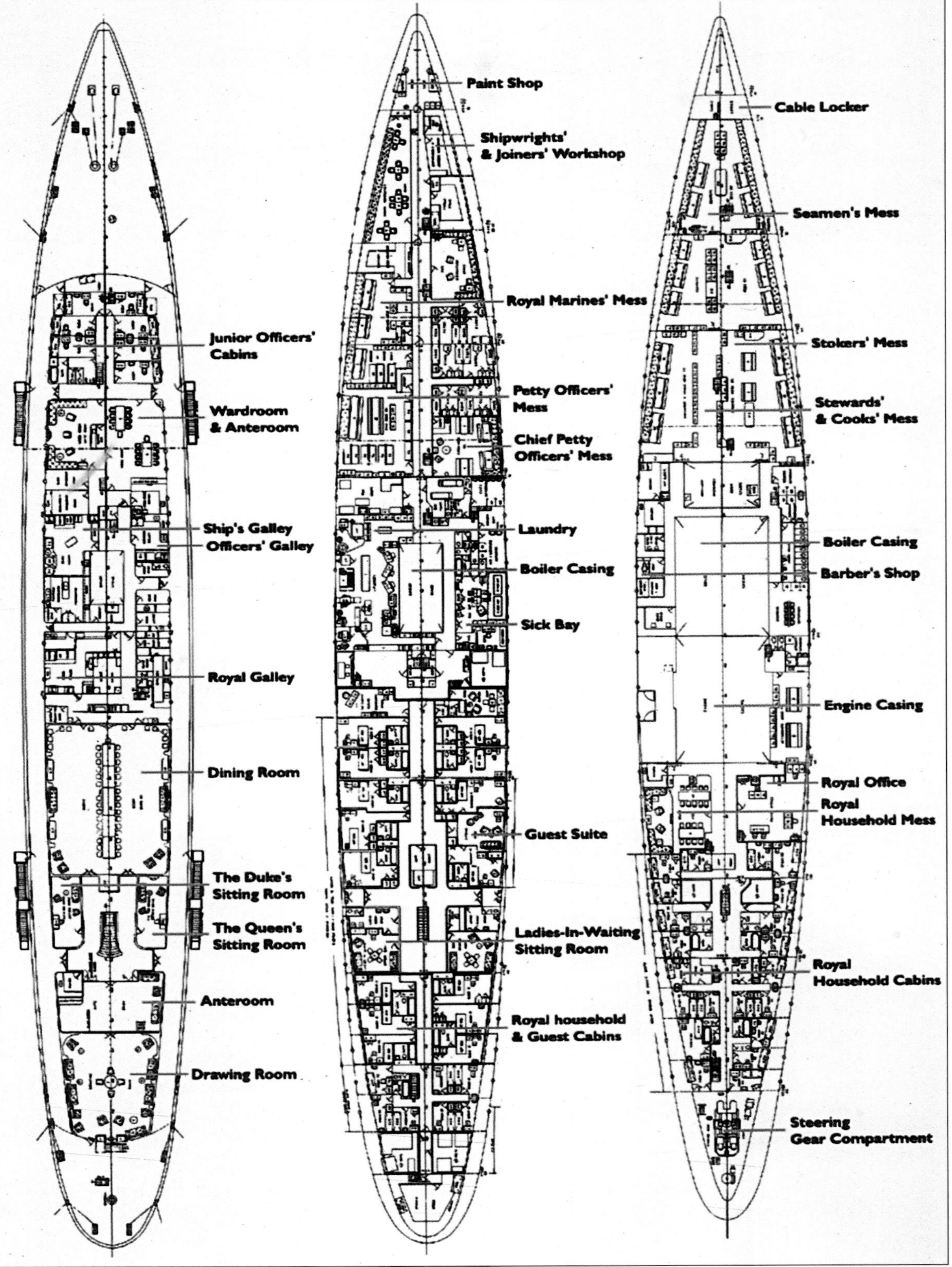
Junior Officers' Cabins
Wardroom & Anteroom
Ship's Galley
Officers' Galley
Royal Galley
Dining Room
The Duke's Sitting Room
The Queen's Sitting Room
Anteroom
Drawing Room
Paint Shop
Shipwrights' & Joiners' Workshop
Royal Marines' Mess
Petty Officers' Mess
Chief Petty Officers' Mess
Laundry
Boiler Casing
Sick Bay
Guest Suite
Ladies-In-Waiting Sitting Room
Royal household & Guest Cabins
Cable Locker
Seamen's Mess
Stokers' Mess
Stewards' & Cooks' Mess
Boiler Casing
Barber's Shop
Engine Casing
Royal Office
Royal Household Mess
Royal Household Cabins
Steering Gear Compartment

THE ANTE-ROOM

The Royal Family gathered in the ante-room for drinks before lunch and dinner in the dining room.[31a] It was connected to the drawing room by large folding mahogany doors, which were usually left open, and at 55 feet long the two rooms could accommodate up to 250 guests.

The fine mahogany bookcase was previously in the King's writing room in the VICTORIA & ALBERT III. Among other things it contained Waterford crystal presented to the Queen by John Brown & Co. when BRITANNIA was launched, and a number of coins. These had been placed under the masts of the VICTORIA & ALBERT III in 1899 for good luck, and recovered when the old yacht was broken up in 1955. On behalf of Queen Victoria were placed one sovereign, one five shilling piece and one penny; similar coins for the Prince of Wales (later Edward VII); and one half sovereign, one five shilling piece and a half crown for the Duke of York (later King George V).

The small, tattered silk White Ensign was once flown on Captain Scott's sledge during his ill-fated Polar expedition, and recovered when his body was found in 1912. Presented in 1913 to King George V by Commander Evans, a member of Scott's expedition, it previously hung in the reception lobby of the VICTORIA & ALBERT III.

The older items of furniture generally came from the VICTORIA & ALBERT III, while the newer furniture was presented to the Queen in 1956 by the Swedish Royal Family.

The silver-grey carpet continued into the drawing room, and was covered by a superb Persian carpet presented to the Queen in 1979.

THE DRAWING ROOM

The drawing room was comfortably furnished with chintz-covered sofas and deep armchairs, with separate sets of covers for use in the tropics. Over the silver-grey carpet were two magnificent Persian rugs, gifts from the rulers of two Gulf States.

The fireplace was electric, although there was much debate as to whether an open coal or log fire could be fitted, as in the previous yacht. But as Sir Hugh Casson recalled: 'I discovered that navy practice meant that if you had an open fire you also had to have a sailor standing by with a bucket. This was clearly ridiculous.' Over the fireplace hung an oil painting by J.A. Wilcox depicting BRITANNIA entering the Pool of London on her return from the Commonwealth Tour of 1954. (see p 241)

The Walmar baby grand piano to port cost £350 when supplied in 1952, and was bolted to the deck.

The small gimballed table, designed by Prince Albert, was originally in his dressing room in the VICTORIA & ALBERT II, and then in the King's writing room of VICTORIA & ALBERT III. It is reputed to hold a glass of whisky safely in anything up to a Force Eight gale! (see p 151, top right)

To the left of the fireplace was a television set and video player, concealed in a cabinet beautifully made by Plymouth Dockyard in 1987 to match the other, older, pieces of furniture. There were several card tables for jigsaws and games of cards, both of which the Royal Family enjoy.

The oldest article on board BRITANNIA was the Lord High Admiral's Verge (rod of office), made for Charles II's brother – the Duke of York – in 1660, when the King appointed him to that office at the Restoration. It was presented by the Lord Commissioners of the Admiralty to the Queen when she became Lord High Admiral in 1964, and is carried at the annual passing-out parade at Dartmouth, the Lord High Admiral's

Drawing room.

Ante-room.

Divisions. The satinwood desk was one used frequently by Queen Victoria on board the VICTORIA & ALBERT II.

Throughout the royal apartments were mementoes collected by or given to the Royal Family throughout their many journeys around the globe. Paintings and photographs, nearly all connected with the present or past yachts, hung on the bulkheads. The decor in the drawing room was continued through the royal apartments, with white bulkheads and deckheads, lustre bronze metalwork and mahogany woodwork.

THE DINING ROOM

This was the State room, used for formal State occasions as well as doubling up as a cinema and for church services on Sundays (from 1986). The panelling and deckhead were white with gold trim, and the carpet was the silver-grey continued from the drawing room. Under the carpet was a dance floor, although it was seldom used.

Dining room.

The table was of mahogany with an ebony edge, made for BRITANNIA in five sections, any of which could be removed to make it smaller for family meals. Fully extended it seated 32 in comfort, which could be increased to 56 for State banquets with the addition of extending tables, two of which were from the VICTORIA & ALBERT III. Prince Philip was convinced the original table was too small, so he assembled 32 Household and staff and had dinner served to them; he was correct, and the two wings were added. Lord Mountbatten designed the electrified pad which ran down the centre of the table, enabling the candelabra to be placed wherever needed. For a State banquet, the table took three hours to lay, with each place setting meticulously lined up and checked. The chairs were of Hepplewhite wheat-ear style, mostly from the VICTORIA & ALBERT III, but with 14 indistinguishable modern copies.[32]

Four nineteenth-century sideboards carved in the style of Chippendale also came from the previous yacht. Numerous mementoes of royal tours adorned the walls and alcoves.

The principal decorations on the table were the silver gilt Nelson and Collingwood vases, presented by the National Patriotic Fund to the families of Admiral Nelson and Lord Collingwood after the Battle of Trafalgar on 21 October 1805. They were subsequently purchased for Edward VII, one being bought at auction, the other from a watch-maker in Portsea. A more recent addition was a solid gold, eighteen-inch high sculpture of a camel and her calf under two palm trees, given to the Queen by the Ruler of Dubai during a State Visit in 1979. The dates in the palm trees are fashioned from 42 rubies, and the piece was said to be worth over one million pounds, one of the most valuable items on board.

When BRITANNIA was decommissioned the dining room was reassembled at Frogmore, Windsor, and is much used by the Duke of Edinburgh for meetings.

HER MAJESTY'S SITTING ROOM

Immediately off the main lobby to starboard was the Queen's sitting room, more of an office with a seven-foot desk, its green leather top complementing the moss-green carpet. Even at sea, affairs of State occupied several hours of the Queen's day, and red boxes containing State papers for Her Majesty's attention were delivered to her anywhere in the world.

Memories of previous tours were retained, for the sofa and armchair were used in the VANGUARD in 1947 and the GOTHIC in 1953. The four light brackets, of carved wood but painted in old silver, came from the Queen's drawing room in the GOTHIC.

Both the Queen's and Prince Philip's sitting rooms were connected by telephone with the offices of the private secretaries, one deck below.

PRINCE PHILIP'S SITTING ROOM

Referred to by Prince Philip as his study, this had teak panelling and a red-topped desk, and was carpeted in grey. The sofa and armchair were covered in oatmeal hopsack, and the curtains were of navy and white printed linen. Above the desk was a model of Prince Philip's first command, HMS MAGPIE.

Prince Philip too spent several hours a day on correspondence, usually in the mornings, for he liked to leave the afternoons free for painting and reading.

THE SHELTER DECK

Approached by the grand staircase (and the lift) this deck contained the bedroom suites of the Queen and Prince Philip – each with its own bathroom. The royal corridor was lit by a large skylight, and to port were

The Queen's sitting room.

The Duke of Edinburgh's sitting room.

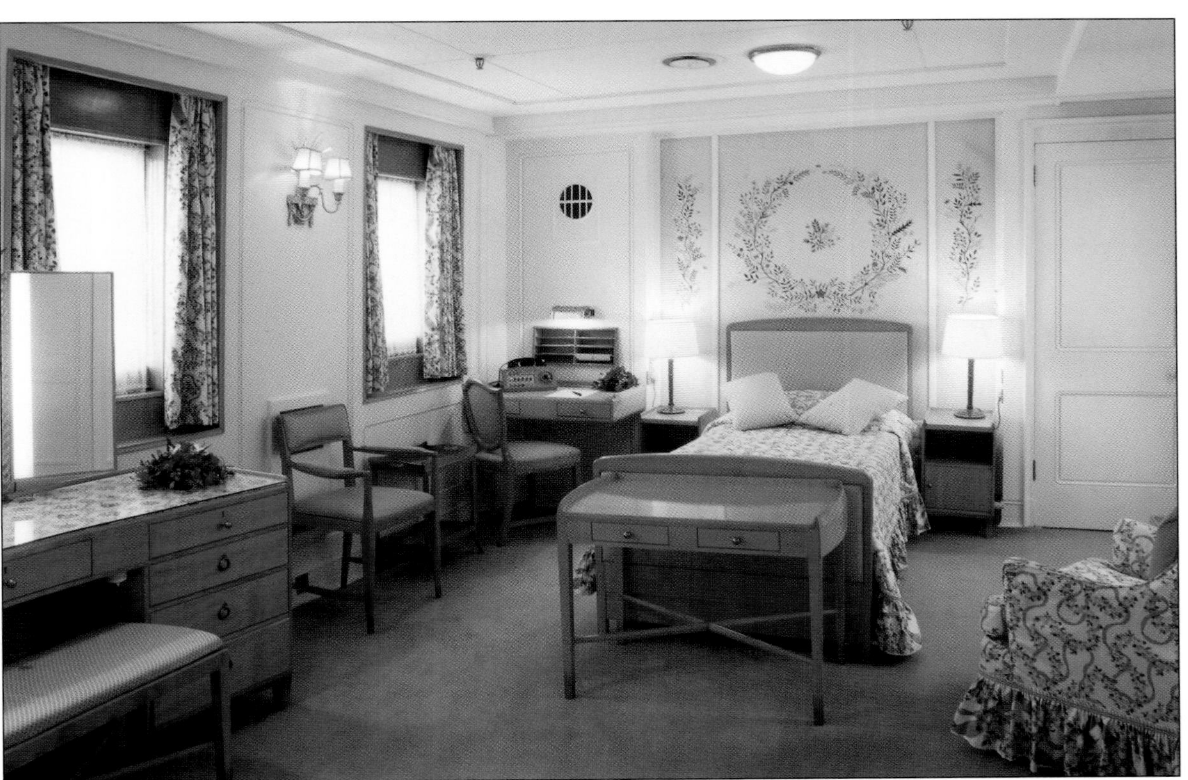

The Queen's bedroom.

Eric Thorburn © The Glasgow Picture Library

Prince Philip's bedroom.

two guest bedrooms (used as nursery suites when the royal children were small), the Queen's wardrobe room, and cabins for dressers and valets. The floors of the bedrooms, being two feet higher than deck level to accommodate the proportions of the main rooms below, benefited from additional privacy, as anyone passing outside could not see in the windows.

At the aft end of the royal corridor was the verandah, fitted with heavy bamboo furniture bought in Hong Kong by Prince Philip in 1959. The Queen and her family often took breakfast and afternoon tea in here with its wide view of sea and sky.

The verandah opened on to the verandah deck, which was above the drawing room. On the verandah deck was an elaborately carved and gilded binnacle, originally one of a pair from the ROYAL GEORGE. It had been installed in successive Royal Yachts, and in BRITANNIA was fitted with a repeater from the Yacht's gyro-compass. Above the binnacle hung the ship's bell, given to the Yacht by Trinity House. The bell was surmounted by the Royal Coat of Arms salvaged from the VICTORIA & ALBERT II.

The verandah.

THE MAIN DECK

Situated below the upper deck, this contained 16 cabins, most with private bathroom and lavatory; two sets of two cabins had shared facilities. All the cabins were furnished to first-class liner standard, and were used by members of the Royal Family, guests and the Royal Household. For important guests there was a suite of two cabins joined by a sitting room, and the Queen herself chose suitable books and selected fresh flowers for her guests.

A large amount of linen came from the VICTORIA & ALBERT; but the total cost for supplying extra linen for the royal bedrooms in 1952 was £498.12.0. This included 170 sheets, 64 pillowcases and 50 bolsters for the Household cabins.

On the lower deck were staff cabins, furnished generally to normal service standard, and the Royal Clerks office; while below that again on the orlop deck were store rooms for the myriad supplies required by the Yacht.

Below left: *Princess Anne on the verandah deck.* Below right: *Prince Charles in the naval uniform of a captain.*

FORWARD

BRITANNIA was the first Royal Yacht to have an ocean-going capacity, and to be an official residence of the Sovereign. She was literally a palace afloat, and to maintain this palace required considerable manpower. Ceremonial arrivals and departures required boats, booms and ladders to be handled quickly and safely, awnings to be furled and unfurled, and flags and standards to be hoisted smartly; all of these functions are very demanding of manpower. There were no women among the officers or crew, for there was no suitable accommodation, nor was there any precedent, that guideline which governed Yacht routine.

Compartments abaft the mainmast were exclusively royal; forward of the mainmast was a naval ship, albeit a very special one. The royal apartments, boiler room and engine room took up roughly half the Yacht. Forward of the funnel was accommodation for the 21 officers and 256 yachtsmen, plus all the essential services and stores to maintain the Yacht's ocean-going capacity. For the officers the accommodation was comfortable; for the yachtsmen it was cramped, even after the 1972/3 refit which gave them bunks instead of hammocks.

ADMIRAL/COMMODORE

By tradition the commanding officers of all Royal Yachts were captains in the Royal Navy. In the seventeenth and eighteenth centuries when there were several Royal Yachts, not all in active service, commands were often given to elderly, distinguished or wounded officers. When questions were raised at the cost of maintaining so many yachts, the Admiralty argued that they had few forms of patronage, whereas the army had many forts or commands to which they could appoint deserving officers!

On 1 January 1893 Captain J.R.T. Fullerton, commanding officer of the VICTORIA & ALBERT II since 1884, hoisted his flag as a Rear Admiral, and thus became the first Flag Officer Royal Yachts (FORY). He continued to retain personal command of the VICTORIA & ALBERT II until his retirement on 1 April 1901. The title lapsed when the VICTORIA & ALBERT III was laid up for the war in 1939,[33] but was revived in 1953 with the appointment of Rear Admiral Conolly Abel Smith. FORY was the most senior independent command afloat, answerable directly to the Queen.

The commanding officer's accommodation was built for an admiral, and was of a standard higher, quite rightly, than normal for a ship's captain, with a large day cabin, night cabin and bathroom. It occasioned the following item under the 'Extras' listed in the building costs: 'Wood lining, ceiling and furniture in lieu of Admiralty Supply Steel furniture; also special electrical fittings; £1120 in materials and a further £845 in labour costs.'[34]

Nine admirals commanded BRITANNIA as Flag Officer Royal Yachts since her commissioning; but in an act of unbelievable parsimony the Admiralty reduced the appointment to a Commodore in April 1995, thus saving a massive £7000 a year. With the Yacht due to decommission in 1997, quite why this decision was taken is beyond the author; the historical precedent alone justified the retention of an admiral until BRITANNIA paid off. The skills and responsibilities of the Commodore were in no way reduced, and this decision gave him far less influence in obtaining the essential services required by the Yacht, particularly abroad.

The Admiral/Commodore was responsible for the efficient running of the Yacht, and when Her Majesty was embarked he had responsibility for the safety of some 300 people. Whilst he had a highly capable team under him, his was the sole responsibility if anything went wrong; if it did, he could be certain that the media would broadcast the fact to the world. As an extra equerry to the Queen he was a member of her Household, and he always accompanied Her Majesty when afloat. The Admiral/Commodore usually dined with the Royal Family when they were on board, otherwise he ate in his day cabin, or, on invitation, occasionally in the wardroom.

Clockwise (from top left):
The Admiral's cabin.
The Commander's cabin.
First Lieutenant's cabin.

His appointment was for several years (about five), and as each admiral retired he was honoured by Her Majesty with a knighthood (Knight Commander of the Victorian Order).

WARDROOM

During the eighteenth and nineteenth centuries appointments were obtained by influence either in the service or at Court. In times of peace promotion was slow, and as Royal Yacht appointments brought automatic promotion they were avidly sought after. In 1923 King George V decided to end this system, and from then on the Admiralty submitted a shortlist of officers, all of whom had been selected for promotion, to the King, who then made his own choice from the list. The use of influence is invidious to present-day thinking, but judging by the number of Royal Yacht officers who reached high rank it was not totally to the detriment of the navy. After all, who is going to recommend a dunce to serve under the very eyes of the monarch.

Appointment to BRITANNIA was purely on merit after interview by the Admiral/Commodore, and was usually for two years. However, the three season officers – junior lieutenants – remained for one year only, as it was not considered good for a young officer to be out of the mainstream navy for more than a year. The term originates from when the VICTORIA & ALBERT was only in commission for the summer season, usually 1 May to 1 October; the Yacht then laid up for the winter and the season officers – at that time sub lieutenants – received automatic promotion to lieutenant.

The five commanders had comfortable, though not luxurious cabins. The junior officers' cabins were decidedly cramped, particularly when the Yacht was overseas and they needed both blue and white uniforms, not to mention the equivalent civilian clothes. The author remembers his cabin as the smallest of any ship in which he served, and not for nothing were the junior officers' quarters nicknamed 'The Ghetto'!

The wardroom.

Eric Thorburn © The Glasgow Picture Library

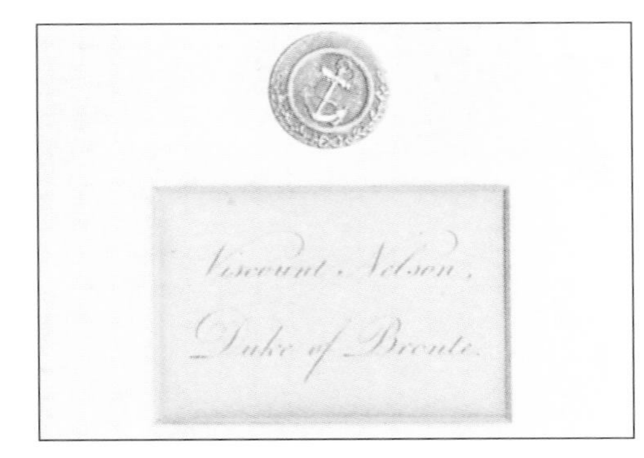

Left: *Wardroom ante-room.* Above: *Nelson's button took pride of place in the anteroom.*

The wardroom and wardroom ante-room were comfortable and welcoming, and the standard of service, food and wine excellent. Most officers ended their appointment to BRITANNIA decidedly poorer, but none would grudge the privilege and experience.

THE COMMANDER

The Admiral/Commodore's team was headed by the Commander of the Yacht, responsible for the daily running of the ship. He was also the Admiral/Commodore's second-in-command, acting for him in his absence in all matters of ceremonial. As Head of the Executive Department he was responsible for routine, safety, organisation, discipline, training and welfare. All seamanship, the appearance and cleanliness of the Yacht, and the maintenance of the upper deck and 'tween decks was also his charge.

Although the other heads of department reported directly to the Admiral/Commodore, as co-ordinator between departments (and as second-in-command) the Commander was *primus inter pares*. He was also President of the Wardroom Mess.

The Commander's team was headed by the First Lieutenant (a Lieutenant Commander), who was responsible for seamanship, the upper deck, and the ship's side. The First Lieutenant was relieved after about a year by the Second Lieutenant, thus ensuring continuity.

The Second Lieutenant (also a Lieutenant Commander) looked after routine and organisation and the 'tween decks, and wrote Daily Orders. The latter was no small task with the constant changes often needed, and their timely issue was the secret of a successful day's Royal Duty.

The Boatswain (a Special Duties Lieutenant or Lieutenant Commander) was responsible for all the ship's boats, rigging and gangways. When anchored or moored BRITANNIA lowered four accommodation ladders; the starboard aft was for the Royal Family, and the port aft for the Household and officials. The starboard forward was for officers, and the port forward for yachtsmen and staff. This procedure was not just elitism, but enabled relatively large numbers of people to disembark from the Yacht in several boats at once.

The Commander had under him 77 yachtsmen for general duties – seamanship, cleanliness, boats crews, gangway staff etc.

COMMANDER (N)

The navigation of the Yacht was entrusted to a specialist Commander (N), who would have completed the navy's Long Navigation Course. He was assisted by a lieutenant, one of the season officers appointed for one year. Whenever the Yacht left Portsmouth on Royal Duty, Commander (N) would have arranged months ahead all the myriad navigational and berthing requirements. For instance, by ancient tradition only Trinity House vessels are allowed to precede the Yacht; tugs were required to have their fenders covered in canvas, and were only used to pull, not push, except in emergency, for the enamel paintwork of BRITANNIA was easily damaged; gangways for the Queen had to have a slope of no more than 15 degrees, and no step higher than eight inches; pontoons placed between the Yacht and any jetty had to be of a certain size; any berth must not be overlooked, both for security and privacy. And so the lists of requirements went on, all of which had to be finalised before the Yacht sailed.

COMMANDER (E)

The Engine Room, Shipwright and Electrical Department was under the control of Commander (E), who had under him a senior engineer (a Lieutenant Commander), four commissioned engineers (lieutenants), a commissioned shipwright (a lieutenant) and 91 yachtsmen. Together they were responsible for maintaining, and in many cases repairing on board, all the machinery and essential services of a Yacht over forty years old, and which had sailed more than a million miles.

From 1984 BRITANNIA burnt diesel fuel in her boilers, but before that she burnt furnace fuel oil (FFO), a thick black oil which had to be heated before it could be sprayed into the boilers. This was one reason she could not be used in the Falklands War, as she was then the only ship in the navy burning FFO; combined with her relatively low passage speed she would have required her own tanker – logistically unrealistic.

The engine room, like the rest of BRITANNIA, was immaculate, and was often the high point of any tour of the Yacht. General Norman Schwarzkopf, when shown the engine room, commented, 'OK, I've seen the showpiece. Now show me the real engine room.' The two-geared steam turbines developed a total of 12 000 horsepower, and drove the Yacht at a maximum of 21 knots. At this speed she burnt 5 cubic meters of diesel per hour (or about 5 tons of FFO), and so, to economise on fuel, cruising speed was invariably less than this. And as the royal apartments were over the propellers they got the worst of any vibration at speed.

Three steam turbo-generators supplied 1500 kW for the lighting and power requirements, for most of the heavy pumps and supply fans were electrically driven. Any two of the steam generators could meet full-load requirements; in addition there was a large diesel generator for harbour use and a small one for emergencies.

In addition to running the main machinery, the engineering department also needed to maintain all the services required by a large village of 300 persons. Galleys, both royal and ship's company; cold and cool rooms carrying thirty days' supplies; air-conditioning, heating and ventilation; fresh water, fire, fuel and sewage systems; capstans for the anchors, derricks for the boats, steering gear for the rudders; and all the complex navigation and radio equipment.

The Duke of Edinburgh with members of the wardroom at Cowes in 1957 wearing 'Cowes Rig'. The rig was only worn at Cowes, and dates back to the early 1900s when it was first worn. A photograph was taken every year at Cowes as a record of officers serving.

The same photograph taken in 1996, the last visit by BRITANNIA to Cowes.

Clockwise (from right):
The bridge.
The wheel, from the Racing Cutter BRITANNIA *(see p 212).*
The engine room.

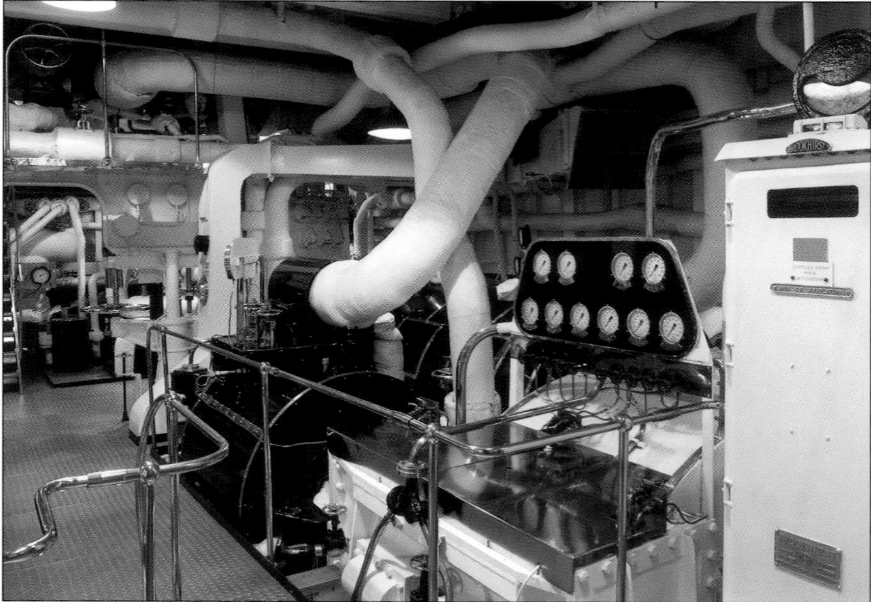

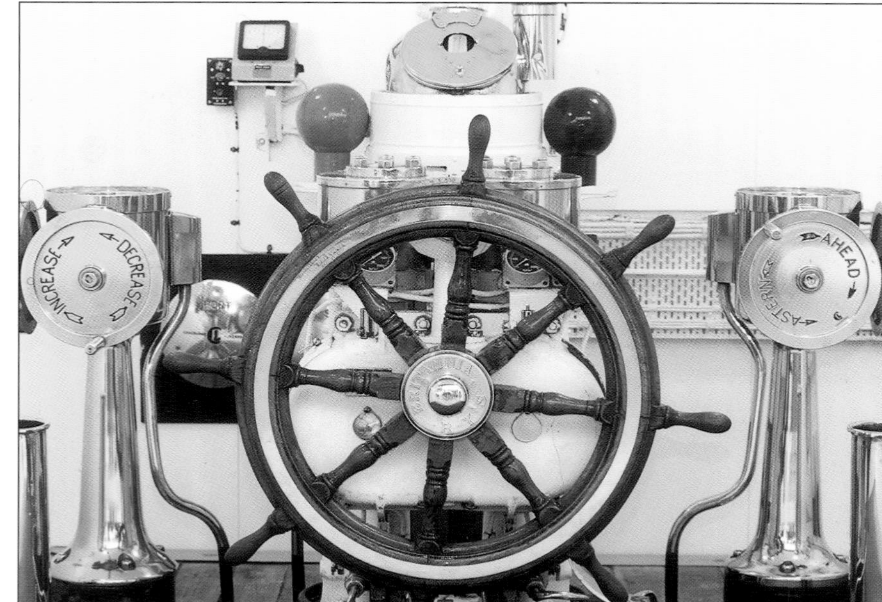

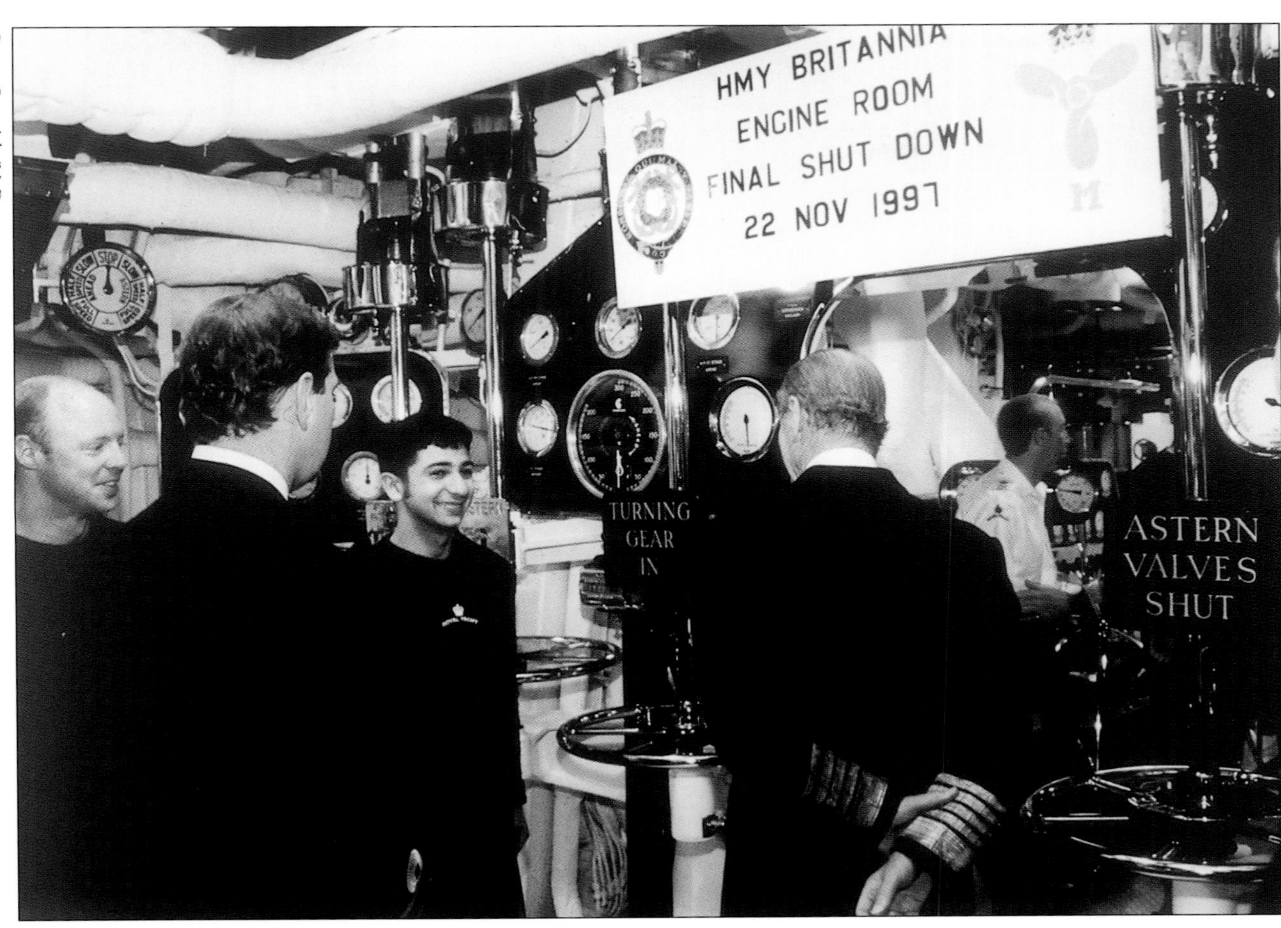

Crown Copyright/MoD

Crown Copyright/MoD

Left: *Prince Philip, CORY and members of the engine room crew at the final shutdown.* Above: *Celebrating one million miles.*

COMMANDER (S)

The Admiral/Commodore's Secretary was also the Commander (S), who had a Deputy Supply Officer (a Lieutenant Commander), together with a department of 57 yachtsmen to supply the needs of the ship and the royal apartments. Preparation for a royal tour involved a veritable mountain of paperwork, and on long tours the storerooms were bursting with provisions, although fresh produce was bought locally wherever possible.

In addition to the highly detailed correspondence necessary for a royal tour the ship's company had to be paid, wherever in the world the Yacht was. Foreign currencies would have to be arranged in as many as seven different coinages, and up to a quarter of a million pounds in total; bills for locally bought stores had to be accounted for and paid; and from small galleys and old fashioned equipment the chefs produced meals to standards higher than any other ship in the Royal Navy.

There was a small printing press on board to cope with the numerous instructions and lists that had to be produced so that everyone knew exactly what was happening. For State banquets the menus were decided by the Palace before BRITANNIA sailed, and the required food and wines embarked. Otherwise menus were approved each day by the Queen, and the menu cards printed on board, in French.

The department was a busy one, and tended to operate behind the scenes unobtrusively and highly efficiently providing logistical support and services to the highest standard.

PRINCIPAL MEDICAL OFFICER

The fifth Commander was the Principal Medical Officer (PMO), responsible for the health of the ship's company, and for the Royal Party when in home waters. When Her Majesty was abroad a physician was included in the Royal Household, known as the 'Medical Officer to the Queen abroad'.

The Communications Department was headed by the Signal Communications Officer (SCO), a Lieutenant Commander, who was also the Royal Cypher Officer, entrusted with decrypting any signals that arrived in code for the Queen. Under him were 25 yachtsmen to operate the complex signals and communications system with its worldwide capability.

The three season officers were Commander (N)'s Assistant, the Household Liaison Officer, and the Royal Barge Officer. The latter probably had the easiest task, for he had a skilled and trustworthy crew, but when any of the Royal Family embarked in the Royal Barge, which travelled at 18 knots, this officer's head was on the line if anything went wrong, even though the Admiral/Commodore invariably also accompanied Her Majesty.

Commander (N)'s Assistant worked out, checked and double-checked, the heights of tide at every port, times of sunrise and sunset, tidal streams and navigational buoys, and any special characteristics of each port. BRITANNIA always arrived to the minute, and so the route must be planned, timed, cross-checked, and often replanned as changes occurred. For longer tours, such as to Australia, this meant an immense amount of detailed planning.

The Household Liaison Officer's job was fraught with potential pitfalls, as woe betide him if he breached the strict hierarchy of the royal staff. Among these, the Travelling Yeoman was responsible for making the travel arrangements of those joining the Yacht, and also for up to five tons of baggage that could accompany the Queen and her Household on a State visit. As his name implies the Household Liaison Officer was in touch with the Palace before a tour started, and once the Household were on board he was the 'fixer' responsible for transport, sport and entertainment of the staff. With up to 25 staff, often with different requirements, plus normal watchkeeping duties, his life could be hectic. One example is that although the staff travel in buses, the Queen's dressers require a car, as they carry the Queen's valuables with them. The needs of the Household itself were generally looked after by the Admiral/Commodore, or the Keeper and Steward of the Royal Apartments.

When BRITANNIA was at sea, all seaman junior officers kept sea watches, and when in harbour all junior officers (i.e. Lieutenant Commander and below) were involved as Officer of the Day.

Responsibility for the royal apartments and their priceless contents rested with the Keeper and Steward of the Royal Apartments – normally a Lieutenant Commander, who remained in post for many years. He reported both to the Admiral/Commodore and to the Master of the Royal Household (and through them directly to the Queen).

For all major tours a Royal Marine band of 26 musicians was embarked; their Director of Music was a commissioned officer (normally a captain). The band practised each day at the forward end of the ship, well away from the royal apartments, and played each morning at the ceremony of Colours. When the Queen was embarked they played in the ante-room during dinner; and of course their ceremonial Beat Retreat was an emotional and unforgettable experience. As President Reagan commented: 'I thought Hollywood was the entertainment capital of the world, but there's no way we could beat this.'

No chaplain was carried, but most Sunday church services were conducted by FORY/CORY. Until 1986 services were held in a variety of places such as the verandah deck, the forecastle, one of the messes or the wardroom. In 1986 Her Majesty gave permission for them to be held in the royal dining room, with the Royal Marine band when embarked.

Royal Barge.

The 1970 Australian Bicentenary Tour.

Clockwise (from above):
Unloading the Rolls Royce, Fiji.
Concert party:
Prince Charles and Lieutenant Commander Jock Slater.
'Dixie' Deane and Tony Herdman.
Niels Westberg supervising the Pacific games.

ROYAL YACHTSMEN

It has to be remembered that BRITANNIA was designed in the early 1950s, and with largely pre-war thinking, when manning standards of ships and machinery were completely different from nowadays. And that to maintain the Yacht in pristine condition, position her from point to point, and to provide all the essential services of an official royal residence took manpower – 256 of them. This included 34 warrant officers, chief petty officers and Royal Marine equivalent ranks; and 26 petty officers and sergeants. It was this seldom changing nucleus of non-commissioned officers who were the heart of the knowledge and expertise that made the running of BRITANNIA so special.

Royal Yachtsmen were split into two; those on the permanent Royal Yacht Service, some 190, and about 50 Ocean Complement drawn from general service for longer tours. Every volunteer for the Yacht was interviewed by the commander in charge of his department; having successfully completed a year in the Ocean Complement he was then eligible to transfer to the Royal Yacht Service when a vacancy arose.

On joining a yachtsman received a small booklet detailing the way the Yacht was run and what was expected of him. The front page carried a message from the Commander: 'You are now a Royal Yachtsman, and it is your privilege to give personal service to Her Majesty the Queen and other members of the Royal Family. Our constant aim is to ensure the privacy, comfort and safety of the Royal Family who are embarked, and to maintain in the Royal Yacht the very highest standard of appearance and efficiency.'

There was no extra pay, leave or other privileges for yachtsmen, but once on Royal Yacht Service they did not have to leave BRITANNIA. This had the distinct drawback that promotion was in 'dead men's shoes', and although most were happy to forgo promotion, some decided to leave the Yacht in order to advance themselves. Exemplary behaviour on board and ashore was expected at all times, and any transgression was followed by dismissal from the Yacht and return to general service; there was no other punishment.

Accommodation until the 1972/3 refit was largely in hammocks – BRITANNIA being the last naval ship to have them. The ship's company's quarters were decidedly cramped, particularly as they were not then air-conditioned. After 1973 all yachtsmen had bunks, except Leading Seaman Jamie Stewart, who was given special permission to retain his hammock, thus becoming the last sailor in the Royal Navy to use one. The yachtsmen's conditions were from 1973 thus largely in line with general service; except that the chief petty officers occupied four-berth cabins due to lack of space. The warrant officers and chief petty officers were combined together in one mess, and the petty officers and sergeants shared another. The junior rates occupied separate messes according to their departments, as in general service; seamen, stokers and supply. There was a large recreation space, where junior rates ate, and a canteen run by the NAAFI.

Nine Royal Marines were part of the complement, living in a separate mess called 'The Barracks'. One was the ship's butcher, one her postman, and the remainder performed security duties, including diving. When on Royal Duty at sea the Marines acted as orderlies for the Royal Family, and in harbour mounted guard at the foot of the gangway. Additional yachtsmen included the Yacht's photographer (Snaps), a physical training instructor, and three NAAFI staff.

All noise was kept to an absolute minimum, and the privacy of the Royal Family respected at all times. When on Royal Duty yachtsmen did not wear caps abaft the mainmast, thus saving the Royal Family from having to return constant salutes. Yachtsmen waited until spoken to by the Royal Family, who knew many of the permanent crew by christian name. All work aft was completed by 9am, and if required to go aft on duty after this time the 'underground route' (main and lower deck passages) was used. Plimsolls were worn for silence, and wherever possible orders were given by hand or flag signals; this was particularly useful when berthing with royalty embarked, as the noise of the welcome often drowned out any spoken order.

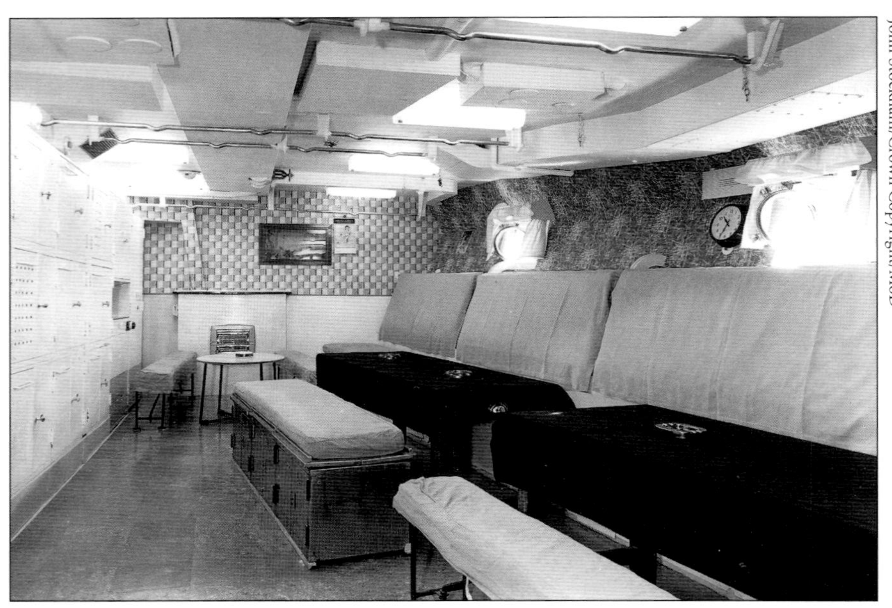

Clockwise (from above):
Above left and right: *The stokers' mess, pre the 1972/3 refit. Note the chromium rails for slinging hammocks, four abreast.*
Yachtsmen's accommodation after the refit.

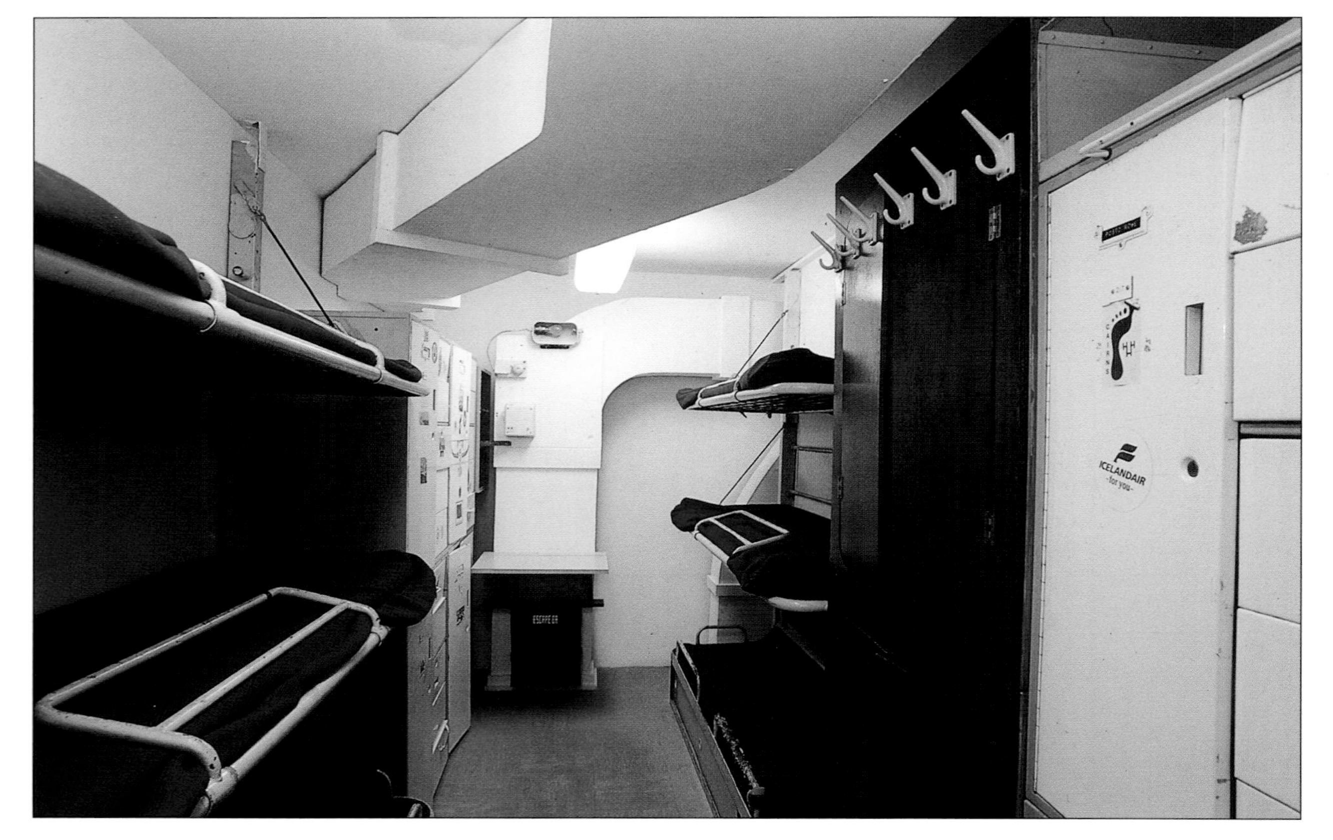

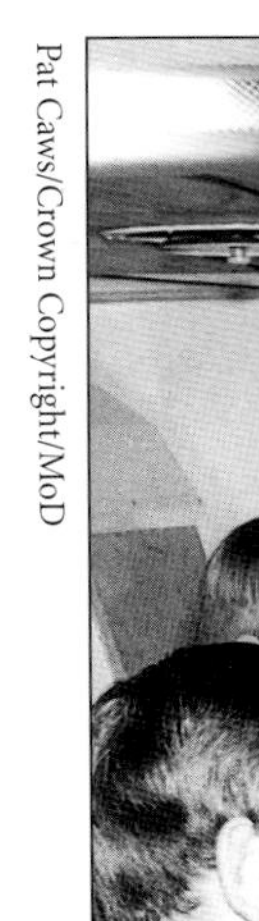

Prince Philip as Commandant General, Royal Marines, celebrates the 313th birthday in 1977 of the Corps with the Royal Marine detachment and Band on board BRITANNIA.

Uniform for yachtsmen was based on service issue, but they wore the jumper inside the trousers instead of outside. This was because a black silk bow was worn on the back of the trousers, reputedly as a mark of respect for Prince Albert, who died in 1861. Like most Yacht myths, this one is hard to verify! White badges were worn instead of red, and on the front of the shirt was a flash with the words 'Royal Yacht' surmounted by a crown.

Shoes with black rubber soles were forbidden on board as they would have marked the teak decks. The plimsolls yachtsmen wore were known as 'pumps,' thought to have been derived from the form of footwear commonly worn at that one-time focus of society – the Pump Room at Bath.

Smoking was allowed below decks, but never on the upper deck at sea or in harbour whenever the Standard was flying; nor when alongside when on Royal Duty with no Standard flying. When ashore in civilian clothes after 6.30pm yachtsmen were required to wear a collar and tie, whatever the climate.

As a privilege yachtsmen could bring relatives and personal friends on board at certain times when not on Royal Duty, but they were never allowed to bring the press on board. Guests could not be taken into the royal apartments, but could be shown round the upper deck and the rest of the Yacht.

BRITANNIA *floating out preparatory to painting during the 1987 refit.*

The Royal Coat of Arms on the bow.

CUSTOMS AND TRADITIONS

Three flags marked the presence of the Queen on board BRITANNIA, the Royal Standard, the Admiralty flag, and the Union flag.

The Royal Standard, always flown from the mainmast-head, is the personal flag of the sovereign, and its use can be traced back to the twelfth century, although the design has changed more than once.

The Admiralty flag, flown from the foremast-head, dates from the early-seventeenth century, and is a yellow anchor with the cable entwined about the stock and shank (i.e. a foul anchor) on a maroon background. It is flown by the Queen as Lord High Admiral, but if the Admiralty Board are also embarked in a ship accompanying the Queen, they too fly the Admiralty flag.

The Union flag, flown from the mizzenmast-head, dates from 1606, when James VI & I ordered the combination of the red cross of St George, for England, and the blue saltire of St Andrew for Scotland. The red saltire of St Patrick, for Ireland, was added in 1801. Initially it was ordered to be flown at sea by all ships of Southern and Northern Britain; later it was flown by HM Yachts to show that persons of importance were embarked. Later still it was flown by the senior admiral of a fleet, and is still today the flag of an Admiral of the Fleet.

As Commander Gavin has recorded, these three flags were first flown together at the Restoration in 1660 of King Charles II. 'It was as though the Royal Standard at the main proclaimed, "I am, by the Grace of God, Charles II, King of England"; the Union flag at the mizzen, "I am the King of Great Britain"; and the Admiralty flag at the fore, "I am Charles, King of England, and Lord High Admiral of the English Fleet."'[35]

Additionally the White Ensign was flown at the stern, and the Union Jack (a smaller Union flag) in the bow, day and night at sea, and between 'colours' and 'sunset' in harbour.

When other members of the Royal Family were embarked, only the Standards appropriate to their Royal Highness' use were hoisted; and the White Ensign and Union Jack as above.

An escort of at least one warship – usually a frigate – was always in attendance whenever the Queen was embarked in BRITANNIA, not only for safety, but also for despatch duties. (King Edward VII when on an official visit to Kiel in June 1904 was escorted by four cruisers and six destroyers.)

The firing of salutes, both royal and naval, was once so joyously and generously given that Pepys, as Secretary to the Admiralty, in 1675 devised a table of salutes to save powder. The Queen is entitled to a 21-gun salute, but as BRITANNIA was not fitted with saluting guns, salutes from other ships or shore batteries were returned by the Royal Escort.

The Queen was the only person piped on board or on leaving the Royal Yacht. However, as a personal mark of favour Her Majesty did give permission for occasional exceptions to be made:

Presidents of the USA on several occasions.
President of the Federal German Republic in 1978.
King Olaf of Norway in 1981.
The King of Spain in 1988.

The boatswain in charge of the piping party used a gold whistle, once the property of John Mair, boatswain of HMS TRIBUTE. He joined the frigate in 1805, just after a large shareout of prize money, and the ship's company decided he too should have a share of the benefit, and purchased the whistle for him. The whistle found its way to the Royal Naval Club, who presented it to the Queen in 1954, whence it came to BRITANNIA.

HMY BRITANNIA *with all flags and standard flying.*

The Trinity House yacht holds the traditional right to lead the Royal Yacht when in pilotage waters, but this is now only exercised on ceremonial occasions. The yacht IRENE is recorded in 1855 as preceding the VICTORIA & ALBERT II, but there are no earlier records.

BRITANNIA had blue mooring ropes, made especially for her. Until she decommissioned on 11 December 1997 she was the second oldest ship in commission in the Royal Navy, and the oldest afloat. HMS VICTORY is still in commission, but is in permanent dry-dock.

The hull of BRITANNIA was royal blue above the waterline and red below. A single band of gold leaf ran round the hull. The upper works were white with buff-coloured funnel and masts. The Royal Coat of Arms was on the bow, and the Royal Cypher on the stern. The ship's name was nowhere displayed on the hull or superstructure.

The Yacht was on Royal Duty when the Standard of Her Majesty the Queen or any other member of the Royal Family was flying; or when the Yacht was proceeding to or waiting to embark royalty.

The Royal Navy enjoys the privilege of drinking the toast to the sovereign whilst remaining seated; this dates from the days of sailing ships and their limited head-room. Conversely, with the increased headroom found in Royal Yachts, the toast to the sovereign was drunk standing up.

HMY BRITANNIA *leaving the Devonport covered dock, 1987.*

Royal Yacht officers wore the evening dress mess jacket (or bum-freezer) without the link buttons. This is reputed to date from when King Edward VII was dining in the wardroom, and his valet forgot to include the link buttons on his jacket – or possibly the jacket could not be done up. The officers of the VICTORIA & ALBERT III surreptitiously removed their buttons to follow the dress of their guest. The wardroom was a veritable treasure trove of traditions, quirks and precedents, and until accustomed to them new officers joining the Yacht found it expensive in 'fines' if adrift by a few seconds or dressed in the incorrect rig! Officers leaving the Royal Yachts traditionally presented the wardroom with a gift, and many fine pieces of silver were thus acquired over the years.

The Royal Yacht Dinner was originally restricted to officers currently serving in the Royal Yachts, and was held on board the ROYAL GEORGE in Portsmouth Harbour on New Year's Eve. It was revived or reorganised in 1887, and opened to past or present officers of the Royal Yachts. It has been held annually most years since then, apart from the First and Second World Wars.

The Board of the Green Cloth got its name from the cloth on which certain allowances were counted out in cash, and applied to officers, ratings and Members of the Royal Household as compensation for meals lost when waiting on royalty. When Queen Victoria was embarked for summer cruises, officers serving in the Royal Yachts were provided with food, wine, linen and plate. This was changed in 1864 to an allowance of three shillings per day, and in BRITANNIA's time was at the rate of 60 pence for officers, 45 pence for royal stewards, and 40 pence for Royal Marines.

When berthed alongside, the after gangway was for the use of the Royal Family only (and accompanying Household), and had a Royal Marine sentry at the shore end. The forward gangway was for the use of all other members of the Yacht.

The 43 flags used in dressing ship were hoisted in three seconds, and spelt no particular message. The line from the mainmast to the mizzen came out of the funnel.

HMY BRITANNIA *at Devonport; evening light.*

A YEAR IN THE LIFE OF BRITANNIA

BRITANNIA visited so many countries in her forty-three-year life that it would be excessively tedious to list her activities yearly in a blow-by-blow account. She made over 600 overseas visits as well as 85 State visits, 110 UK visits and 186 sea days/seminars/diplomatic receptions. In all she steamed 1 086 041 nautical miles, and circumnavigated the world eight times.

There were obviously highlights: her World Tour with the Duke of Edinburgh for the Olympic Games at Melbourne in 1956, the Yacht later visiting Antarctica; Canada in 1959 for the opening of the St Lawrence Seaway, when it is estimated half-a-million people saw the Yacht; her first visit to Australia and New Zealand in 1963; the Bicentennial of Captain Cook's discovery of Australia in 1970; Eastern Arabia in 1979; the evacuation of over 1300 people from the civil war in Aden in 1986; China and Hong Kong the same year; the USA in 1991; the memorable D-Day commemorations in 1994; and her final State role, the handing back of Hong Kong to China in 1997.

The Jubilee Year tours in 1977, coming almost exactly half-way through the Yacht's life, illustrate her role so admirably that it is worth recounting them in some detail, for they give an excellent illustration of how the Yacht was employed. During that year when on Royal Duty she visited several Pacific Islands, Australia, New Zealand, the east and west coasts of England, Northern Ireland, Scotland and the West Indies.

As the Flag Officer Royal Yachts, at that time Rear Admiral Sir Hugh Janion, KCVO, wrote:

'Never, perhaps, has HM Yacht BRITANNIA in her long career enjoyed such a magnificent year as this one in which we have celebrated the Silver Jubilee of Her Majesty's accession to the Throne. We have crossed the Atlantic, Pacific and Indian Oceans to complete our sixth circumnavigation and, as I write this, we are crossing the Atlantic again. By the end of the year, we shall have steamed 42 000 miles and visited 72 harbours and anchorages throughout the Commonwealth.'[36]

BRITANNIA slipped her moorings and sailed from Portsmouth on 28 December 1976, briefly refuelled at Madeira, then called at Antigua where the Band had three engagements; playing at the local cricket ground, the Governor's cocktail party and finally the ceremony of Beat Retreat.

On Saturday, 15 January 1977, she transited the Panama Canal and visited the Rodman Naval Base, embarking the British Ambassador, the Defence Attaché in Bogotá and the Commander of US Forces South for the canal transit.

The Yacht was accompanied by RFA GREY ROVER, enabling her to refuel at sea on passage to Tahiti, reached on 30 January, where much hospitality was exchanged with the French Naval Base.

A day was spent at Rarotonga in the Cook Islands (3 February), probably the perfect Pacific Island. A strong sports contingent went ashore for cricket, soccer, rugby, sailing, golf and tennis, and for the less energetic there was swimming from white sandy beaches. A cocktail party was given on board BRITANNIA, followed by 'Refreshment and Entertainment' ashore.

Palmerston Atoll (4 February) was settled by a Gloucestershire ploughman in 1861, and his grandson Ned Masters still ruled the island in 1977. BRITANNIA made a point of calling at this isolated island whenever

Clockwise (from right):
Crossing the line ceremony, 1970.
Princess Anne about to be dunked.
Princess Anne being dunked.

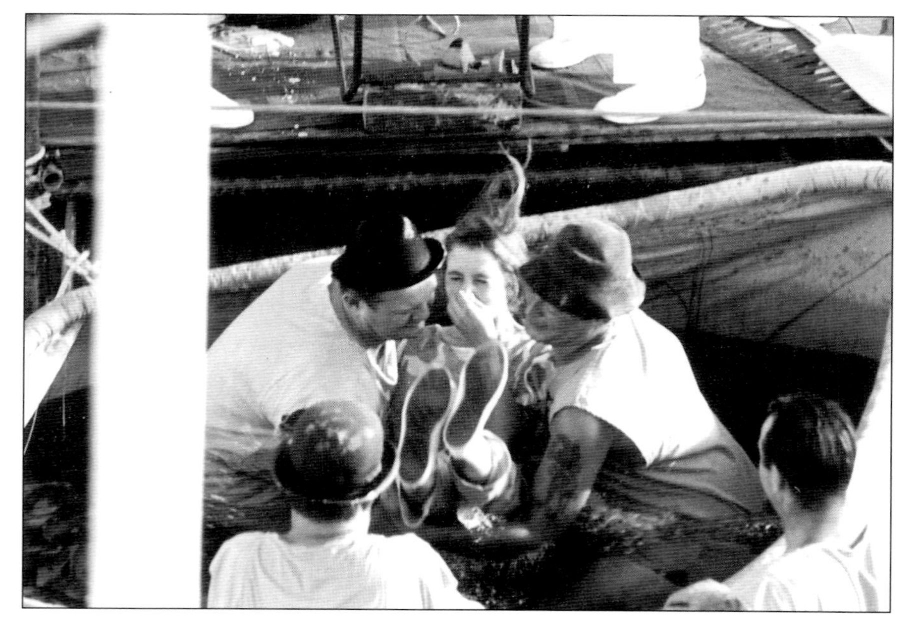

Prince Philip and Princess Anne during the Crossing the line ceremony, South Pacific 1970.

she was crossing the Pacific; the Yacht's doctor went ashore as usual, for it would probably be several months before the next ship called.

The period 6-10 February was spent at Pago Pago in American Samoa for a boiler clean and to make final preparations for the arrival of the Queen and the Duke of Edinburgh. During the next six weeks of Royal Duty the Yacht was to call at 18 ports, a tight schedule with little margin for bad weather.

On 10 February, after a twenty-three-hour flight from Britain, the Royal Party arrived at 9.40am. The Queen and the Duke of Edinburgh were accompanied by nine members of the Household, eight officials, two police officers and 25 staff. The Queen was received by the Governor, and later entertained him and a small group of Samoans to coffee on board; meanwhile the Yacht embarked five and a half tons of baggage. BRITANNIA sailed two hours after the Royal Flight had touched down, and after months of planning, the Silver Jubilee Tour of the Pacific started.

When royalty were embarked in BRITANNIA a warship escort was provided, not only for safety but for despatch duties. For the first stage of the Tour HMNZS TARANAKI was the Royal Escort, in company for the Queen's first visit to Apia, the capital of Western Samoa. The Royal Yacht was met by a fleet of Fautasi, enormously long war canoes propelled by up to 40 paddlers, who then escorted BRITANNIA into harbour.

The Yacht berthed at 6.30pm, and later that evening the Queen gave a dinner party for 40 guests, followed by the ceremony of Beat Retreat performed by the Royal Marine Band (and this, don't forget, after a 23-hour flight for the Royal Party).

The next day the Queen had a full programme of engagements ashore before the Yacht sailed that evening. One day at sea followed, Sunday 13th being lost when they crossed the International Date Line; King Neptune's Court duly assembled and initiated newcomers to his realm (those who had not previously Crossed the Line). The Royal Family were enthusiastic participants in this good-humoured ritual, and most of them have by now 'suffered' the lathering and shaving, followed by ducking in a canvas tank of sea water. The Queen, as Princess Elizabeth, was initiated along with her sister, Princess Margaret, when HMS VANGUARD Crossed the Line with the Royal Family embarked in 1947 en route to South Africa.

Monday, 14 February saw the Yacht berthed at Nuku'alofa, following a 21-gun salute from HMNZS TARANAKI in honour of the King of Tonga, and a reply from the shore battery. The Queen and the Duke of Edinburgh were guests of the Tongan Royal Family for the day, including a traditional feast of roast pig and fruits; those remaining on duty were not forgotten, for the King ordered ample supplies to be sent on board the Yacht. Her Majesty entertained the King and Queen to dinner on board, followed by Beat Retreat. BRITANNIA sailed at 11pm, and the author recalls the previous departure of the Yacht from Tonga in 1970:

> The wharf was packed with Tongans, and we sailed to the singing of a choir. Otherwise all was silence, and as we moved slowly from the pier we could see the shores of the bay lined for miles with flaming torches held aloft by the islanders, their total silence a sign of respect for royalty. It was among the most moving sights of the Tour.

The 15th was spent at sea on passage to Fiji, where BRITANNIA anchored in Suva Harbour the following day to an escort of yachts and canoes. At 10am Fijian chiefs embarked to perform the welcoming ceremony of Cavuikelekele on the verandah deck, following which the Queen and Prince Philip proceeded ashore by Royal Barge for a full day of engagements, ending with a State dinner given by the Prime Minister. BRITANNIA meantime had berthed alongside King's Wharf, and the next day, Thursday 17 February, the Queen and the Duke of Edinburgh flew to the neighbouring island of Valua Levu for engagements. That evening they hosted a return dinner on board BRITANNIA for the Prime Minister, followed by Beat Retreat before the Yacht sailed at 11pm.

Thirty-six hours later, on 22 February, BRITANNIA arrived at Auckland, New Zealand, to an impressive aquatic welcome. It would be incredibly tedious to both author and reader to list every single day's engagements, but an indication is given from the programme opposite.[37] After a full day for the Queen and the Duke of Edinburgh ashore there was a reception on board, following which the Yacht sailed with the Prime Minister and Mrs Muldoon embarked.

HMNZS CANTERBURY took over as Royal Escort, and the Yacht visited a further seven ports in the next fourteen days: Whangerei, Napier, Gisborne, Dunedin, Timaru, Lyttleton and Akaroa. Nearly all passages had to be carried out at a demanding high speed to meet the royal programme ashore, leaving little margin for bad weather. The Queen and the Duke of Edinburgh visited numerous places ashore, using the Yacht as a base, and hosting receptions, dinners and the ceremony of Beat Retreat. The Maori welcome to the Queen this time was at Gisborne, as always a very moving ceremony.

The Royal Party disembarked at Lyttleton on 7 March to fly on to Australia, and BRITANNIA bade farewell to New Zealand and sailed across the Tasman Sea, being joined by HMAS VAMPIRE off Newcastle, New South Wales. The Queen and the Duke of Edinburgh meanwhile visited Canberra, Queanbeyan, Brisbane, Tamworth and Williamtown before rejoining BRITANNIA at Newcastle on 11 March. The Prime Minister of Australia and Mrs Fraser embarked with the Royal Party, and the Yacht sailed that evening for Sydney. After a peaceful day at sea BRITANNIA entered Sydney Harbour on Sunday 13th to a tumultuous welcome and a hectic programme ashore which ended with a supper party on board for 100 guests.

The Queen and the Duke of Edinburgh flew to Tasmania on the 14th for a two-day visit, and BRITANNIA sailed for Melbourne, arriving early on the 16th to avoid becoming embroiled in a union dispute. The UK

NEW ZEALAND

Tuesday, 22nd FEBRUARY, 1977
Auckland

[8.30 a.m. 21 gun salute from shore saluting battery.]

9.30 a.m. H.M.Y. BRITANNIA anchors off H.M.N.Z. Naval Base, Auckland.

10.00 a.m. The Queen and The Duke of Edinburgh leave H.M.Y. BRITANNIA by barge.
Dress: U.1/S.B.J.

10.05 a.m. Arrive H.M.N.Z.S. Philomel landing.
Received by Sir Denis Blundell (Governor-General) and Lady Blundell and the Rt. Hon. Robert Muldoon (Prime Minister) and Mrs. Muldoon.
The Prime Minister presents Commander E. D. Deane (Commanding Officer, H.M.N.Z.S. Philomel).
Leave by car.

10.10 a.m. Arrive Naval Base Review Area.
Royal Salute.
The Queen, accompanied by The Duke of Edinburgh, inspects Tri-Service Guard of Honour by landrover.
Address of welcome by the Prime Minister.
(S) The Queen replies.

10.30 a.m. Military Review.
Official presentations.

11.15 a.m. Leave by landrover.

11.20 a.m. Arrive H.M.N.Z.S. Philomel landing.
Sir Patrick O'Dea presents Mr. J. M. Foster (Chairman of the Organising Committee for "The Two Man Round the North Island Race").
Leave in Royal Barge, passing through the entrants for the race en route.

[11.25 a.m. H.M.Y. BRITANNIA berths at Princes Wharf East.]

11.25 a.m. Arrive Devonport Wharf.
Received by the Hon. G. F. Gair (Minister of Housing) and Mrs. Gair.
The Duke of Edinburgh fires the final gun to start the race.
Mr. Gair presents Mr. P. G. Sheenan (Mayor of Devonport) and Mrs. Brougham (Mayoress).
Walk down wharf to car.

11.40 a.m. Leave by car.

50

NEW ZEALAND

Tuesday, 22nd FEBRUARY, 1977—*continued*

12.10 p.m. Arrive Auckland reception point.
Received by the Prime Minister and Mrs. Muldoon.
The Prime Minister presents Sir Dove Myer Robinson (Mayor of Auckland) and Lady Myer Robinson.
Walk among people down Queen Street, through Queen Elizabeth II Square.

12.30 p.m. Arrive Trillo's reception lounge.
Civic presentations.
Sign visitors' book.
(The Duke of Edinburgh changes out of uniform).

12.55 p.m. Attend civic luncheon. *Dress: L.S.*

2.15 p.m. Retire.

2.25 p.m. Leave by car.

2.45 p.m. Arrive Ellerslie Racecourse.
Received by the Prime Minister and Mrs. Muldoon.
Attend young people's gathering.

3.30 p.m. Leave by car.

3.45 p.m. Arrive Overseas Passenger Terminal.
Received by "Representatives of the Guards Association and Royal Marines Association will be assembled at the Terminal."

The Duke of Edinburgh

(S) **4.30 p.m.** Presentation of Gold Awards (40) onboard H.M.Y. BRITANNIA. *Dress: L.S.*

The Queen and The Duke of Edinburgh

5.30 p.m. Reception for Royal Visit Officials and spouses. *Dress: L.S.*

6.00 p.m.– 6.30 p.m. Press reception.

8.00 p.m. Dinner party onboard H.M.Y. BRITANNIA for the Governor-General and Lady Blundell and the Prime Minister and Mrs. Muldoon and the Cabinet and wives. *Dress: D.J.*

10.00 p.m. Reception onboard H.M.Y. BRITANNIA.
Beat Retreat.

11.30 p.m. H.M.Y. BRITANNIA sails.
(The Prime Minister and Mrs. Muldoon are embarked).

52

Extracts of the day's programme.

papers tended to concentrate on the Republican dissenters, who were a small but vociferous minority, whilst the Melbourne papers gave massive favourable cover to both the Queen and her Royal Yacht. The Royal Party spent the afternoon at Melbourne races, then hosted a dinner on board BRITANNIA; a busy day on the 17th, then the Yacht sailed for the two-day passage to Adelaide, arriving at 10am on Sunday 20 March. That day repeated the full pattern of so many others, ending with a formal dinner and Beat Retreat.

The Yacht sailed on 22 March, the Queen and the Duke of Edinburgh having moved ashore to Government House before leaving for engagements in Northern Australia, including Port Moresby and Darwin, intending to rejoin BRITANNIA at Geraldtown. A cyclonic storm when the Yacht was crossing the Great Australian Bight caused this plan to be cancelled, and BRITANNIA sailed direct to Fremantle, arriving on 26 March for a hectic week of public and private engagements.

Opposite: *HMY* BRITANNIA *leaving Sydney.*

After a final reception and formal luncheon, Royal Duty was over with the departure by air for England of the Queen and the Duke of Edinburgh on 30 March. All that remained for BRITANNIA to do was sail back to Portsmouth, half the world away. This she did by way of Diego da Garcia, the Suez Canal, Malta and Gibraltar, arriving on 2 May after four months away and having steamed 28 107 miles.

Throughout the Tour BRITANNIA was accompanied by the RFA GREY ROVER, refuelling the Yacht and her escorts 31 times. The Flag Officer Royal Yachts later wrote: '…in retrospect I do not know how I would have met Her Majesty's programme if I had had to rely on local arrangements for refuelling and revictualling, naval and NAAFI stores.'[38]

The Tour is best summed up in part of a letter FORY wrote to the First Sea Lord the day before the Yacht returned to Portsmouth:

> BRITANNIA, in the past four months since sailing from Portsmouth on 28 December 1976, has undoubtedly done nothing but good for the British cause abroad, both on and off Royal Duty. Appealing to both young and old alike from Heads of State to young children on the jetty, they are all fascinated by the Yacht. When on Royal Duty the attraction is obvious, but at other times they still appear in their hundreds to admire 'The Queen's Yacht'. It could of course be argued that this is so for any visiting warship; however they are usually open to visitors and not the subject of the security measures necessary to keep the general public at a respectful distance.
>
> In conclusion I doubt whether the Yacht has ever been seen by so many people, not only in the countries visited but also on television all over the world. Whilst it is the Queen's Jubilee Year and therefore very special, I think the Yacht is an integral and invaluable part of the Queen's activities both abroad and at home and we all look forward to our next spell of Royal Duty in the United Kingdom. The part we have to play is perhaps summed up by the following message to all Royal Yachtsmen from Her Majesty the Queen.
>
> 'The success of our visits in the Pacific and to Australia and New Zealand is due in no small measure to the splendid service of all Royal Yachtsmen.
>
> 'Apart from providing us with a most welcome home from home, the Yacht has never failed to impress all who have seen her and all the guests who have been on board. We look forward to seeing you all again in June and wish you a comfortable and safe passage home. Splice the Mainbrace.'[39]

BRITANNIA was at Portsmouth for a month, giving well-earned leave, preparing for the summer tour of the United Kingdom and having a gleaming coat of new paint applied by the Dockyard. On Sunday 5 June she sailed from Portsmouth to a mooring in the Pool of London and the week celebrating the Silver Jubilee. The Yacht provided officers and yachtsmen for official duties at the Service of Thanksgiving at St Paul's Cathedral on the 6th. On the 9th the Queen and the Duke of Edinburgh, accompanied by 39 Household and staff embarked on BRITANNIA; that day they gave a formal luncheon for 54 guests, including the Archbishop of Canterbury and Mrs Coggan and the Prime Minister and Mrs Callaghan. As BRITANNIA was moored in the Pool of London, all the Household and guests had to be embarked by the Yacht's boats – no small task.

Returning to Portsmouth BRITANNIA prepared for the first of the United Kingdom Tours, this being to the West Coast and Wales; Liverpool on 20/21 June, Holyhead on the 22nd, Pembroke Dock and Barry on the 23rd and Cardiff on the 23rd-25th, embarking the Prime Minister and Mrs Callaghan for the last visit of the Tour. The programme usually included a full day of engagements ashore for the Queen and the Duke of Edinburgh, a formal dinner for up to 50 guests in the evening, followed by a reception for 200 guests on board ending with Beat Retreat.

The Queen Reviewing the Fleet, 28 June 1977 embarked in HMY BRITANNIA.

Then followed a fast passage back to Portsmouth for the Silver Jubilee Fleet Review at Spithead on the 28th, the largest gathering of Royal Naval, Commonwealth and foreign ships since the Coronation Review of 1953. Naval reviews have a long tradition stretching back to Roman times, for they were not only a display of naval strength but were also an occasion for the monarch to thank the fleet after a battle. On ceremonial occasions such as this they were a chance for the Royal Navy to parade before the Lord High Admiral, and as the Prince of Wales said: 'When the Queen reviews her ships today she will be reviewing, in human terms, the continuation of that great maritime spirit which has proved to be the strength and saving grace of this island on so many previous occasions and which is still the envy of so many navies throughout the world.'

There were 101 ships and two hovercraft from the Royal Navy, the only survivor from the 1953 Review being HMS RECLAIM, the diving trials ship. Seventy-nine ships represented the navies of Commonwealth, NATO, CENTO and EEC nations, as well as many vessels representing the Merchant Navy and the Fishing Industry and organisations like Trinity House, Sail Training Associations and the RNLI. Closer inshore were anchored a myriad of yachts representing yacht clubs from around Britain. Dressed overall the ships were anchored in ten lines, seven miles long, and at 11am BRITANNIA sailed to commence the Review.

On board were Her Majesty the Queen, Admiral of the Fleet the Duke of Edinburgh, Commander the Prince of Wales, the Princess Anne, the Prince Edward, the Duke of Gloucester, the Duke of Kent, Prince Michael of Kent and Admiral of the Fleet Earl Mountbatten of Burma. Among the guests were the Prime Minister

Group photo – ship's company.

and Mrs Callaghan, Admiral of the Fleet Sir Edward Ashmore (Chief of the Defence Staff) and Admiral Sir Terence Lewin (First Sea Lord).

Exercising their traditional right to lead the sovereign were the Elder Brethren of Trinity House embarked in the PATRICIA, and BRITANNIA was followed by the Type 42 destroyer HMS BIRMINGHAM with the Board of Admiralty embarked. Three RFA's, LYNESS, SIR GERAINT and SIR TRISTRAM had sailed earlier from Southampton; embarked were ministers, MPs, ambassadors, naval holders of the Victoria Cross and George Cross, and well-known figures from public life.

As BRITANNIA passed Spit Refuge buoy the fleet fired a Royal Salute, and the Yacht then anchored at the head of the review lines and dressed overall. The Queen gave a luncheon on board for the Admiralty Board and Flag Officers, then at 2.30pm the Review Column weighed and proceeded for the two-hour, fifteen-mile journey through the lines. Sadly it was a dull and overcast afternoon, which caused the cancellation of the fly-past, apart from a reduced complement of helicopters. BRITANNIA anchored on completion of the Review, and after the helicopter fly-past Her Majesty entertained 200 naval ratings from the fleet. That evening, according to tradition, the Queen had dinner with her admirals and captains in the upper hangar of HMS ARK ROYAL, following which a splendid display of fireworks from Southsea preceded the signal for the fleet to be illuminated. The end of a most memorable day.

The following day BRITANNIA berthed at South Railway Jetty and Her Majesty landed for an official visit to the City of Portsmouth, allowing the Yacht two weeks to prepare for the next tour of the United Kingdom. The East Coast Tour started on 10 July, and visited Felixstowe on the 11th, Grimsby on the 12th, Hull on the 12th and 13th, Middlesbrough on the 14th and Newcastle on the 15th. Receptions, audiences, walkabouts, luncheons and dinners followed one another at each port, and the Royal Marine Band lost count of the number of times they Beat Retreat.

BRITANNIA returned to Portsmouth on the 19th, and sailed ten days later for Cowes Week, by now a tradition with the Royal Family; on board were the Duke of Edinburgh, Prince Andrew, Prince Edward, Princess Alexandra, Mr Angus Ogilvy and their children. The Queen embarked at Southampton on 4 August for the final United Kingdom tour, this time to the West Country and Northern Ireland. Torbay and Plymouth were visited on the 5th, Falmouth the 6th, Lundy Island the 7th, Avonmouth the 8th, Ramsay Island the 9th, Belfast the 10th (where the Queen made her first helicopter flight) and finally Portrush on 11 August.

The Western Isles Cruise following Cowes Week was by then well established as the start of the Royal Family's holiday at Balmoral, and on 12 August the Queen was joined by Princess Anne, Princess Margaret, Viscount Linley and Lady Sarah Armstrong-Jones. This was a time for the Family to relax, going ashore for picnics or barbecues, visiting old friends and enjoying the magnificent scenery. When on royal tours it was unusual for junior officers to dine with the Royal Family, but on this cruise each officer was invited aft at least once.

The final day was always spent visiting the Queen Mother at her remote and romantic Castle of Mey. So at exactly 11am on 15 August – the ritual never varied, although the dates did – the Royal Family mounted the steps of Scrabster Harbour to greet the Queen Mother. After lunch, a walk round the grounds, and tea, the Royal Family embarked in the Yacht, and as she sailed away the Queen Mother sent off multi-coloured rockets from the castle turrets, while BRITANNIA replied by igniting flares in a dramatic farewell ritual. BRITANNIA docked as usual at 6am in Aberdeen, as silently as possible so as not to wake the Queen. By mid-morning the Royal Family had left for Balmoral, and BRITANNIA was free to return to Portsmouth.

At the end of that summer BRITANNIA had steamed 4264 miles in eleven weeks of extensive tours of the United Kingdom and as one officer commented, 'we were able to witness much of the tremendous warmth of the British people extended to the Queen during her Silver Jubilee Year.'[39a]

After giving summer leave BRITANNIA sailed again on 30 September for the Silver Jubilee Tour of the Caribbean, fuelling in the Azores before arriving in Bermuda on 9 October. The Yacht made final prepara-

Caribbean Tour 1977, First Day covers.

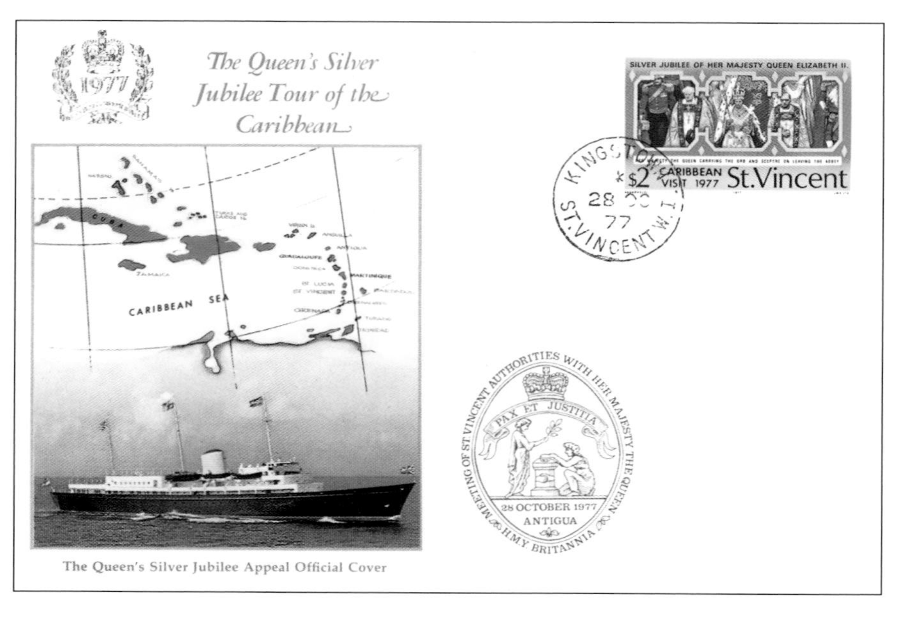

HMY BRITANNIA *in the Western Isles 1974.*

tions for the arrival of the Queen and the Duke of Edinburgh, who were visiting Ottawa. Hospitable as ever, the island entertained yachtsmen for three days before BRITANNIA sailed to Freeport to refuel briefly, then it was on to Nassau on the 15th for a tumultuous welcome.

HMS ANTRIM joined as Royal Escort, and on the afternoon of 19 October the Queen and the Duke of Edinburgh arrived at Nassau after a full four days in Ottawa; with Her Majesty came nine members of the Household, nine officials and 22 staff. That evening the Queen and the Duke of Edinburgh attended a dinner and reception at Government House. The following day was a typical one, as shown by the programme opposite, ending with a dinner on board for 40 guests, a reception afterwards for 200, and, finally, Beat Retreat. The islanders were not to be outdone however, for as BRITANNIA sailed 'they packed the jetty swaying and singing to the music of the Police Band. Alongside them leapt and gyrated the colourful, excited "Junkaroo"; men and women dressed in wonderful replicas of Beefeaters, Yeomen of the Guard and the Crown Jewels. A warm and moving send off for the Queen at the end of a remarkable occasion.'[40]

Five days at sea followed, cruising south through the islands, with time for picnics, barbecues and swimming ashore. On the 25th the Queen and the Duke of Edinburgh attended a dinner in the wardroom to commemorate the Immortal Memory of Admiral Lord Nelson's victory at Trafalgar,[41] then on the 26th BRITANNIA arrived at Tortola. As usual there was a full day of engagements, including a dinner on board for 40 guests representing Tortola, the Turks and Caicos, the Cayman Islands and Anguilla. This was followed by a reception for 200, ending with Beat Retreat before the Yacht sailed. Another day at sea, then on the 28th the pattern of engagements was repeated at Antigua. Three further days were spent cruising, during which the Queen and the Duke of Edinburgh visited the messdecks on BRITANNIA, enabling nearly every yachtsman to meet Her Majesty. Whilst with the Royal Marine detachment the Duke of Edinburgh (Commandant General of the Royal Marines) cut a cake to celebrate the 313th birthday of the Corps of Royal Marines (see p 267). On the 30th a private visit was paid to the island of Mustique, where the Princess Margaret welcomed the Queen ashore.

Barbados was reached on Monday 31 October, preceded by a fly-past by Concorde, arriving to take the Royal Party back home. BRITANNIA berthed at 2pm, and the Queen had engagements ashore followed by a press reception on board; later there was a dinner and reception at Government House, the latter involving 1000 guests. The 1st of November was again a full day of engagements, and the following day Her Majesty departed for London, Concorde whisking her home in four hours to attend the State Opening of Parliament.

This was the end of Royal Duty for BRITANNIA in Silver Jubilee Year, but she had two more days in which to enjoy Barbados before sailing for home on 5 November. She called at Madeira to refuel on the 13th, and arrived back at Portsmouth on 18 November, having sailed 9718 miles in six weeks. As the detailed itinerary above shows, it was not all sun and lazing on tropical beaches, although there was a certain amount of that to compensate for the hard work of Royal Duty. There was a more serious diplomatic role to be played, binding these islands closer to the Commonwealth; the enthusiastic welcomes given to the Queen wherever she called showed that BRITANNIA helped to achieve that aim.

When she secured to her mooring in Portsmouth BRITANNIA had in Silver Jubilee Year steamed 42 000 miles circumnavigating the world, visiting 72 harbours and anchorages. The circumnavigation was her sixth, and she had run a total of 569 400 miles since her launch twenty-four years earlier. Meeting an exact and exacting timetable was not all plain sailing, as one wag in the engineering department wrote:

> And still it keeps going – the machinery easily maintains full power, the air conditioning keeps you fresh, the First World War vintage evaporators give you almost unlimited quantities of sparkling fresh water, and all the services you've come to accept are, thanks to us, working away down there, twenty-four hours a day, seven days a week, your interests at the forefront of our minds...

The electrical department too had its problems: 'The usually calm exterior was ruffled however when the main armament (stabilisers) failed. Fortunately spares were available from the Science Museum as were the two members of the department old enough to remember how to fit them!'[42]

In her farewell message to FORY the Queen surely expressed her feelings for all those years of BRITANNIA's service when she said: 'Prince Philip and I wish to thank you and all Royal Yachtsmen for your outstanding contribution to the celebration of my Silver Jubilee. Our visits both at home and overseas were made all the more comfortable and impressive by the presence of the Yacht. We appreciate that this has meant a great deal of hard work. God speed your passage home and may you have a happy Christmas. Splice the Mainbrace.'

THE BAHAMAS

Thursday, 20th OCTOBER, 1977

New Providence

10.40 a.m.	Leave H.M.Y. BRITANNIA by car. *Dress: M.D. (Decs.) (T)/U.1*
10.45 a.m.	Arrive at the Senate. National Anthem.
(S)	Opening of Parliament. Balcony appearance.
11.15 a.m.	Leave by car.
11.20 a.m.	Arrive H.M.Y. BRITANNIA.
12.15 p.m.– 12.45 p.m.	Press Reception on board H.M.Y. BRITANNIA. *Dress: L.S.*
1.00 p.m.	Private lunch.
2.40 p.m.	Leave H.M.Y. BRITANNIA by car.
2.50 p.m.	Arrive Broadcasting Corporation of The Bahamas. Tour the building. Unveil a plaque and open the ZNS TV Station. Sign visitors' book.
3.20 p.m.	Leave by car.
3.40 p.m.	Arrive Nassau Harbour. Walk from entrance to Prince George Wharf to H.M.Y. BRITANNIA (200 yards).
3.55 p.m.	Arrive H.M.Y. BRITANNIA.
	The Queen
4.15 p.m.	Investiture on board H.M.Y. BRITANNIA (17 recipients).
	The Duke of Edinburgh
4.15 p.m.– 5.00 p.m.	Embark in Royal barge and sail past assembled boats in Nassau Harbour.
	The Queen and The Duke of Edinburgh
8.00 p.m.	Dinner on board H.M.Y. BRITANNIA (40 guests). *Dress: D.J. (Decs.) (T)*
9.45 p.m.	Reception on board H.M.Y. BRITANNIA (200 guests).
10.45 p.m.	Beat Retreat.
11.15 p.m.	Farewells.
Later	H.M.Y. BRITANNIA sails.

30

An extract of the day's programme in the Bahamas.

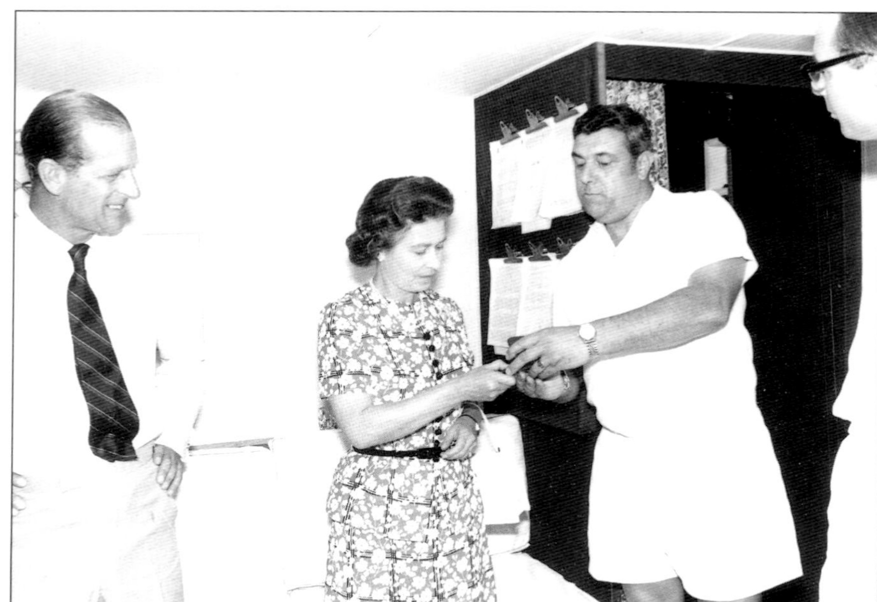

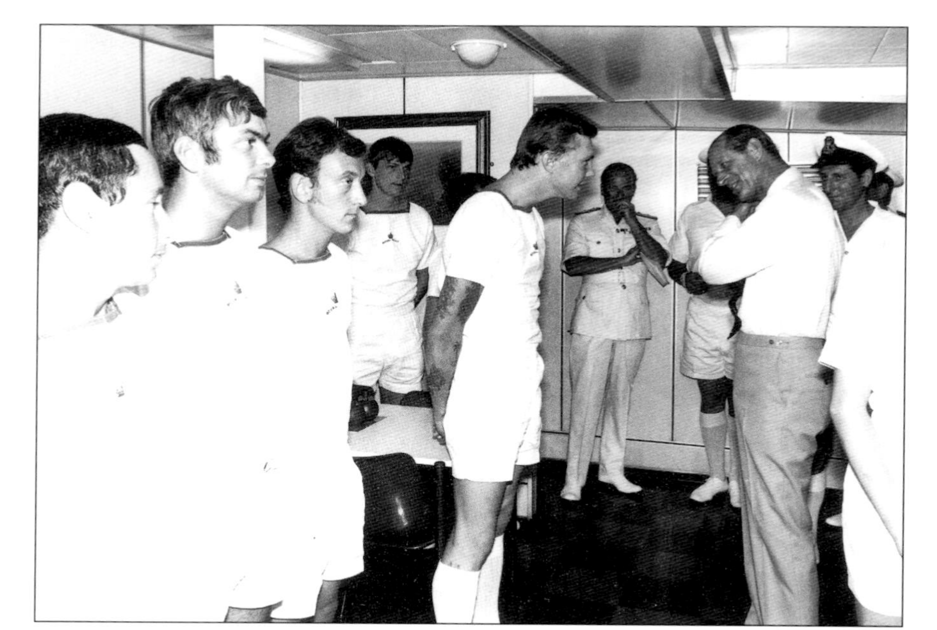

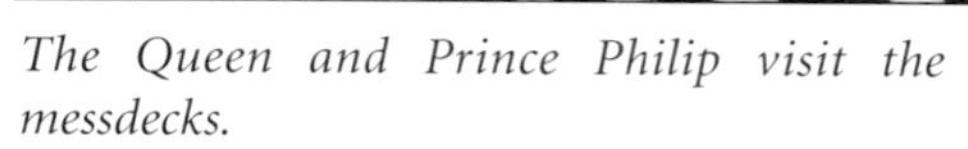

The Queen and Prince Philip visit the messdecks.

THE FINAL YEARS

Following the Jubilee Year Tours BRITANNIA settled into the familiar pattern of State visits, overseas visits to both Commonwealth and non-Commonwealth countries, diplomatic receptions, sea days and seminars – and, of course, Cowes Week each August, followed by the Western Isles Cruise.

Increasingly the Yacht was used for diplomatic and embassy receptions aimed at the commercial and trade sectors, along with sea days, when top businessmen were invited for a day on board BRITANNIA to promote British trade. They were started in a small way in 1963 when Prince Philip presided over a round-table talk on industrial and commercial relations with 60 employers and trade unionists in Australia.

In 1968 BRITANNIA was used to promote British trade following a State visit to Brazil, but the true potential of the Yacht as a business and seminar vessel was not fully appreciated until the State visit to Mexico in 1975. Since then BRITANNIA was used many times to promote British trade, often at the end of a State visit overseas. The trick was to balance promoting business with the aura of the Royal Yacht, for as one courtier said: 'You have to keep the gravitas of the Royal Yacht, and bear in mind the serious fact that she is the Queen's residence at sea.'[43]

In 1981 BRITANNIA played host to Italian businessmen when she cruised round the Bay of Naples for a day with the British Invisible Exports Council. As the Council's Director General William Clarke said: 'We carefully checked the business coming from that cruise and 500 million US dollars can be directly attributed to face-to-face contacts on BRITANNIA. It is the ideal forum for the kind of business that depends on personal contact. The charisma of the Royal Yacht attracts high-calibre decision makers who wouldn't normally come to this kind of conference if it was held in a top hotel.' As a past FORY put it: 'It's one thing to turn down a five-star hotel, quite another to refuse an invitation to come on board BRITANNIA.'[44]

In 1983 70 Swedish top businessmen were invited for a sea day in BRITANNIA to meet 20 London bankers, and not one of those invited refused. 'The result is expected to be in hundreds of million pounds sterling,' said Mr Clarke. Business included a £32 million equity issue for a Swedish construction company by a London bank, financial co-operation in a Bombay port development bid, and an Indonesian hydro project. 'A significant proportion originated from contacts made on board the Royal Yacht,' said Mr Clarke.[45] BRITANNIA's presence at the Anglo-Indian trade summit in 1993 is credited with finalising contracts worth more than £1 billion. Companies that had been haggling over the small print for years were told that if they completed their deals in time, they could sign their contracts with a ceremony on board the Yacht; the arguments were soon resolved.[46] The return of the Royal Yacht in diplomatic terms was immense, but sometimes difficult to quantify in terms of hard cash.

A more tangible return was shown from the costing exercise of a State visit by the Queen to Japan in 1991. It emerged that it was cheaper to locate BRITANNIA halfway across the world than to hire a local hotel with all its attendant security problems.[47] A Royal Yacht provides a familiar, secure base for the sovereign, complete with the communications and entertaining facilities required by a Head of State. Many smaller countries, particularly in the Commonwealth, would balk at the costs and responsibilities involved in a State visit were it not for the Royal Yacht.

There is no doubt of the immense diplomatic and political gains that BRITANNIA brought to Britain; what was impossible to quantify were the financial returns. However, *The Times* of 11 December 1996 reported that BRITANNIA through sea days had earned £2 billion in trade deals during the previous five years; i.e . £400 million per annum. Her annual running cost was £10 million, but this figure took no account of taxation on the crew's pay, on the Yacht's maintenance, or on the £400 million earnt above. Rather than being a charge to the nation, it is far more likely that BRITANNIA was a net earner.[48]

In 1997 the Secretary of State for Defence, Mr Michael Portillo said: 'BRITANNIA has lent her prestige to the promotion of British exports worldwide and the attraction of inward investment to Britain, and she has hosted numerous commercial events. The benefits that BRITANNIA has brought to the British economy *are invaluable*.'[49] (My italics.)

Every country needs to advertise its wares, and there was no greater advertisement for Great Britain Ltd than the Royal Yacht, encapsulating as she did engineering excellence, tradition and stability in a changing world. Even if one accepted the annual running cost of £10 million (which was highly debatable as a net sum) the cost of running BRITANNIA was less than half Sainsbury's 1997 advertising budget. Which gave better value to the Nation?

On 23 June 1994 the Secretary of State for Defence, Malcolm Rifkind, announced to the House of Commons that the Government had decided to decommission BRITANNIA in 1997. Her last major refit was in 1987, and a further one in 1996/7 would be necessary at an estimated cost of £17 million, which would only prolong her life for a further five years.

Mr Rifkind went on to say that the Queen, 'had made it known that in the light of changes in the pattern of Royal visits since the Yacht was built, she does not consider a Royal Yacht to be necessary in future *solely* (my italics) for the purpose of foreign travel... Nonetheless the Government believes it is right to consider, without commitment, whether there should be a replacement at some future point...'[50]

The Queen and the Royal Family were saddened at the decision, but they had known for some time that the ship could not last for ever. They were well aware that public opinion probably would not countenance a new Yacht from the State purse, and, contrary to popular belief, the Queen certainly could not afford to build or run a new Yacht. The divorces of the Prince of Wales and the Duke of York, along with the behaviour of certain junior members of the Royal Family, had led to widespread anti-Royalist feelings, although the monarchy was, in fact, changing and adapting, as it has done throughout the centuries. The result in some quarters was a perception of a Royal Family out of touch with reality, expensive to maintain, frivolous in the lower ranks, and largely irrelevant to the closing years of the twentieth century. However debatable some of these opinions may have been, they certainly did not help the cause of a replacement for BRITANNIA.

The Queen and Prince Philip had a deep affection for BRITANNIA, for they had been very closely involved with her building and use, literally from the keel upwards. As Prince Philip said: 'Almost every previous sovereign had been responsible for building a church, a castle, a palace or just a house. The only comparable structure built in the present reign is BRITANNIA.'[51] BRITANNIA had served them well, averaging for the Queen two State visits and six overseas visits per year – in addition to eleven overseas and UK visits per year by other members of the Royal Family. However, the Queen was getting older, the patterns of travel and diplomacy were changing, and however much BRITANNIA provided a 'home-from-home' during arduous overseas visits it was questionable whether a Royal Yacht was still an essential. If the concession for a new Yacht was increasing trade and commercial use, maybe the time had come to draw a line.

The Government argued that refitting BRITANNIA at a cost of £17 million was not viable. Details of how this estimate was arrived at were not given, but several eminent naval architects found the sum difficult to justify in the light of commercial practice; say for a cruise liner being refitted to meet current SOLAS (Saving of Life at Sea) standards. BRITANNIA was cosseted all her life, and although forty-three years old the hull was in excellent condition, as was found in the 1991/2 docking and inspection. In the tender documents

HMY BRITANNIA

Watercolour by Colin M. Baxter – 'HMY Britannia entering Portsmouth Harbour'.

relating to future use of BRITANNIA the Government stated: 'Despite expected wastage, due to age, no cracking has been detected in the main hull girder... In general, much of the structure is in mint condition...'

However, the internal equipment, particularly on the electrical side, required major refitting, even though the document went on to detail all the major upgrading work since the Yacht was built – an impressive list. Still, it is difficult to see how the sum of £17 million was arrived at, unless for Treasury or political motives. Certainly the political will at the time seemed to be lacking to make a sensible, or indeed any, decision, for it was not for another two and a half years that one was made.

Sir Donald Gosling, the well known industrialist and yachtsman, was absolutely correct when he commented that BRITANNIA was a classic, with a line and style no modern yacht could reproduce. The dramatic presence she created was an essential part of her 'cachet', as was the interior, right down to the light and bathroom fittings.

Even if the £17 million refit would only prolong the life of BRITANNIA for five years, at £3.4 million a year that would have been considerably less than the interest charge on the estimated £80 million for a replacement. (No one in marine circles believed the Government's estimate of £60 million for a new yacht.) Given the royal and political will the sensible course would have been to refit BRITANNIA for a further five years' life, during which time a new yacht could have been designed and built for joint use of the sovereign and industry.

From the June 1994 announcement to decommission BRITANNIA until January 1997 there seemed to be almost total lethargy from the Government. This was in sharp contrast to a flurry of activity from private firms eager to promote an alternative new Royal Yacht. However, the All Party Royal Yacht Parliamentary Group reported to the Prime Minister, and a financial strategy was commissioned from Singer & Friedlander to examine the possibility of a new yacht costing about £80 million.

There were also the inevitable questions as to the need for, and cost of, a Royal Yacht. Ever since Charles II built his first yacht in 1661 there have been complaints in Parliament and the country against the expense of the upkeep of nearly all successive yachts.

The Admiralty has always been responsible for the building and upkeep of Royal Yachts, although they were usually made available to the navy in times of need. BRITANNIA was built with a dual-role as a Royal Yacht and as a hospital ship for the Royal Navy, and for most of her life it was technically feasible for her to achieve that role. Any new Royal Yacht would not have been dual-role, but one option was for the Yacht to be firmly on commercial and industrial promotion lines in addition to royal use.

The Royal Navy had to man and maintain BRITANNIA from a shrinking budget of manpower and money, when she had no military effectiveness whatever. In the annual Defence Budget of £23 billion (1994), the cost of running the Yacht was insignificant, but a more equable method would have been to allocate the State Visit costs to the Foreign Office, and sea days to the Department of Trade and Industry.

The arguments against a new Royal Yacht were well paraded. The contentions ran that she was an anachronism, a relic of Empire; that she was elitist in an age of democracy; that the need for a yacht in an age of air transport was no longer necessary; that she was expensive to run in both men and money; and that she was no longer required with the shrinking ties of the Commonwealth.

Less well paraded were the reasons for a Yacht; that she represented stability in a changing world; that all Heads of State are, by definition, elitist, and that Britain should suitably maintain the Head of State of a major maritime power; that she was cost effective, impressive, and provided a 'home-from-home' for the monarch on State visits, which are frequently gruelling; that a new yacht could be run for half the manpower and cost of BRITANNIA, who was herself a net earner to the nation; that 95 per cent by quantity and 77 per

IWM – CT1496

HMY BRITANNIA *at Dartmouth, with Britannia Royal Naval College behind. Compare this with the* VICTORIA & ALBERT II *on p 165, before the college was built in 1902.*

50th anniversary of D-Day.

Imperial War Museum, London. CT 1592

The Queen and Prince Philip.

Imperial War Museum, London. CT1590

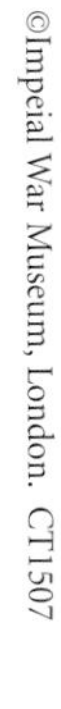

HMY BRITANNIA, *London.*

HMY BRITANNIA *at Tower Bridge.*

cent by value of Britain's imports and exports were carried by sea;[52] and that the Queen is Head of a Commonwealth of 51 states, and Head of State of 16 of them; and that the UK conducts many billion pounds' worth of trade with the Commonwealth. In maintaining those ties and that trade BRITANNIA played no small part.

The arguments further ran that nearly three-quarters of the earth's surface is covered by water; on these seas passed most of the country's vital interests – food, fuel, trade. That Britain was an island nation dependent on the sea, and we forgot that at our peril. That we were still a major maritime force, and as such a Royal Yacht for the sovereign and head of the Commonwealth was not a luxury but a vital component of our image and prestige abroad.

Prince Charles was not alone in being unhappy with the decision to scrap BRITANNIA, noting the 'genius' of the British for failing to appreciate their national assets. Numerous captains of industry felt the same; as one wrote to *The Times* of 25 October 1995: 'Our company, like many others in foreign trade, is heavily reliant on icons of British quality to project an image and create an environment for trade in technological goods and services, and BRITANNIA serves as a splendid venue in which the sovereign and head of the Commonwealth can preside when abroad. BRITANNIA uniquely encapsulates tradition, engineering excellence and continuity at a time when there are fewer instantly recognisable British products in the world markets. Many exporters – and others – feel betrayed and dismayed by the Yacht's decommissioning.'

The *Daily Telegraph* leader of 2 August 1996 stated:

> Retention of the Royal Yacht has nothing to do with the public's changeable sentiments towards individual members of the Royal Family; it has everything to do with the dignity of the sovereign of a still-important maritime nation, as it has been since 1660. HM Yacht BRITANNIA may indeed be a useful platform for promoting British exports, and it may serve practical purposes other than that for which it was built. But these are subsidiary matters, and the Government would do the monarch a disservice if it justified the replacement chiefly in utilitarian terms. The real point is that the Royal Yacht confers prestige, as was movingly demonstrated when the Queen hosted world leaders in BRITANNIA during the 1994 D-Day celebrations. A Royal Yacht should also serve as a reminder to the world of the proficiency of British engineering and seafaring skills.

The author and journalist, Brian Hoey, looked at both sides of the argument when preparing his book *The Royal Yacht Britannia*, and concluded: 'If we accept the need for a continuing role for the monarchy in Britain, it is important that we do not allow any devaluation in that role.'[53]

During the period 1994-97 several designs were put forward for a new Royal Yacht, and interesting options on how to pay for the vessel. Banks were keen to provide the finance, and although attractive figures could be produced they were in fact poor value, as the capital allowances used would ultimately be funded by the taxpayer. Government can in any event borrow money more cheaply than the commercial sector; and to borrow money from the private sector for a national asset would surely have sent up the wrong signals. The Queen too felt that a national asset such as a yacht should be funded by the State; to resort to private finance or even sponsorship by industry would diminish the monarchy.

THE CADLAND SHIP

This was one of the more appealing designs, so called because many of the meetings were held at Cadland Manor, home of the main promoter, Maldwin Drummond, then Commodore of the Royal Yacht Squadron. This was a radical design for a Royal Sail Training Ship, designed by Colin Mudie. The elegant vessel would have been one of the largest sailing ships in the world, and drawn admiration wherever she went. At 370 feet long (112 metres) the ship would have been some 40 feet shorter than BRITANNIA, but the royal accommodation was to be of much the same size and standard.

The Cadland Ship, proposed Royal Sail Training Vessel.

A flagship for the youth of the nation and Commonwealth, the ship would have been UK built and equipped to the highest standards of British maritime technology in all areas. Three-masted, square-rigged and multi-engined, the ship was designed to have a speed under computer-controlled sails of 12-15 knots, an economic cruising speed of 15 knots, and a top speed of 20 knots. Her range of 6000 miles would give a worldwide capability, and she would meet all known environmental requirements.

The ship was to have secure royal accommodation aft, with reception rooms for State, ceremonial and promotional occasions, guest suites for visiting Heads of State and cabins for members of the Household and staff. Forward was accommodation for the 60 permanent crew and 180 trainees, who would be selected as 'Queen's Cadets' after previous sail training experience. Some 3500 fee-paying cadets per year would train on board, with bursaries for those unable to meet the cost.

British companies would install the very best of their products, so that the ship would be a permanent floating advertisement. Two theatres, one of 144 seats forward and one of 36 seats aft would enable sales presentations to be made, and the ship would have full communications and business facilities. A hold, serviced by a crane, would allow bulkier items of equipment to be carried for exhibitions overseas.

The Cadland Ship was costed at £65 million, all privately funded, and her annual operating costs of £5 million would have meant she was self-financing. Government would pay for the 15 days a year planned for State and royal use and industry for the 20 days of Commerce and Arts. Cadet days would number 280 per year, and the ship would be open to the public for 30 days a year. Other than State and royal costs, the ship would have cost Government nothing, neither capital for building nor expenditure for running, apart from the permanent staff for the royal accommodation.

The journalist Libby Purves was a strong supporter of the plan, and her article in *The Times* of 19 April 1996 concluded: 'The Royal Sail Training Ship is the synthesis between old technology and new, between our history and the nation we want to be. It is conservative and socialist, ancient and modern, royal and democratic.'

Yet as Vice Admiral Sir Ian McGeoch said: 'Analysis of the sail training task and how exacting it is, in terms of programming, would show that it is incompatible with that of a Royal Yacht. Besides, risk to life and limb cannot be entirely eliminated without prejudice to the raison d'être of sail training – imagine the media feast which would be provided by "Lad falls to his death in the Royal Yacht".'[54]

Press reports at the time indicated the project was blocked by Mr Michael Heseltine, who preferred to see a motor yacht. If true, it is a great shame, as Britain lost both a Royal Yacht and a National Sail Training Ship.

DML SHIP

Devonport Management Ltd (DML), the private firm running Devonport Dockyard, put forward a plan for a total refit of BRITANNIA, and then to charter her back to the Government for State use. This proposal generated far more interest than the new build option, but sadly was not accepted by Government.

DML had carried out the major refit to BRITANNIA in 1987, and had developed a steady market for refitting the world's 'superyachts'. Shortly after the 1994 announcement to decommission BRITANNIA the yard liaised with Sir Donald Gosling by inviting designers to propose a new BRITANNIA. Sir Donald had been a keen promoter of the need for a Royal Yacht representing Britain's commercial and diplomatic interests overseas, and offered to put up the first £5 million.

Four designs were considered, of which probably the most appropriate and elegant was from John Munford, released to the press in August of that year. At 459 feet (140 metres) long and displacing 8250 tons the new yacht would have been larger than BRITANNIA, allowing the increased accommodation to include a lecture room/theatre seating 120 for commercial presentations. The vessel would have been manned by the Royal Navy, but with modern and more efficient design half the number of yachtsmen would be needed. The royal apartments would remain for the exclusive use of the Royal Family, but the guest suites and other areas would be available for charter by captains of industry on promotional tours.

John Munford Design wrote at the time of the proposed new yacht:

> The word 'yacht' perhaps gives the wrong idea of what BRITANNIA is. She is a ship which is majestically styled and for a small proportion of time serves the State's requirements for the Royal Family. For the majority of the time this yacht is a pedigree business machine serving the industries of our country. It represents in itself the best of British shipbuilding and engineering and serves as a platform to promote British industries abroad. It is known that £2 billion worth of orders have been signed on board (the present) BRITANNIA over the last ten years, but it is hard to tell the true amount of orders in the wake of the Royal Family's work and BRITANNIA's presence.

DML felt it was politically unacceptable for public or Crown money to be used, but that private sources should be used. Lloyds Bank offered 100 per cent finance on the estimated cost of £70 million, and DML would then charter the yacht back to the Crown, State or industry as appropriate.

Income was projected from chartering to:

- the Royal Family for private use.
- the Foreign Office for State use i.e. overseas visits.
- the Department of Trade and Industry for promoting British interests abroad.
- the Ministry of Defence (Navy) for officer training packages.
- extended training for Commonwealth cadets.

Charter rates of £100 000 per day were at that date commonly obtained for 'superyachts', but Government was reported to be sceptical of the income projections. Much work was done by DML on the political and industrial fronts, but in spite of the latter's avowed need of an icon such as BRITANNIA to further British

DML Ship, proposed new Royal Yacht. Designed by John Munford.

products and prestige abroad, industry was slow in coming forward with firm proposals or finance. Government too was singularly lacking in providing the positive lead so critically needed for the project to gel, with the inevitable result that it too failed.[54a]

BRITISH EXPORTERS ASSOCIATION CRUISE ROYAL YACHT

Promoted by the British Exporters Association, this project took the form of a mini cruise liner of about 10 000 tons (i.e. twice the size of BRITANNIA), with separate areas of royal accommodation and other cruise ship standard accommodation. It was envisaged that when on Royal Duty part of the cruise accommodation would be available for the Royal Household and staff, the remainder being occupied by paying guests made up from industry, business and trade delegates.

The proposal appeared to have missed the essential requirements of a Royal Yacht – that she must be a secure and private palace for the Head of State, and that to attract commerce and industry for sea days it is vital to maintain the gravitas and aura that surrounds royalty and a Royal Yacht – factors incompatible with a cruise ship and paying passengers.

THE PARLIAMENTARY MARITIME GROUP

This is an all-party group of both Houses of Parliament and British Members of the European Parliament. It represents certain companies, professional research, and other organisations involved in maritime activities and affairs. It was involved from the start in promoting a new Royal Yacht, and quickly established parameters of use and design. The Group settled on a larger motor yacht, similar in size to BRITANNIA, and designed by Alasdair Burns of Dundee, which they actively promoted. At a cost of £60-80 million, and with 2000 square metres of exhibition space, the Group proposed that the vessel should be financed privately and chartered back to the Government.

After two and a half years of prevarication by the Government, and with BRITANNIA due to decommission in less than eleven months, a decision was finally made. The Secretary of State for Defence, Mr Michael Portillo, announced on 22 January 1997:

> The decision stands to decommission BRITANNIA. However, the Government have decided to commission a new purpose-built Royal Yacht, and have so informed Her Majesty the Queen. We have taken the decision because we believe that a Royal Yacht is an important national asset, which projects a prestigious image of Britain, adding powerfully to official occasions and assisting greatly in promoting British economic interests. Her Majesty the Queen has made it clear that she expects such a role to be the primary purpose of a new yacht. Moreover, the new yacht will at times provide Her Majesty with a suitable residence overseas, thus contributing to the impact of her visits and enabling her to represent our nation in an appropriate setting. The Ministry of Defence will procure the new Royal Yacht. After a study to enable us to draw up a formal specification and a competition, a contract will be placed with a British shipyard. She will be crewed by the Royal Navy and fly the White Ensign. The Queen will contribute to the furnishings and fittings of the State rooms and royal apartments, drawing some items from BRITANNIA... The Government... believe that a new Royal Yacht – a symbol of the nation's pride – should be funded not by sponsorship or subscription, but by the nation. The capital cost will be met from public funds in the reserve.

He went on to say:

> We have considered what would be appropriate for BRITANNIA after decommissioning. The Government do not consider it would be appropriate to sell her to a new owner for private use. She will not put to sea again, but we are interested in proposals for a suitably prestigious use for BRITANNIA in the public interest in the United Kingdom. Such a scheme would need to take account of the plan to transfer royal fittings to the new yacht. Any proposals for BRITANNIA would need to guarantee that

> the Yacht would be kept in excellent condition. If that cannot be assured, it would be better to see her scrapped than to see her deteriorate.[55]

Almost immediately a political row developed, for the Conservative Government had deliberately failed to consult the Labour Opposition, as was normal on matters affecting the monarchy. With a general election due in May, they had instead sought to make political capital from the announcement. Not only that, they also failed to consult the Prince of Wales, who would have counselled against the spending of public money on a new yacht. The Queen was informed at Sandringham by telephone, and was thus given little time for discussion; a more suitable way would have been by the Prime Minister at his normal weekly meetings when Her Majesty had returned to Buckingham Palace. The Queen was said to be 'pleased' at the decision, based on the belief that a new Royal Yacht would be a valuable national, not personal, asset.

Yet the Queen was reported to be deeply distressed at the way the monarchy was drawn into the row, and she was not alone. Sir Edward Heath described Mr Portillo's actions as 'not honourable'; Lord Armstrong, a former Cabinet Secretary, commented that '...he would have urged ministers to consult opposition leaders...'; and Field Marshal Brammall, former Chief of the Defence Staff, said: 'By involving the Royal Family in this controversy, so close to a general election, the Government has created the impression it was trying to score a fast one over the Opposition.'[56]

There was obviously sadness that BRITANNIA was to go, but this was mixed with relief that a new Royal Yacht was to replace her. Since the 1994 announcement to decommission BRITANNIA she had undertaken two State visits (to Russia and South Africa); deployed to the Mediterranean and Eastern Coast of the USA and Canada; was in London for the VJ Day celebrations; and had undertaken sea days and other commercial seminars.

As if Government at last realised what a priceless asset they were discarding, BRITANNIA's final year was crammed with over 80 diplomatic and commercial events during 28 visits to 17 countries. She sailed from Portsmouth for her last overseas voyage on 20 January 1997 via the Mediterranean, the Gulf States, India, Malaysia, Singapore, Thailand, The Philippines, Japan and finally Hong Kong for the handover to China.

BRITANNIA sailed from Hong Kong shortly after midnight on 30 June with the Prince of Wales and the last Governor, Chris Patten, and his family embarked. To the sceptics watching it was a symbolic act, this relic of Empire leaving Britain's last major colony; but to many others it was an intensely moving scene, and a reminder of Britain's role in the world. We neglect the lessons of history at our peril.

Speaking of her final deployment to the Far East, Lieutenant Commander Dickie Randall, her last Senior Engineer, wrote:

> We visited 18 countries on a commercial trip, including four ports in Japan, and everywhere we went people said they were coming to the presentations because they were on the Royal Yacht. We've had orders for British firms worth £2 billion signed on board the Yacht since January, and massive crowds everywhere even though we were not open to the public.
>
> There have been 110 major commercial and diplomatic events this year, 99 per cent of them trying to get people to invest in Britain. We've been away from our base port for about eight months.
>
> From Manilla to the Suez Canal we did the fastest passage in her 44-year history, and the engines ran as sweetly as you could wish. We kept up the highest sustained average speed we've ever done, (a continuous 8435-mile passage from Manila to Gibraltar at an average speed of 14.6 knots) for more than two weeks in the monsoon season. This is the most reliable ship I've ever served in. She's very well-built and well-maintained – she has to be, because she's hard-worked, not a plaything. The communications

The handover of Hong Kong.

> are a bit antiquated – we had to go to the GEC/Marconi museum earlier this year to borrow some spares for different units.[57]

Six days after arriving back at Portsmouth on 1 August BRITANNIA was on duty at Cowes Week, where her presence attracted, as always, much attention – and trade. From Cowes the Yacht sailed for her last Western Isles Cruise; 19 members of the Royal Family were on board at various times.

Whilst the Yacht was away a new Labour Government had been elected in May, pledged to conserve public funds, and the future of any new Royal Yacht was thus in the balance. A tedious and ill-informed public debate – both over the future of BRITANNIA and of any new yacht – flared and died throughout the summer. The previous Conservative administration totally lacked the 'spin-doctor' expertise of New Labour; otherwise they would have paraded the exceedingly valid commercial arguments for a new Royal Yacht, backed by facts and figures showing what BRITANNIA had actually earned, as opposed to a perceived cost. The very public divorces of the Prince of Wales and the Duke of York, together with, in some quarters, a perception that the Royal Family were an extravagant luxury, had not helped engender a sympathetic public feeling.

And whereas the Prime Minister, Tony Blair, was reported to have been 'astounded' with BRITANNIA, and very much for a new yacht, he was strongly opposed by Chancellor Gordon Brown. In June Lord

Watercolour by Colin M. Baxter – 'HMY Britannia at South Railway Jetty, HMS Victory in the background.'

Gilbert, Defence Procurement Minister, told the House of Lords: 'There is no question whatever of the value which we recognise BRITANNIA has produced for the country over the last forty years or so. The only question is what form should the successor be, whether or not we should have one, and how it should be financed.'[58]

As BRITANNIA's hull was sound, Sir Donald Gosling proposed a total refit of the interior, involving completely new electrics and re-engining with diesel-electric engines or the gas turbines in common use throughout the Royal Navy. The reduced engine room and redundant boiler room could then have been converted to a theatre for commercial presentations. Manning levels could have been reduced through a radical rethink of the Yacht's role for the future. Such a plan, at a cost of £50 million, could have been funded from the public-private initiative; and as the return on private investment, the ship could be chartered out for six months of the year, at £70 000 per day. Sir Donald also offered to underwrite such a plan by personally chartering seventy days a year for the first five years. However, a briefing to five Sunday newspapers by the Chancellor's 'spin doctor' (Charles Wheelan) 'spun out of control,'[59] and the idea was dropped.

A Ministry of Defence Project Team consulted with representatives of the Royal Family, the Foreign Office and the Department of Trade and Industry, and produced plans for a new yacht codenamed 1997 MVD (for Minimal Viable Design). The new design was based on a shorter vessel than BRITANNIA, with reduced royal accommodation and increased business area, including a 100-seat conference hall. With a crew of 120, range of 6000 miles and annual operating costs of £5 million the yacht would have cost £64 million to build. Yet by the time the report was presented to Ministers the Chancellor appeared to have made his mind up, for in early October he said that it was not possible to replace or refurbish BRITANNIA.[60]

Geoffrey Robinson, MP, was then a Minister and part of the committee deciding the future of the Yacht, and his memoirs shed an interesting light on the deliberations. The Queen's representative, Sir Robert Fellowes, was 'at pains to make it clear right from the outset that the Queen was making no request for a BRITANNIA II. It was entirely up to the Government... (and)... she would consider whatever proposition was put to her, but, he cautioned, we must not take her approval for granted.' As Robinson continued: 'In the end it was the death of Diana, Princess of Wales, that killed off the new *Britannia*. The impact of Princess Diana's death touched every part of British life, not least the monarchy itself. A new Royal Yacht, the refurbishment of the present one, it all seemed out of place in the post-Diana atmosphere.'[59a]

Coupled with Treasury insistence that public money could not be used, this spelt the death knell for any replacement yacht, even though the Ministry of Defence was all for one.

Confirmation of BRITANNIA's fate came on 10 October, when the Defence Secretary, George Robertson, told the Commons that after detailed consideration of all the options and widespread consultation across Government and with Buckingham Palace, the Royal Yacht would not be replaced or rebuilt. He went on to say:

> BRITANNIA has served the nation well for over forty years and earned a special place in many people's affections. We made clear that we would not spend public money on a Royal Yacht and I am keeping that promise. We in the MoD have to justify every penny of the taxpayer's money that we spend and in this case I could not do so, particularly – as the Queen has made clear – since a yacht is not needed for royal travel. We considered in detail all private finance options, but these would only have been viable with a substantial annual subsidy from public funds.[61]

From the wealth of newspaper comment that followed it emerged that the Queen personally had vetoed any replacement for BRITANNIA. Her Majesty was anxious to avoid any accusation of extravagance, for opinion polls had shown widespread public feeling against a new yacht paid for by the taxpayer. Whatever her personal feelings, the Queen announced that she considered the decision 'understandable and appropriate'.

Clyde Heritage Trust proposal to dry-dock BRITANNIA *in Glasgow at Govan.*

For those favouring a new yacht Menzies Campbell, Liberal Democrat foreign affairs spokesman, encapsulated their thoughts when he said: 'A great opportunity has been lost to show all that is best in British engineering and shipbuilding. A national yacht could have been a great advantage to UK plc. Use by the Royal Family could have been subordinate to the opportunity of promoting Britain.'[62]

The journalist Robert Hardman had earlier written: 'It is sad that a party with such a love and talent for public relations, led by a man with such a pronounced national vision, cannot see the huge national public relations benefits of a flagship for a great maritime nation.'[59b] He had identified the problem accurately, for whereas the nation was not prepared to fund a new Royal Yacht, it might have accepted a National Flagship – like the Cadland Ship. Without royal or political approval, however, both were non-starters.

In addition to his statement Mr Robertson went on to add that the Government was looking with great care at options for BRITANNIA's future, including preservation, and were examining a short-list of proposals. These included:

- The Clyde Heritage Trust, with plans to dry-dock BRITANNIA permanently in Glasgow at Govan as the focal point of a Maritime Centre.
- Forth Ports mooring her at Leith alongside the new Cruise Liner Terminal for corporate hospitality and public access.
- Placing the Yacht at the centre of the display of maritime history in Portsmouth naval dockyard.
- Conversion to a floating museum alongside the Millennium Dome, with conference and banqueting facilities.
- Using her for a Royal Yacht Visitor Centre near Canary Wharf in Docklands.
- Mooring her in the Upper Pool of London for use as a conference and international trade centre, with public access.

Most of the Royal Family, as well as many senior naval officers and Royal Yachtsmen were against preserving BRITANNIA, feeling that she should be scrapped or scuttled, as her namesake had been in 1936. They were concerned that it would be difficult to maintain the Yacht's pristine condition, and not easy to find a dignified role for her future. Others considered that the previous BRITANNIA had been the personal property of King George V, whereas the Yacht was a national asset, deep in the affection of many. If a suitable dignified role could be found for her, and her upkeep guaranteed, they thought BRITANNIA deserved to be saved, and to continue giving pleasure to many thousands at closer quarters.

From 20 October to 22 November BRITANNIA circumnavigated Britain for her last Tour, visiting eight major ports – Plymouth, Cardiff, Belfast, Glasgow, Aberdeen, Newcastle, London and Portsmouth. The Queen, the Duke of Edinburgh, the Duke of York, Prince Edward, the Princess Royal and Princess Alexandra were embarked at various times. Huge crowds welcomed her everywhere, and there were particularly emotional scenes on the Clyde, where she had been built in 1953.

BRITANNIA lay in the Pool of London for eight days, which coincided with the celebrations to mark the Golden Wedding Anniversary of the Queen and the Duke of Edinburgh, and the Yacht provided accommodation for various members of European Royal Families. The Queen, Prince Philip and the Prince of Wales also hosted a lunch for serving and past Chiefs of Defence Staff, First Sea Lords and Chiefs of Staff.

On the evening of 21 November massive crowds witnessed BRITANNIA's floodlit departure, her 410 feet long Paying-off Pennant flying (one foot for every foot of her length), and the Royal Marine Band playing. The next morning, as she entered Portsmouth for the last time, she was escorted by HMS SOUTHAMPTON with the Commander-in-Chief Fleet embarked. She was accompanied by a mass of small craft, while every vantage point and the shore were crowded with well-wishers. As she berthed at South Railway Jetty, home to so many Royal Yachts, Commodore Morrow rang down for the final time 'Finished with Main Engines'.

HMY BRITANNIA *leaving Portsmouth for her final overseas tour, 20 January 1997, flying the flag of Commodore Royal Yachts (CORY), Commodore A.J.C. Morrow, CVD.*

The Paying-off Ceremony on 11 December 1997 was always intended as a family event for both the Royal Family and the families of past and present Royal Yacht officers and yachtsmen – and that was how the day turned out, with well over 2000 people present. That morning the Royal Family toured the Yacht and chatted informally with officers and yachtsmen, but inevitably there was an underlying note of sadness.

Paul Reynolds, the BBC Court Correspondent, wrote to the author: 'The Royal Family left BRITANNIA (at 1500), the Queen being piped ashore for the final time. The Yacht looked splendid in the afternoon sun and the clouds whipped up by the Force Seven from the west. The short service went well, with the usual hymns, followed by Beat Retreat, which always strikes a chord. Then the flags came down, with Commodore Morrow saluting, and the Queen fighting back the tears, and the two thousand yachtsmen and families feeling rather special.'

In a message to the ship's company of BRITANNIA, the Queen and Prince Philip commented:

> Looking back over forty-four years we can all reflect with pride and gratitude upon this great ship which has served the country, the Royal Navy and my family with such distinction. BRITANNIA has provided magnificent support to us throughout this time, playing such an important role in the history of the second half of the twentieth century. Steaming over one million miles she has proudly carried out over seven hundred royal visits at home and overseas as well as numerous highly successful commercial programmes. Her achievements are a great testament to those who designed and built her, and to those craftsmen and artisans who have maintained her with such dedication over all these years.

Crown Copyright/MoD

HMY BRITANNIA *entering Portsmouth for the last time, 22 November 1997, flying her 410-foot Paying-off pennant.*

Her Majesty and Prince Philip went on to thank the Officers and Royal Yachtsmen for their unfailing loyalty, dedication and commitment to the Royal Yacht Service:

> ...We would also wish to thank the wives and families who have quietly but strongly supported the Royal Yacht over the years and often during periods of long absence. It is with sadness that we must now say goodbye to BRITANNIA. It is appropriate that with this final event she bows out with the style which is so typical of the manner in which her business has always been conducted.

A dismal period of indecision followed, for BRITANNIA's future was still uncertain. On 10 October the Secretary of State for Defence had announced the two preferred bidders: Forth Ports in Leith, and a bid received well after the official deadline from the Manchester Ship Canal Company. The latter proposal was for BRITANNIA to be at the centre of a £48 million 'Heritage Centre', but thankfully was rejected.

In the author's view, the most suitable bid, given adequate funding, was from the Clyde Heritage Trust, where BRITANNIA would have rested in Glasgow at the A-listed Govan drydock, then lying derelict. BRITANNIA would have provided the catalyst for an imaginative scheme to record and celebrate the maritime history of the Clyde, and also to renovate a rundown area and provide much-needed jobs. Lack of capital left the project relying too much on grants and Lottery funding, and Mr Robertson rejected the bid.

In Portsmouth BRITANNIA had been towed to a corner of the dockyard, and the dispiriting task of de-storing proceeded. There was much to remove, for apart from the fittings in the royal apartments there were all the cabins to be stripped, and stores for the ship's company of 250 men to go ashore. The more valuable items were returned to the Royal Collections Trust, and the dining room was re-assembled at Frogmore, where it is much used by Prince Philip for meetings.

Decommissioning ceremony, 11 December 1997.

Certificate of Handover.

SCHEDULE 4 TO D/DS(S)/528/24/75

MINISTRY OF DEFENCE

CERTIFICATE OF HANDOVER

I, the undersigned, being an authorised Officer of Disposal Sales (Ships) certify, on behalf of the Secretary of State for Defence that The Former Royal Yacht BRITANNIA Trust, (the Purchaser), has purchased from the Secretary of State for Defence the former Royal Yacht BRITANNIA "as seen as lying" at Her Majesty's Naval Base PORTSMOUTH together with the former Royal Barge and other associated equipment as described at Annexes B and C of Schedule 1 to contract D/DS(S)/528/24/75 dated 29th April 1998.

I further certify that the said Purchaser has paid to the Accounting Officer, Ministry of Defence the amount of the purchase money of the said equipment and that the Secretary of State for Defence and The Purchaser have agreed that title, ownership and risk in it shall transfer to The Purchaser at Portsmouth Naval Base 1220 ***Hours on*** 1 May 1998 ***1998.***

Authorised Signature

Name: M. W. Robinson

Appointment Director of Ships, Armaments + Aircraft.

I, being an authorised representative of The Former Royal Yacht BRITANNIA Trust, (the Purchaser), do hereby accept title, ownership and risk in the former Royal Yacht BRITANNIA and associated equipment as described above.

Authorised Signature

Name

Appointment DIRECTOR

And so the months dragged by whilst BRITANNIA and her few remaining crew awaited a decision as to her future, until finally, on 8 April 1998, Mr Robertson announced that Forth Ports at Leith was the successful bidder. He refused on grounds of 'commercial confidentiality' to divulge why the other bidders had been unsuccessful, but it was reported that Forth Ports' financial standing as a major UK port, coupled with their plans to leave BRITANNIA largely unchanged, justifiably won the day.

Forth Ports was already building at Leith a £75 million Cruise Liner Terminal and residential development, and it was not a difficult task to include a permanent berth for BRITANNIA. Apart from essential modifications for visitor access the Yacht would remain as she always had been; a visitor centre, exhibition hall, shop and restaurant would all be ashore. Ownership of BRITANNIA was to be transferred to a charitable trust, and her upkeep would come from the £1.2 million per year she earned, as well as from the profits of the shoreside facilities. It was estimated that BRITANNIA would inject £3.5 million per year into the local economy, and create a total of 180 jobs.[63]

On 1 May 1998, exactly one year after the general election that sounded the death knoll for British Royal Yachts, BRITANNIA left Portsmouth for Leith – 'flagless, powerless and an empty shell' – towed by a German tug.

HMY BRITANNIA *at Leith with Edinburgh in the background.*

Crown Copyright/MoD

EPILOGUE

BRITANNIA is almost certainly the last British Royal Yacht, for the royal and political will for a replacement is lacking. Even though she earned many millions of pounds each year in commercial and diplomatic terms, these facts were not widely understood, and much of the British public regarded the Yacht as an extravagance. Thus ended many centuries of history and tradition, and it is fitting that BRITANNIA has returned to the country of her birth.

BRITANNIA is now owned by The Royal Yacht Britannia Trust, a non-profit making charity whose sole remit is to maintain BRITANNIA in keeping with her former role. This it does by operating as one of Scotland's few five-star visitor attractions, and one of the UK's top corporate event venues.

After arrival at Edinburgh's historic port of Leith on 5 May 1998, BRITANNIA underwent a general refit, but apart from essential adaptions for safety and access she remains almost exactly as she was when in commission as a Royal Yacht. BRITANNIA opened to the public on 19 October 1998 and since then over one million visitors have enjoyed their tour of the main upper decks and all the royal apartments.

At the end of September 2001 BRITANNIA moved to her final berth at Ocean Terminal in Leith Harbour, with a purpose-built Visitor Centre ashore. As part of the relocation much of the Main Deck was opened to the public, giving them an insight into life below decks.

When BRITANNIA decommissioned in 1997 there was very deep concern felt by many that she would not be properly maintained in a dignified role. The fact that she won the Best New Visitor Attraction of 1999, and that her upkeep has gained the approval of numerous former Royal Yachtsmen is reassuring to us all.

FOOTNOTES

PART ONE – THE SAILING YACHTS

CHAPTER 1 – THE KING'S SHIPS

Section 1: Anglo-Saxons to the Early Stuarts

1. *The Royal Navy – A History vol. I* p 71.
2. *Royal Yachts* p 21.
3. *Classic Ships* p 123.
4. *Naval Chronicle* 1800 p 315.
5. *Royal Yachts* p 25; *The Royal Navy – A History vol. I* p 81.
6. *The Royal Navy – A History vol. I* pp 116-7.
7. *The Royal Navy – A History vol. I* p 117.
8. *The Royal Navy – A History vol. I* p 121.
9. *Royal Yachts* p 27.
10. *Royal Yachts* p 27; *The Royal Navy – A History vol. I* p 121.
11. *Royal Yachts* pp 27-8; *The Royal Navy – A History vol. I* p 130.
12. *Royal Yachts* pp 28-9.
13. *Royal Yachts* p 29.
14. *The Royal Navy – A History vol. I* p 144.
15. *A Few Naval Customs, Expressions, Traditions and Superstitions* p 6.
16. *The Royal Navy – A History vol. I* p 144.
17. *Royal Yachts* p 32; *The Royal Navy – A History vol. I* p 341.
18. *Royal Yachts* p 32; *The Royal Navy – A History vol. I* pp 357-8.
19. *The Royal Navy – A History vol. I* p 366.
20. *The Royal Navy – A History vol. I* pp 372-3.
21. *Royal Yachts* p 33.
22. *Royal Yachts* p 21.
23. *The Royal Navy – A History vol. I* p 349.
24. *The Royal Navy – A History vol. I* p 447.
25. *Royal Yachts* p 37.
26. *The Royal Navy – A History vol. I* p 407.
27. *Royal Yachts* p 38.
28. Alan Hamilton – Cowes Week – *The Times* 22 July 1996.
29. *Royal Yachts* p 38.
30. *Royal Yachts* pp 43-4.
31. *Anne of Denmark* p 147, quoting the Autobiography of Phineas Pett p 81.
32. *Royal Yachts* p 44.
33. *Royal Yachts* p 38.

Section 2: Royal Yachts in Scotland

1. *Canna,* J.L. Campbell p 21.
2. Personal letter from Dr Norman Macdougall. See footnote 8

[2a] Personal letter from Dr Norman Macdougall. See footnote 8
[3] Alexander Lindsay. *A rutter of the Scottish Seas* circa 1540. See footnote 9
[4] *Scotland at War* pp 36-56.
[4a] *Scotland at War* pp 36-56.
[5] *Scotland, James V & VI* p 121.
[6] *History of Scotland*, Robert Chambers 1832.
[7] The oddly named MORSENER was either a corruption of Monsieur, or a variation on Morse, a seahorse.
[8] Personal letter from Dr Norman Macdougall, St Andrew's University.
1: Accounts of the Lord High Treasurer of Scotland, Ed. T. Dickson and Sir J. Balfour Paul (Edinburgh 1877-1916) vols. vi, vii, viii.)
2: Letters & Papers, Foreign and Domestic, of the reign of Henry VIII, Ed J.S. Brewer et al. (1862-1932)
3: Crown – magnate relations in the personal rule of James V, 1528-1542; James S. Cameron, unpublished PhD thesis, St Andrews University 1995.
[9] Alexander Lindsay. *A rutter of the Scottish Seas* circa 1540. National Maritime Museum monograph No. 44-1980 p 13. And Accounts of the Lord High Treasurer of Scotland, 1538-1541, pp 337, 402, 420, 421, 445, 480 etc. And *Scotland, James V & VI* p 162.
[10] *The Girlhood of Mary Queen of Scots* p 9.
[11] *The Girlhood of Mary Queen of Scots* p 370.
[12] *The Girlhood of Mary Queen of Scots* p 371.
[13] *Anne of Denmark* pp 15-25 (Murdin, State papers p 637.)
[13a] *Anne of Denmark* pp 15-25 (Murdin, State papers p 637.)
[13b] *Anne of Denmark* pp 15-25 (Murdin, State papers p 637.)

CHAPTER 2 – CHARLES II (1660-1685)

Section 1: The Principal Yachts

- Where dimensions differ I have selected them in the order National Maritime Museum, Lyon, Gavin.
- Length is length on the keel.
- Tonnage of sailing yachts is shown as tons burden. That of steam-yachts is shown as tons displacement, in common with normal warship practice.
- Rebuilding involved carefully dismantling the old yacht and reusing sound timbers. Invariably the new vessel was of different dimensions, and thus a new ship. To differentiate between successive yachts of the same name I have numbered the later ones as II, III etc.

[1] *Royal Yachts,* McGowen p 1.
[2] Rates of pay: Admiral £4/day. Vice-Admiral £2 to £2 10s. Rear-Admiral £1 to £2. Gunners, carpenters and bo'suns from £2 to £4/month. Able-seamen 24s/month. Ordinary seamen 19s/month. Boys 9s 6d/month. Captains of flag-ships on half-pay £150 per annum. Service Pay – Captain Russell Grenfell, R.N.

MARY
[3] Dimensions from Pepys's Register of Ships of the Royal Navy from 2 May 1660 to 18 December 1688.
[4] *Royal Yachts,* p 47.
[5] CSP, 17 April 1657.
[6] P. N. Davies, 1973 International Journal Of Nautical Archaeology & Underwater Exploration 2. 1: pp 59-73.

KATHERINE
[7] *Royal Yachts* p 52.
[8] Nicholas Witsen, later Burgomaster of Amsterdam, described her at the time of her capture: 'On the 4th September, 1673, there was to be seen at Amsterdam in front of the Palisades a very costly yacht of His Majesty the King of England. It is low in the water, carries 10 brass guns, and is so shaped and built that it can keep the sea. Sail, mast and gaff of the shape that is usual in this country. The stem is upright, after the new fashion, formed of a strong piece. Has a fine yellow-painted head supported by sea-nymphs and goddesses; it spreads out wide, but below, it is sharp and of a good shape, very proper to cut the water and make good speed. All

round on the outside for two feet below the rails it is covered with costly sculptures and gold-painted carvings of grotesque figures and plants. It has no lee-boards. Is also not tarred outside, as one is accustomed to do to ships here, and this is very elegant, for the Irish timber of which it is made shows all the better its nature and ruddy colour which is agreeable to the sight; to tar this wood or preserve it with paint or otherwise is not necessary, for it is the finest wood to be found in Europe, and resists all worm and rot. It is true that this wood is not so flexible as the oak that is used for ship-building in this country, and therefore this yacht is not of such a curved shape as those that are built in this country, but more straight-sided, which nevertheless does not look bad, though many masters consider this the important feature of a ship. It has low bulwarks. The mast is stepped in such a way that it can be moved to and fro to seek sailing power; from the truck flies a silk streamer which in calm hangs down to the water, and it is on all sides proudly decked with flags. The lower part of the stern is round, and it spreads out high and broad (after the English fashion). At the top it boasts three round, gilded lanterns; a maiden in stately dress, representing England as it seems, finely carved and gilded stands against it (the stern), bearing in her raised right hand the arms of his Majesty; in her left hand she holds a sceptre with a lily on it; this hand holds down a stooping monster; the rest of the stern below is decorated with birds and other fine carved work, and the whole is covered with a royal crown. The deck of the yacht is almost flat.

One goes down some steps into two rooms aft, the foremost is a brave hall, painted all round with works of art, gilded and decorated with carvings; the after cabin which one enters from the other is up a step or two; here there is a nice bedstead, and it looks out aft with windows being decorated all round with gold leather. Above this room, which is raised some feet above the deck, stands the helmsman; the iron tiller is conveniently bent so that it can be handled by a man standing upright. The after end of the roof over this stern cabin is higher than the fore end for the sake of appearance.

Below these two rooms in the bottom of the ship are spaces for stowing rigging gear and tools. In the fore hall is a staircase with a door by which one goes down into a room whose floor is the ship's bottom; through this one enters another, and thus reaches the caboose which is the fore part of the ship; these rooms have beds all round, separated by screens painted with the King's arms and gilded.

The two after galleries are not placed as high as they usually are in yachts in our country, since they keep the sea more with them than we are wont to do with ours; there are skylights on deck to give light to the rooms below. On the upper deck aft, as well as on the orlop, there are cupboards built against the bulwarks and closed with gilded doors. Hatches and covers can be used to keep out the sea.

(*Mr Pepys's Navy* pp 149-151; Gavin pp 252-3; this differs in detail from the account given in Gavin, but not importantly so.)

HENRIETTA

9 I am inclined to HENRIETTA being named after Charles's favourite sister Henriette Anne, Duchess of Orleans; he was distraught when she died in 1670 aged only twenty-six. With his mother, Queen Henrietta-Maria, he had a difficult relationship; she tended to be possessive of all her children, and the years of exile and poverty only made the rift between mother and son deeper.

10 See building costs for the ANNE yacht.

11 *Royal Yachts*, p 55.

12 *Pepys's Diary*, 14 June 1667.

13 *Royal Yachts*, p 67.

14 PRO Adm. 51/3876.

KATHERINE II

15 At the National Maritime Museum, this rigged model of a Stuart Royal Yacht circa 1674 probably represents the KATHERINE II, built that year. The model represents a design for one of the fourteen large yachts built by Charles II, of which a number of representations survive in the works of Van de Veldes, father and son. The decorations of the stern are not, however, indentical with any of those sketched and named by those artists, although the dimensions correspond very closely with those of the KATHERINE and the PORTSMOUTH, both built for the king at Woolwich in 1674 by Phineas Pett.

As actually built, nearly all these Stuart Royal Yachts carried a large carving of the Royal Arms in the stern. The figure of a draped woman and two naked boys, which here take the place of that design, seem to indicate that the present model represents a projected rather than a completed vessel. The carving, which is excellently preserved, is delicate and elaborate, the sleeping boys above the windows of the cabin being particularly charming. The mast, gaff and lower yard are all original, whilst the sails and rigging have been added by the museum. The three stern lanterns, sloping back, but apparently globular, as seen from the waterline, were discovered in the hull of the model.

The dimensions of the yacht represented, measured from the model, are approximately: burden 130 tons, length of keel 56 feet, length on deck 70 feet, breadth 20 feet 4 inches, depth in hold 8 feet 2 inches. The model is on scale of 1:30, and is made of boxwood, with open timbering in the hull.

It is unlikely this model was for the PORTSMOUTH yacht, because only £26 was expended on her carving work, and that shown on the model would cost many times as much, especially if the inboard carving was elaborate as the outboard. By comparison, the carving on the FUBBS cost £300.

From the quality of the carving, and a Van de Velde drawing of the KATHERINE's stern, it is probable the model represents that yacht.

PORTSMOUTH

16 *Royal Yachts,* p 61.

17 Commander Gavin gives the naming of the PORTSMOUTH as after the Duchess of Portsmouth in his text, but after the town of Portsmouth in his List of Yacht Names. I am inclined to the former, as Louise was still very much in favour at the time of the yacht's launching, and she had been created Duchess of Portsmouth only a year previously.

18 *Charles II,* Antonia Fraser p 230.

CHARLOT

19 *Royal Yachts,* McGowan p 4.

MARY II

20 *Royal Yachts,* Naish plate 3.

HENRIETTA II

21 Personal letter to author from Major Grant Walker, U.S. Naval Academy, Annapolis.

FUBBS

22 Pepys; Minute January 1681-2.

23 *Royal Yachts,* p 254.

24 In 1705 the Duke of Richmond – then also Duke of Lennox – resigned all his heritable estates to the crown, including that of Hereditary High Admiral of Scotland. The crown continued to appoint a vice-admiral for Scotland until some time after the abolition of the Scottish Admiralty Court in 1830.

25 *Royal Yachts,* p 255.

Chatham, 17 May 1682

GENTS,

In answer to yours of 10th inst.,… I do desire the following materials to be speedily put in hand at the places and by the persons nominated-viz.:

That her masts and yards etc., should be made in HM Yard at Deptford.

That the rigging be ordered to be made of fine yarn (as the MARY yacht was) at the King's Ropeyard at Chatham of such dimensions as I shall advise, and to be fitted in the loft there.

That the block and pumps be made by Mr (Master) Smith at Chatham of such sizes and nature as shall be signified by me.

That the lead for ballast shall be cast in HM Yard where she is now building.

That the carved work may be performed by young Mr Fletcher, which may be worth of, est. £300.

That the painting and gilding works may be done by Mr Walker of Deptford and may be worth £350.

That the sails be made by Mr Edmondson with His Majesty's canvas of such dimensions and sorts of cloth as I shall advise.

As to the other works to be performed as directed by the Lords Commissioners of the Admiralty I shall timely give you notice thereof.

PHIN. PETT

Greenwich, 13 July 1682

His Majesty having commanded me to launch his new yacht building here the first spring in August I entreat you to favour me with the loan of the following provisions for her launching from His Majesty's stores at Chatham, which I shall take care to return again once she is launched:
The yachts bilgeways.
Launching planks 640 feet in length.
Ways and capps, 80 No.
Ribbons, 260 feet in length.
Compass spurs to run from the bilgeways up to the weale [wale] to be in length 13ft to 15ft, 12 in No.
A piece of old mast for her windlass of 18ft long and 2ft through, wrought.

PHIN. PETT
Navy Office, 7 August 1672

At my late waiting on His Majesty at Windsor he was pleased to command me to launch his new yacht building at Greenwich on the 23rd inst, and that his Majesty may meet with no disappointment therein do lay before you the following particulars for which I desire you will please give your speedy directions:

1st. For launching the yacht the day above said that the respective officers of Deptford be directed to take charge of her and to go on with the setting of her masts and rigging and fitting her for sea with all possible speed.
2nd. To direct young Mr Walker, the painter, to hasten the works of said yacht in such a manner as I shall direct by time of launching, he expecting your order for same before he will go on with gilding works.
3rd. Direct officers at Deptford to send to Greenwich the ways, ribbons, bilgeways and piece of mast for said yacht which are now coming from Chatham in the Lighter HOY.
4th. That orders may be sent to Chatham for supplying the thimbles and hooks wanting for the said yacht's rigging.

I enclose a letter from Master Attendant Chatham and that the rigging and blocks for said yacht may be hastened to Deptford, it being requested that they be at Deptford some days before her launching in order to the landing of her shrouds fixed to the head of mast, to be in readiness to set as soon as she is launched, and the officers at Deptford may be directed to fit her with ensign-staff, flag-staffs and trucks for them and the silk colours or such others as are necessary out of the stores for her launching as also with the loan of two old 4th Rates mainsails for the gilding of the yacht, which I do take care to see safe return into stores.

PHIN. PETT

ISABELLA

[26] Gavin does not include the ISABELLA in his list of Principal Yachts, but from her size and appointment I have done so.
[27] *Royal Yachts* p 268.
[27a] *Royal Yachts* p 268.
[28] *Mariner's Mirror* Vol. 85 No 4 (November 1999), p 456.
[29] *Royal Yachts,* p 68.
[30] ADM 42 & 4115.
[31] *Charles II,* Antonia Fraser p 225.
[32] *Charles II,* Antonia Fraser p 225.
[33] *Royal Yachts* p 60.
[34] *Charles II,* Antonia Fraser p 224.

Section 2: The Secondary, Surveying and Dockyard Yachts

[1] *Saltwater Palaces* p 15.
[2] *Mr Pepys's Navy* p 149.
[3] *Saltwater Palaces* p 16.

ROYAL ESCAPE

[4] The SURPRISE is variously described as a coasting brig, collier, or fishing smack. Being single-masted she was not a brig, and although she may have occasionally carried coal she was probably not a collier as such, or she would have been described as a keel. It is likely she was incorrectly called a fishing smack following the 1660 classification; a smack then was a small vessel of 15-50 tons. The SURPRISE was probably a hoy or smack engaged in the coastal trade.
[5] *Royal Yachts* p 253.
[6] *Charles II,* Antonia Fraser p 224.

ANNE

[7] *Royal Yachts* p 51.
[8] *Royal Yachts* p 68.

BEZAN

[9] The painting of the BEZAN flying Dutch colours shows another yacht to port with an even shorter gaff, almost a perfect Bermudan rig.

SAUDADOES

[10a] *Royal Yachts* pp 56-7.
[10b] *Royal Yachts* pp 56-7.
[11] Figures in brackets before rebuilding.

Length on gundeck	–	Length by the keel	74 feet (50′)
Beam	21 feet 6 inches (18′)	Depth in hold	10 feet (8 feet)
Tons burden	180 (86)	Crew	75 (40)
Guns	16 three-pounders		

There is a Van de Velde drawing at the National Maritime Museum of SAUDADOES as a sixth-rate.

[12] *Royal Yachts* p 58.

KITCHEN

[13] *Saltwater Palaces* p 12.

NAVY

[14] Gavin gives her date of building as 1666, but it is now accepted as 1673 – *Great Ships* by Fox; and Major Grant Walker, U.S. Naval Academy, Annapolis.

ISABELLA BEZAN

[15] The second BEZAN is shown in Pepys's list as the ISABELLA BEZAN, 52 tons.
[16] P.R.O., Ind. 10704(1).
[17] *Mariners Mirror* Vol. 18 pp 197-8.
[18] *Royal Yachts* pp 257-8.

DOCKYARD YACHTS

[19] *Royal Yachts* p 68.
[20] *Pepys's Diary* 9 November 1664.
[21] A 'hythe' was a small backwater shut off from the main stream by a gate; hence Rotherhythe – now Rotherhithe – and Billingsgate. The gate gave a measure of security for loading and unloading against river pirates.
[22] *Saltwater Palaces* p 17.

MERLIN

[23] *Royal Yachts* p 251.

CHAPTER 3 – THE LATER STUARTS

Section 1: James II (1685-1688)

[1] *Royal Yachts,* p 68.

Section 2: William and Mary (1688-1702)

[2] *Royal Yachts,* p 70.
[2a] *Royal Yachts,* p 70.
[2b] It was to be his last sail in the ROYAL TRANSPORT, for Tsar Peter continued overland to Russia, whilst the ship sailed round the top of Europe to Archangel. There she languished for fifteen years, her draught too deep for the

shallow rivers to proceed further inland. Finally, in 1715, Peter ordered the ship westward round the North Cape to meet him in the Baltic; off Marstrand, on the coast of Sweden, she ran into a storm and sank to the bottom.

PEREGRINE GALLEY

[3] Peregrine Osborne was confirmed as Viscount Osborne of Dunblane soon after his father was created Earl of Danby. Lord Dunblane became Marquess of Carmarthen when his father was created 1st Duke of Leeds on 4 May 1694. *The Works of the Van de Veldes*, M.S. Robinson, p 993.

Section 3: Queen Anne (1702-1714)

[4] *Royal Yachts,* pp 70-71.

CHAPTER 4 – GEORGE I (1714-1727)

[1] James, third Earl of Berkeley, shortly to become First Lord of the Admiralty, and to remain in office throughout the King's reign.

[2] *Royal Yachts* p 77.

CHAPTER 5 – GEORGE II (1727-1760)

ROYAL CAROLINE II

[1] Deptford Dockyard estimated £1494 for the work of converting the yacht CAROLINA into an armed sloop. Amongst other things this involved lengthening the vessel by 3 feet, and the yard advised against the work, as the cost was almost that of a new sloop. The Admiralty however ordered them to proceed (letter 11 July 1749); the final cost was £3331. The renamed PEREGRINE SLOOP was lost with all hands in the Bay of Biscay en route to the West Indies in 1762 (not captured by the French as noted in the Progress Book). *The Royal Yacht Caroline*, p 13.

[2] NMM document ADM/A2395.

[3] *The Royal Yacht Caroline* p 14.

[4] PRO ADM 33/414.

[5] and 4, *Royal Yachts* p 83.

[6] *The Royal Yacht Caroline* var. pp.

DORSET

[7] *Royal Yachts* p 94.

CHAPTER 6 – GEORGE III (1760-1820)

[1] ROYAL CHARLOTTE, MARY III, KATHERINE II, AUGUSTA and FUBBS III; and the warships NOTTINGHAM (60 guns), WINCHESTER (50 guns), MINERVA (32 guns), TARTAR (28 guns), HAZARD (14 guns) and LYNX (14 guns).

PRINCESS AUGUSTA

[2] ADM 52/1163.

[3]

Sir Charles Molloy	1749-	
Sir Piercy Brett	-1760	RA 1762, Ad Blue 1778
Sir Peter Denis	1760-1770	RA, VA 1778
John Campbell	left to command VICTORY as a RA	
Sir William Cornwallis	-1787	RA 1793
Sir Hyde Parker		RA 1793, Ad WI Fleet 1799
Henry Trollope	1797-	RA 1801, Admiral 1812

Sir Henry Neale	1801-1803	RA 1810
Sir Edward James Foote	1806-1807	RA 1812

[4] The First Lord of the Admiralty (Aylmer, Torrington, Berkeley, Anson, Delaware etc.) performed this duty. The Earl of Sandwich returned to the Admiralty as First Lord in 1771 determined to stimulate royal interest in the Navy. He arranged royal visits to the fleet and dockyards, and eventually presented George III with detailed scale models of the six Royal Dockyards.
[5] *George IV, Prince of Wales* p 140.
[6] *Royal Yachts* p 93.
[7] *Royal Yachts* p 94.

ROYAL SOVEREIGN
[8] *Royal Yachts* p 95.
[9] *Annals of our Royal Yachts* p 35.
[10] *Royal Yachts* p 96.
[11] *Naval Chronicle* 1801 vol. 4 appendix 1.

WILLIAM & MARY
[12] Both Gavin and Lyon have the work of 1764/5 as 'great repairs', but since all her dimensions have altered I have classed it as a rebuild in accordance with the National Maritime Museum.

CHATHAM III
[13] These dimensions are according to Lyon. Gavin gives:

Length on gundeck	58 feet 10 inches	Length by the keel	47 feet 3 inches
Beam	–	Depth in hold	–
Tons burden	90	Crew	9
Guns	6 two-pounders		

1842 repaired and lengthened
1867 taken to pieces
[14] *The Naval History of Great Britain* vol. IV, p 96.
[14a] *The Naval History of Great Britain* vol. IV, p 96.

PLYMOUTH II
[15] These dimensions according to Lyon. Gavin gives:

Built 1796 at Plymouth.		Surveyor Sir John Henslow.	
Length on gundeck	64 feet 8 inches	Length by the keel	52 feet 7¼ inches
Beam	18 feet 6 inches	Depth in hold	10 feet 1 inch
Tons burden	96	Crew	–
Guns	–		

1830 taken to pieces

WILLIAM & MARY III
[16] George IV, Regent and King, p 145.

CHAPTER 7 – GEORGE IV – REGENT (1811-1820) AND KING (1820-1830)

[1] *George IV, Regent and King* p 31.
[1a] *George IV, Regent and King* p 35.
[2] *Royal Yachts* p 120.
[3] *Annals of our Royal Yachts* p 36.
[4] *George IV, Regent and King* p 73.
[5] *The Unruly Queen* p 283.
[6] *The Unruly Queen* p 287.
[7] *The Unruly Queen* p 363.

[8] *George IV, Regent and King* p 152.
[9] *George IV, Regent and King* p 207.
[10] *George IV, Regent and King* p 209.
[11] *George IV, Regent and King* p 222.
[11a] *George IV, Regent and King* p 222.
[12] *George IV, Regent and King* p 231.
[13] see below.
[14] *Royal Yachts*, p 110. The full account reads:
It being my turn with the other two lieutenants, I took command of our tender, the SEAGULL, a cutter of fifty tons only, a good sea-boat, but very wet in the winter months. She was a sort of half-tide rock, as much under as above water. I wore fisherman's boots above the knees, as the only way of keeping tolerably dry. My first movement was to the Nore, and there with the ROYAL SOVEREIGN and two or three men-of-war to wait for the ROYAL GEORGE yacht, with the King on board, coming down the Thames in tow of a steamer. It was a dark and very still night, and the measured strokes of the paddle-wheels were a new and most peculiar sound to us. Steam then was in its very infancy.
[15] *The King's Jaunt*, p 343.
[16] *The King's Jaunt*, p 352.
[17] Progress Book ADM 180/13; Logs ADM 51/3365 & ADM 52/4594.
[18] *George IV, Regent and King* p 335.
[13] *Royal Yachts* pp 100-110. A fuller text reads:
Early in June I received an unexpected order to join H.M. Yacht ROYAL SOVEREIGN, fitting for sea at Deptford Dockyard, taking with me three midshipmen... We found the yacht in the basin, being regilded and painted, the hull purple, the royal colour. She was a beautiful ship richly gilt, with a family head, as it is termed, the King, Queen and two or three children in a group. Her ports were all circular, with carved figures round them, the size of a two-year-old child; her stern was covered with figures.

I do not remember the number of our crew [67], but they consisted of dockyard riggers, all old men-of-war's men, thorough seamen, of good character, and mostly married men. Our proper captain was Charles Adams, commonly called Charlie Adams, more like a midshipman than a staid post-captain...

In two or three days I was sent for to the Admiralty and saw Sir George Cockburn, the senior naval lord, about our mess arrangements. He said that 'hitherto the yachts had been paid under the Board of Greencloth, that was all wrong. Would you believe it, sir, the mess expenses were nearly £1000 in six weeks? I shall give you £100, you will keep the main bills only, as vouchers, the smaller may go as extras. You will keep a gentlemanly table, your fish, soup, joint, and occasional game, and for wine, port and sherry; and if you have a friend at table, a little champagne and claret will do no harm.' I told him I perfectly understood him, and would allow no extravagance.

When moored in the river we had several visitors, and one day a large wherry with silk awnings and cushions, and with six men in nautical dresses, and a party of ladies, rowed slowly round us. I invited them to see the yacht, and offered my arm to the best-looking lady, and took her round the ship. All at once there was shout of, 'A man overboard!' The cries ran like wildfire; the ladies began to scream. I ran on deck, found the master, a fiery-eyed, red-faced little Welshman in a great state of excitement. 'What's all this Franklin?' 'I couldn't help it sir; he began to abuse the King, and I hustled him to the gangway meaning to kick him into his boat, but she had dropped astern and overboard he went.' And there he was, his bald head above water, paddling and splashing like a dog. A wherry took him up, and he would be landed. By this time some of the other men began to show their teeth. I told them to be silent, that any person who presumed to abuse His Majesty on board his own yacht would inevitably be kicked overboard by the officers, and so they all with great haste hustled into their boat... they were not gentry.

Once Captain Brenton had joined, 'the Duke and Duchess (of Clarence) and party came off. It turned out an ugly night, blowing hard, with many squalls of rain; and there was much sea on. The Duke, Sir Edward (Owen, a noted pilot), and our captain were on deck all night, and of course I could never go below. The yacht had the character of being, and was, a most excellent sea-boat, but she did kick and roll about famously.'

In fact the crossing was so rough that the Dukes's two daughters were pitched out of George III's four-poster bed, and 'found in the lee scuppers, rolling over each other'. No harm was done, and the party was safely landed at Antwerp.

Whilst the ROYAL SOVEREIGN was in Antwerp, Boteler and some fellow officers hired a carriage intending to visit the battlefield of Waterloo. In Brussels he learnt that the captain of the yacht, whose permission he had failed to obtain for his leave of absence, was staying in the same hotel. It was with some trepidation that Boteler sent up his card, but Captain Brenton thought it a splendid idea, and joined the party.

At Waterloo, seven years after the battle, they saw, 'branches torn off the trees, walls broken down… and barn doors riddled with bullets'. In the church they were shown a small slab over the Marquess of Anglesey's leg, and in the fields he noted the corn grew a foot higher where the bodies of men and horses were buried.

Returning to the yacht he found 'the crew stupid as owls from the lot of Holland's drunk; very cheap here so I at once took strong measures against any further tippling, by having the Master At Arms at the gangway, knocking holes in stone jars and slitting bladders of spirit. I was informed that this was only meant for their wives at home. After a little I thought it a pity to waste so much good stuff, so had all future seizures put into 'breakers' and when any extra work or bad weather happened, the 'main brace was spliced', in plain English a tot was served all round; this quite won the hearts of our fine crew and won me high praise.

When our captain returned we up anchor, worked down river, and in quick time were up the Thames again, expecting to be laid up, instead of which to our great delight, for yacht service was very fascinating, our captain Charlie Adam joined, and we next day were off for Dover Roads, and in a day or so embarked the Crown Prince of Denmark and suite for Calais. On their leaving the yacht a diamond ring was presented to the captain and 100 sovereigns to me for the ship's crew, and which I gave the purser to be distributed among them as prize money.

While at Calais the officers invited Beau Brummel, resident there to escape his creditors, to dinner, and found him 'most entertaining'. We returned to England and were ordered to Sheerness to be in readiness to join the ROYAL GEORGE yacht, about taking the King to Scotland. It was blowing very strong, and we had to beat from the Nore into Sheerness Harbour; the yacht worked like a top, tack and tack without a fault.

CHAPTER 8 – WILLIAM IV (1830-1837)

[1] *King William IV* p 71.
[2] *King William IV* p 115.
[3] *King William IV* p 116.
[4] *King William IV* p 139.
[5] *King William IV* p 144.
[6] *King William IV* p 289.

CHAPTER 9 – THE LORDS LIEUTENANT OF IRELAND'S YACHTS

I am much indebted to *The Rise and Fall of Parkgate, Passenger Port for Ireland, 1686-1815,* by Geoffrey Place, published by The Chetham Society 1994. Much original research went into this very readable account of Parkgate.

Manchester University Press.

[1] *The Rise and Fall of Parkgate* p 61.
[2] 'The Lion's Whelp', by John Wassel, Mariner's Mirror 63 (1977) p 368.

MARY

[3] P. N. Davies, 1973 Int. Journal Of Nautical Archaeology & Underwater Exploration 2. 1:59-73 p 63.
[4] ibid. p 67.
[5] ibid. p 60.
[6] ibid. pp 63-70. Her wreck was rediscovered on 11 July 1971 by divers from the Chorley and Merseyside branches of the British Sub-Aqua Club, and a considerable number of artefacts recovered.

MONMOUTH

[7] *The Rise and Fall of Parkgate* p 68.
[8] ibid. p 69.
[9] ibid. p 72.

PORTSMOUTH

[10] *The Rise and Fall of Parkgate* p 69.
[11] PRO, ADM 51/3943.
[12] *The Rise and Fall of Parkgate* p 71.
[13] Strengthened and fitted with a mortar for shore bombardment.

NAVY

[14] Gavin gives her date of building as 1666, but it is now accepted as 1673. vide *Great Ships* by Fox; and personal letter to author by Major Grant Walker, U.S. Naval Academy, Annapolis.
[15] PRO ADM 51/3918.
[16] *The Rise and Fall of Parkgate* p 73.
[17] ibid. p 78.
[17a] ibid. p 78.

SOESDYKE

[18] The dimensions for the SOESDYKE are those given by Lyon in *Great Ships*. They differ from those given by Gavin, but I have been unable to trace either primary source. However, as Lyon is more accurate on his history (The List of the Navy ADM 180/20), I have taken his dimensions.
[19] *The Complete Peerage* - Royal Archives.
[19a] *The Complete Peerage* - Royal Archives.
[20] PRO. ADM 51/4344.
[21] Deptford letters ADM 106/293.

CHARLOT

[22] *The Rise and Fall of Parkgate* p 74.
[23] ibid. p 74.
[24] ibid. p 75.
[25] ibid. p 75.
[26] The CHARLOT was rebuilt and enlarged to new dimensions at Deptford in 1710; rigged as a ketch in 1736; lengthened in 1747; renamed AUGUSTA in 1761; and rebuilt again in 1771 at Deptford. In 1773 she was renamed PRINCESS AUGUSTA, and rated a ship, not a yacht, she continued to do duty as the principal yacht of George III. She was finally sold in 1818, parts of her having served seven monarchs over 141 years. Some record!

DUBLIN

[27] PRO. ADM 51/280.
[28] *The Rise and Fall of Parkgate* p 79.
[29] ibid. p 77.

DORSET

[30] *Royal Yachts* p 83.
[31] *The Rise and Fall of Parkgate* p 81.
[32] ibid. p 84.
[33] ibid. p 83.

WILLIAM & MARY III

[34] Lyon says beam 23 feet 2½ inches
[35] Following Joseph Hume's querying the need for five Royal Yachts - *Royal Yachts* p 112.
[36] *The Rise and Fall of Parkgate* p 85.
[37] The first WILLIAM & MARY was built 1694; rebuilt to new dimensions 1764, and sold in 1801.
[38] *The Rise and Fall of Parkgate* p 76.
[39] ibid. p 87.

ROYAL CHARLOTTE II

[40] Lyon says beam 23 feet ½ inch

[41] Progress Book ADM 180/13; Logs ADM 51/3365 & ADM 52/4594.

[42] *Royal Yachts* p 112.

PART TWO – THE STEAM YACHTS

CHAPTER 10 – QUEEN VICTORIA (1837-1901)

Section 1: Victoria and Albert

[1] *Viscount Esher – A selection of Her Majesty's diaries* 1832-1840 p 49.

[2] *Royal Yachts* p 119.

[3] *The Luxury Yachts* p 63.

[4] *The Royal Yacht Britannia* – Morton p 77.

[5] Adm. 51/3743, 31 August 1843.

[6] *The Life of the Prince Consort* – p 174.

[7] The French King had evidently spared no thoughts as to the comfort of his guests, for as Sir Robert Peel wrote to Lord Aberdeen, somewhat tongue in cheek I assume: 'I see for the purpose of doing honour to his royal visitors and their companions that he [King Louis] sent a very large order to England for bottled beer and cheese. I hope you will have had calm weather so that you may all enjoy these delicacies.' *Annals of our Royal Yachts* p 40 quoting from The Peel Papers.

[8] On the journey to Brighton the Queen and her party were sitting out of the wind by one of the paddle-boxes, unwittingly blocking the rum locker. Seeing the crew standing in groups and whispering, the Queen feared a mutiny and summoned the Captain. When he explained the situation, the Queen said she would move on condition she could have a drink as well. She sipped the proffered glass of grog [rum and water mixed] and remarked, 'I'm afraid I can only make the same remark I did once before, that I think it would be very good if it were stronger.' The crew, naturally, were delighted.

Grog: after Admiral Vernon, whose nickname in the fleet was 'Old Grogram', from the material of which his boat cloak was made. In 1740 Vernon, in an attempt to reduce drunkenness, directed that the pint of neat rum per man per day (half a pint for boys) should be diluted with a quart of water. This watered down mixture was speedily given the nickname 'grog'. – *The Oxford Companion to Ships and the Sea.*

[9] *The Royal Yacht Britannia* - Hoey p 129.

Section 2: Victoria and Albert II

[10] Captain The Hon. Joseph Denman, commanding officer of the VICTORIA & ALBERT, wrote on 14 June 1854 to Lieutenant Colonel Phipps, Private Secretary to the Prince Consort, that, 'The scientific people at Portsmouth Dockyard are to investigate rolling,' as influenced by screw or paddle propulsion. The Commander-in-Chief Portsmouth, Admiral Sir Thomas Cochrane, had already despatched a small team [Commander Crispin, additional Captain of the VICTORIA & ALBERT; Mr Aylen, the Master; and Mr Partridge, Assistant Engineer at Woolwich Dockyard] on board the screw vessel HIMALAYA to report on her behaviour in all sea conditions, and to assess the relative propulsion methods for a Royal Yacht.

Admiral Cochrane had posed ten questions for the team to consider, including vibration from the engine and screw in various parts of the ship; noise or other inconvenience caused by the screw; the motion of the ship; her dryness in all conditions; and her manoeuvrability. The party joined the HIMALAYA at Southampton for Malta, and Commander Crispin, additional captain of the VICTORIA & ALBERT, reported that for the first day the weather had been 'very boisterous with much sea; the remaining 7 days exceeding fine and the sea very smooth'. He concluded his report: 'For Her Majesty's Yacht I am of opinion as regards "safety and comfort" the paddle wheel is decidedly superior to the screw – first, from the lighter draft of water, enabling the paddle to keep closer to the shore, and entering shallow harbours – secondly – because the "shock", "shake" and "noise" occasioned by the screw are decidedly opposed to the personal comfort of Her Majesty, and I particularly remarked that, "these palpably increased as the ship lightened and the sea became rougher although her speed averaged only 10-9 knots between Queenstown and Malta."'

With the capability of constructing a vessel whose outward form shall be faultless – because freed from the unsightly yet most useful paddle boxes; with a speed of propulsion equal to the fastest paddle, with much greater space for cabin comfort from the compactness and position of a screw engine, with sailpower far superior – if fitted with a "trunk" for lifting the screw; it may be asked why, with all these admitted and important advantages, a screw ship should not be preferable to a paddle-wheel ship for Her Majesty's Yacht, I answer and very reluctantly so – from all my well known predilections in favour of the screw generally speaking over the paddle- because I am convinced till further improvements shall have much lessened, or entirely removed the shock and vibration from the screw itself – a screw ship as a yacht will in that vital and all important point – the personal comfort of Her Majesty, prove a total failure.' *Royal Yachts,* McGowan pp 4-5.

[11] *Naval Architecture,* W.H. White 3rd edition 1894 p 374.
[12] *Royal Yachts,* McGowan p 5.
[13] *The Royal Yacht Britannia,* Hoey p 96.
[14] *The Royal Yacht Britannia,* Hoey p 97.
[15] *Royal Yachts* pp 135-42.
[16] As were the Captain and Commander of the VICTORIA & ALBERT II, Prince Leiningen and Commander Fullerton.
[17] *Annals of our Royal Yachts* p 42. Quoting from *Letters of Queen Victoria*, edited by G.E. Buckie, second series vol. ii (John Murray 1924).
[18] OSBORNE II. Trials as reported in the *Illustrated London News* of 26 August 1871:

Measured mile:	15. 294 knots at steam-pressure of 24 lbs/sq in (maximum pressure 30 lbs/sq in).
Paddle-wheels:	27ft 6in diameter; 11ft 6in length; 3ft 7in breadth; immersion 2ft 3in at load line. Revolutions 28/minute (maximum 31/minute).
Boilers:	Four, each having 450 brass tubes, loaded to 30lbs on the safety valves. The superheaters have flattened tubes, the steam passing through the tubes at the funnel root. The superheaters can be shut off very easily when required and with the boilers at work.
Funnels:	Two, each 72in in diameter, and standing 46ft above the fire grate.
Engines:	Two oscillating engines from Maudslay, Son & Field. 80 inch diameter, with a stroke of 7ft.
Coal:	'Very limited' at 200 tons, giving 30 hours at full speed. 'At ten knots her coal would carry her over long distances.'

The figurehead from OSBORNE II was presented by King Edward VII to RNC Osborne, and transferred to BRNC Dartmouth in 1921. 'Weather and time took their toll, and some years ago a fibreglass replica replaced it.' [Curator, The Britannia Museum, 17 January 2000.]

[19] *Royal Yachts* p 144.
[19a] *Royal Yachts* p 144.
[20] *Royal Yachts* p 145.
[21] *An Admiral's Wife In The Making* pp 162-200.
[21a] *An Admiral's Wife In The Making* pp 162-200.
[22] *Royal Yachts* p 148.
[23] In March 1893 Commander Fortescue became an Equerry to the Prince of Wales, and 'for the next seventeen years until the day of his death… [I] was thus a personal servant to the kindest and most considerate of masters that ever a man was fortunate to serve.' *Looking Back* pp 173-199.
[23a] *Looking Back* pp 173-199.
[24] *Roger Keyes*, by Cecil Aspinal-Oglander, pp 22/3.
[25] *300,000 Miles at Sea* pp 66-78, and personal family letters.
[26] Ships Log: Tuesday 3 April 1900. Her Majesty The Queen accompanied by their Royal Highnesses Princess Christian and Princess Henry of Battenburg and attended by their suites embarked. ADM 53/16490.
[27] ADM 53/16490.
[28] Sir Francis Larking and Captain Ponsonby. ADM 53/16490.
[28a] *300,000 Miles at Sea* pp 66-78, and personal family letters.
[29] ADM 53/16490.
[30] The date would appear to be wrong, for the following days entries are headed Thursday 31 October.

Section 3: Victoria and Albert III

[31] Unknown.
[32] *Royal Yachts* p 297.

[33] *300,000 Sea Miles* pp 64-70.
[33a] *300,000 Sea Miles* pp 64-70.
[34] *Pembrokeshire County History, Volume IV* p 166.
[35] The yacht suffered for the rest of her life from this piece of whimsy; the steam capstan that replaced the hand windlass proved under-powered, and weighing anchor was a lengthy process.
[36] As originally designed she had a metacentric height of two feet, 'to secure steadiness and ease of motion at sea', as Sir William White explained. As built, the yacht had an excess 771 tons, much of it above the waterline, and her metacentric height when fully laden was reduced to three inches. When lightly laden, she was largely unstable, as was demonstrated in the dry dock. Altogether 260 tons were removed by lightening the masts, fo'c'sle deck, funnels, casings, watertight doors, and boat-hoists. Ballast totalling 250 tons was placed in the double bottoms, and although the yacht ended up with 14 inches more draught than designed, her metacentric height was restored to 2. 4 feet when laden, and never less than 18 inches when light. *Royal Yachts* p 304.
[37] *Royal Yachts* p 300.
[38] 'It may be asserted confidently that there is no safer vessel afloat. Her stability as completed is in all respects most satisfactory. When fully laden the metacentric height, which measures the stiffness, is about 2 3/4 feet. As coal and fresh water, etc., are consumed, being stowed low in the ship, the stiffness diminishes somewhat; but the metacentric height never falls below 1½ feet. All conditions of service are thus amply provided for.

Her high freeboard makes her 'uncapsizeable'. If it were possible to heave her down and lay her absolutely on the beam-ends, she would move back to the upright immediately she was released. On service no such condition could be approached, of course; and the fact is stated simply as an indication of the enormous margin of stability.

Commodore Lambton reports her to be an excellent sea-boat so far as the trials have gone. This was the opinion formed during her steam trials and on the passage round to Portsmouth, when fairly heavy weather was met.' *Royal Yachts* p 309.
[39] In his definitive volume, *Royal Yachts*, Commander Gavin firmly states Sir William White designed the VICTORIA & ALBERT III, and at no time in his lengthy appendix on the building of the yacht is there any mention of outside plans. Although the boxes at the National Maritime Museum do contain plans of the STANDART, they were almost certainly for comparison – it is, after all, standard practice to find out what the opposition is up to!

There is no doubt that in lightening the VICTORIA & ALBERT the removal of the cowled intakes and the booms led to cleaner lines. But I can find absolutely no documentary evidence to support the story.
[40] *Footprints in the Sea* pp 161-66.
[41] *The Royal Yacht Britannia,* Hoey p 100.
[41a] *The Royal Yacht Britannia,* Hoey p 100.
[41b] *The Royal Yacht Britannia*, Hoey p 100.
[42] The carpets were later protected by mackintosh covers during rain: the author discovered them in 1970, carefully stowed away in BRITANNIA's lay-apart store 'just in case ever needed'!
[43] *Footprints in the Sea* pp 161-66.

CHAPTER 11 – KING EDWARD VII (1901-1910)

[1] *Daily Graphic* of 11 April 1902: 'It carries us back a long way to recall that July day [actually August] at Deptford Dockyard when the ROYAL GEORGE was sent afloat with martial pomp and ceremony in the presence of the then Duke of York, The Lords of the Admiralty, and a great assemblage of notabilities long since gone to their graves.'
[2] *Royal Yachts* p 222.
[3] *Britannia and Her Contemporaries* p 7.
[4] DAGMAR (1866), PRINCESS (1869), ALEXANDRA (1871), ZENOBIA (1872), HILDEGARDE (1876), FORMOSA (1880), and ALINE (1882).
[5] Reference lost.
[6] Built for Albert Edward Prince of Wales, registered in his name 19 May 1893.
1. Sold to John Lawson Johnston, of Kingswood, Sydenham Hill, London, registered in his name 16 December 1897.
2. Sold to Martin Diederich Rucker, of 28 Ely Place, London, on 2 April 1898 (and mortgaged).
3. Sold to Daniel Cooper, of Warren Tower, Newmarket, Suffolk, on 20 July 1898.
4. Sold to Albert Edward Prince of Wales 20 May 1899.
5. Sold to Sir Richard Bulkeley, Bt, of Baron Hill, Beaumaris, Anglesey, on 18 October 1900.

6. Sold to King Edward VII in 1902, but not registered.
7. 11 March 1911. Registered in the name of His Majesty King George V.
8. Sea-burial off St Catherine's Light, 10 July 1936, at the express wish of King George V – see under King Edward VIII.

[7] The Royal Tour 1901, or the Cruise of HMS OPHIR: no pagination.

[8] It appears that the VICTORIA & ALBERT II was merely used as accommodation ship, as she was not used to lead the OPHIR to sea next day, that duty falling to the ALBERTA. I assume that the VICTORIA & ALBERT was not in full commission, it being out with the summer season.

[9] The Royal Tour 1901, or the Cruise of HMS OPHIR, last page.

[10] ADM53 31571.

[11] *The Royal Yacht Britannia,* Hoey p 100.

[12] *Royal Yachts* p 305.

[13] *300,000 Miles at Sea* p 81.

[14] The Royal Tour 1901, or the Cruise of HMS OPHIR, no pagination.

[15] *The Royal Yacht Britannia,* Hoey p 102.

[15a] *The Royal Yacht Britannia,* Morton p 19.

[16] *Royal Yachts* p 159. There is a splendid painting by Eduardo de Martino titled 'King Don Carlos visits His Majesty's Yacht Victoria & Albert on the River Tagus, 2nd April 1903' in the Royal Collection. [RC450786]

[17] Details in *Royal Yachts* p 319.

[18] Her wardroom plate and silver was sent to the First Lord's house; it had initially been supplied to the room allocated for the Lords and Ladies-in-waiting. When the Lord's room became the wardroom in 1874 the silver and plate remained. *Royal Yachts* p 319.

CHAPTER 12 – KING GEORGE V (1910-1936)

[1] *Royal Yachts* p 167.

[2] *Annals of Our Royal Yachts* p 57.

[3] Two carved gilt panels from the ALBERTA flank the entrance to the mess room of HMS NELSON; and were presented by George V.

[4] 5 August 1919, HMS RENOWN with the Prince of Wales embarked sailed from Portsmouth.
11 August, arrived at Conception Bay, Newfoundland.
21 August, at Quebec. RENOWN then sailed for the West Indies and South America whilst the Prince of Wales toured Canada and parts of the United States. 1 December 1919, RENOWN with HRH arrived at Portsmouth.

[5] 16 March 1920, RENOWN with the Prince of Wales embarked sailed from Portsmouth via the West Indies, Panama Canal, San Diego, Honolulu, the Pacific to Australia and New Zealand.
11 October 1920, RENOWN with HRH arrived at Portsmouth.

[6] 26 October 1921, departed Portsmouth, HRH and his suite (including Lieutenant The Lord Louis Mountbatten MVO RN) occupying the admiral's quarters. Called at Gibraltar, Malta, Port Said, Suez, Aden before reaching Bombay 17 November. HRH spent four months in India; it is probable RENOWN was deployed elsewhere, as for the Calcutta-Burma-Madras voyages HRH embarked in the Royal Indian Marine troopship DUFFERIN.
17 March 1921, departed Karachi for Japan, calling at Ceylon, the Federated Malay Straits, the Straits Settlement and Hong Kong; arrived Yokohama 12 April 1921.
9 May 1921, departed Kagoshima, calling at Manila, Labuan, Jesselton, Brunei, Penang, Trincomalee, Great Hamish (for oil), Suez and Gibraltar; arrived Plymouth 20 June 1921.

[7] For visits to Belfast to open the Northern Parliament; to Guernsey and Jersey; and to Southend and Harwich for the King to attend the East Coast regattas and race BRITANNIA.

[8] Once to visit the Atlantic Fleet at Portland and Torbay, and the second time for Cowes Week.

[9] Where considerable deterioration in the steelwork of her frames was found, but only what might be expected in a composite vessel of her age. As well as repairing or replacing steelwork, all of which was galvanized, the cedar topsides and many of the bottom planks were replaced. By April 1923 the old ship was as good as new, and in exactly the same trim as regards her hull as when she was built thirty years previously. Her sliding hatch had been replaced by a doghouse just before the Great War, otherwise she remained largely unaltered.

[10] *Footprints In The Sea* p 166.

[11] *Footprints In The Sea* p 160.

[12] *Sacred Cowes* p 89.
[13] *The Royal Yacht Britannia,* Morton p 21.
[14] *Footprints In The Sea* pp 189/90.
[15] They had with them a small suite of half-a-dozen equerries and ladies-in-waiting, for this was to be a convalescent cruise with no official functions whatever. The yacht sailed at once for Leghorn, where a week was spent visiting Pisa and the surrounding countryside. The King visited the Leaning Tower of Pisa, but nothing would persuade him to ascend it; Queen Mary, whose energy was indefatigable, went more than half way up.

'Queen Mary loved the shopping expeditions which ended usually about five o'clock, in time to be back on board the yacht for tea when everyone, including the Queen herself, compared their purchases from the local shops and how much they had paid for them. …The King seldom went on shore, spending most of the day in one of the pavilions on the boat deck reading, writing and often talking to the officers.' *Footprints In The Sea* pp 190.
[16] *Footprints In The Sea* p 171.
[17] In 1927 Fife further increased the height of the mast, the boom was shortened, and the gaff lengthened. To take full advantage of these alterations to the sail plan a slight deepening and straightening of the keel of BRITANNIA was carried out, the whole effect of the changes being a considerable improvement to her performance in light winds. However in a race at Cowes a sudden squall hit the fleet:
'The BRITANNIA was obviously out of hand. Caught in this way with the big sail-plan they had let her luff too heavy, and she had borne away suddenly, and heeled to a great angle, flooded her decks, and come to again. They [The King and Sir Philip Hunloke] soon got her going again… and she came thundering through the line… the winner of the match.' *Britannia and her Contemporaries* p 98.
[18] *The Royal Yacht Britannia*, Morton p 22.
[18a] *The Royal Yacht Britannia,* Morton p 22.
[19] Probably following the squall at Cowes the previous year [see note above] and further rough weather at Ryde. The height of the gaff was lowered, and a 'Marconi' or one yard-topsail fitted i.e. the entire height of the mast from deck to top was in one straight line. This not only reduced top weight, but was an approach to the 'triangle' of the Bermudan rig, which was to be the last change to her rig in 1931.
[20] *Britannia and her Contemporaries* pp 135-6.
[21] VELSHEDA, ASTRA, CANDIDA, SHAMROCK, ENDEAVOUR and BRITANNIA.
[22] *Royal Yachts* p 203.
[23] *The Luxury Yachts* pp 150/51.
[24] *Annals of Our Royal Yachts* p 59.

CHAPTER 13 – KING GEORGE VI (1936-1952)

[1] The 300ft NAHLINE was built for Lady Yule on the Clyde by John Brown & Co. in 1930. Photographs taken of King Edward and Mrs Simpson were widely publicised in the United States, but suppressed in Britain; the photographs precipitated the King's decision to abdicate. NAHLINE was sold in 1937 for £120 000 to King Carol of Rumania at the insistence of his mistress, Magda Lepescu, who had been intrigued at the romantic part the yacht played in the affairs of the King Edward and Mrs Simpson. On King Carol's abdication in 1940 the yacht became state property; from about 1980 she was a floating restaurant on the Danube, and this saved her from modernisation. In 1999 she was bought by the yacht broker Nicholas Edmiston and brought to Devonport for survey and full restoration.
[2] The *Financial Times* 11 June 1994.
[3] EMPRESS OF BRITAIN, 1931, 42 348 tons gross, quadruple screw, largest British post-war steamship. Canadian Pacific Railway Company [Managers, Canadian Pacific Steamship Company]. Sunk October 1940 off the coast of Ireland. Attacked by aircraft and left ablaze, she was taken in tow the following day but sunk by U-32.

EMPRESS OF AUSTRALIA, 1914. [ex-EMPRESS OF CHINA, ex-TIRPITZ. Canadian Pacific Railway Company (Managers, Canadian Pacific Steamship Company).]
[4] Personal letter to author from Lt Cdr Stevens. Lieutenant Commander A.W.A. 'Steve' Stevens, MBE, joined the VICTORIA & ALBERT as a boy seaman on 1 May 1939, and left on 23 September that year following the outbreak of war. He was also a messenger on board the above ships to and from Canada. He went on to become a Petty Officer A. A.2, then via the Upper Yardman scheme obtained a commission on the General List. He had many executive officer jobs, commanded a destroyer, and ended his career as RNO Loch Ewe. During the war when the VICTORIA &

ALBERT was used as overflow accommodation for HMS EXCELLENT he found himself back on board the yacht whilst doing a gunnery course. 'It was nice to have my own cabin instead of slinging a "mick" across the bathroom, but the old ship was full of the ghosts of a splendid past.'

5 Admiral North was dismissed from his post as Flag Officer Commanding the North Atlantic Station after British and Free-French forces failed to capture Dakar for De Gaulle. Although he had orders not to interfere with any French naval force unless it was sailing for a German-held port, Admiral North was accused of allowing a Vichy French force to pass through the Straits of Gibraltar. Up to his death in 1961 Admiral North fought to vindicate his conduct, and it is now generally accepted that he was used as a scapegoat for the failure of Dakar.

6 Letter from Captain HMS EXCELLENT.

7 *That Day in Gibraltar*, p 97.

8 Navy List.

9 The most valuable pieces were transferred to HM Yacht BRITANNIA or Buckingham Palace; the following went to: the Maritime Museum – an anchor; the wardroom stove; a fireplace and surrounds from the Queen's drawing-room; two semi-circular cupboards from the base of the mizzen-mast; and the Royal Arms and scroll from the stern:

- the RN Barracks, Portsmouth – panelling and wall-lights from the royal accommodation; some cannon; a bell; and the figurehead (strictly speaking, a scroll-head).
- the Merchant Taylor's Company - the silver ship's bell, which they originally presented to the yacht.
- HMS EXCELLENT – the main staircase and doors from the royal apartments.
- HMS ROYAL ARTHUR – the Petty Officer's school – some upper-deck gear, including davits.
- various naval barracks and shore establishments – a number of ornamental lanterns of Grecian design.

10 Dates Royal Yachts ceased to be as such:
King Manuel of Portugal's AMELIA III in 1910.
Tsar Nicholas II of Russia's STANDART to the minelayer MARTI in 1917. Refitted in 1930s; scrapped 1963.
The German Kaiser's HOHENZOLLERN laid up 1914, scrapped in 1923.
Mohamed V, Sultan of Turkey's ERTHOGROUL in 1918.
Archduke Charles Stephen of Austria's UL in 1918.
King Alphonso of Spain's GIRALDA in 1931.
Prince Paul of Yugoslavia's DRAGO and VILA in 1939.
King Carol of Rumania's LUCEAFARUL in 1940.
King Boris II of Bulgaria's NADIEJDA in 1943.
King Victor Emmanuel of Italy's SAVOIA II in 1943.
King Farouk of Egypt's MAHROUSSA in 1952.

CHAPTER 14 – QUEEN ELIZABETH II AND HM YACHT *BRITANNIA*

Section 1: Britannia – Building and Her First Year

1 *The Royal Yacht Britannia* - Morton p 32.

2 *The Royal Yacht Britannia* - Hoey p 107.

3 *The Royal Yacht Britannia* - Morton p 25.

4 *The Royal Yacht Britannia* - Morton p 25. This remark was occasioned by Prince Philip querying the design of the 'battleship' embarkation ladders. He knew from past experience that these took 'a huge gang of seamen and a long time to put together'. The ladders were retained but the design improved for taking them apart and for storage; and by installing power winches these could also be used for the forward ladders, the main derrick and other purposes.

5 *The Royal Yacht Britannia* - Morton p 132.

6 *The Royal Yacht Britannia* - Morton p 29.

7 *The Royal Yacht Britannia* - Hoey p 108.

8 Personal letter to the author, 19 September 1996, from Captain J. Mott, Royal Navy, who stood by BRITANNIA whilst she was building.

9 *The Life Story of a Fish* p 132.

10 *The Life Story of a Fish* p 132.

11 *The Life Story of a Fish* p 135.

12 *The Life Story of a Fish* p 134.

13 *The Life Story of a Fish* p 140.

[14] HMS SURPRISE (ex-GERRANS BAY; ex-LOCH CARRON). Temporary Royal Yacht for the Coronation Naval Review at Spithead on 15 June 1953. The twin 4-inch gun mounting in B position was removed to provide an inspecting platform for the Queen. Laid down in 1944, HMS ALERT and HMS SURPRISE were originally to have been 'Loch'-class frigates; then to have been completed as 'Bay'-class frigates; but finally modified with reduced armament and increased accommodation as Despatch Vessels or Commander-in-Chief's 'yachts' for the Far East (ALERT) and Mediterranean (SURPRISE) stations. SURPRISE was rated as a Despatch Vessel until 1961, then reclassified as a Flag Frigate.

[15] *The Life Story of a Fish* p 133.

[16] *The Life Story of a Fish* p 135.

[17] *The Royal Yacht Britannia,* Morton p 32.

[18] *The Life Story of a Fish* p 137.

[19] *The Royal Yacht Britannia,* Hoey p 104.

[20] *The Life Story of a Fish* p 142.

[21] *The Life Story of a Fish* pp 141/4.

[22] *The Life Story of a Fish* p 146.

[22a] When *Britannia* was first designed, the boats were to be hoisted in and out by hand-operated davits. This would have required many yachtsmen to turn out whenever a boat needed to be lowered or hoisted – clearly impractical. Prince Philip persuaded the Admiralty to install merchant-ship type powered davits, which could be operated by one man.

[23] *The Life Story of a Fish* p 150.

[24] Britannia Newsletter No 17 & 19.

[25] *The Life Story of a Fish* p 156.

[26] *The Royal Yacht Britannia,* Morton p 97.

[27] *The Life Story of a Fish* p 159.

[28] *The Royal Yacht Britannia,* Morton p 33. 'Not so,' said Captain John Mott (personal letter to author).

[29] *The Life Story of a Fish* p 161.

Section 2: The Layout of *Britannia*

[30] *The Royal Yacht Britannia,* Hoey p 108.

[31] *The Royal Yacht Britannia,* Morton p 32.

[31a] The original plans made no provision for a pantry to contain drinks and glasses for the ante-room and drawing room.

[32] The dining room has been recreated at Frogmore by command of the Duke of Edinburgh, and is much used for meetings.

[33] 18 September 1939 FORY, Vice Admiral Sir Dudley North, CSI, CMG, CVO, struck his flag as FORY at sunset.

5 December RY VICTORIA & ALBERT laid up for the war, and Lieutenant W.G.C. Crouch, MVO, DSC, appointed in command with a skeleton crew.

August 1945 Admiral Sir Dudley North was reappointed Admiral Commanding Royal Yachts at the express command of His Majesty, and drew up a 'skeleton Royal Yacht Service so that the benefit of… long experience was not lost to the Admiralty.'

16 May 1947 Admiral Sir Dudley North retired as Admiral Commanding Royal Yachts, and the appointment was thereafter in abeyance at the wish of King George VI.

2 February 1953 Vice Admiral E.M.C. Abel Smith CB, CVO, appointed as FORY, with a full complement of officers appointed to the V. & A. Lt Cdr Woodford remained in command of the VICTORIA & ALBERT III until she was broken up in 1955.

[34] *The Royal Yacht Britannia,* Hoey p 109.

[35] *Royal Yachts* p 230.

Section 3: A Year in the Life of *Britannia*

[36] Foreword to 'HM Yacht BRITANNIA Silver Jubilee Tours 1977' – printed privately by HM Yacht BRITANNIA.

[37] The Blue Book. Printed by Buckingham Palace for each Royal Tour to collate engagements.

[38] FORY to the First Sea Lord 1 May 1977.

[39] HM Yacht BRITANNIA Silver Jubilee Tours 1977 p 28.

[39a] HM Yacht BRITANNIA Silver Jubilee Tours 1977 p 28.
[40] HM Yacht BRITANNIA Silver Jubilee Tours 1977 p 39.
[41] In the Wardroom hung a small frame containing a gold button cut from Nelson's uniform, and one of his calling cards inscribed 'Viscount Nelson, Duke of Bronte'. They were presented in 1925 to the wardroom officers of HM Yacht VICTORIA & ALBERT by The Hon. Sir Alexander Nelson Hood, KCVO, Duke of Bronte.
[42] HM Yacht BRITANNIA Silver Jubilee Tours 1977 p 40.

Section 4: The Final Years

[43] *The Royal Yacht Britannia,* Hoey p 119.
[44] *The Royal Yacht Britannia,* Hoey p 119.
[45] *The Royal Yacht Britannia,* Morton p 187.
[46] The *Daily Telegraph* 9 August 1996.
[47] *The Royal Yacht Britannia,* Hoey p 121.
[48] Assume, as widely reported, that BRITANNIA was responsible for £400 million a year of contracts. Of that, (on a very simplistic basis) at least one quarter (£100 million) was wages, on which Government recovered 35 per cent in direct and indirect taxation, i.e. £35 million. Assume a company profit on £400 million of 10 per cent, on which Government recovered 40 per cent Corporation Tax, i.e. £16 million.

BRITANNIA's running costs were reputed to be £10 million per year, including refits. Of this, half was pay for the ship's company, on which Government recovered 35 per cent in taxation. And half was maintenance, on which it recovered company taxation from services provided. So the net figure was more likely to have been under £7 million.

From an earnings figure of £400 million per annum, Government recovered £54 million in taxation (£35 + £16 +£3), against a running cost of £10 million per annum – a net balance of £44 million, apart from the immeasurable diplomatic and political prestige the Yacht conferred. I appreciate these are simplistic figures, but why on earth did no one high in the pro-Royal Yacht lobby refine such figures and parade them? Far from being a burden to the tax-payer, BRITANNIA was a very substantial net earner.
[49] *Hansard* 22 January 1997.
[50] *Hansard* 23 June 1994.
[51] *Financial Times* 11 June 1994.
[52] 1994 Department of Transport Statistics Report 7. 352 million tons worth £217 billion.
[53] *The Royal Yacht Britannia,* Hoey p 154.
[54] Vice Admiral Sir Ian McGeoch KCB, DSO, DSC, 12 May 1996.
[54a] The DML Ship may well have stood a chance, but one flaw lay in that DML proposed to arrange the charters, whereas, for obvious reasons, the Ministry of Defence should have assumed that responsibility.

Probably the most practical secondary role any new Royal Yacht would have been for training – either Naval Cadets or 'postgraduates' from other training ships, such as the Sail Training Association. With reduced permanent complement there would never be enough hands for ceremonial, social and commercial events. Training could also have continued while the Yacht was sailing to or returning from State or commercial functions, so there would have been no loss of instruction.

Whether a sailing or motor yacht would best provide the combination of roles required is now – unfortunately – academic.
[55] *Hansard* 22 January 1997.
[56] *The Times* 28 January 1997.
[57] *Navy News* Britannia Supplement January 1998.
[58] *Daily Telegraph* 12 June 1997.
[59] *Daily Mail* 19 October 2000. Extract from *The Unconventional Minister* by Geoffrey Robinson, published by Michael Joseph in 2000.
[59a] *Daily Mail* 19 October 2000.
[59b] *Daily Mail* 19 October 2000.
[60] *Daily Telegraph* 2 October 1997.
[61] MoD News release 10 October 1997.
[62] *The Guardian* 10 October 1997.
[63] *Glasgow Herald* 9 April 1998.

APPENDIX ONE

YACHTS CHRONOLOGICALLY BY MONARCH

CHARLES II 1660-1685

MARY, 1660.
ROYAL ESCAPE, 1660.
KATHERINE, 1661.
ANNE, 1661.
BEZAN, 1661.
CHARLES, 1662.
JAMIE/JEMMY, 1662.
HENRIETTA, 1663.
MERLIN, 1666.
MONMOUTH, 1666.
SAUDADOES, 1670.
KITCHEN, 1670.
CLEVELAND, 1671.
QUINBOROW, 1671.
NAVY, 1673.
DEALE, 1673.
ISLE OF WIGHT, 1673.
KATHERINE II, 1674.
PORTSMOUTH, 1674.
CHARLES II, 1675.
CHARLOT, 1677.
MARY II, 1677.
HENRIETTA II, 1679.
ISABELLA BEZAN, 1680.
FUBBS, 1682.
ISABELLA, 1683.
(Coronelli's Yacht)

WILLIAM & MARY 1689-1702

SOESDYKE, 1692.
WILLIAM & MARY, 1694.
SQUIRREL, 1694.
SCOUT, 1695.
PEREGRINE GALLEY, 1700.
FUBBS II, 1701.
QUEENBOROUGH, 1701.
ISLE OF WIGHT II, 1701.

QUEEN ANNE 1702-1714

PORTSMOUTH II, 1702-3.
ISABELLA II, 1703.
DRAKE, 1705.
DUBLIN, 1709.
BOLTON, 1709.
CHARLOT II, 1710.

GEORGE I 1714-1727

CAROLINA, 1716.
CHATHAM, 1716.
QUEENBOROUGH II, 1718.
KATHERINE III, 1720.
FUBBS III, 1724.
MARY III, 1727.

GEORGE II 1727-1760

DRAKE II, 1729.
ROYAL CAROLINE, 1733.
CHATHAM II, 1741.
OLD PORTSMOUTH, 1741.
PORTSMOUTH III, 1742.
ROYAL CAROLINE II, 1749.
DORSET, 1753.
PLYMOUTH, 1755.

GEORGE III 1760-1820

ROYAL CHARLOTTE, 1761.
AUGUSTA, 1761.
BOLTON II, 1763.
WILLIAM & MARY II, 1765.
AUGUSTA II, 1771.
MEDINA, 1772.
PRINCESS AUGUSTA, 1773.
CHATHAM III, 1793.
PORTSMOUTH IV, 1794.
PLYMOUTH II, 1796.
ROYAL SOVEREIGN, 1804.
WILLIAM & MARY III, 1807.
ROYAL GEORGE, 1817.
PRINCE REGENT, 1820.

GEORGE IV 1820-1830

ROYAL CHARLOTTE II, 1824.

WILLIAM IV 1830-1837

ROYAL ADELAIDE, 1833

QUEEN VICTORIA 1837-1901

VICTORIA & ALBERT, 1843.
FAIRY, 1845.
ELFIN, 1848.
PRINCE OF WALES, 1850.
VICTORIA & ALBERT II, 1855.
OSBORNE, 1855.
ALBERTA, 1863.
OSBORNE II, 1870.
VICTORIA & ALBERT III, 1899.

EDWARD VII 1901-1910

VICTORIA & ALBERT III.
Racing Cutter BRITANNIA, 1893.
ALEXANDRA, 1907.
OPHIR

GEORGE V 1910-1936

VICTORIA & ALBERT III
MEDINA
RENOWN
Racing Cutter BRITANNIA

EDWARD VIII 1936

GEORGE VI 1936-1952

VICTORIA & ALBERT III

QUEEN ELIZABETH II

VICTORIA & ALBERT III
BRITANNIA, 1953.

APPENDIX TWO

A LIST OF ROYAL YACHT NAMES AND THEIR DERIVATIONS

From 1660-1997, in alphabetical order, with their year of building and subsequent history.

ALBERTA, 1863, probably after Princess Louise Caroline Alberta, Duchess of Argyll: possibly after Princess Victoria of Hesse (Victoria Elizabeth Mathilde Alberta Marie) afterwards Marchioness of Milford Haven, born that year; or after Prince Albert, who had died in 1861, two years prior to ALBERTA's launch. Broken up 1913.

ALEXANDRA, 1906, after Queen Alexandra, wife of Edward VII. Sold 1925.

ANNE, 1661, after the Duchess of York, wife of Charles II's brother, James, Duke of York, later James II. His personal yacht. Sold 1686.

AUGUSTA, 1761, renamed (ex CHARLOT II) to free the name for the ROYAL CHARLOTTE; after George III's eldest sister, later the Duchess of Brunswick, and mother of Caroline, future wife of George IV. Rebuilt 1771.

AUGUSTA II, 1771, rebuilt and named after her predecessor. Renamed PRINCESS AUGUSTA 1773.

BEZAN, 1661, after Bezaan, in Dutch a mizzen-sail. Sold 1686.

BOLTON, 1709, after the Dukes of Bolton, for many years hereditary Governors of the Isle of Wight. Governor's yacht. Rebuilt unofficially 1763.

BOLTON II, 1763, after her predecessor. Taken to pieces 1817.

BRITANNIA, the name given to Britain by the Romans.
1893, The Prince of Wales's racing cutter. Given a sea-burial at King George V's wishes in 1936.
1953, HM Yacht BRITANNIA. Paid-off 11 December 1997.
The first warship to bear the name was a first-rate of 1682. The present HMS BRITANNIA is the Royal Naval College, Dartmouth.

CAROLINA, renamed 1716 (ex-PEREGRINE GALLEY of 1700) in honour of the Princess of Wales, and George II's future Queen, Caroline of Anspach. Quite why it is difficult to understand, for George I's dislike of his daughter-in-law was a public scandal – 'cette diablesse Madame la Princesse'. Rebuilt and renamed ROYAL CAROLINE 1733.

CHARLES, 1662, after King Charles II. Exchanged with the Office of Ordnance 1668 for the TOWER smack.

CHARLES II, 1675, after her predecessor. Wrecked on the coast of Holland 1678.

CHARLOT, 1677, possibly after Charlotte, Countess of Yarmouth, second daughter of Barbara Villiers by Charles II. Rebuilt 1710.

CHARLOT II, 1710, rebuilt and named after her predecessor. Converted to a ketch 1736; lengthened 1747. Renamed AUGUSTA 1761 to free the name for the ROYAL CHARLOTTE, 1761 (ex-ROYAL CAROLINE).

CHATHAM, 1716, Chatham Dockyard Commissioner's yacht. Sold 1742.

CHATHAM II, 1741, after her predecessor. Large repairs 1765; rebuilt 1793.

CHATHAM III, 1793, rebuilt and named after her predecessor. Taken to pieces 1867.

CLEVELAND, 1671, after the notorious Duchess of Cleveland, formerly Barbara Villiers, later Lady Castlemaine. She was created Duchess of Cleveland, Countess of Southampton and Baroness Nonsuch in August 1670; more of a golden handshake, as she was soon to be ousted by Louise de Kéroualle. Sold 1716.

DEALE, 1673, probably after the town of Deal in Kent. Probably Chatham or Sheerness Dockyard yacht. Sold 1698.

DORSET, 1753, geographical, but why is unknown, as she was the Viceroy of Ireland's yacht to replace the DUBLIN. Sold 1815.

DRAKE, 1705, after Sir Francis Drake. Plymouth Dockyard Commissioner's yacht. Rebuilt 1729.

DRAKE II, 1729, rebuilt and named after her predecessor. Sold 1749.

DUBLIN, 1709, after the city. Viceroy of Ireland's yacht. Taken to pieces 1752.

ELFIN, 1848, probably a pun, as she was one-third the size of the FAIRY yacht, whom she replaced. Broken up 1901.

FAIRY, 1844, unknown. Broken up 1868.

FUBBS, 1682, after Charles II's mistress, Louise de Kéroualle. Her portrait shows a baby face with fat cheeks surrounded by a halo of curls, which led the King to nickname her Fubbs (for chubby). Louise outlived both her yacht namesakes, (see PORTSMOUTH) and died in Aubigny, France, aged eighty-five, 'very old, very penitent, very poor'. Rebuilt 1701.

FUBBS II, 1701, rebuilt and named after her predecessor. Rebuilt 1724.

FUBBS III, 1724, rebuilt and named after her predecessor. Taken to pieces 1781.

HENRIETTA, 1663, possibly after Charles II's mother (1609-1669) or more probably his sister Minette, the Duchess of Orleans (1631-1660). I am inclined to the yacht being named after Charles's favourite sister Henrietta Anne, Duchess of Orleans; he was distraught when she died in 1660 aged only twenty-nine. With his mother, Queen Henrietta-Maria, he had a difficult relationship; she tended to be possessive of all her children, and the years of exile and poverty only made the rift between mother and son deeper. Sunk in action against the Dutch at the Battle of Texel 1673.

HENRIETTA II, 1679, after her predecessor. Sold 1720.

ISABELLA BEZAN, 1680, probably after the Duke of York's daughter, born in 1676. Sold to Sir Phineas Pett 1683.

ISABELLA, 1683, probably after the Duke of York's daughter. Broken up 1702.

ISABELLA II, 1703, rebuilt and named after her predecessor. Sold 1715/16.

ISLE OF WIGHT, 1673, geographical. Governor of the Island's yacht. Rebuilt 1701.

ISLE OF WIGHT II, 1701, rebuilt, named after her predecessor. Sold 1712.

JAMIE/JEMMY, 1662, either after James, Duke of York, or more likely after the Duke of Monmouth, Charles II's favourite, and natural, son by Lucy Walter. The yacht was sometimes called JEMMY, so I am more inclined to the latter choice. Broken up 1721.

KATHERINE, 1661, after catherine of Braganza, Infanta of Portugal, affianced to Charles II. Captured by the Dutch 1673 at the Battle of Texel; returned the following year. To general service 1674.

KATHERINE II, 1674, after her predecessor. Rebuilt 1720.

KATHERINE III, 1720, rebuilt and named after her predecessor. Ketch-rig 1736; sold 1801.

KITCHEN, 1670, aptly named, as she accommodated the royal cooks and galleys in attendance on the principal Royal Yachts. Made a bomb-vessel 1692; sold 1698.

MARY, 1660, after Charles II's sister, the Princess Royal, widow of the Prince of Orange and mother of the future William III. Mostly employed on despatch duty to Ireland. Wrecked off Holyhead 1675.

MARY II, 1677, after her predecessor. Rebuilt 1727.

MARY III, 1727, rebuilt and named after her predecessor. Converted to ketch-rig 1735; taken to pieces 1816.

MEDINA, 1772, great repairs and renamed (ex-OLD PORTSMOUTH 1741, ex-PORTSMOUTH II 1702-3) after the river at Cowes, as she was the Governor of the Isle of Wight's yacht. Taken to pieces 1832 after one hundred and thirty years' service.

MERLIN, 1666, probably after the bird of prey, for Charles II was a keen falconer. Sold 1698.

MONMOUTH, 1666, after James, Duke of Monmouth, Charles II's natural son by Lucy Walter. Sold 1698.

NAVY, 1673. Charles II took a deep interest in the navy, and it was under him it became known as the Royal Navy. Sold 1698.

OLD PORTSMOUTH, 1741, renamed, ex-PORTSMOUTH II, 1702-3. Great repairs and further renamed in 1772 as the MEDINA.

OSBORNE, renamed in 1855, (ex-VICTORIA & ALBERT I), named after Osborne House, the residence on the Isle of Wight bought by Queen Victoria and Prince Albert in 1845 and subsequently much enlarged into an Italianate villa. Broken up 1868.

OSBORNE II, 1870, after her predecessor. Sold 1908.

PEREGRINE GALLEY, 1700, after her designer, Peregrine, Lord Danby, later Marquess of Carmarthen. Renamed CAROLINA 1716.

PORTSMOUTH, 1674, after Charles I's mistress Louise de Kéroualle. Louise had been introduced by Louis XIV to Charles's court with the intention of gaining his bed, his confidence and his secrets. She became his mistress in 1671, and within eighteen months (February 1673) had been created Duchess of Portsmouth, Countess of Fareham and Lady Petersfield. Made a bomb-vessel 1688, and wrecked in the great gale at the Nore in 1703.

PORTSMOUTH II, 1702-3, after the town. Portsmouth Dockyard Commissioner's yacht. Renamed OLD PORTSMOUTH 1741 to free the name for PORTSMOUTH III.

PORTSMOUTH III, 1742, after her predecessor. Rebuilt 1794.

PORTSMOUTH IV, 1794, rebuilt and named after her predecessor. Taken to pieces 1869.

PRINCE REGENT, 1820, after the Prince Regent. Refitted 1836 and presented to the Iman of Muscat. (There is some doubt she was ever delivered, and may have been broken up in 1847)

PRINCE OF WALES, 1850, after the Prince of Wales (later Edward VII) born on 9 November 1841. Miniature corvette, probably intended for Virginia Water. Fate unknown.

PRINCESS AUGUSTA, 1773, renamed (ex-AUGUSTA II) for the royal review of the fleet at Portsmouth 22-26 June; and rated a ship not a yacht. Principal yacht of George III. Sold 1818.

PLYMOUTH, 1755, after the town. Commissioner of Devonport Dockyard's yacht, built to replace DRAKE II. Taken to pieces 1793.

PLYMOUTH II, 1796, after her predecessor. Taken to pieces 1830.

QUINBOROW, 1671, after the village of Queenborough, on the Isle of Sheppey near London. Probably a survey yacht. Sold 1719.

QUEENBOROUGH, 1701, after the village on the Isle of Sheppey. Rebuilt 1718.

QUEENBOROUGH II, 1718, rebuilt and named after her predecessor. Sold 1777.

ROYAL ADELAIDE, 1833, after Queen Adelaide, wife of King William IV. Miniature frigate on Virginia Water. Broken up 1877.

ROYAL CAROLINE, 1733, rebuilt and renamed (ex-CAROLINA, ex-PEREGRINE GALLEY). Named after Queen Caroline, wife of George II. Converted and renamed PEREGRINE SLOOP in 1749; lost with all hands in the Bay of Biscay in 1762.

ROYAL CAROLINE II, 1749, built (not rebuilt) and named after her predecessor. Renamed ROYAL CHARLOTTE 1761.

ROYAL CHARLOTTE, 1761, renamed (ex-ROYAL CAROLINE) in honour of George III's bride Princess Charlotte of Mecklenburg-Strelitz. Taken to pieces 1820.

ROYAL CHARLOTTE II, 1824, after the Prince Regent's only child by the Princess of Wales. Princess Charlotte had married Prince Leopold of Saxe Coburg-Saalfeld (later King Leopold of the Belgians), and died on 5 November 1817 after giving birth to a stillborn boy. Taken to pieces 1832.

ROYAL ESCAPE, 1660, renamed (ex-SURPRISE) and converted to a yacht by Charles II to commemorate his escape in her to France in 1651 after defeat at the Battle of Worcester. To general service 1673; rebuilt 1714.

ROYAL GEORGE, 1817, after George, Prince Regent. To an accommodation ship for the Royal Yachts 1843. Paid off 1902; broken up 1905.

ROYAL SOVEREIGN, 1804, after George III. To a depot ship at Pembroke 1832; broken up 1850.

SAUDADOES, 1670, meaning 'intense longing' in Portuguese. Named by Charles II's Queen, catherine of Braganza, to whom he gave the yacht. Rebuilt and enlarged as a sixth-rate of 180 tons, 1673.

SAUDADOES II, 1673, rebuilt as a man-of-war, although nominally, for a time at least, still the Queen's yacht. Captured by the French 1693.

SCOUT, 1695, unknown. Sold 1703.

SOESDYKE, 1692. Named after a royal palace near Soest, east of Hilversum, Netherlands; in modern Dutch 'Soestdijk'. Sold 1713.

SQUIRREL, 1694, unknown. Sold 1714.

VICTORIA & ALBERT, 1843, after Queen Victoria and Prince Albert. Renamed OSBORNE 1855; broken up 1868.

VICTORIA & ALBERT II, 1855, after her predecessor. Broken up and burnt 1904.

VICTORIA & ALBERT III, 1899, after her predecessor. Broken up 1955.

WILLIAM & MARY, 1694, after the reigning monarchs. Great repairs 1737 and 1746; rebuilt 1764/5.

WILLIAM & MARY II, 1764/5, rebuilt and named after her predecessor. Very large repairs 1783. Sold 1801.

WILLIAM & MARY III, 1807. Built, not rebuilt, and named after her predecessor. Taken to pieces 1849.

83 yachts.

BIBLIOGRAPHY

Gavin C.E., *Royal Yachts.* Rich & Steele 1932.
Drummond Maldwin, *Saltwater Palaces.* Debretts 1979.
Smith Beckstall, *The Britannia and her Contemparies.* Methuen & Co 1929.
Morton Andrew, *The Royal Yacht Britannia.* Orbis Publishing Ltd 1984.
Hoey Brian, *The Royal Yacht Britannia.* Patrick Stephens Ltd 1995.
Britannia 1959, printed privately 1959.
Her Majesty's Yacht Britannia, printed privately 1970.
GrisbyJ.E., *Annals of Our Royal Yachts 1604-1953.* Adlard Coles 1953.
Crabtree Reginald, *Royal Yachts of Europe.* David & Charles 1975.
Naish G.P.B., *Royal Yachts.* National Maritime Museum/HMSO 1953.
McGowan A.P., *Royal Yachts.* National Maritime Museum/HMSO 1977.
Rousmaniere John, *The Luxury Yachts.* Time-Life Books 1982.
Price Harry, Petty Officer, *The Royal Tour 1901* or *The Cruise of HMS OPHIR.* Webb & Bower 1980.
Bellarbarba S. & Osiulati G., *The Royal Yacht Caroline.* London 1989.
Marwick Arthur ed., *Dictionary of British History.* Thames & Hudson 1980.
Chambers Dictionary of World History 1994.
The Old Scots Navy 1689-1710, Navy Records Society 1912.
LindsayAlexander, A Rutter of the Scottish Seas c.1540. National Maritime Museum monograph No. 44-1980.
Accounts of the Lord High Treasurer of Scotland, 1538-1541, pp 337, 402, 420, 421, 445, 480 etc.
Walker & Manning, *British Warship Names.* Putnam 1959.
Martin J.H., *Pictorial History of Ships.* Sundial Books Ltd 1976.
Bell Douglas, *Seamen of Britain.* Nelson 1943.
Trotter W.P, *The Royal Navy in Old Photographs.* J.M. Dent & Sons 1975.
Kemp Peter ed., *The Oxford Companion to Ships and the Sea.* Oxford University Press 1976.
White W.H., *Naval Architecture.* John Murray 3rd edition 1894.
Greenhill Basil, *The Evolution of the Wooden Ship.* Batsford 1988.
Cowburn Philip, *Charles II's Yachts.* History Today, Volume XII 1962.
Faith Nicholas, *Classic Ships.* Boxtree Limited 1995.
Lyon D., *The Sailing Navy Lists.* Conway Maritime Press 1993.
Fox Frank, *Great Ships.* Conway Maritime Press 1987.
Beckett Commander W.N.T., *A few Naval Customs, Expressions, Traditions and Superstitions.* Messrs Gieves about 1925.
Dalglish Captain J.S., *The Life Story of a Fish.* The Adelphi Press 1992.
Grenfell Captain Russell, *Service Pay.* Eyre & Spottiswoode 1944.
The Naval Chronicle, 1799-1801.

Poore Lady, *An Admiral's Wife In The Making.* Smith Elder & Co., 1917.
Agar Captain Augustus, *Footprints in the Sea.* Evans Brothers 1959.
Pembrokeshire County History, Volume IV. The Pembrokeshire Historical Society 1993.
Pelly Admiral Sir Henry, *300,000 Sea Miles.* Chatto & Windus 1938.
Fortescue Captain The Hon. Sir Seymour, *Looking Back.* Longmans, Green & Co. 1920.
Clowes Laird, *The Royal Navy – A History*, vol 1. London 1877.
Anderson R. C., *Oared Fighting Ships.* Perceval Marshall 1962.
James William, *The Naval History of Great Britain.* 1837.
Heckstall-Smith Antony, *Sacred Cowes.* Allan Wingate 1955.
Wilson Timothy, *Flags at Sea.* HMSO/National Maritime Museum 1986.
Place Geoffrey,*The Rise and Fall of Parkgate, Passenger Port for Ireland, 1686-1815.* The Chetham Society 1994.
Thorpe Lewis, *The Bayeux Tapestry and the Norman Invasion.* The Folio Society 1973.
Prebble John, *The Lion in the North.* Martin Secker & Warburg 1971.
Campbell J.L., *Canna.* Oxford University Press 1984.
Chambers Biographical Dictionary.
Armstrong G., *Scotland, James V & VI.*
Fraser Antonia, *Mary Queen of Scots.* Wiedenfield & Nicholson 1994.
Stoddart Jane, *The Girlhood of Mary Queen of Scots.* Hodder & Stoughton 1908.
The Diary of Samuel Pepys. Everyman edition, J M Dent 1950
Wilcox L.A.,*Mr Pepys' Navy.* G. Bell & Sons 1966.
Williams Ethel Carleton, *Anne of Denmark.* Longman 1970.
Fraser Antonia, *Charles II.* Weidenfield & Nicholson Ltd 1979.
Gregg Edward, *Queen Anne.* Ark Paperbacks 1984.
Brooke John, *King George III.* Constable & Company 1972.
Hibbert Christopher, *George IV, Prince of Wales.* Longmans 1972.
Hibbert Christopher, *George IV, Regent and King.* Charles Allan 1975.
Prebble John, *The King's Jaunt – George IV in Scotland 1822.* Collins 1988.
Fraser Flora, *The Unruly Queen.* Macmillan 1996.
Ziegler Philip, *King William I.* Collins 1971.
Marshall Dorothy, *The Life and Times of Queen Victoria.* George Wiedenfield & Nicholson 1972.
Bennett Daphne. *KingWithout a Crown.* William Heinemann Ltd 1977.
Dimbleby Jonathan, *The Prince of Wales – A Biography.* Little, Brown & Co. , 1994.
Millar Sir Oliver, *The Tudor, Stuart and Early Georgian Pictures in the Collection of Her Majesty The Queen.*
Millar Sir Oliver, *The Later Georgian Pictures in the Collection of Her Majesty The Queen.*
Millar Sir Oliver, *The Victorian Pictures in the Collection of Her Majesty The Queen.*
The Concise Catalogue to Paintings in the National Maritime Museum. Antique Collectors Club 1988.
Robertson M.S., *The Paintings of the Willem Van de Velde.* National Maritime Museum/Royal Dutch Petroleum Company/Sothebys 1990.

INDEX

( ) = main details or description.
[ ] = illustrations.
Upper case = vessels